To my wife Liz,
our children and grandchildren
in the hope they will enjoy and learn from
the lives of these great  men and women

# AUTHOR'S NOTE

Balquhidder is a small village standing at the head of Loch Voil nestling among heather-clad mountains.

Sixty years ago the kirkyard at Balquhidder was softened by the evening light as Dad and I searched amongst the graves of MacLarens and Stewarts, Fergussons and MacGregors for the grave of my great great great great grandfather, Robert Fergusson, who had been born in Balquhidder in 1725. I think that's the right number of 'greats.'

We may not have found his grave but what we did find was the grave of Rob Roy MacGregor, the famous Jacobite outlaw who had died in 1734. The MacGregors had settled in Balquhidder Glen in 1558 by the simple and tried expedient of massacring eighteen families of the clan MacLaren and taking their land.

Dad wondered whether as a small boy Robert would have been told of the exploits of Rob Roy, and recounted the history of this legendary figure.

Rob Roy was the son of Donald MacGregor, chief of the MacGregors of Glengyle; the 'Roy' referred to his red hair, Ruadh in Gaelic. Strictly, Rob Roy was not a MacGregor but took the Campbell name of his mother, Margaret, as the entire MacGregor clan had been outlawed and the use of their name proscribed in 1603 by James VI after a particularly bloody murder by the MacGregors of eighty Colquhouns in a clan feud.

The MacGregors were famous for their skills in droving cattle and raising money from lowland farmers by a charge levied to provide protection for their herds from the reivers (raiders), principally, it must be said, the MacGregors themselves. It was an early and lucrative example of the protection racket and the charge was known appositely as 'black mail.'

Rob Roy was a skilful swordsman, a talent he had learned as a boy fighting with a stick and practising the cuts and thrusts which would later make him one of the finest swordsmen of his age. He fought and won more than twenty duels with his mighty broadsword, duels in which he was never scratched, nor ever killed his opponent as the duel was decided when blood was first drawn.

He had fought at the Battle of Killiecrankie in 1689 in the first Jacobite uprising when wild Highlanders, under the command of 'Bonnie Dundee,' charged the red-coated government troops and slaughtered them before they could draw their bayonets. Rob Roy was not, however, outlawed for taking part in the Jacobite rising but later when he crossed the powerful Duke of Montrose.

Rob Roy had become a successful cattle trader and at the peak of his fortunes he owned six thousand acres on the eastern shore of Loch Lomond and the slopes of Ben Lomond. Every year he would borrow substantial sums of money from Montrose as a loan to fund the purchase of cattle which he would drive to market for sale, using the proceeds to repay the loan. One year his chief drover absconded with the money, one thousand pounds, and Rob Roy was unable to repay. His plea to Montrose for time to pay was rejected and he was precipitately bankrupted and outlawed, his name 'put to the horn.' While he was away trying to raise the money, his house was burned down and his wife and four boys had to flee for their lives through the snow to take shelter with her kinfolk. Rob Roy himself took to the hills and from then on lived on his wits, pursued relentlessly by his creditors and only avoiding capture through a succession of daring escapes.

Eventually pardoned, he died in peace in his house at Inverlochlarig at the head of Balquhidder glen. What young boy could not have their imagination fired by a tale such as this?

My father also told me the stories of the great Scots who had changed the world, of James Watt and the steam engine, of the stories of Sir Walter Scott and Buchan, and of the poems of Burns, the ideas of James Hutton, the skills of James Young Simpson and the travels of David Livingstone.

For many years work intervened, but with retirement came the opportunity to study Scottish history.

I became fascinated with the Scottish Enlightenment, that time when the intellectual giants of the period such as David Hume, Adam Smith, Mary Somerville and Joseph Black produced ideas and works of the greatest cultural, philosophical, and scientific importance that still inform and influence contemporary Western society today.

Scotland at the time was an impoverished country, worn out by centuries of war and coming to terms with its loss of nationhood through the Act of Union with England. I became fascinated with the paradox whereby this flowering of intellectual thought took place in a country which was internationally backward and remote from the stimulating atmosphere of the major European capitals.

Within these pages I attempt to resolve and bring a human face to that paradox. This book is designed for those who desire to know more about the Enlightenment, and in particular, about the lives of these Scots who contributed so much to the world through their ideas, art and inventions. It is written as a digestible survey in an attempt to distil the 'magic' ingredients of the period without becoming overly academic, while extending the historical scope to include other notable men and women who contributed something special to our lives.

Within this framework I present five questions for consideration: What special circumstances in Scotland nurtured this explosion of talent? Are there common themes which influenced these men and women, and if so, are there essential elements we could use to encourage intellectual and artistic development today?

Would the application of the principles of reason and rational thought, practiced by the philosophers of the Scottish Enlightenment be helpful in deciding the political and economic choices faced today? This carries a special resonance with the proposed referendum on Scottish independence planned for the autumn of 2014. While this book deliberately does not take a position on the referendum itself, the opportunity is used to apply the reasoned thought typical of the Enlightenment to some of the issues.

Could the principles of the Scottish Enlightenment provide a guide for the development of a new form of post–industrialisation society?

Is it possible for the conditions which gave birth to the Scottish Enlightenment to be replicated, leading to a re-Enlightenment?

## Acknowledgements

Above all, this book intended to be an accessible, readable account of the figures of the Scottish Enlightenment, rather than an academic text, and as such there are no references or footnotes. Each chapter does, however, contain a suggestion for further reading; these books are acknowledged as being amongst the many sources used for the material.

On a personal note, I would like to recognise the outstanding commitment to the project of my publisher, Martin Belk, who has unstintingly given his advice and support and whose company, stimulating conversation and friendship have been a continual pleasure.

I also thank my wife, Liz, who has been ever tolerant of the long periods of time spent on research and writing, and has provided a steady diet of coffee and support when she hasn't otherwise sought refuge on the golf course – I am pleased to report that her golf has improved tremendously throughout the process.

Andrew Ferguson

## Sir Eduardo Luigi Paolozzi: a Great Scot

'Sir Eduardo Luigi Paolozzi' by Ida Kar;  National Portrait Gallery, London

Who better to illustrate a conversation on the dynamic figures of the Scottish Enlightenment than Scotland's own pioneer of Pop Art?

Eduardo Paolozzi was born on 7 March 1924 in Leith, the eldest son of Italian immigrants. He studied at the Edinburgh College of Art before moving to London, then Paris where he came under the influence of the Surrealists such as Georges Braque.

Upon Paolozzi's return to London, he interpreted many Enlightenment themes in his work—such as his homage to Adam Smith with the sculpture 'The Wealth of Nations.' He was obsessed with the links between man and machine which he epitomized in pieces such as 'Secrets of Life: The Human Machine and How it Works.'

Paolozzi would have been comfortable in the company of the intellectual giants of the Enlightenment. A selection of Paolozzi's sculpture is presented throughout *Scots Who Enlightened the World*, a fitting continuum to the robust historical, cultural and creative history of Scotland.

–Martin Belk

## A Word from the Publisher

*Scots Who Enlightened the World*, an historical yet timely book, marks a new milestone in collaborative twenty-first century independent publishing. Thanks to the enthusiasm, expertise, dedication, skill and devoted support of Patricia Belk, Patrick Berry, John Calder, Matthew Collier, Shona Corner, Mary Folliet, Chris Hardie, Christopher Harvie, Jim Haynes, Thomas Haywood, Philip Hunt, Kirsty Kerr, Jonathan Pryce, National Galleries of Scotland, First Minister Alex Salmond, Graeme Smith & Jan Smith we bring you this informative and inspiring account of men and women from the Scottish Enlightenment, who continue to contribute to the pursuit of knowledge for the benefit of humanity.

—MLB

Scientific discovery, and perhaps more importantly, a vision of the power of science, were arguably the most defining features of the Scottish Enlightenment.

The Enlightenment was driven by a remarkable collection of intellectuals – scientists, philosophers, economists and literati. David Hume, a philosopher rather than a scientist, championed the scientific method. Many others, including James Hutton, Joseph Black and James Watt gave us important scientific principles, discoveries and innovations that underpin so much of what we now take for granted in our modern world and the impact of these great Scots continues to resonate today. At the time of course, many did not appreciate the significance of these ground breaking ideas, and it is only with hindsight that we can fully recognise the magnificent contribution Scotland has made towards enriching the daily lives of many people across the world.

I hope you enjoy reading Andrew Ferguson's explorations of these extraordinary figures in Scottish history.

ALEX SALMOND, FIRST MINISTER OF SCOTLAND

# CONTENTS

## Part 3: Doctors & Surgeons

## Part 4: Poets & Writers

# CONTENTS
(alphabetical by person)

# GUIDE TO COLOUR PLATES

**1. Frances Hutcheson**
Allan Ramsay, 'Frances Hutcheson'
(1694–1746) oil on canvas c.1740-45
Hunterian Museum and Art Gallery,
University of Glasgow

**2. Henry Home, Lord Kames**
David Martin, 'Henry Home, Lord Kames'
(1696–1782) oil on canvas 1794
Scottish National Portrait Gallery

**3. David Hume**
Allan Ramsay, David Hume (1711–1776) oil
on canvas 1766
Scottish National Portrait Gallery

**4. James Hutton**
Sir Henry Raeburn, 'James Hutton'
(1726–1797) oil on canvas c. 1776
Scottish National Portrait Gallery

**5. Mary Somerville**
Thomas Phillips, 'Mary Fairfax, Mrs
William Somerville' oil on canvas 1834
Scottish National Portrait Gallery,

**6. James Watt**
James Eckford Lauder, 'James Watt and the
Steam Engine: the Dawn of the
Nineteenth Century' 1855.
Scottish National Portrait Gallery

**7. James Hogg**
Sir John Watson Gordon, James Hogg,
(1770 - 1835) Poet;
'The Ettrick Shepherd' oil on canvas 1766
Scottish National Portrait Gallery

**8. Sir David Wilkie, 'The Honours of
Scotland'**, 1822
Scottish National Portrait Gallery

**9. Robert Louis Stevenson**
Count Girolamo Nerli, 'Robert Louis
Stevenson' oil on canvas 1892
Scottish National Portrait Gallery

**10. Anne Bayne**
Allan Ramsay, 'Anne Bayne, Mrs Allan
Ramsay' oil on canvas c.1743
Scottish National Portrait Gallery,
Edinburgh

**11. Archibald Campbell**
Allan Ramsay, 'Archibald Campbell / Mac
Cailein Mòr, 3rd Duke of Argyll
(1682–1761) oil on canvas c.1744
Scottish National Portrait Gallery

**12. Alan Ramsay**
Allan Ramsay, 'Allan Ramsay' (Self-portrait)
, (1713–1784) pastel on paper c.1756
Scottish National Portrait Gallery

**13. Margaret Lindsay**
Allan Ramsay, 'The Artist's Wife: Margaret
Lindsay of Evelick'oil on canvas c.1758 •
National Gallery of Scotland

**14. David Hume**
Allan Ramsay, David Hume (1711–1776) oil
on canvas 1766
Scottish National Portrait Gallery

**15. Jean-Jacques Rousseau**
Allan Ramsay, 'Jean-Jacques Rousseau'
(1712–1778)oil on canvas c.1766
National Gallery of Scotland

**16. Niel Gow**
Sir Henry Raeburn, 'Niel Gow' oil on
canvas 1787
Scottish National Portrait Gallery

**17. The Skating Minister**
Sir Henry Raeburn, 'Revd Dr Robert
Walker Skating on Duddingston Loch'
oil on canvas c. 1795 • National Gallery of
Scotland, Edinburgh

1690  1700  1710  1720  1730  1740  1750  1760  1770  1780  1790  1800  1810  182

Francis Hutcheson 1694 - 1746

Henry Home, Lord Kames 1696 - 1782

David Hume 1711 - 1776

Allan Ramsay 1713 - 1784

Adam Smith 1723 - 1790

James Hutton 1726 - 1797

Robert Adam 1728 - 1792

Joseph Black 1728 - 1799

• 1695 Bank of Scotland founded          James Watt 1736 - 1819
  by an act of the Scottish Parliament
                                     Robert Fergusson 1750 - 1774

                                        Archibald Menzies 1754 - 1842

                                        William Murdoch 1754 - 1839

• 1697 Thomas Aikenhead, age 19, controver-   John Loudon McAdam 1756 - 1836
  sially executed in Edinburgh
  for 'blasphemy' by Presbyterian Kirk       Sir Henry Raeburn 1756 - 1823

                                        Thomas Telford 1757 - 1834

                                        Alexander Nasrnyth 1758 - 1840

• 1707 last meeting of                       Robert Burns 1759 - 1796
  Scottish Parliament until 1999
                                         John Rennie 1761 - 1821

                                      William Symington 1763 - 1831

                                       Charles Macintosh 1766 - 1843

                                          James Hogg 1770 - 1835

1767 Allan Ramsay appointed court painter    Mungo Park 1771 - 1806
              to King George III •
                                          Sir Walter Scott 1771 - 1832

                                          Robert Stevenson 1772 - 1850

                                             Sir David Wilkie 1785 - 1841

                    American Revolution |——————|
                            1775–1783

• 1725 'The Odyssey' by Homer translated

• 1725 Frances Hutcheson: 'An Inquiry into the Original of Our Ideas of Beauty and Virtue'

                              French Revolution |——————|
                                      1789–1799

1782 James Watt invents steam engine •

1730 Edinburgh Royal Infirmary founded •

1789 Mutineers of 'The Bounty' settle on Pitcairn Islands •

1746 Wearing of Tartan prohibited in Britain •

• 1717 first Scottish-Irish emigrations to US after failed harvest
• 1720s-30s mass Ulster Scots emigration to Carolinas and Virginia in the US

• Scottish Highlanders join US emigration

1690  1700  1710  1720  1730  1740  1750  1760  1770  1780  1790  1800  1810  182

830 1840 1850 1860 1870 1880 1890 1900 1910 1920 1930 1940 1950 1960

*1874 First Impressionist exhibition in Paris •*

*• 1896 first modern Olympics held in Athens*

*1883 Brooklyn Bridge opens •*

*1952 Queen Elizabeth II coronation •*

World War I |———|
1914–1918

821 Bay Company & Northwest Company merge in North
merica, Scotsman George Simpson named president; territory
lmost ten times' that of Roman Empire

World War II |———|
1939–1945

*1929 Great Depression begins in the US •*

*• 1838 'New York Herald' first US newspaper
to employ European correspondents*

*• 1933 first rumours of
'Loch Ness Monster'
reported by press*

*• 1839 Scottish inventor Kirkpatrick Macmillan
constructs first bicycle*

*1924 Britain's elects first working-class Prime
Minister, Ramsay MacDonald, an illegitimate
child born in Lossiemouth, Scotland •*

Korean War |—|
1950–1953

*1949: The National Covenant for Home Rule is
launched by John MacCormick in Scotland •*

Mary Somerville 1780 - 1872

*1950 'Stone of Destiny' Scotland's Coronation stone,
taken by the English in 1296, stolen from
Westminster Abbey by four Scottish Nationalist students.
A rumoured copy was recovered from Arbroath Abbey.
The stone was handed back to Scotland in 1996by the
British Government and is now at Edinburgh Castle •*

Robert Napier 1791 - 1876

Thomas Carlyle 1795 - 1881

nes Young Simpson 1811 - 1870

James 'Paraffin' Young 1811 - 1883

David Livingstone 1813 - 1873

William Thomson, Lord Kelvin 1824 - 1907

*• 1935 Radar invented by
Sir Robert Watson-Watt*

Joseph Lister 1827 - 1912

James Clerk Maxwell 1831 - 1879

Andrew Carnegie 1835 - 1919

Alexander Graham Bell 1847 - 1922

Sir Thomas Lipton 1850 - 1931

Robert Louis Stevenson 1850 - 1894

Sir Ronald Ross 1857 - 1932

Elsie Inglis 1864 - 1917

John Buchan 1875 - 1940

Alexander Fleming 1881 - 1955

John Logie Baird 1888 - 1946

Robert Watson-Watt 1892 - 1973

Eric Liddell 1902 - 1945

830 1840 1850 1860 1870 1880 1890 1900 1910 1920 1930 1940 1950 1960

# Scots Who Enlightened the World

ANDREW FERGUSON

Polwarth Publishing

# What is the Scottish Enlightenment?

*It is a principle innate and co-natural to every man to have an insatiable inclination to truth and to seek for it as for hid treasure.*
— Thomas Aikenhead

In the latter part of the eighteenth century there was a flowering of new ideas in philosophy, literature, architecture, science and technology. Many of these originated in Scotland and soon spread throughout the world. This historic epoch has become known as the Scottish Enlightenment.

*'Master of the Universe'* Eduardo Paolozzi, a mechanised interpretation of the drawing by William Blake of Sir Isaac Newton. Scottish National Gallery of Modern Art. photo: Thomas Haywood

Two main factors characterised the Enlightenment. The first was a reliance on reason, which encouraged the re-examination of many ideas that had been held before to be universal truths, but which could not stand up against the remorseless spotlight of reason. The second was a freedom to express ideas, which in an earlier age would have been considered heresies, often punishable by torture and death.

## Enlightenment: The French Dimension

For many, the term 'Enlightenment' is defined by the period of intellectual development in eighteenth century France which, in 1789, culminated in the destruction of *l'ancien régime* and the horrors of the French Revolution. The spirit of the French Enlightenment was encapsulated in the *Encyclopédie* produced in Paris by Diderot and others between 1751 and 1772, and ambitiously intended to summarise and analyse the sum total of human knowledge. The first edition comprised twenty-eight volumes with a further seven volumes added later. By comparison the first edition of the Encyclopaedia Britannica which was produced between 1768 and 1771 in Edinburgh by William Smellie, a master printer and friend of Robert Burns, ran to a more modest three volumes. Smellie was sometimes idiosyncratic in his views; an example was his definition of 'woman,' a word which he defined succinctly but with undeniable accuracy, as 'the female of man.' Feminists might justifiably consider that this substantially understates the contribution of women.

'Reason' was the mantra of the French philosophers, coupled with a belief in individual liberty and in the right to follow the dictates of one's conscience. This emphasis upon reason as an end in itself contrasts with the Scottish Enlightenment where reason was just the tool to better understand human behaviour, the study of the 'science of man.' It was the remorseless exercise of reason by the French *philosophes* that inexorably led to their renunciation of religion. They were not just opposed to the rigidity and extremes of the Catholic Church but often to Christianity itself. Voltaire was typical of the views of many when he declared that 'every sensible man, every honourable man, must hold the Christian sect in horror,' as quoted in *The Enlightenment* by Peter Gay. Voltaire was well aware of the importance of religion in binding society and believed in the concept of a God, unlike many of his atheist counterparts, but he retained a narrow definition of 'a sensible man.' Cynically he wrote, 'I want my lawyer, my tailor, my servants, even my wife to believe in God, because it means I shall be cheated and robbed and cuckolded less often.' He concluded with his famous epigram, 'If God did not exist it would be necessary to invent Him.'

In this hostility to Christianity the French philosophers were far more sceptical than their Scottish counterparts. Hutcheson and Kames, both practising Christians, were more interested in the moral study of man and in the debate as to whether God was an inherently benevolent being, or the harsh deity as portrayed by the Calvinists than in any doubt as to His existence. Even Hume was probably an agnostic rather than a confirmed atheist.

A further key differentiator between the French philosophers and their Scottish counterparts was a denial of the important role that universal education, as promoted by Adam Smith, could have in enriching the lives of the people. Voltaire saw no point in educating agricultural workers, writing that 'the cultivation of the land required only a very common kind of intelligence.' Arrogantly, the French philosophers argued that the 'people' could not be educated because they were 'unenlightened' (unlike of course the philosophers!) as they had been prejudiced against the pursuit of reason by the dogmas of religion.

There was a powerful sub-text to the French Enlightenment which was a belief in liberty, the freedom to follow one's conscience. This championship of the concept of liberty, both civil and political, brought the philosophers in conflict with the State, although many of the philosophers somewhat paradoxically believed in the rule of a benign despot, as epitomised by the king, whilst disparaging the role of the nobility. Cynics might point out that many of these same philosophers were members of the Royal Academies from which they received their salaries. Rousseau took a more extreme view, believing controversially in the authority of the 'general will.' The general will, as he characterized it in his book, *The Social Contract*, was a mythical concept, the imaginary 'will' of the people derived from some inherent concept of universal rights and aspirations, but certainly not equivalent to the 'sum-total' of the wills of individual people and even less to the 'greatest happiness for the greatest number,' as espoused by Francis Hutcheson. Rousseau even propounded the concept of a 'civil religion' to replace the discredited Church. As a consequence of these implicit attacks on the authority of the State, Rousseau, like Voltaire, was forced to spend some time overseas – in the case of Rousseau as the guest of David Hume with whom he later irrationally and ungratefully quarrelled.

These convictions of the philosophers, their contempt for religion, for religious belief and for the Catholic Church; the belief in the authority of the 'general will' as espoused by Rousseau, even his idea of a civil religion — would all be contributors to the spiritual anarchy which helped to breed the French Revolution and to create the moral vacuum which allowed the eventual Reign of Terror — although it was all done, at least initially, with the intention of transforming a 'corrupt' society into the 'new Jerusalem' of the philosophers.

## Why Scotland?

The French may have tried to claim the Enlightenment as their own, but there was at the same time a powerful intellectual movement in Scotland encapsulated in the works of such internationally acclaimed moral philosophers as David Hume and Adam Smith, both of whom had spent some time in Paris. Hume corresponded extensively with Voltaire, although interestingly never met him, claiming that his diplomatic responsibilities confined him to Paris; Hume met and befriended Rousseau, but to his later cost. Smith met and admired Voltaire – an admiration which was reciprocated by Voltaire who said of Smith, 'We have nothing to compare with him'. There is no record of Smith meeting Rousseau, but his opinion of his intellectual ability was disparaging, considering him 'more capable of feeling strongly than of analysing accurately.'

France, a wealthy and cultured country at the heart of Europe, was perhaps a natural place for new intellectual ideas to flourish, but Scotland, a country on the periphery of Europe, was in many ways an unlikely country in which to find the vigorous challenge of established doctrines and beliefs through the application of implacable reason and painstaking observation.

By the end of the seventeenth century Scotland had become the poor relation of Europe, unsure of its national identity, dominated by the rigours of a harsh religion, intellectually backward and economically one of the poorest of Europe's nation states. Edinburgh was a medieval slum, characterised by rat-infested tenements where the ritual was to throw human waste out the window each evening to be swept down to the Nor' Loch, an open sewer. The glory of the New Town was not even a dream. The century had started with such hopes.

## The Union of Crowns and the Stuarts

On 4 March 1603, Queen Elizabeth I of England died and James VI of Scotland started his leisurely journey to London to be crowned as James I of England. The Union of the Crowns of England and Scotland would surely bring an end to the centuries of fighting between the two countries and Scotland would enjoy peace and prosperity as a full partner with England under the sympathetic rule of a Scottish king. Or there again, perhaps not.

James had promised to return regularly to his native land, but he became enraptured by the wealth and opportunities of the English Court and preferred to govern Scotland from afar. It was much easier. 'Here I sit,' he said, 'and govern [Scotland] with my pen; I write and it is done.' Only once would he revisit his native country before his death in 1625.

Scotland fared little better under Charles I, who attempted to foist upon the Scottish Kirk a new Book of Common Prayer, seen by the Scots as an attempt by the king to impose upon them the 'outlandish' Roman practices of the English Church in place of the austere form of religion practised in Scotland. It is an understatement to say this was not well received; there were riots in the streets of Edinburgh when the new Prayer Book was first used in St Giles.

A National Covenant was prepared for signature by the Scottish ministers, nobles and people, who joined together in a pledge to preserve the laws and liberties of the kingdom and to defend the Presbyterian Church 'against all sorts of persons whatsoever', by whom, of course, they meant the king. Thousands of people signed in this early example of a national referendum. There could be only one outcome from this act of defiance: war, with the king pitched against the Scottish people.

King Charles raised an English army and sent them north to subdue his troublesome Scottish subjects, but there was no enthusiasm amongst his troops for the fight and the king was forced to agree to peace. He even had to agree to pay the costs of the Scots Covenanter army which had been raised against him. His troubles were only just beginning. Charles recalled the English Parliament to raise funds to pay off the Scots. When Parliament refused to do his bidding, he marched with four hundred cavaliers to Westminster to take control and seize his opponents. Typically, he arrived too late and the birds had flown the coop.

In 1642 Charles again raised an army, this time to impose his will upon the English Parliament and the people. The Civil War had begun; it was King matched against Parliament. After a series of battles, Charles I and his Cavaliers were defeated by the Parliamentarians under Oliver Cromwell, supported by a Scots army of Covenanters. Charles himself surrendered to the Scots army at Newark in 1646 with the hope he would be able to play the Scots against the English. His ploy failed when the Scots agreed to transfer the king to the Parliamentarians for a price – three hundred thousand pounds – and agreed to withdraw their army to Scotland. King Charles was kept as a prisoner until on a cold January morning in 1649 he was taken from the Banqueting House in Whitehall to the scaffold, wearing two shirts so that he would not shiver in the winter cold and appear frightened of his impending death.

His son, the young Prince Charles, was in exile. Five days after his father's death, the Scots, perhaps regretting their betrayal of his father and shocked by the execution, proclaimed the young prince Charles II, King of Scotland, on the understanding he would sign the Covenant and enforce the Presbyterian faith, not just in Scotland, but throughout the kingdom of Britain. This was a direct threat to the rule of Oliver Cromwell and the Commonwealth.

Cromwell marched north with an army of seventeen thousand battle-hardened troops to face a Scots army of twenty-two thousand led by the experienced commander David Leslie. Cromwell camped outside Edinburgh but was unable to tempt the Scots to battle and so, with his army drenched by the incessant rain and weakened by illness, he withdrew to Dunbar. The Scots army which Leslie had carefully positioned on the Doon Hill to the south of Dunbar was protected by a steep slope from attack by the English to the north and barred Cromwell's line of retreat to England. The Scots just had to wait and victory would be theirs.

Just one problem; Leslie had not taken into account the religious fervour of the leaders of the Kirk, the effective rulers of Scotland. They believed there should be a pitched battle between the forces of good and those of evil, when naturally the godly would triumph. In a decision of unbelievable naivety, Leslie was ordered to lead his troops down from their impregnable position and confront the 'heathen' on the plains below. Cromwell watched in amazement as the Scots slithered down the slippery slope of Doon Hill to spend the night in the open, where to add to their misery they were soaked by the heavy rains. 'The Lord hath delivered them into our hand' was Cromwell's verdict. He had known that he needed a miracle to defeat the Scottish army and ironically it was the religious fanatics in power in Scotland who delivered it to him. At dawn, the English artillery pounded the Scots on their right and the English cavalry attacked their front. The Scottish army was broken; four thousand Scots died and another ten thousand were taken prisoner.

It was not, however, the end of Charles's adventure. The next spring Cromwell moved his army to Perth, leaving the way to England temptingly unguarded. Charles took the bait and marched south with an army of thirteen thousand but his Scottish army was defeated by Cromwell at the Battle of Worcester in 1651 and after months in hiding Charles fled to France. He would not return until 1660, two years after the death of Oliver Cromwell.

Charles II might have been expected to show some gratitude to the Scots for their earlier support, but like his father he had no love for the Presbyterian Church and he appointed his own bishops, brutally suppressing the Covenanters during the Killing Times. He was, in turn, succeeded by his Catholic brother James VII, but when his queen at the advanced age of forty gave birth to a son, Prince James, better known in later life as 'The Old Pretender', it was for many Protestants in England the last straw. They foresaw a future threatened by the prospect of permanent Catholic rule. In despair they turned to the Protestant William of Orange in the Netherlands. William was married to Mary, who herself as the daughter of James VII, had been the heir to the throne until the birth of the young prince. In 1688 William and Mary sailed with a fleet of sixty warships to England. James was paralysed. He asked his army for their loyalty but when they deserted him he accepted the inevitable and fled with his wife and baby son to France.

In February 1689 William and Mary were crowned King and Queen of England. The Glorious Revolution was complete.

But what of Scotland? Nobody had bothered to ask the Scots for their opinion. After a delay of two months for proper deliberation, Scotland meekly, if somewhat reluctantly, followed suit and accepted the monarchy of William and Mary; James was conveniently assumed to have 'forfeited' the Scottish crown. Thus the Stuart dynasty ended with a whimper and any pretence of political influence for Scotland died with it.

## The Darien 'Adventure'

Politically it had not gone too well. How had the country fared economically from the Union? Scotland had been very much the junior partner in the Union of the Crowns. England had gained great wealth through trade with her overseas colonies, but this trade was restricted to the English, with Scottish merchants explicitly excluded. The Glorious Revolution did not bring either peace or prosperity to Scotland as William had no love for Scotland or the Scots and never even visited the country, following the unpopular Stuart policy of basing the Secretary of State for Scotland in London. By the end of the century Scotland had become one of the poorest countries in Europe and what was desperately needed was a money-making scheme to bring prosperity to a country mired in poverty. Along came a man with just such a scheme – but sadly without a 'caution' printed on the label.

William Paterson had been born in 1658 in Dumfriesshire but had fled to England for safety during the Killing Times. From there he went to the West Indies, where he made a small fortune as a merchant. It was while he was in the West Indies that Paterson first heard of Darien from a group of pirates. They described an 'idyllic' place strategically situated on the coast of what is now Panama where the earth was rich, the forests plentiful, and there was even talk of gold. Sadly, and fatally, Paterson had never been there himself and relied for his information on the stories he was told.

He returned to England in 1687 and set himself up in London as a merchant. He built a reputation as a successful trader and banker. In 1691 he was one of the promoters of the Bank of England, raising the immense sum of one million two hundred thousand pounds as capital. He was, however, a quarrelsome soul and after a disagreement with his fellow directors he resigned and returned to Scotland, where in 1695 he helped to found the Bank of Scotland. The Scots were well aware of the wealth that had been gained by the English and the Dutch through their colonies overseas. Trading was the rage – the way for a country to become wealthy – and in 1695 an Act was passed forming a new trading company, grandly called the Company of Scotland Trading to Africa and the Indies.

The company aimed to raise the huge sum of six hundred thousand pounds; half of this sum, three hundred thousand pounds, had been promised in London, but the promise would not be honoured. The mighty East India Company feared this new rival as a threat to their monopoly and objected, successfully, to the king. William was not sympathetic to the ambitions of his Scottish subjects. 'I have been ill-served in Scotland' said the king. 'I hope some remedy may yet be found to meet the inconvenience that may arise from this Act.'

And a remedy was found, simple but brutally effective. A decision was made in the English Parliament that anyone residing in England who subscribed money to the new company could be prosecuted as a criminal. The three hundred thousand pounds promised in London vanished overnight.

Paterson came to the rescue. He wanted the Scots to have the same opportunity to profit from overseas trade as the English were enjoying. He proposed that the Company of Scotland Trading to Africa and the Indies should form a colony in Darien, providing a strategic land bridge between the Pacific and the Atlantic.

He talked of an idyllic country with white sands, blue seas and fertile land which as an international trading post would bring unimaginable wealth to the colonists and the investors who took part in the venture. He omitted to mention, or more probably did not know, that in Darien it rained from April to December, not just showers, but unremitting tropical rainstorms. Nor did he mention the endemic fever.

Scotland was in a fervour of excitement. Undaunted by the collapse of their financing in England, the promoters determined to raise the money in Scotland and the Scottish people responded enthusiastically both to invest and to put themselves forward as colonists. It is estimated that one quarter of Scotland's wealth was invested in the venture. Darien was the opportunity which would make Scotland and its people rich.

By 1698 twelve hundred had signed up for the expedition which set sail in July in five ships, led by the fifty ton Caledonia. William Paterson and his wife were among the colonists as they sailed from Leith, cheered on by massive crowds.

The expedition was sadly ill-prepared. They carried biscuits, beef and beer for the voyage but much of it was already mouldy when they set sail. They planned to obtain provisions by trading goods and carried a cargo which bizarrely included tartan cloth, powdered wigs and bonnets, goods for which there would be little demand. They had no idea of the conditions that would greet them on arrival.

The little fleet was beset by storms. The voyage took sixteen weeks, punctuated by the burial at sea of those who died of fever during the long crossing. The survivors arrived on the north coast of Panama in November and sailed on to the sheltered inlet at Darien. There they set to building a township of huts, which they optimistically named New Edinburgh, and a fort. They did not care, or perhaps they didn't even know, that the land they were building on was claimed by Spain. Worse, they were not aware that King William was trying secretly to arrange a treaty with the Spanish. Spain shipped vast quantities of gold and silver from its empire in Peru through Panama and William did not wish to upset the Spaniards by supporting a colony on their land. An order was issued forbidding English subjects in the Americas to sell arms or provisions to the new Scottish colony or to deal with it in any way. Ruthlessly, the Scottish settlers were sacrificed to the demands of English politics.

Darien was not the tropical paradise Paterson had painted. The impenetrable jungle, alive with poisonous snakes, made the growing of crops almost impossible. Food was running out and that which was left was heaving with maggots; not unsurprisingly there were no buyers for the tartan cloth and bonnets, so there was no money to buy more supplies.

Some progress had been achieved by the great efforts of half-starved and sickly men. The fort had been finished and the guns put in place. A protective ditch had been dug across the neck of land joining Darien to the mainland. But that was all. No land had been cleared, no crops sown and no trade developed. Then, worse still, the rains came, a solid, continuous downpour. Fever raged, first evidenced by a rash of red blotches covering the body, followed by violent vomiting of yellow bile, by aching limbs, and then, usually, by death. Many died including Paterson's own wife, who had died soon after they had arrived in Darien. The remaining settlers were in despair. In June 1699, under threat of an attack by the Spanish, the decision was taken to face the realities and sail home. It was a disaster. Only one ship, the Caledonia, reached Scotland, with just three hundred survivors from the twelve hundred who had set out full of hope just a year before.

But worse was still to come. As no news of the disaster had yet reached Scotland, a second group of hopeful settlers had already set sail for Darien wishing to share in the imagined prosperity. They set out in a fleet of four ships, including the company's flamboyant flagship, the Rising Sun, which had thirty-eight guns and was richly decorated with a gold rising sun painted on her bows and boasted rich gold carvings. Soon after the second fleet had set sail the true fate of the first expedition was learned from the survivors of the Caledonia. The directors of the company were appalled and promptly dispatched a further ship with two hundred soldiers on board to give support. They arrived to find a deserted settlement. The huts were rebuilt, but the new settlers fared no better than their predecessors.

To make things worse the Spanish now decided to act to protect their rights. They sent a fleet of twelve ships and an army of two thousand men to Darien. The settlers resisted bravely but they were hopelessly outnumbered and after resisting the siege for a month they surrendered and set sail back to Scotland. Only a handful of survivors and none of the four ships reached home.

It was one of the worst disasters in Scottish history. There had been a terrible loss of life and of money that Scotland could ill afford. The nine ships bought or chartered by the company had sunk or been abandoned and any pretence that Scotland could challenge the trading might of England had sunk with them.

This was a severe blow to Scotland. The nation's pride and confidence took a critical hammering and its economy was left in tatters. Even God seemed to have deserted the Scots. Through the 1690s wet summers, early frosts and long cold winters, the results of a change in the sun's pattern, brought seven lean years. Crops did not ripen and Scotland suffered badly from famine, with thousands dying of starvation. The President of the Royal College of Physicians in Edinburgh, Sir Robert Siddall, graphically described the sufferings of the people:

> 'death in the faces of the poor that abound everywhere; their ghostly looks, their feebleness, their agues and their fluxes threaten them with sudden death. Some die by the wayside, some drop down in the streets, the poor sucking babes are starving from want of milk which the empty breasts of their mothers cannot furnish. Crowds of men and women are forced to prowl and fight for food like beasts'.

By the time the famine had ended, a third of the population had been lost – through starvation, through disease or through forced migration. Union with England had become the only choice.

## The Act of Union

Perhaps it was the only choice, but it was not to be a union of equals. The terms were dictated by Scotland's powerful southern neighbour and the package was gift wrapped with cash to encourage acceptance by Scotland's leaders; 'such a parcel of rogues in a nation', as Robert Burns wrote.

On 16 January 1707, the Treaty of Union became law and the Scottish Parliament voted itself out of existence. In the strangely downbeat words of the Lord Chancellor, it was 'the end of an auld sang.'

From that date all decisions would be made by the parliament in Westminster, a parliament in which Scotland had only a minority role, with forty-five Scottish representatives out of a total of five hundred and fifty-eight members. Scottish interests soon became an irrelevance and politically, Scotland became a backwater.

Moreover, it was a backwater dominated by a strict Calvinist tradition based on the Reformation and the teachings of John Knox.

## Calvinism

The Reformation derived from the ideas of Martin Luther who was disillusioned by the excesses of the Catholic Church and preached of a Christian Church based on simple faith, with Jesus Christ at its head and with its ministers merely acting as His officers. This was in direct conflict with the Catholic Church, which believed the Pope was God's representative on earth.

People had begun to question the beliefs of the Catholic Church, asking if the bread and wine taken at Mass really were the body and blood of Christ, why services were held in Latin so that only the priests could understand them, and whether it was right for the Church to raise money by encouraging nobles to pay large sums for the forgiveness of their sins in this life and for the promise of entry to heaven in the next. The Catholic Church in Scotland, as indeed in Europe, had become corrupted by power and wealth. Churchmen enjoyed all the pleasures of life: fine clothes, rich jewels and good food – even the enjoyment of women, despite their vows of celibacy.

John Knox had learnt his Reformation ideals from John Calvin whilst in exile in Geneva, encountering in his words 'the most perfect school of Christ that ever was on earth since the days of the Apostles.' The power of his preaching changed Scotland forever from a Catholic into a Reformist country. Gone was the absolute authority of the Pope; gone were bishops appointed by the king; and in their place was a vision of an all-powerful God, represented on earth by His ministers.

Calvinism in its pure form was a harsh religion. There was strict observance of the Sabbath, with all work, dancing, music and games forbidden. Any transgression was severely punished; the penalty for blasphemy was death. This was the religious background to Scotland at the end of the seventeenth century and this was the belief which had driven the Covenanters who stood against the armies of Charles I and Charles II. It was only a few years before the Union, in 1697, that an unfortunate theology student, Thomas Aikenhead, had been taken, shivering on a cold January morning, to the gallows to be hanged for profaning the name of God. His crime was that on leaving an ale house with other students on a cold August evening he had jested that he wished he 'was now in the place called Hell to warm myself there.' One of his 'friends' reported his words and his troubles began. It seemed Aikenhead had made other rash statements, calling the Bible a book of romances and the disciples a 'company of silly witless fishermen.'

Foolish, certainly, but he was probably just a young man trying to impress his friends. In vain he recanted, for his accusers would not move from the view that he had broken God's Law and must be punished by being put to death by hanging. Thomas spoke movingly from the scaffold, first accusing the friend who had borne witness against him of uttering similar blasphemies, but then forgiving him. In words which startlingly foreshadow the belief in reason enshrined in the Enlightenment he stated in his defence, 'It is a principle innate and co-natural to every man to have an insatiable inclination to truth and to seek for it as for hid treasure.' His last words were to commend his soul into the hands of God, saying, 'And now, O Lord Father, Son and Holy Ghost, in thy hands I recommend my spirit.' As he uttered these words the hangman pulled tight the noose and this poor, perhaps misguided, boy was hanged for the crime of blasphemy.

## The Birth of the Scottish Enlightenment

Scotland had lost its wealth, its national identity and the independence for which so many Scots had fought and died over so many years. It was one of the poorest countries in Europe and was beset by religious intolerance.

It is difficult to conceive that such a background of poverty and of religious intolerance should provide fertile ground for an explosion of new ideas. But it did. Scotland had many latent advantages which now began to bear fruit.

*An Educated and Literate Society* — There was a well-established educational system which provided virtually universal education throughout the country, encouraged by the ideals of the Reformation.

John Knox, in the First Book of Discipline, had envisaged universal schooling, demanding that a school be set up in every parish, although in practice implementation of this worthwhile objective had been hampered by lack of funds. Various Acts in the seventeenth century further encouraged the development of schools and in 1696 an Act was passed requiring each parish to set aside a sizeable house for use as a school and to provide a salary for a schoolmaster.

A lasting benefit of Calvinism was the translation of the Bible into English. Previously, the Bible had only been read in Latin and was, therefore, the sole preserve of the priests. Now every home had a Bible and every father was responsible for teaching the Scriptures to his family. Reading became widespread, not only of holy works but of the new writings of the philosophers, the historians and the scientists. Lending libraries developed and all classes of society could access the latest ideas.

Scottish universities were a part of the spread of knowledge. They were happy to embrace new ideas, whereas, by comparison, the ancient universities of England had become outdated in their thinking and self-obsessed with their perceived importance. The Scottish universities encouraged the challenging of accepted beliefs and provided excellent teaching in 'useful' subjects like medicine, science and the law, with entry available to all who could afford the modest lecture fees or who could obtain a bursary. In a daring break with tradition, lectures were even given in English rather than in Latin! As a result, by the eighteenth century the Scottish people were amongst the most literate and best educated in Europe.

***A Legal System based on the Exercise of Reason*** — England had a legal system based largely on common law, whereby the law developed through a basis of precedent and argument. By comparison, Scotland had its own well-established legal system based on the exercise of reason and this independent legal system had been specifically protected in the Act of Union. Scottish lawyers were used to reasoned argument and through the exercise of reason would contribute strongly to the development of new political and economic ideas.

***Prosperity*** — Scotland was gradually becoming more prosperous after the disastrous end to the seventeenth century. The Union with England — which in the early years had been seen as an economic threat with Scottish merchants finding it difficult to compete with their English counterparts — became an opportunity.

Trade opened up with the colonies previously closed to Scottish merchant venturers. The Clyde became an international port capturing a large share of the trade in importing tobacco from Virginia, and Glasgow grew rapidly to become Britain's second city. The 'tobacco lords', who would boast their inordinate wealth by swaggering ostentatiously around the Trongate with their silver-topped canes, tricorn hats and red cloaks, not only brought riches to the city, but also through their international experiences the influence of new ideas and opportunities to which Glasgow was instinctively receptive.

***The 'Select Society'*** — Edinburgh was less commercial, less exposed to external influences than Glasgow, but it became a powerhouse of intellectual thought rivalled only by Paris and London. In a stroll through the city's streets a visitor would pass in just a few minutes the houses where lived eminent philosophers, lawyers and men of letters. There was a close circle of men of intellect, friends who met regularly at dinner or through the societies they had set up, and who would discuss and argue in depth the new ideas and theories put forward, their discussions enlivened by a bottle – or two or three – of claret wine. In terms of proximity and the ability to gather, Scotland's small size became in itself an advantage. As William Smellie, the first editor of the *Encyclopaedia Britannica*, observed:

> *'Here I stand at what is called the Cross of Edinburgh, and can, in a few minutes, take fifty men of genius and learning by the hand… In Edinburgh, the access of men of parts is not only easy, but their conversation and the communication of their knowledge are at once imparted to intelligent strangers with the utmost liberality.'*

***The Scottish Enlightenment*** — These two strands, the practical application of new ideas in Glasgow and the intellectual theorists of Edinburgh, came together to bring about not only a golden period in Scotland's history but also a flowering of thought and of new ideas based on reasoned argument and deduction which would change the world and the way we think. This was the Age of Enlightenment. Even the Church became less hostile to new thinking.

With this growing prosperity and intellectual activity, the country became more confident in its future. The Jacobite Rising in 1745 under Bonnie Prince Charlie was almost an irrelevance, a throwback to an earlier time and age. However romantic the story, the campaign was in truth fought by Highlanders for a prince in whose cause they did not believe and for a way of life that had already been left behind. It was a brave but largely irrelevant last throw of the dice.

Scotland was not alone in entering on a period of exciting intellectual development as new ideas flourished throughout Europe. Scots, however, made a great contribution, not just relative to the size and importance of the country, but absolutely by making major contributions to philosophy, to the sciences and particularly the application of science to everyday needs, to literature, to art and architecture, and to the social sciences.

The ideas of the Scottish philosophers spread throughout the world, influencing in particular the development of intellectual thought in America, even the wording of the American Constitution. Benjamin Franklin had visited Edinburgh in 1759, meeting with the leading figures of the Enlightenment, and many Scots went to America and served in positions where their ideas could influence the 'new' Americans. After independence from British rule, America had the opportunity as Thomas Paine said of 'seeing government begin, as if we had lived in the beginning of time.' The American Constitution could be designed from scratch and much of the thinking inherent therein derives from the ideas of the Scottish Enlightenment, constructing a strong government, but with safeguards for the rights of the individual and the interests of the individual states. It recognised, unlike the French Enlightenment philosophers, the importance of religion within society – as John Adams wrote, 'Our constitution was made only for a moral and religious people. It is wholly inadequate to the government of any other' - and, influenced by the Scottish Enlightenment, recognised also the benefits of a universal education. In this again the new Americans differentiated themselves from the French philosophers who considered the 'education of the masses' a waste of time, for as Voltaire had disdainfully remarked, 'As for la canaille (the rabble) I have no concern. It will always remain la canaille.' The American Constitution also had the unusual virtue of being commendably brief, and America today has embraced the ideas of Adam Smith more wholeheartedly than Britain itself - perhaps the 'American Dream' should in reality have been the Scottish Dream?

The Scottish Enlightenment was an outstanding contribution for a country which not many years before had been on the verge of collapse. Philosophers such as David Hume and Adam Smith achieved worldwide renown and influence, whilst engineers such as James Watt provided the power for the Industrial Revolution, which would change both Britain and the world forever.

The story of the Enlightenment can be told through the individual accounts of these philosophers, scientists, engineers, writers and artists, collectively: the Scots who enlightened the world.

Their ambitions and achievements are diverse, but there are common themes which run through many of their lives: a desire for self-improvement; the quality of Scottish education in the towns, in the countryside and in the universities, an education which was available to all of merit; a belief in hard work and its rewards, based on well-entrenched Calvinist ideals; and the development of ideas based on the exercise of argument and reason.

The Age of Enlightenment is usually taken to be the development in the eighteenth century of radical philosophical concepts through the 'study of man,' particularly through the works of philosophers such as Hutcheson, Kames, Hume and Smith.

It is with these prominent thinkers that we begin that we begin.

**Further Reading**
Alexander Broadie (Ed), *The Scottish Enlightenment: An Anthology*
Michael Fry, *The Union*
Arthur Herman, *The Scottish Enlightenment:*
                *The Scots' Invention of the Modern World*
Gertrude Himmelfarb, *The Roads to Modernity*
Rosalind Marshal, *John Knox*
John Prebble, *Darien, The Scottish Dream of Empire*

**Online Resources**
Education Scotland
http://www.educationscotland.gov.uk/scottishenlightenment/index.asp
http://www.historytoday.com/roy-campbell/scotlands-neglected-enlightenment

'Newton' Eduardo Paolozzi - 1995
British Library, London
photo: Thomas Haywood

EDUARDO PAOLOZZ

Paolozzi interprets William Blake's 1795 print 'Newton' illustrating how Sir Isaac Newton's formulas shifted the conventional view of the world to being determined by mathematics.

# Thinkers & Philosophers

## Part 1

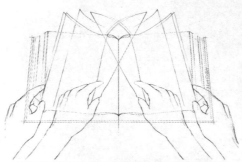

# THINKERS & PHILOSOPHERS

**Francis Hutcheson**
*PIONEER OF THE STUDY OF MAN AND HIS MOTIVATION*

**Henry Home**
*PHILOSOPHER AND LAND IMPROVER*

**David Hume**
*PHILOSOPHER AND HISTORIAN WHO STUDIED
'THE SCIENCE OF MAN'*

**Adam Smith**
*ECONOMIST AND PHILOSOPHER WHO IDENTIFIED
THE 'INVISIBLE HAND'*

**Joseph Black**
*THE FATHER OF MODERN CHEMISTRY*

**Mary Somerville**
*THE 'QUEEN' OF SCIENCE*

# Part 1 • Thinkers & Philosophers

## Thinking the Unthinkable

*'We look to Scotland for all our ideas of civilization.'*
—Voltaire

At the heart of the Scottish Enlightenment was the desire better to understand human behaviour and man's motivation by the application of reason based upon experience. The inexorable pursuit of reason would lead the philosophers and scientists of the Enlightenment to challenge the very basis of Christian doctrine, a radical approach which only a few years earlier would have been regarded as heresy. This required a new openness to ideas which was an essential component of the Enlightenment.

It was the force of reasoned thought which would lead Hutcheson to query the harsh doctrine of predestination and it was reasoned thought which led Hume to question the existence of God. Hutcheson preached an early form of Humanism, arguing 'that action is best which procures the greatest happiness for the greatest numbers,' implicitly contradicting the Calvinist certainties, while Hume was bold enough to question the existence of miracles, writing 'there is not to be found, in all history, any miracle attested by a sufficient number of men, of such good sense, education, and learning, as to secure us against all delusions in themselves; of such undoubted integrity, as to place them beyond any suspicion of any design to deceive … and at the same time attesting facts, performed in such a public manner, and in so celebrated a part of the world, as to render the detection (of falsehood) unavoidable.'

The questioning of religious 'certainties; is probably not so shocking to us today as it was in the time of Hutcheson and Hume but it was not only religious teaching which was held up to the light of reason and found wanting.

Many of these philosophers were concerned with the 'science of man', endeavouring to explain the behaviour and motivation of men. Smith, who thought of himself as a philosopher rather than an economist – indeed the 'dismal science' of economics had not yet been invented – wrote the 'Wealth of Nations' in an attempt to explain how man behaving rationally was not inherently selfish but would through his logical behaviour assist in the betterment of mankind.

Questioning of accepted beliefs was not left to the philosophers. Scientists such as Black and Hutton would apply reasoned thought to the world about them, discovering the concept of latent heat and explaining the Earth as a 'living body' which had existed, not for just a few thousand years as the scriptures taught, but for uncountable millions of years.

These were exciting times indeed and the ideas of these men would change both the world and the way we think about it.

And so we begin with Hutcheson, the 'Father of the Enlightenment.'

# Francis Hutcheson
1694–1746

PIONEER OF THE STUDY OF MAN AND HIS MOTIVATIONS

Francis Hutcheson, for many the 'Father' of the Enlightenment, was a Scottish philosopher who became Professor of Moral Philosophy at Glasgow University. He was described as 'the never to be forgotten Hutcheson' by his pupil Adam Smith. Hutcheson changed the way people thought, challenging the harsh certainties of Calvinism and the doctrine of predestination, and, by creating a new understanding of man and his role in society, paved the way for the ideas of David Hume, Adam Smith and others. He believed in the inherent goodness of mankind and in man's ability to make moral choices, believing 'that action is best which produces the greatest happiness for the greatest number.'

## Early Life

Hutcheson was born in Ulster, that Protestant part of Ireland which had been settled by Scottish Presbyterians who followed the fanatical 'hard-line' Calvinist religious teachings of John Knox. Hutcheson's father was a minister of the church, as was his grandfather, and both were committed Calvinists who believed in the doctrine that man was inherently a sinner who from birth was predestined for either heaven or hell.

Although a belief fervently held by many, strict Calvinism was inherently perverse as it meant that man could not improve upon the fate ordained for him even by the exercise of good deeds. If that were God's intention then what would be the point of moral behaviour or benevolence? This inherent illogicality was later satirised by James Hogg in his book, *The Private Memoirs and Confessions of a Justified Sinner.*

It was at his grandfather's house that Hutcheson received his first lessons in religious teachings. It was expected that the young Francis would follow his father and become a minister, sharing his father's belief in Calvinism. That was not to be. In 1711 Francis went to Glasgow to continue his studies and there learned to question the harsh views of the committed Calvinist.

Allan Ramsay, Frances Hutcheson. Hunterian Gallery, Glasgow

Francis Hutcheson
*see: colour plate 1*

## Hutcheson Learns a Different View of God

At that time Glasgow was a graceful city with wide streets very different from the mean and smoky wynds of medieval Edinburgh. Merchants from Glasgow had for many years ventured abroad to trade with the colonies in the New World of America and as a flourishing 'new' city, its citizens were more receptive to ideas which challenged accepted beliefs than the more settled Edinburgh folk.

When Hutcheson joined, the University of Glasgow had about four hundred students and suffered far less than its east coast counterpart in Edinburgh from interference from the Kirk or by the townsfolk, so that ideas could flourish unchecked by the forces of conservatism. Hutcheson enrolled as a theological student and was taught a very different form of religion from the strict Calvinism of his father. He learned that the world about us with all its beauty and variety reflected the God who had created it, a kind and gentle God who watched over his people. The harsh teaching of the Calvinists was rejected by new thinkers, who wondered what had happened to the belief that man was made in the image of God and by his good works and his acceptance of Jesus could enter heaven. What was the point of living a moral life if your fate was predestined from birth and you could in no way alter your destiny?

Some went even further, believing that God was so removed from the world that man was left on his own to find a way to survive. Religious thought had moved a long way in the few years since the unfortunate Thomas Aikenhead had been sentenced to death and hanged for blasphemy.

Hutcheson believed there must be a path between the two extremes, that there was a moral law which guided men's behaviour but neither the Calvinists nor the 'free thinkers' were right; man was a creature guided by an implicit 'moral law' but this was by choice, not by accident. The very functioning of society demands certain codes of behaviour such as respect for your fellow man and his rights. His ideas challenged the harsh Calvinism of his roots. After completing his time at university he was asked by his father to preach in his stead at Armagh and after the service his father hurried over to hear the verdict of the congregation. They were not best pleased; 'Your silly loon, Frank,' said one disgusted Scottish elder of the church in his local tongue, 'has fashed a' the congregation wi' his idle cackle; for he has been babbling this oor aboot a gude and benevolent God, and that the sauls o' the heathens themsels will gang to Heeven, if they follow the licht o' their ain consciences. Not a word does the daft boy ken, speer, nor say aboot the gude auld comfortable doctrines o' election, reprobation, original sin and faith. Hoot mon, awa' wi' sic a fellow.'

The liberal concept of a benevolent God that Hutcheson had embraced at Glasgow was obviously somewhat out of kilter with the views of that member of the congregation–where was that reassuringly familiar Hell and Damnation? In order to broaden his studies and take his ideas forward, Hutcheson went to Dublin, where he had been asked to set up a Presbyterian Academy as an alternative to Trinity College, Dublin, where entrance was restricted to Catholics. In Dublin he found a vigorous free-thinking society and he was able to enjoy the company of many leading intellectuals. He developed the idea that man was born to be free and to make his own choices. If a man chose to do a good deed, for example by helping another, that was his own choice and he did it because he derived satisfaction from the act of kindness.

Hutcheson published his ideas in two books, *An Inquiry into the Original of Our ideas of Beauty and Virtue* (1725) and an *Essay on the Nature and Conduct of the Passions and Affections* (1728). In the *Inquiry* he set out his concept of Virtue or Moral Good. He defined the difference between 'moral goodness,' evidenced by actions of which we instinctively approve, and 'moral evil.' Our reaction to moral good or evil is innate so that an act of benevolence without thought to reward excites our instinctive approval whilst we recoil against an act of evil such as treachery. He believed that all men are born with an innate sense of right and wrong; that they operate according to a moral law and gain satisfaction from the good they do to others. The goal of man is happiness, not in the contemporary sense of a superficial happiness derived from acquisitions and material wealth, but in the idealistic sense of achieving happiness by making others happy. He believed 'that action is best, which provides the greatest happiness for the greatest number.'

Hutcheson was, however, a realist; he understood that men did not always act from good motives and that this in itself was the result of moral choice. He had moved a long way from the Calvinist view of predestination.

In the *Inquiry* he also set out his belief that the concept of Beauty was dependent upon its perception, writing that 'were there no mind with a sense of beauty to contemplate objects, I see not how they could be called beautiful.' He envisaged a sixth sense, a sense of beauty, to add to the five senses of sight, touch, smell, feel and hearing and attempted to define the concept of beauty which he felt should imply a regularity of form spiced by diversity.

Further, Hutcheson then rather strangely tried to analyse the relative beauty of various geometrical forms. He thought that 'variety increases the beauty in equal uniformity' so that he held the pentagon to be more beautiful than the square and the cube more beautiful than the pyramid. His ideas on the intrinsic beauty of 'uniformity' do however have some substance in that researches into the perception of the beauty of the human form do show a predilection towards symmetry provided, as he wrote, 'no other inconvenience ensues; as when the eyes are not exactly like, or one arm or leg is a little shorter or smaller than its fellow.'

In his *Essay on the Nature and Conduct of the Passions and Affections* Hutcheson expanded his classification of senses, defining a sense as 'every determination of our minds to receive ideas independently of our will.' He identified five 'classes' of senses; the first the external senses of touch, taste, etc.; the second the sense of 'beauty;' the third a public sense, 'our determination to be pleased with the happiness of others, and to be uneasy at their misery;' the fourth a moral sense whereby 'we perceive virtue or vice, in ourselves, or others' and the fifth a sense of honour, pleasure at the approbation of others for our benevolent acts or shame at our wickedness. He distinguished between the 'calm desire' of benevolence, desiring the happiness of others, and the 'passions' aroused by our 'appetites' such as 'hunger and thirst (and) the desires between the sexes.' It was necessary to keep a just balance between our appetites and our passion.

It is perhaps no perhaps no coincidence that it was about this time he married Mary Wilson, perhaps accounting for the passage in the *Inquiry* 'Love itself gives a beauty to the Lover, in the eyes of the person beloved … And this perhaps is the strongest charm possible and that which will have the greatest power.' They would have seven children but only one, a son, survived.

## Professor of Moral Philosophy at Glasgow University

His ideas were well received and when the position of Professor became available at his old university he was a strong candidate despite holding views which challenged the establishment. He was appointed and proved himself an excellent teacher, carefully avoiding contentious religious issues and attracting a wide audience for his ideas. He believed it his duty not just to open the minds of his students to new thinking but to care for them also in a pastoral way, often lending them sums of money to sort out their affairs; perhaps unsurprisingly, he found the Irish students the most wayward and headstrong.

Hutcheson brought about the modernisation of university teaching, firstly by lecturing in English rather than in Latin, which before had been the custom, and secondly, by extending the scope of the curriculum to include the study of the classics, particularly Greek. He encouraged his students to reject the harsh dogma of Calvinism and decide for themselves the answers to the moral questions of the day, regarding the Church as a moral guide and a keeper of conscience.

He taught that all human behaviour was part of an overall 'law of man' which covered not only moral but also economic behaviour, how people act and trade with each other in the real world. It was these ideas which inspired one of his pupils, Adam Smith, to produce some years later his groundbreaking work on economics.

Hutcheson died of a fever in Dublin in 1746. He had published little during his time at Glasgow, concentrating instead on his teaching. As his biographer William Scott wrote, 'Hutcheson's strength lay in his personality. His personal magnetism and method of lecturing were his main influences. The first brought him his audience and the second taught it.' He believed that philosophy was not dry theory to be taught through learned works but a living subject. He left his progressive mark on ideas and on the method of education in Scotland, not through his published works but through the power of his teaching. It would be nine years after his death before his final work, *A System of Moral Philosophy in Three Books*, was published by his son, also Francis.

## Hutcheson's Legacy

Hutcheson had led the way in fresh thinking on moral issues, questioning the harsh certainties of the Calvinists. Although it would be left to others such as David Hume and Adam Smith to take these ideas forward, his teaching, his challenge to established ideas, and his inspiration of those who followed in his path justify the claim that he had 'fathered' the Scottish Enlightenment.

He was in another way ahead of his time. His belief in the basic principle of liberty challenged the existing status of women and he saw women as in every way the equal of men in their rights. This applied also to slavery; he wrote that 'nothing can change a rational creature into a piece of goods void of all rights.' His views would later inspire the abolitionists and for these ideas alone he has earned his place in history.

### Further Reading
Francis Hutcheson, Philosophical Writings
William Robert Scott, *Francis Hutcheson: His Life, Teaching and Position in the History of Philosophy*

### Online Resources
University of Glasgow
http://www.universitystory.gla.ac.uk/biography/?id=WH0191&type=P
Francis Hutcheson Institute
http://www.fhinst.co.uk/

# *'Fare ye a' weel, ye bitches!'*

## Henry Home, Lord Kames
### 1696–1782

PHILOSOPHER AND LAND IMPROVER

*'We must every one of us acknowledge Kames for our master.'*
—Adam Smith

Henry Home wrote extensively on legal and philosophical subjects, in addition to carrying out innovative agricultural improvements on his lands, but is best remembered as one of the early and most influential figures of the Scottish Enlightenment. He acted as a mentor for a number of key Enlightenment figures, including David Hume, Adam Smith and James Boswell, the biographer of Dr Johnson. Thomas Reid, the 'common sense' philosopher, was another regular visitor to his home.

His reach was international. He entertained Benjamin Franklin on his visit to Edinburgh in 1759 at his house at Kames. Home and Franklin became close, exchanging views and ideas. Home sent Franklin a copy of his *Elements of Criticism*, which examined what characterised 'good' literature and art and tried to define the nature of beauty, admittedly in a somewhat didactic style; Franklin protested at the omission of music. Home would again entertain him at Blair Drummond in 1771 on his second visit to Scotland.

### Training in the Law

Henry Home (pronounced 'Hume.' Henry Home and David Hume, also born 'Home', were related) was born in 1696 in Kames to a landed Berwickshire family of modest but comfortable means. He was tutored at home and as a bright boy who enjoyed books and learning, it seemed logical that a career in the law would best fit his talents. Accordingly, at the age of sixteen he was packed off to Edinburgh to join the chambers of a writer to the signet.

Scottish law had developed along a very different path from English law. Although in both there was a distinction between the lawyer who acts for an individual, in England called a 'solicitor,' but in Scotland a 'writer to the signet,' and the representative who pleads the case before a judge in a court of law, in England called a barrister but in Scotland an advocate, the theory and practice of the two legal systems were and remain very different.

Scottish law was based initially on the laws of the Romans and as such is closer to the law as practised in continental countries than to that practised in England. The exercise of law is based on reason; the decision of a Scottish judge in either a civil or a criminal case looks beyond the facts in an attempt to find the truth. As such there is a third option of a verdict of 'non proven' in addition to the 'guilty' and 'not guilty' verdicts available to an English court.

By contrast, English law developed on the principle of legal precedent; that is, a case is decided on the basis of decisions made previously in similar cases. This is called 'common law', although over time it has been overlain by immense legislation. An English court is not required to exercise reason or look behind the facts presented in an endeavour to discover the truth; the decision of the court is made only on the evidence presented. The procedure in court is essentially adversarial, with each side represented by a barrister who argues, often aggressively, his client's case and tries to disprove or cast doubt on the case of the opposition.

These fundamental differences in the operation of the law were jealously guarded by the Scots and together with the Scottish Church and university system were the only parts of Scottish life expressly excluded from the Act of Union.

Henry Home had originally planned on becoming a writer to the signet. He decided to change to become an advocate as a result of a visit to the house of Sir Hew Dalrymple, Lord President of the Court of Sessions, which opened his eyes to the 'ease and affluence' of an advocate's life. He immediately resolved to become an advocate and undertake the extra studies required. These took time and Home was twenty-seven years old before he finally qualified as an advocate, having then satisfied the last requirement of making a speech in public on a specific item of civil law.

## Life as an Advocate

Home prospered as an advocate. He had a quick intellect with an impressive power of persuasive reasoning, noting that Scottish law is 'grafted' upon the laws of Rome and that 'Roman law is illustrious for its equitable rules affording great scope for acute reasoning.' It is this core belief in reason that enabled Scottish lawyers to contribute so significantly to the ideas of the Scottish Enlightenment, based likewise upon the exercise of reason. He believed that decisions in law should be based upon the exercise of principles but going further, he asserted that 'if the decision be founded upon wrong principles, or concludes falsely from true principles, it can signify nothing.'

In 1737 Home was asked to become curator of the Advocates' Library. He approached his task with characteristic vigour, making the library not just a source for legal works but also for works on philosophy, history and geography so that the Library became in time one of the principal collections of learned works within Scotland and indeed Britain. David Hume, himself later a keeper of the Advocates' Library, used its resources extensively to expand his reading and ideas, as did many other Enlightenment figures. It is no exaggeration that the resources of the Advocates' Library were a key factor in the development of the Scottish Enlightenment, and it was the efforts of Henry Home which established its foundation.

David Martin, Henry Home, Lord Kames, Scottish National Portrait Gallery

Henry Home, Lord Kames
*detail, see: colour plate 2*

In 1741, the year his father died, Henry Home married Agatha Drummond, who was not only acclaimed as one of the beauties of Edinburgh but was heiress to the estate of Blair Drummond. They had two children; the younger, Jean, would marry a rather boring husband and, somewhat unconventionally, took her pleasures elsewhere causing a major scandal. Home was totally unsympathetic and sent her off to France.

A frenetic worker, Home usually woke before 6.00 a.m. to prepare for his day. When the court adjourned at 3.00 p.m. Home would spend the rest of the afternoon reading and writing. His evenings were spent with friends, developing ideas over numerous bottles, until he retired to bed round midnight.

Home came to dislike claret, 'that liquor without which no Scotch gentleman in those days could be exhilarated,' and instead preferred port, chosen in support of Britain's oldest ally. The serving of port led to a bon mot by Henry Erskine who, when asked by his host for news of the French fleet in the West Indies, replied wittily 'Confined to port, my lord, as we are at present.'

Home would invite young men of ideas to join him and his evening gatherings included such figures as Adam Smith, David Hume, Allan Ramsay and James Boswell. This method of encouraging serious discussion in convivial surroundings became a key feature of the Enlightenment. David Hume was a special favourite, although the two frequently quarrelled; Home was a strict Episcopalian and could not accept the agnosticism of Hume. David Hume in turn called Home the 'best friend I ever possessed' but also 'the most arrogant man in the world.' James Boswell was another protégé of Home, perhaps seeking in him a father figure to replace his own father, Lord Auchinleck, from whom he was estranged. Boswell did contemplate writing a biography of Home but instead moved to London where he came under the spell of Dr Johnson and wrote the famous *Life of Johnson* – but not before he had sampled the illicit pleasures of Home's daughter, Jean.

Henry Home's first published work was a legal text in which he annotated and discussed past legal decisions to help in the development of Scottish law. He realised that the law was a 'living' body, developing as society developed. This led him to the idea that society too developed over time and that the development of law was an essential part of this process.

Home was fascinated by the way his ideas were developing but he was constrained by the time he could spare from his busy legal career. In 1752 he was appointed a judge and took the honorary title of Lord Kames after his birthplace.

## The Concept of Property, the Rule of Law and the Development of Society

Home, or as we shall now call him, Kames, wrote a number of further legal works before turning in 1751 to the study of man and society in his *Essays on the Principles of Morality and Natural Religion*, a book which provided the foundation for the later 'common sense' school of philosophy.

Kames believed in predestination, that the destiny of each soul was unerringly guided and foreseen by God. He recognised the paradox that man believed he had freedom of choice and reconciled this apparent contradiction by the somewhat tortuous argument that, although his destiny was preordained, man was unaware of this and therefore believed in ignorance that he could exercise free will, or, as he put it, that free will is a delusion given to man by a benevolent Deity.

Kames drew on his experience of law to ask the question: 'Why do laws exist within a society?' Kames thought that laws developed to protect the concept of property; certain objects belong to certain people and this concept of ownership needs to be recognised and respected. It was not enough to think, as Hutcheson had taught, that man was inherently moral. Kames had seen too much of the world going through his courts to accept that notion. Rather it was in man's interest to create laws to respect the concept of private property, for without property there would be no point in working, or as he put it, 'labour and industry [would be] in vain.' Kames believed that the desire to own and accumulate property was a fundamental feature of human society. Kames further recognised that the concepts of property and of law had developed as society had developed. He proposed the idea that society advanced through four stages. In the first men lived by hunting and fishing and as such lived in small family groupings. The next stage was a nomadic one, where families followed herds of animals, later domesticating some;

this pastoral stage required larger groupings but was still based around an extended family community or clan. The third stage was cultivation, where crops were sown and reaped by and for the community. New trades now developed such as ploughman and blacksmith to serve the wider community; 'contracts' had to be formed to recognise the various tasks performed and 'rights' were needed to reward the efforts of individuals within the community.

The final stage was the development of commerce, trade and industry, which could only operate in a world where property rights were respected and laws enforced. This stage represented a fundamental break with the past, requiring the imposition of law and government. The concept of property rights was essential to the development of this fourth stage; as Kames identified, 'Without private property there would be no industry and without industry men would remain savages for ever.'

These four stages of society were all represented in Scotland at the time of Kames. In the Hebrides there were poor fisher folk who gathered seaweed and shellfish to eke out their wretched lives; in the Highlands small groups of clan members lived as cattle drovers; and in the lowlands there was settled agriculture with herds of cattle, flocks of sheep and the growing of crops. The final stage was found in the cities, such as Glasgow, whose merchants had become wealthy through the burgeoning tobacco trade with the colonies, and Edinburgh, where the form of 'polite' society had fully developed.

Hutcheson had wondered why if every man had the desire to be free there was still so much oppression. Kames supplied the answer; in primitive societies there was a need to work together to survive and to sometimes accept harsh rule as protection against marauding tribes. But as a society develops and becomes wealthier, so individual freedoms will flourish in an environment where the individual is protected by and respects the rule of law.

This thinking had an unexpected result. Scots could look at other races and judge them purely by the stage they had reached along the process of evolution. With this philosophy there was no suggestion that an African, for example, was in some way inferior to a white man, merely that the African was some stages behind in the process of social evolution. This implied there was no justification for the slavery of Africans as a perceived 'inferior' race and in the course of time led to an epoch-making judgement.

Joseph Knight, an African-born slave, had been transported to Jamaica where he was sold to his master, who in 1769 brought Knight with him to Scotland. Knight learned of a decision in the English courts that slavery was against the law of England and so approached his master and asked for wages for all the service he had given over the years. When his master refused he ran away but he was caught and arrested. The Sheriff of Perth first heard the case and held that as there was no slavery in Scotland and the slave laws of Jamaica did not apply in Scotland, Knight should be freed. His master then appealed and took the case to the Court of Sessions in Edinburgh where Kames sat as one of the judges.

The proposition was put to the court that 'the law of Jamaica [should not be supported] because it is repugnant to the first principles of morality and justice' and that furthermore 'no man is by nature the property of another.' Kames, by now an old man of eighty-one years, agreed. 'We sit here,' he declared, 'to enforce right, not to enforce wrong.' Slavery was declared illegal in Scotland and Joseph Knight was set free. It was a decision based on reason, not precedent, and underlined the belief first expressed by Hutcheson that every man had the right to be free.

## Judge of the Criminal Court

In 1763 Kames was appointed Lord Commissioner of High Court of Justiciary. In more simple terms, he became a judge of criminal cases, travelling around Scotland and trying cases which ranged from theft of sheep to murder. Kames was a harsh judge with a taste for conviction and a mordant sense of humour, although in his defence it must be said he would often pass a lesser sentence of whipping or transportation rather than the ultimate punishment of death by hanging.

His caustic sense of humour is illustrated by the trial of Mathew Hay, a farmer in the Borders who was a frequent chess companion of Kames. Hay was accused of the murder by poison of the daughter of one of his tenants, Elizabeth Wilson, whom he'd impregnated. For good measure, he was also accused of the murder of the tenant together with his wife and their other daughter. Evidence in the case was given by Dr Joseph Black who found traces of arsenic in the samples sent to him for examination. Hay was duly found guilty and sentenced to death. 'That's checkmate to you, Mathew!' Kames commented as the guilty man left the court.

## Kames the Land 'Improver'

Improvement, the modernisation of farming techniques, was very much a part of the Enlightenment. It embraced not just the enclosure of lands but also the introduction of farm machinery, admittedly primitive, and more advanced methods of farming.

Despite his busy life in the law Kames had found time to become an 'Improver,' bringing agricultural improvements to his estate in Berwickshire. He enthusiastically adopted the new ideas being introduced, including rotating his crops, raising turnips in drills as fodder, using the plough in the cultivation of potatoes and utilising fertilisers to improve the yield from his lands. The estate at Kames was sold in 1775 after he had inherited through his wife the family property at Blair Drummond in Perthshire. Kames enthusiastically set out to 'improve' his new estate, building new farm houses and introducing innovative methods of cultivation and breeding; he wrote The Gentleman Farmer to encourage other landowners to embrace the new ideas and put aside their 'stupid attachment to ancient habits and practices.'

Kames became a member of the Edinburgh Society for Encouraging Arts, Sciences, Manufactures and Agriculture, a 'daughter' of the Select Society, and in 1755 a Commissioner for the Forfeited Estates. These were estates which had been transferred to the Crown after the failed Jacobite Rising and considerable efforts were put into improving conditions for the tenants, including the introduction of longer tenancies, the provision of education, the building of roads and instruction in improved agricultural methods. Later emphasis was given to the cultivation of flax, which would lead in time to the development of a prosperous linen industry.

## 'Fare Ye a' Weel'

Kames died in his eighty-seventh year. He had worked to the last and his words of farewell to his fellow judges on leaving court for the last time were, characteristically, 'Fare ye a' weel, ye bitches.' He told his doctor two days before his death that 'he earnestly wished to be away because he was exceedingly curious to learn the nature and manners of another world,' and there would be work to be done there.

## Kame's Legacy

Henry Home was a hard man, a man of iron constitution and sardonic wit who combined erudition with bawdy humour and refinement with coarseness, treating his errant daughter with brutal disdain. He read extensively, filling every hour of his day with reading, with writing, with the exercise of the law and with intellectual discourse. He had above all a fine intellect and was able through the exercise of reason to promote ideas concerning the form of society, man's role within it and the part played in the advancement of society by the development of a system of law.

Home also encouraged many younger intellectuals, famously David Hume and Adam Smith, both through his evening gatherings and his 'legacy' of the Advocates' Library, to advance thinking in all areas of life. If Hutcheson was the 'father' of the Enlightenment, perhaps Kames was its foster father.

**Further Reading**
Henry Home, Lord Kames, *Essays on the Principles of Morality and Natural Religion*
Ian Simpson Ross, *Lord Kames and the Scotland of His Day*

**Online Resources**
International Association for Scottish Philosophy
http://www.scottishphilosophy.org/lord-kames.html

## David Hume
### 1711–1776

PHILOSOPHER AND HISTORIAN WHO STUDIED THE 'SCIENCE OF MAN'

*'There is no question of importance whose decision is not comprised in the science of man and there is none which can be decided with any certainty before we become acquainted with that science.'*

— David Hume, *A Treatise of Human Nature*

David Hume believed in the study of man. He was primarily a philosopher but also an historian who believed that history was the product of human nature.

His clear exercise of reason and desire for evidence led him to challenge accepted beliefs dear to the Church, such as the belief in miracles or in the existence of an after-life. These views brought him the opposition of Church leaders and Establishment figures and Hume in his day was perceived to be an atheist, although today he might be more correctly described as an agnostic. This perception undoubtedly hindered his advancement, and as a result he was in his lifetime probably regarded more highly as an historian than as a philosopher.

He has now received the recognition he deserves as a great philosopher, perhaps the greatest to write in the English language, and one of the leading lights of the Scottish Enlightenment.

### Childhood

David Hume was born in Edinburgh in 1711, the son of a successful Edinburgh lawyer who died when Hume was only two years old, leaving his mother a widow with three young children to support. She moved her young family to their estate in the Borders. Hume did not go to the local school but was taught at home, learning also to enjoy the country pleasures of riding, shooting and fishing.

At the age of eleven he went to Edinburgh University, where he learned Greek, Logic and Natural Philosophy, living with his mother in their house in Edinburgh. He studied Law and it was naturally assumed that he would follow his father into that profession, but he had no taste for it. He read widely at this time, particularly the writings of philosophers, and became so wrapped up in his books that he fell ill, his mind over-stressed by his obsessive and lonely studies.

It was during this period that Hume became an atheist, losing his belief in the existence of a god. This may be a little extreme; it may rather be that he could not be persuaded that the existence of God could be supported by reasoned argument or factual evidence and as such we would today characterise him as an agnostic, one

David Hume
*colour plate 3*

Allan Ramsay, David Hume. Scottish National Portrait Gallery

who 'does not know.' It is a mark of the more liberal times that these views expressed by Hume could be published, if not endorsed. It was not that many years earlier that Thomas Aikenhead had been hanged for blasphemy.

### A Treatise on Human Nature

In 1734 Hume moved to France to study and there wrote his first book, *A Treatise on Human Nature*, in which he attempted to set out a complete system of philosophy based on the science, or study, of man. The *Treatise* is comprised of three books. The first, *Of Understanding*, deals with the origin of ideas and the process whereby one attains knowledge. Hume argues that knowledge is not gained solely by the exercise of reason but by reason moulded by experience, by watching and learning. He wrote that 'The idea of cause and effect is derived from experience,' giving as an example one billiard ball striking another: each time the former strikes the latter, the stationary ball moves. We therefore learn that a stationary billiard ball when hit by a moving ball will itself move; we have learned this not through the power of reason but through experience.

The second book, *Of the Passions*, sets out to explain the emotional side of man. Hume realised that man cannot be controlled by reason alone; as he wrote, 'Reason is and only ought to be the slave of the passions.' It is our emotions, such as aspiration for success, a wish to be loved, a craving for fame, even anger or greed, which determine our desires, but it is reason which determines our actions, the course of action by which we endeavour to achieve those desires. It is therefore in the final reckoning self-interest which drives men's actions, even if that self-interest might be the pleasure derived from philanthropy.

The third book, *Of Morals*, was published some time later; in it Hume considers the concept of 'goodness' and the effect of human behaviour both on the individual and on others. Hume recognised that men have a 'sense of virtue', of what is right and what is wrong, but wondered whether this sense was inherent (existing from birth) or learned; in modern terms, did it come through nature or nurture? Hume did not know; 'I am of the opinion,' he wrote, 'that it is impossible for me at present to give any precise answer to this question.' In fairness to Hume the issue is still debated today – and still undecided!

He did recognise that men from the earliest times had to work together in a form of society and as such had to respect each other's feelings. 'There is no human and indeed no sensible creature whose happiness or misery does not in some manner affect us when brought near to us.'

It took two years for Hume to find a publisher for the *Treatise* and when he did his book was at first a failure, or, as Hume himself said, it fell *'dead-born from the press.'* He had expected over-night fame but his book was greeted with the worst of receptions, deafening silence. As he wrote, wryly, 'Authors have this … in common with lovers and founded on the same reason, that they are both besotted with a blind fondness of their object.' Yet this was the book which was identified two hundred and fifty years later by Bertrand Russell to be 'by common consent the greatest work of philosophy … in the English language.'

The ideas expressed by Hume challenged accepted religious beliefs. His arguments made no allowance for inherent knowledge, but only knowledge which could be derived from experience. It came close therefore to denying the existence of the immortal soul and indeed of God, for no proof of His existence could be derived from experience. The world was not 'God-created' but created by man through knowledge derived from experience. The Church was not impressed.

Disappointed with the lack of response he received from the publication of the *Treatise* and, not least because he needed some money, Hume decided to produce a work of more immediate popular appeal. Accordingly, in 1742 he published his next work, a series of essays entitled *Essays, Moral and Political*, in which he dealt with a number of subjects such as *'Love and Marriage,' 'Impudence and Modesty,'* and *'Moral Prejudice.'* These receiveded much more attention. Hume had written a best seller. As a result of this success he was invited to apply for the position of Professor of Moral Philosophy at Edinburgh University, but his past came back to haunt him and he was eventually turned down; twelve of the fifteen ministers deciding his appointment voted against him because they did not approve of his rejection of the Church and its teachings, and his presumed avowal of atheism.

## Return to France

Hume had a position, briefly, as a tutor to the Marquess of Annandale; 'briefly' because the marquess proved inconveniently to be insane. He returned to France after this, perhaps surprisingly for a philosopher, as secretary to General James St Clair.

General St Clair had been instructed to lead an expedition to Canada to fight the French and seize Quebec but bad weather made the ocean crossing impractical so the general, whose expedition had reached no further than the Isle of Wight, was given new orders, fairly vague it must be said, to 'Make a descent on some part of the Western coast of France ... which might greatly annoy the French!'

The orders were imprecise, and to make matters worse the general was not allowed for reasons of secrecy to obtain a map of France and so had to rely on a map in a book purchased by one of his officers. Perhaps more by good luck than good navigation he stumbled upon the town of L'Orient on the west coast of France, which he promptly besieged. The siege was not a great success as the British twelve pounder guns, just four in number, made little impact on the walls of the town and the British were, in any event, heavily outnumbered by the defenders. Nevertheless the citizens of the town, terrified by the haphazard firing of the guns, resolved to surrender. Even this did not work out for the poor general who had retired with his troops before the French commander could find him to give him the surrender.

Somewhat surprisingly the general succeeded in returning with his men to England, but Hume was not impressed by his first-hand experience of the British military. Undismayed, he travelled again with the general, this time on a mission as ambassador to Vienna and Turin. This was much more to Hume's taste; he could enjoy the company and conversation of civilised minds.

During this period Hume found time to write more essays, one of which, *On Miracles*, raised further controversy. Hume declared there had been no miracle of which the existence could be proved by evidence and thus no justification for the miracles which formed a cornerstone of Christian faith — a fair if challenging requirement for proof....

> *There is not to be found, in all history, any miracle attested by a sufficient number of men, of such unquestioned good sense, education and learning as to secure us against all delusion in themselves; of such undoubted integrity, as to place them beyond all suspicion of any design to deceive others...*

## The Scottish Enlightenment

Hume returned to Edinburgh, where he joined the circle of thinkers and scientists who formed the Scottish Enlightenment, of which Hume himself had become a key member. In 1752 he published a series of essays under the title *Political Discourses*. In these he dealt with a number of issues, including economics, where he favoured free trade and was opposed to government borrowing. Wise words indeed, which should perhaps be placed on the desk of every Chancellor of the Exchequer:

> *Why should the case be so different between the public and an individual as to make us establish different maxims of conduct for each? It would scarcely be more prudent to give the prodigal son a credit in every banker's shop in London than to empower a statesman to draw bills [raise money] in this manner upon posterity.*

When Adam Smith gave up the Chair of Logic at Glasgow University, he proposed his friend Hume for the vacant professorship. Again, however, Hume's reputation as an anti-establishment atheist was held against him and his application was denied. He did eventually secure a post in 1752 as keeper of the Advocates' Library, which gave him unlimited access to its collection of more than thirty thousand books. He used this position to good effect, publishing over the next ten years his *History of England* in six volumes, which brought him greater fame in his lifetime than any of his philosophical treatises, so much so that Hume himself always claimed to be an historian rather than a philosopher, albeit an historian whose interest in history was philosophical. He wrote:

> *[The] chief use [of history] is only to discover the constant and universal principles of human nature ... These records of wars, intrigues, factions and revolutions are so many collections of experiments by which the politician or moral philosopher fixes the principles of his science.*

In 1754 Hume became one of the founding members of the Select Society, a society formed by his friend Allan Ramsay, the painter, to receive and discuss papers from its illustrious members, who included Adam Smith and the historian William Robertson, and later Lord Kames and Adam Fergusson. For ten years the Select Society formed the centrepiece for intellectual discussion in Edinburgh and many theories later published were first floated before its members.

## Le Bon David and the Salons of Paris

Hume was invited in 1763 to return to France as Secretary to the British Ambassador and with many happy memories of his earlier time there he accepted. Hume's reputation as a philosopher had preceded him and he was fêted in the salons of the great and the good, thoroughly enjoying the attention and fame he received. Somewhat surprisingly, this plump and ageing philosopher who spoke

French with a broad Scots accent became the idol of the Paris salons and the darling of the fashionable ladies of France who called him 'le bon David.'

During his life Hume had always enjoyed the company of ladies, but more through the pleasures of conversation than any more intimate attachment. It is recorded that when he was a young man he had paid his 'addresses' to a lady who had rejected him, possibly because of his doubtful prospects. With the onset of his later fame it was hinted by a mutual friend that the lady might now have changed her mind. Hume replied somewhat ungallantly, *'So have I!'*

While still in Scotland he had been receiving admiring correspondence from a lady known rather elegantly as Marie-Charlotte-Hippolyte de Campet de Saujeon, or more succinctly as the Comtesse de Boufflers, who at the time had the double inconvenience of being married and also the mistress of the Prince de Conti. She had written:

> *For a long time, Sir, I have struggled with conflicting sentiments. The admiration which your sublime work has awakened in me and the esteem which it has inspired me for your person, your talents and your virtue, have frequently aroused the desire of writing to you, that I might express these sentiments with which I am so deeply smitten.*

Confused and flattered by this approach, Hume replied that as a long-term bachelor he had 'rusted amid books and study.' The relationship between Hume and the Comtesse blossomed at a safe distance through the regular exchange of letters and ideas, but now that he was in France he met her in person, attending her salon to exchange ideas on philosophy and the latest gossip, even joining a house party at the Prince's hunting lodge outside Paris. Correspondence at long range was one thing, but close personal contact took what had been a purely intellectual friendship into a dangerous new phase, a little overheated for Hume who in 1766 decided to retreat to Edinburgh, but not without a complication on the way.

Hume was accompanied on his return by Jean-Jacques Rousseau, the French *philosophe*, who in 1762 had published the *Social Contract* which opened with the bold statement that 'Man is born free, and everywhere he is in chains' and which advocated the principles of liberty, equality and fraternity which would later become the rallying call for the French Revolution. Rousseau did not extend his admiration for the innate wisdom and ability of the 'common people' to his private life; he had a long term affair with an illiterate maid, Therese, by whom he sired five children, all of whom were taken from their mother at birth and given to a foundling hospital because, or so he claimed, Thérèse was incapable of raising the children.

Not surprisingly Rousseau's revolutionary ideas were not well received in aristocratic France and he had fled into exile to the distress of Hume, appalled at the treatment of his fellow philosopher. Hume had been warned that in befriending Rousseau he was 'warming a viper in his bosom,' but he nevertheless took him back with him to London. In no time the petulant Rousseau had quarrelled with his benefactor and they carried out a bitter argument by letter which Hume eventually terminated by writing to his former friend that through his words and deeds he had 'become the enemy of your own repose, fortune and honour. I cannot be surprised after this that you are my enemy. Adieu, and for ever.'

## Hume's Death and After

Hume returned finally to Edinburgh where he rejoined the intellectual elite, enjoying the pleasures of fine clarets, good food and the company and conversation of his fellow intellectuals. Hume was in particular much impressed by Adam Smith's writing on economics, *The Wealth of Nations*, writing to Smith to warmly praise his work.

By 1775 Hume had become seriously ill and realised his life was nearing its end. His friend and fellow philosopher Adam Fergusson wrote, 'David I am afraid loses ground. He is cheerful and in good spirits but I confess that any hopes ... have very much abated.'

Hume bore his impending death stoically. Just before the end he wrote to the Comtesse de Bouffleur, with whom he had continued to correspond from a safe distance, that:

> *Tho' I am certainly within a few weeks, dear Madam, and perhaps within a few days, of my own death, I could not forbear being struck with the death of the Prince of Conti – so great a loss ... My distemper is a diarrhoea, or disorder in my bowels, which has been gradually undermining me these last two years but within these six months has been visibly hastening me to my end. I see death approach gradually, without any anxiety or regret. I salute you with great affection and regard, for the last time. David Hume.*

He died of intestinal cancer on 25 August 1776, saddened he had not finished the great work of delivering his countrymen from Christian superstition. He died as he had lived, unconvinced of the existence of a god but nonetheless at peace with himself and the world. David Hume's doctor, who was present at his death, wrote to Adam Smith saying that he 'died in such a happy composure of mind that nothing could have made it better.'

But the controversy which had been a part of Hume's life did not end with his death. He had left three works to be published posthumously, *Dialogues Concerning Natural Religion, On Suicide* and *Of the Immortality of the Soul*, knowing the reaction they would provoke. Of suicide Hume had written, 'If suicide be considered a crime 'tis only cowardice can impel us to it. If it be no crime both prudence and courage should engage us to rid ourselves at once of existence when it becomes a burden.' He could find no trace in the Scriptures which forbade suicide. The banning of suicide was therefore not based on the Scriptures but on the ideas of men and did not in Hume's view have any basis in reason.

The idea of immortality on the other hand is rooted in the Scriptures, but in Hume's view the concept of immortality could not be supported by evidence or reason and should therefore be dismissed. Both ideas were deeply shocking to religious believers. The old philosopher could still shock from beyond the grave. But did he know the shock he caused – or was he right that there is no such thing as immortality?

## Hume's Legacy

David Hume was one of the leading members of the Scottish Enlightenment, regarded by his friends as a great and original thinker. His belief was in reason based on experience. Reason would lead man to create a world best suited to his desires, ideally to a world of peace and friendship. It is the belief in the power of reason which defines the Enlightenment.

Hume is now best remembered as, arguably, the greatest of British philosophers – but in his lifetime he was more famous as a historian. Hume viewed history from the viewpoint of the philosopher, defining history as 'so many collections of experiments by which the moral philosopher fixes the principles of his science.' Hume's biographer Nicholas Phillipson is clear of his importance in both roles. In his book, *David Hume: The Philosopher as Historian*, Phillipson traces 'the step-by-step progress by which one of the greatest of Western philosophers turned himself into one of the greatest historians of Britain, a progress that was entirely natural and awesome in its demand on a remarkable intellect.'

Adam Smith wrote a fine epitaph for a man whose reputation today stands as probably the greatest of British philosophers, with his thoughts on philosophy as relevant now as when they were first written:

> '...the extreme gentleness of his nature never weakened the firmness of his mind or the steadiness of his resolution.' Smith concluded, 'I have always considered him both in his lifetime and since his death as approaching as nearly to the idea of a perfectly wise and virtuous man as perhaps the frailty of human nature will permit.*

Further Reading
Roderick Graham, *The Great Infidel: A Life of David Hume*
David Hume, *Essays, Moral, Political and Literary*
Nicholas Phillipson, *David Hume: Philosopher as Historian*

Online Resources
David Hume texts web site
www.davidhume.org

## Adam Smith
### 1723–1790

ECONOMIST AND PHILOSOPHER WHO IDENTIFIED THE 'INVISIBLE HAND'

*Little else is required to carry a state to the highest degree of opulence from the lowest barbarism, but peace, easy taxes, and a tolerable administration of justice.* — Smith

Adam Smith was a notable philosopher and an economist before economics had been invented. He had strong views about the role of government within society and earns his place as one of the cornerstones of the Scottish Enlightenment as the author of one of the most influential books ever written, *An Inquiry into the Nature and Causes of the Wealth of Nations.* In this groundbreaking book, known more commonly as *The Wealth of Nations*, Smith explores for almost the first time the science of economics and sets out convincingly the case for a market economy. The ideas and arguments he advances are as influential and relevant today as when they were first written.

*'Wealth of Nations'* Eduardo Paolozzi, South Gyle, Edinburgh. Inscribed: 'KNOWLEDGE IS WONDERFUL BUT IMAGINATION IS EVEN BETTER -Albert Einstein' photo: Thomas Haywood

## Childhood, School and University

Smith was born in Kirkcaldy in June 1723. His father had died six months before his birth and he was brought up by his mother, to whom he remained closely attached throughout his life.

His career nearly came to an early end. When he was only three years old it is said that he was kidnapped by a group of tinkers or gypsies, but fortunately he was quickly found by his uncle and brought safely back to his mother's house. It was as well; as Smith's biographer wrote, 'he would have made, I fear, a poor gypsy.'

Smith was a clever child, learning Latin and Greek at school; he went on to Glasgow University at fourteen, an age which seems very young to us today but was normal at the time. Glasgow was then a lovely city of twenty thousand people set by the Clyde, described by Daniel Defoe as 'one of the cleanliest, most beautiful and best-built cities in Great Britain,' and in the early eighteenth century its university was one of the most intellectually adventurous of the universities of northern Europe, dynamic in comparison with the sterile dogmatism of Oxford.

At Glasgow Smith read moral philosophy, the study of the principles which guide human behaviour, where his teacher was Francis Hutcheson, an original thinker whose ideas were to influence many of his famous pupils. Hutcheson taught that moral decisions, choices between right and wrong, were in-built through an innate moral sense rather than deduced by reason.

Smith went on to study at Oxford University, which he described caustically as a 'sanctuary in which exploded systems and obsolete prejudices find shelter and protection, after they have been hunted out of every other corner of the world,' a contrast to the much more enlightened teaching and receptive approach of the Scottish universities. Despite his views he remained for six years at Oxford, complaining that the level of teaching was 'very poor' after Glasgow. Smith thought he had identified the reason: he observed that at Oxford the professors were paid a salary by their colleges whereas at the Scottish universities they received fees paid by their students; as a result the Oxford professors were too often content just to receive their salary and gave up any pretence of teaching. Smith wrote acerbically that 'it will be his own fault if anyone should endanger his health at Oxford by excessive study!'

## Professor of Moral Philosophy

On his return to Kirkcaldy Smith was invited by Henry Home to give two series of lectures to students at Edinburgh University, on rhetoric and jurisprudence. It was in these lectures that he first outlined his belief that governments should not involve themselves in the affairs of business. His lectures were well received and as a result he was invited in 1750 to become the Professor of Moral Philosophy at Glasgow University.

Corbis Images

Adam Smith, author of *The Wealth of Nations*,
by John Kay

There were about four hundred students at Glasgow University at the time, and of these roughly eighty attended Smith's classes. Within the umbrella of moral philosophy Smith taught natural theology (the study of the knowledge of God derived from observation and from reasoning), ethics (the study of moral questions) and jurisprudence (the study of law and government). The lectures started at seven thirty in the morning and it must sometimes have been challenging for his students to stay alert in view of the early hour, the academic nature of the lectures and possibly their excesses of the night before! As a professor he had to capture and hold their attention which he did by illustrating his ideas by history and example. His success is evidenced by James Boswell who wrote, 'My greatest reason for coming (to Glasgow) was to hear Mr. Smith's lectures which are truly excellent. His sentiments are striking, profound and beautiful, the method in which they are arranged clear, accurate and orderly, his language correct, perspicuous and elegantly phrased.'

The ideas he had expressed in his lectures inspired Smith to write his first book, *The Theory of Moral Sentiments*, published in 1759, in which he attempts to explain how man derives a sense of morality, setting out not to define whether one action is right and another wrong but to explain how people form a judgement as to what is right and what is wrong, attempting to bridge the gap between Hutcheson's belief in an innate moral sense and Hume's less idealistic view of man driven by reason but ruled by his passions.

Smith put forward the view that we are guided in our behaviour by the way others judge us; in the words of Burns's poem To a Louse - 'O wad some Pow'r the giftie gie us, to see oursels as others see us!' Smith believed that we first form a judgement of the morality of others from an assessment of their words and deeds and then use that judgement to gauge our own actions. He believed that man is essentially self-interested – that is, a man will take that course of action which gives him the greatest benefit – but that this self-interest is modified by 'sympathy,' an understanding of the effect our actions will have on others, which affects the actions we take. But it is not enough to receive the approval of our fellows; we need also to gain self-approval based on our own judgement of our words and deeds.

Smith mixed widely with the leading figures of his time, becoming a close friend of the philosopher David Hume, the geologist James Hutton and the chemist

James Black, all themselves leading contributors to the Scottish Enlightenment. He regarded the thirteen years he spent as a professor at Glasgow University as 'by far the happiest period of my life,' but nevertheless accepted in 1763 an offer to become the travelling tutor to the young Duke of Buccleuch, who was just leaving Eton for a European tour. For this Smith would receive a salary of five hundred pounds a year and a pension of three hundred pounds, making him comfortably off. He left without completing the year's course of lectures but his moral sense was so ingrained – in line with his beliefs, he was obviously concerned as to how others would view his decision to leave halfway through the course – that at his last lecture he insisted on returning to his students the fees they had paid for the unfinished part of their course, forcing it into their pockets despite their protests.

Smith travelled in Europe with the young duke for nearly three years, meeting some of the great French philosophers, such as Voltaire, before the tour ended abruptly on the death of the duke's younger brother, who was travelling with them. The young duke had appreciated the genius of his companion and in gratitude provided Smith with a substantial sum of money, enough that he no longer needed to work. Smith would now be able to live in comfort to the end of his days, but more importantly he had the time and freedom to write the book that would change the world.

## The Wealth of Nations

In 1767 Smith returned to Kirkcaldy to live with his mother. His thinking was now done; it was time to put his ideas on paper. It would take him nine years to write his masterpiece. *The Wealth of Nations* was published in March 1776.

The book which runs nearly nine hundred pages, has been described as, after the Bible, the most influential book ever written. One of its early readers was the Prime Minister, William Pitt, who adopted one of Smith's core beliefs, the benefits to be gained from free trade. Pitt was so impressed with the work that when Adam Smith joined him and some friends for dinner they all stood waiting until Smith was seated. When Smith asked them to be seated Pitt replied, 'No, we will stand till you are first seated, for we are all your scholars.'

## What is the 'Wealth' of a Nation?

In *The Wealth of Nations* Smith sets out his views on what he called 'political economy,' defining first the 'wealth' of a nation. Before this, the 'wealth' of a nation was measured by the amount of gold it could accumulate, gold which would enable a king to build and furnish his palaces or to raise an army to defend his country or invade a neighbour. Exports, goods sold to other countries, were therefore seen as a 'good thing' as they increased the amount of gold in the country, whereas imports, goods bought from abroad, were a 'bad thing' because gold left the country in payment. This view, the 'mercantilist' theory, led to the creation of a network of export subsidies, of import duties and of taxes and regulations, all designed to protect domestic industry by encouraging exports and reducing imports, thereby supposedly increasing the 'wealth' of the country. In practice, however, these restrictions distorted trade and created inefficiencies which held back the real growth of the economy.

Was the amount of gold possessed by a nation the true measure of its wealth? Smith believed not. He viewed the wealth of a country in a dynamic rather than static way, putting forward the idea that the 'wealth' of a nation was not the sum of its gold but the total of the goods and services it produced; its people were enriched from the 'annual product of land and labour' and a country became wealthy through the industry of its people. The more that a country produced, the greater the 'surplus' and the wealthier it would become through the investment of the capital created. The true measure of the wealth of a country was not therefore the static sum of its stock of gold but the dynamic value of its annual output, or as we would say now, its 'gross domestic product.'

Smith recognised the importance of a working population who shared in the wealth of society. He explained:

> *Servants, labourers and workmen of different kinds, make up the far greater part of every great political society.... No society can surely be flourishing and happy, of which the far greater part of the members are poor and miserable. It is but equity, besides, that they who feed, clothe and lodge the whole body of the people should have such a share of the produce of their own labour as to be themselves tolerably well fed, clothed and lodged.*

Smith also recognised that the desire for betterment was an inherent characteristic of mankind:

> *...a desire which, though generally calm and dispassionate, comes with us from the womb, and never leaves us till we go into the grave.... An augmentation of fortune is the means by which the greater part of men propose and wish to better their condition.*

It is this desire for betterment which drives improvement, increasing annual output and thus the true wealth of a country, which may seem self-evident now, but at the time was groundbreaking. Scotland was then one of the poorest countries in Europe and Smith had realised why: the absence of wealth creation.

**The 'Division' of Labour** — Even in the relatively simple economy of the time there was a great reliance on the skills and efforts of the many to contribute towards the overall good. A simple 'woollen coat,' wrote Smith, 'is the product of the joint labour of a great multitude of workmen': the shepherd, the shearer, the spinner, the weaver, the dyer, the tailor, the carter who transports the wool and the ironworker who makes the shears; the list goes on. It is the combined output of all these people that creates the wealth of a country.

He believed that production could be increased if tasks were broken down into smaller units to be carried out by specialists. As an example he instanced the manufacture of pins, which he had watched near his home in Kirkcaldy. He observed that a total of eighteen different operations were required to make a pin; the drawing of the wire, straightening, cutting, making the point, making the pinhead and so on. One man working on his own could produce perhaps twenty pins in a day, but ten men, working in a group and each with a special task and skill, could produce as many as forty-eight thousand pins! The value of this higher output not only paid for the time of the men, their training and their tools, and for the materials, but provided a surplus in the form of profit to the employer. This surplus gave greater wealth to the nation and a sum which could be invested in the future.

The art, Smith believed, was to persuade everyone to contribute to the overall good. Each individual has an interest in working to achieve reward. 'It is not from the benevolence of the butcher, the brewer, or the baker that we expect our dinner, but from their regard to their own interest,' he wrote. The market worked through what Smith called the 'invisible hand' to encourage people to earn money by plying their trade and thus to contribute their part to the overall wealth of the country. Smith recognised the danger that too much specialisation might in time make man a drudge to his labour, a point later picked up by Adam Fergusson.

***The Benefits of Free Trade and a Market Economy*** — Smith wrote that when there was free trade and competition, the working of the market, the interaction of buyers and sellers, would produce the most efficient outcome. In a free exchange both buyer and seller gain, as otherwise they would not trade. When an item is scarce and hard to come by its price goes up; others will then be encouraged to produce that item, increasing the supply and meeting the demand. Freedom and the self-interest of the individual need not lead to chaos but can produce a better outcome, as if guided by an 'invisible hand.'

Markets, Smith believed, worked best if they were left alone; they should be freed from any restriction or influence that would prevent their natural working. Smith believed that all too often the actions of the state, however well intentioned, interfered with the free working of the market.

However, he did realise the dangers of leaving markets entirely to themselves, or as we would say today, letting them function 'unregulated.' Smith recognised that by themselves people would not necessarily work in the best interests of all; there would be a temptation for manufacturers to get together to try to restrict trade so that they could increase the prices of their manufacture. He wrote rather cynically that 'people of the same trade seldom meet together, even for merriment and diversion, but the conversation ends in a conspiracy against the public or in some contrivance to raise prices.' Smith realised this could also apply to special skills and professions; by restricting the number of trainees a trade or profession could keep, its rewards higher than would otherwise have been the case. Ironically these restrictions on practising a profession are often enforced by the state.

*The Benefits of Free Trade Between Nations* — Smith believed that specialisation, where each person does what he does best, should extend also to countries, so that each country should specialise. Smith therefore believed in free trade; he thought trade between countries increased global wealth and that duties and restrictions on trade should therefore be abolished.

> *By means of glasses, hotbeds and hotwalls, very good grapes can be raised in Scotland, and very good wine too can be made of them at about thirty times the expense for which [wine] at least equally good can be bought from foreign countries. Would it be reasonable law to prohibit the importation of all foreign wines merely to encourage the making of claret and burgundy in Scotland?*

Therefore Smith supported the colonists of America in resisting the attempts of the British government to restrict their trade in manufactured goods. He foretold the growth of America and of its influence, writing well before the event that:

> *...such has been the progress of that country in wealth, population and improvement that in the course of little more than a century, perhaps, the produce of America might exceed that of British taxation so that the seat of empire would then naturally remove itself to that part of the empire which contributed most to the general defence and support of the whole.*

Government attempts to increase trade by subsidy could often have the opposite effects from those intended and desired. Smith cited the support given by payments or 'bounty' to the white herring industry.

> *The bounty to the white herring fish industry is a tonnage bounty proportioned to the burden [size] of the ship, not to her diligence or success in the fishery; it has, I am afraid, been too common for vessels to be fitted out for the sole purpose of catching not the fish but the bounty!*

This is the law of unintended consequences; all too often an action taken by government with the best of motives results in totally unintended outcomes.

*The Role of the State* —Smith believed the state should have just two objectives; to create an environment where the individual could provide for himself and to supply the public only  with those services such as defence of the kingdom, education and the rule of law which an individual could not himself provide. He was not a believer in state spending.

> *Public services are never better performed than when their reward comes only in consequence of their being performed and is proportioned to the diligence employed in performing them.*

Most government expenditure is spent on '*unproductive hands,*' those who do not create value above cost but whose benefit (if any) is immediately consumed. He therefore declared:

> *It is the highest impertinence and presumption … [for governments] to pretend to watch over the economy of private people. They are themselves always, and without any exception, the greatest spendthrifts in society.*

Public investment should only take place where private individuals have failed; 'a great bridge cannot be thrown over a river at a place where nobody passes.' Much wasteful government expenditure would be avoided if this lesson were simply followed.

Taxes are needed for the state to provide those services – one example is defence – which the private individual cannot. A tax should be fair, certain, easy to collect and equitable; that is, the rich should pay more tax as a share of their income than the poor. Smith wrote cynically that 'there is no art which one government sooner learns of another than draining money from the pockets of the people,' or as Colbert, the French Minister of Finance under Louis XIV, had earlier picturesquely explained, 'The art of taxation consists in so plucking the goose as to obtain the largest amount of feathers with the smallest amount of hissing.'

Smith did, however, believe strongly in the importance of free education, based on his experience of the parish schools in Scotland, which have 'taught almost the whole common people to read and a very good proportion of them to write and account [mathematics].' Without a good system of education a nation would fail.

**The Impact of 'The Wealth of Nations'** — Sometimes Smith's work is portrayed as promoting a heartless world where man is driven by profit alone, but Smith realised that the motives which drive people are complex. It is not the thought of profit that would prompt somebody to enter a burning building to save a person trapped inside. Man is a complex of motives and has 'sympathy' for his fellow men and the effect of his actions upon them. *The Wealth of Nations* has had a profound effect on how the world works, and has been translated into many languages.

## Smith's Last Years

Smith was by now a reasonably wealthy man and enjoyed the fruits of his success and fame. He dined with friends and enjoyed good discourse. He was very well read, with a huge library, and planned to write further works in which he would deal with the arts and with the role of government and the law. However, as he grew older he became less able in terms of physical health, and was increasingly aware that he would never complete the full body of works he had set out to achieve. At supper with friends on 17 July 1790 Smith excused himself and retired early to his bed, saying, 'I believe we must adjourn this meeting to another place.' He died that night and was buried in Canongate churchyard.

## Smith's Legacy

Adam Smith saw himself as a philosopher rather than as an economist. As such he tried to understand and explain the motives for human behaviour, bridging the gap between Hutcheson's belief in the innate 'goodness' of man and the cynicism or perhaps realism of Kames and Hume. Smith believed that man was not totally selfish but derived pleasure and satisfaction from helping others, a view far removed from the harsh self-interest often wrongly attributed to *The Wealth of Nations*. We first judge other people's actions and then we carry out our own to meet those standards and the perceived judgement of others.

It is, however, as an economist that he is best remembered — setting out his belief in free markets and the working of the 'invisible hand' to create a more prosperous world. His ideas have had a fundamental impact throughout the world.

Smith's views are often criticised because of the potential for people to exploit the system by acting selfishly or by abusing the freedom of the market. But he foresaw this and recognised that there must be rules in place to prevent individuals from interfering with the free operation of the market or from harming others or the general good. This regulation, or as he put it the administration of justice, is needed to prevent potential abuse because if justice is removed, 'the great, the immense fabric of human society … must in a moment crumble into atoms.'

**Further Reading**
James Buchan, *Adam Smith*
John Rae, *Life of Adam Smith*
Adam Smith, *An Inquiry into the Nature and Causes of the Wealth of Nations*
Nicholas Smith, *Adam Smith: An Enlightened Life*

**Online Resources**
Adam Smith Institute
www.adamsmith.org

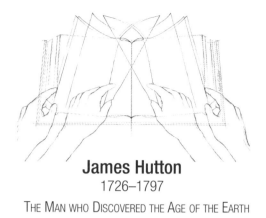

## James Hutton
### 1726–1797
#### THE MAN WHO DISCOVERED THE AGE OF THE EARTH

### Challenge to the Church

For a long time, the Church based its teaching as to the origin of the earth upon beliefs derived from a literal reading of the Bible. The first of these beliefs was that the Earth had been created in six days. According to the accepted biblical doctrine, it was a busy few days. The first day God created Day and Night; the second day he made the firmament which He called Heaven; the third day the waters were gathered into the seas and dry land appeared covered with grass and fruit trees; the fourth day He created the Sun, Moon and stars; the fifth day was somewhat more relaxing, just encompassing the creation of all the birds and the creatures who live in the seas with the sixth day reserved for creating all the beasts who live on the land, including Man. On the seventh day, Sunday, not unreasonably He rested.

With the exception of Creationists who believe implicitly in the timetable set out in Genesis, the majority of Christians now recognise that this account of the creation of the Earth is an allegory, not meant to be interpreted literally, but for many years this was accepted as truth.

The second belief concerned the age of the Earth. It was believed it had been formed about six thousand years ago, an estimate made after meticulous study of the Bible by James Usher, Archbishop of Armagh. To be exact his calculations showed that the Earth had been formed at noon on 23rd October 4004 B.C., conveniently a Sunday. Even such a great scientist as Newton accepted these as truths but one man questioned these beliefs, both as to the true age of the Earth and as to its creation, implicitly challenging the Church. James Hutton realised that the Earth had been formed not in six days but over innumerable years. He also realised that the centre of the Earth was hot and that the hot magma forced itself through the Earth's crust in a continuing process of renewal whilst the crust itself was the product of millions of years of geological upheaval and glacial erosion. The Earth was not six thousand years old but had existed for millions of years. As he wrote, there is 'no vestige of a beginning – no prospect of an end.'

These discoveries are fundamental to our understanding of the earth but strangely Hutton did not receive acknowledgement of his ideas in his lifetime, possibly because when Hutton published his ideas in 1795 in his book *Theory of the Earth* it was written in such an opaque style as to be virtually unintelligible. It was only when one of his 'disciples,' John Playfair, wrote a simplified version a few years after Hutton's death that the world could at last understand what Hutton had been saying.

James Hutton
*detail, see: colour plate 4*

### Searching for a Way of Life

James Hutton was born in 1726 into a family of wealthy merchants and as such his career and life were mapped out almost from birth. He would be a lawyer.

In a strange parallel with David Hume and Adam Smith, Hutton's father died when he was still young and he was brought up by his mother. After school Hutton went to Edinburgh University, where his interest was stimulated by chemistry, both as a science in itself and as a method of discovery by the exercise of logic. He then trained, as did so many, to become a lawyer. The law however did not interest him and in 1744 he changed to the study of medicine, first in Edinburgh, then in Paris, and finally in Leiden. It may have been his understanding of the body as a living and organised mechanism that later led to his thinking of the earth as a dynamic 'living' system.

On his return to Edinburgh he decided not to practise as a doctor but joined in business with a former school friend to make sal-ammoniac, a flux used in welding together metals, out of coal soot. They were pioneers of the chemical industry and prospered, not least because the principal raw material was virtually free to them.

## 'Improvement': A Revolution in Agriculture

Hutton now had the benefit of a steady income and decided that the proper life for a gentleman was to become a farmer on the family estate near Duns in the Borders which he had inherited from his father. As always he did nothing by halves. New ideas were coming into the traditional and centuries-old industry of farming and Hutton went to Norfolk to learn the most advanced farming methods, such as the rotation of crops, which he then introduced to his estate in Scotland. He dug drainage ditches to improve his land, enclosed his fields with low stone walls and ploughed with the new-fangled 'Suffolk' plough, which needed just one man and two horses rather than the three men and six horses of the traditional cumbersome Scottish plough. He rotated the crops grown in his fields, one year wheat, the next turnips, and then barley, to allow the land to recover. The turnips were planted late to allow the fields to lie fallow for six months. While the land was fallow he would graze his cattle to allow for natural fertilisation through manure. He followed his scientific instincts by experimenting with different varieties of crop and by developing fertilisers.

This improvement in agricultural practices based on the scientific study of crop selection, and the improvement in the quality of crops and livestock by the practise of selective breeding, is called, rather unimaginatively, 'The Improvement,' and formed a key component of the Enlightenment. Hutton understood the principles of selective breeding. He used to tell with warm approval the story of a Chinese emperor who when walking in the spring through his rice fields had noticed that one stalk of rice had grown far taller than the others. The emperor realised this stalk had ripened earlier than the others and he ordered that a new strain of rice be bred from it. Because this strain ripened earlier it could be grown in the cold lands north of the Great Wall, where it could mature before the icy weather came.

Hutton also understood, long before Darwin, the principle of the development and diversification of species by natural selection.

> *We are to consider, that in the infinite variation of the breed, that form best adapted to the exercise of those instructive arts by which the species is to live will be most certainly continued in the propagation of this animal, and will be always tending to perfect itself by the natural variation which is continually taking place* [author's emphasis]. *Thus for example where dogs are to live by the swiftness of their feet and the sharpness of their sight, that form best adapted to that end will be the most certain of remaining, while those forms that are least adapted ... will be the first to perish.*

This was development of the species by natural selection, which predated Darwin by almost a century. Hutton stayed on his farm for thirteen years, living alone and meeting few people but learning about the land and its formation. In a further parallel with Hume and Smith he never married; is this perhaps a precondition for the expression of genius? Hutton did not have a very favourable view of women, possibly as a result of an unhappy experience.

> *If the ladies were but capable of loving us men with half the affection that I have toward the cows and calfies that happen to be under my nurture and admonition, what a happy world we should have!*

His interests were not, however, limited to farming. He wanted to find out how the earth had formed and he learned this through observation as he walked about his farm, realising that most rocks were sedimentary – that is, made of deposits of layers of different materials — and that the surface of the earth is changing continually through constant erosion from glaciers, water and wind. The material that was 'lost' replaced by molten rock forced up from below the earth's surface. This was an extremely slow process and meant that the earth must be very old, although how old he could not determine.

## Scientific Enlightenment

By 1768 Hutton had got his estate in good shape and decided to rent it out for a substantial sum. He returned to Edinburgh to set up house with his sisters and develop his interests in science.

It is a nice coincidence that Edinburgh itself exhibits so clearly the process of evolution of the earth. The shiny black rock that supports Edinburgh Castle was formed from the magma that remained at the core of an ancient volcano. It is so hard that during the last ice age the ice sheet moving eastwards could make no impression on the rock and left behind a 'tail', a steep-sided ramp running down what is now the route of the Royal Mile to Holyrood House. But that was not the reason that Edinburgh was an inspired choice.

With the Scottish Enlightenment in full flourish, Hutton had chosen well. He became a close friend of Joseph Black and was instrumental with Black and Adam Smith in the formation of the Oyster Club, a dining club which met every Friday in a tavern in the Grassmarket for the discussion of ideas.

Hutton wanted to understand the forces that had formed the earth as we know it today, how volcanoes worked and what caused earthquakes. Many days he would walk on Arthur's Seat and he eventually realised that the exposed dark rocks known as Salisbury Crags were different from and younger than the other rocks thereabouts. What were the forces that had caused this?

One of the earliest writers on the science later known as geology was an Italian, Nicolaus Steno, who had realised in the seventeenth century that sedimentary rocks had been formed over years by the deposit and then consolidation through pressure of mineral and organic material. He understood that they had been created in layers and that the bottom layer must have formed before the next layer was laid upon it. Sedimentary rocks are important because they contain significant information about the history of the earth. Steno also realised that the fossils found in sedimentary layers were not just oddly shaped rocks, as was until then believed, but the petrified remains of once-living plants and creatures, able to tell us about the flora and fauna of prehistoric times; for example, our knowledge of dinosaurs comes from their fossilised remains.

Robert Hooke, a brilliant English scientist, had realised that earthquakes and other cosmic upheavals had raised rocks above sea level in past years, and a Venetian, Moro, realised that the molten lava which is thrown out when a volcano erupts comes from deep within the earth. But all these scientists, despite their insights about the formation of the earth into the state it is in today, believed in the 'history' of the earth as set out in the Book of Genesis and that the age of the earth was around six thousand years. Even the brilliant Isaac Newton, the man who discovered gravity and invented calculus, developed the science of mechanics and derived the composition of light, believed in the strict Biblical chronology of the formation of the earth. Hutton was the first man with the intellectual honesty and bravery to challenge the existing beliefs. He realised that the formation of the Earth must have taken place not in six thousand years but over innumerable ages.

## The Age of the Earth

Hutton explained his ideas to Joseph Black and together they applied the principles of chemistry to their investigation of how rocks were formed. In his *Theory of the Earth* Hutton discussed the characteristics of crystallised substances such as pyrites, quartz, fluor and galena (Iron pyrites is a sulphide of iron, quartz is a crystal of silica sometimes containing gold, fluorspar is calcium fluoride and galena is a common lead ore, lead sulphide – all are combinations of more than one element), and wrote that:

> *unless every one of these different substances may be dissolved in water, and crystallised from it, it is vain to look for the explanation of these substances in the operations of nature, by the means of aqueous solutions. On the other hand, heat being capable of rendering all these substances liquid ... no further conditions are required than the supposition of a sufficient intensity of subterraneous fire or heat, and a sufficient degree of compression upon these bodies.*

More simply, the various mixes of minerals occurring naturally on Earth could not have been caused by the action of water as they are not soluble, but only by fusion, the application of great heat and pressure from below the surface of the earth which caused them to erupt in the form of molten rock to the surface.

The Royal Society of Edinburgh had been formed in 1783 to encourage scholarship in the sciences, history, philosophy and literature. Inevitably it included among its distinguished members Adam Smith, Joseph Black, Adam Fergusson and James Hutton, and in 1784 Hutton was invited to make a presentation to the Society on his ideas as to the origins of the earth. In March 1785 he presented his first paper, delivered on his behalf by Joseph Black.

Black, an eminent scientist in his own right, was an inspired choice for the delivery of Hutton's paper as he had a commanding presence, was well used to delivering lectures and had the respect of the scientific community. If anyone could sway the audience it would be him. Black began:

> *The purpose of this Dissertation is to form some estimate with regard to the time the globe of this earth has existed, as a world containing plants and animals; to reason with regard to the changes which the earth has undergone; and to see how far an end or termination to this system of things may be perceived.*

This first paper dealt with Hutton's observation that most of the land where people lived was made up of stratified rocks representing the 'waste' of past land, consolidated not as generally believed by flood but by heat and pressure. Hutton himself delivered the second lecture. He asked how new strata of rock could rise from the sea to form new land. It could not just be the receding waters, because if it were then the new strata rocks would lie flat, and yet it was known through observation that strata were found in every degree of 'fracture, flexure and contortion.' Fossils of all vegetable types can be found in the strata or layers of rock and they must have been formed in underwater sedimentary deposits later pushed up as new dry land.

There had to be some immense force pushing the rock upwards. Hutton realised that hot liquid rock or magma was being forced up from the centre of the earth. The proof of this could be found where rocks contained veins of another, very different rock; these veins must have come from hot liquid rock which had been pushed up from underneath, forcing its way into the older stratified rocks and lifting the strata above the sea. Volcanoes such as Etna and Vesuvius had long been observed in eruption, spouting molten rock into the sky. Hutton realised the creation of mountain ranges could be explained through the outpouring of molten rock where there were live or extinct volcanoes, but there were mountain ranges where there was no evidence of volcanic activity. What immense force had created these? Unwittingly he had identified the effect of the impact of tectonic plates, but long before the existence of these plates had been recognised.

Hutton was by now in failing health, but he carried out a geological expedition into the Highlands and found evidence of granite veins invading the stratified rocks from below, 'terminating in a thread where it could penetrate no further,' proving his ideas that the internal heat of the earth had forced molten granite into the strata above.

Hutton then asked: 'a question naturally occurs with regard to time; what has been the space of time necessary to accomplish this great work?' Observation of erosion in itself indicated the length of time the process took. No one could give with certainty the age of the earth, but simple observation determined that it must be ancient, hundreds of thousands or even millions of years old. (Current thinking is that the earth is between four and a half and five billion years old.)

In 1795 Hutton published his ideas in his *Theory of the Earth*. Sadly, as already mentioned, although a gifted conversationalist Hutton had never been able to express his ideas clearly or concisely on paper and his book was largely impenetrable to the general reader. A full understanding of his thoughts and discoveries would have to wait until the work of his 'disciple', John Playfair, was published after Hutton's death in March 1797. He was buried in Greyfriar's Churchyard in Edinburgh. His friend, James Black, would be buried beside him just two years later.

### Hutton's Ideas Become Accepted

The controversy did not end with Hutton's death as others continued to challenge his views. It was left to Charles Lyell, a Scottish geologist who was born in the year of Hutton's death, finally to put the argument to rest. Lyell was initially a disbeliever; he had been taught as a student at Oxford that Hutton was wrong and the earth as we know it had been created by a 'Great Deluge' five thousand years ago; Hutton's theory that the earth had evolved through continual change and had an age of incalculable years was poppycock!

Lyell wanted to see for himself, so he travelled Europe in search of the truth. He found in the Isle of Wight evidence of the fossils of land-based plants and freshwater shells beneath the chalk which it was known had been formed in the deep sea. The land must have been submerged in ancient times, covered by the sea and then raised again, just as Hutton's theory predicted. In Italy on an island in the Bay of Naples, known then to the locals as the Isle of Isk, he found traces of shellfish eight hundred metres above sea level; the whole island had been pushed up from the Mediterranean by huge underground forces. Lyell had become convinced that Hutton had indeed been right. He wrote these and other findings in *Principles of Geology*, which strongly supported Hutton's theories and became the standard textbook for geology for more than a century. Hutton was at last vindicated.

Charles Darwin was another sceptic until he was given Lyell's book, which he read during his voyage on the Beagle. One of the first islands he reached on the voyage was St Jago in the Cape Verde Islands. It was a barren island with little to interest Darwin as a naturalist but nevertheless he went ashore. While collecting corals on a beach he noticed a small cliff behind the beach with a wavy white band stretching along it about ten metres above sea level. Darwin climbed to reach the band and was astonished to realise it was made up from the crushed but still recognisable remains of coral and shells. Darwin immediately realised this could not be the result of falling sea levels as the band was not level but varied in height above sea level along its length. Neither could it have been formed by a 'catastrophe', the catch-all excuse of the traditionalists, because the shells and coral were perfectly formed. The answer could only be that the land had been pushed upwards by huge subterranean pressures exactly as Hutton had said.

Darwin realised with a shock of astonishment that Hutton was right! The earth was constantly evolving from a natural and constant process of erosion, storms, earthquakes, volcanic eruptions and the upwards pressure of molten rock.

## Hutton's Legacy

True to the principles of the Enlightenment, James Hutton used observation and reasoning in his quest to determine how and when the earth was created. He was the first to realise that the heat and pressure from the centre of the earth forced out molten rock to replace that lost through erosion from the effects of glaciers, water and wind in a continuing cycle of evolution. Further developing his ideas, Hutton proposed a theory that the earth was an 'organized body,' thereby pre-dating the Gaia theory of James Lovelock by nearly two hundred years. He wrote:

> But is this world to be considered thus merely as a machine, to last no longer than its parts retain their present position, their proper form and qualities? Or may it not also be considered as an organized body? Such as has a constitution in which the necessary decay of the machine is naturally repaired, in the exertion of those productive powers by which it had been formed.
>
> This is the view in which we are now are to examine the globe; to see if there be, in the constitution of this world, a reproductive operation, by which a ruined constitution may be again repaired, and a duration or stability thus procured to the machine, considered as a world sustaining plants and animals.

Hutton realised this continuing cycle of evolution took place over an enormous period of time and that the earth could not be just six thousand years old as taught by the Church, but must be hundreds of thousands or even millions of years old. He identified that the 'marks of marine animals in the most solid parts of the earth' and the 'immense quantities of calcareous bodies' found in the strata predated by millions of years the first traces of man.

The earth had not come into being in five days, with man appearing on the sixth, but had existed for millions of years before the appearance of man and would probably last for millions of years after the last man had disappeared. As he wrote, 'we find no vestige of a beginning – no prospect of an end.'

**Further Reading**
James Hutton, *Theory of the Earth*
Donald McIntyre and Alan McKirdy, *James Hutton: The Founder of Modern Geology*
Jack Repcheck, *The Man who Found Time*

**Online Resources**
Education Scotland
http://www.educationscotland.gov.uk/scottishenlightenment/jameshutton/index.asp

## Joseph Black
### 1728–1799

THE FATHER OF MODERN CHEMISTRY

Joseph Black

Joseph Black trained and practised as a doctor and was 'much employed as an able and most attentive physician.' As a doctor he treated a number of the key participants in the Scottish Enlightenment including his close friends David Hume, Adam Fergusson and Adam Smith. It is not however as a doctor that he is now remembered but as a scientist.

He introduced into science the discipline of scientific method, using precise measurement and the exercise of logic to understand the processes of chemical reaction, and by these methods he discovered the gas carbon dioxide and the principle of latent heat.

According to Black, the benefits of science were not derived from the abstract solution of theoretical problems but by applying scientific methods to find solutions to the problems experienced in the everyday world, or, as we would say today, he believed in 'applied science'.

### Boyhood and Training as a Doctor

Born in 1728 in Bordeaux in south-west France, Black was the son of a Scottish mother and a Belfast father who traded as a wine merchant in Bordeaux where he owned a vineyard on a hill overlooking the river Garonne. Joseph's parents, John and Margaret, had a total of thirteen children; perhaps the wine agreed with them!

Young Joseph was first taught at home by his mother, though one wonders how she found the time between childbearing and child-rearing. At the age of twelve he was sent to school in Belfast; in the days before the railways travel by sea was easier than travel by land. At eighteen he went to Glasgow University to study languages and philosophy. His father then decided he should learn a useful career so he trained as a doctor under the tutelage of Dr William Cullen, the Professor of Medicine. William Cullen had joined the university as a lecturer in chemistry. In the early sixteenth century, medicine had been transformed by the introduction of chemical treatments such as opium, mercury and antimony, therefore, a link between chemistry and medicine had been made. Cullen was one of the first to lecture on medicine, previously held to be the preserve of practising doctors, and thereby effectively started the School of Medicine.

Cullen was one of the first people to observe that 'water, and perhaps other fluids, in evaporating … generated some degree of cold.' He demonstrated this by dipping the ball of a thermometer repeatedly in water, then waving it vigorously in the air to evaporate the water and watching the recorded temperature fall. He repeated the experiment using an air pump to evacuate the air in a chamber containing a vessel of water, with another smaller vessel containing ether inside that. Ice formed on the outside of the vessel containing the ether. Cullen had unknowingly invented the refrigerator. He had observed the phenomenon but it would remain for Black to explain the science.

### Black's Thesis on Magnesia: The Discovery of Carbon Dioxide

After three years as a student of Cullen, Black moved to Edinburgh to complete his training. He then published the thesis which first brought him fame, entitled rather forbiddingly, *Dehumore Acido a Cibis Orto, et Magnesia Alba*. It was one of the few papers that Black published as he believed the practical application of his ideas was more important than any transient fame derived from the publication of learned papers. At the time many people suffered from kidney stones. The treatment was to prescribe caustic alkalis to give relief from the pain; the problem was that the alkalis themselves were painful and damaging to the body. Black wondered whether magnesia, already used to treat acid in the stomach, might prove a less aggressive cure.

Typically, he wanted to understand how this would work. He discovered that the magnesia (magnesium carbonate), when treated with an acid such as sulphuric acid, quickly dissolved, giving off an effervescence or violent bubbling. He also noted that if he heated the magnesia it would turn into a white powder that would be dissolved by acids but without giving off bubbles. He carefully weighed the powder created and found it was five-twelfths of the weight of the original magnesia. He realised he was extracting a gas from the magnesia, a gas he called 'fixed air' as it was believed at the time that all gases were forms of air. He determined by experiment that this 'fixed air' was denser than air itself and that it supported neither plant life nor naked flame.

Black repeated the experiment with limestone, calcium carbonate, and got the same results. If he then bubbled the gas through an aqueous solution of lime, calcium hydroxide, calcium carbonate would be precipitated. He had discovered was a gas which could be extracted from a compound by heating or by chemical reaction and that the compound could then be reconstituted by chemical reaction. But what was this gas? Black, through precise experimentation and accurate measurement, had discovered carbon dioxide.

## The Discovery of Latent Heat

In 1755 William Cullen was appointed to the Chair of Chemistry at Edinburgh University. A year later Black took his mentor's place as Professor of Medicine and Lecturer in Chemistry at the University of Glasgow where he became a close friend of Adam Smith, who by then had been a professor for five years.

Black lectured lucidly on the then established rules of medicine and set up a private medical practice, but it was not in medicine but in chemistry that his genius lay. He worked further on 'fixed air', determining it was produced by breathing and could be derived from burning charcoal. He realised there might be many other fixed airs or gases still to be discovered, laying the path for the later discoveries of Priestley and Cavendish.

The prosperity of Glasgow was growing based on its developing industries but these encountered technical difficulties. Black had already worked on the problem of bleaching in the linen industry but now the growing whisky distilling industry sought his help. Large quantities of energy were required to heat the whisky to produce distillation and then vast amounts of water were required to cool and condense the vapour. Distilleries therefore required large resources of cheap water.

It had already intrigued Black that snow would continue to lie on the mountains long after the spring sun had arrived and temperatures had risen above freezing. Conversely, he had noted that a freezing night did not immediately cover the ponds with ice. Surely it would have been logical for the water to freeze totally when the temperature fell. Conversely when ice melted the water around it was cooled but the remaining ice stayed at the same temperature. The question he asked himself was, where does the heat go?

The explanation could only be that the physical change from the solid to the liquid state itself required heat. The resultant liquid must therefore possess this 'heat,' a heat which could not be detected by the thermometer and which he called 'latent heat.' Conversely the move from a liquid state to a solid state, such as the freezing of water, required the 'extraction' of this latent heat which explained why water did not immediately freeze over.

A vapour such as steam must have the same property of latent heat, in this case demonstrated by the large amount of cold water required to condense it. Conversely, because of latent heat, much more heat is required to turn boiling water into steam than is required to boil the water in the first place. By experimentation he determined that however long it took to heat a given volume of water to boiling point, the same amount of heat must be applied for roughly five times as long to convert the boiling water into steam. This time his findings were published, but typically not until after his death, as a series of lectures on the *General Effects of Heat*. The discovery of the concept of latent heat was fundamental in helping the young James Watt improve the performance of the steam engine. Watt had already realised that it was massively inefficient to condense the steam on each stroke of the engine by cooling it in water, as in the design of existing steam engines, and then reheating it as steam. Black now explained why — it was the loss of latent heat in the steam each time the steam was condensed and it was this understanding that inspired Watt to introduce a separate condenser in his steam engine. Black had discovered the science which enabled Watt to design and build the more efficient steam engines which would power the Industrial Revolution. In his studies he also discovered the concept of specific heat, that different materials of identical mass require a different amount of heat to raise their temperature by the same one degree and was one of the first to suggest using hydrogen in balloons to provide lift.

## Professor of Chemistry at Edinburgh University

In 1766, Black was appointed Professor at Edinburgh University, forgoing original research, concentrating instead on elegant lectures for his students, for which he was greatly admired. He would begin his courses by explaining that 'Chemistry, like all other sciences, had arisen from the reflections of ingenious men on the general facts which occur in the practice of the various arts of common life.' It was not an abstract science but an attempt to explain the world around us.

In common with most of the professors of medicine and science, Black did not receive a salary but was paid by the students at a rate of three guineas each for a year's course. He was a popular lecturer and had as many as two hundred students at a time, so he received a good income. Henry Brougham noticed when he attended Black's course that there was a small brass scale which Black used to weigh the guineas he was paid. Black explained that it was needed because some of the gold coins provided by his students were of less than the legal weight so, true to his scientific principles and perhaps his canny Scots background, Black measured the weight of each coin he was given.

He continued to give practical advice on the application of science to real-life problems, advising on a multitude of practical engineering problems covering the manufacture of glass, the problems of corrosion, the distillation of tar, the bleaching of linen and the refining of sugar. In all cases he followed his precept of applying science to the betterment of mankind.

## Dr Black's Distinguished Patients

Black continued during this time to practice medicine, famously treating his friend David Hume, whom he had met three years after his appointment as professor when Hume had finally returned to Edinburgh. He also treated his cousin, philosopher Adam Fergusson who was born in 1723 and a member of the Select Society, of which Smith and Hume were members. He succeeded Hume as librarian of the Advocates' Library and in 1759 he became Professor of Natural Philosophy at Edinburgh, although he had not studied philosophy since his student days. He had just three months to master the subject before he was required to teach it. Another of Black's patients was Adam Smith, and he would be doctor to each of his dearest friends, present to ease their final hours.

## Honoured by the World

The first honour Black received came not from the British scientific world but from Russia. In 1783 he was elected an Honorary Member of the Academy of Sciences in St Petersburg, and in 1789 he was elected one of the eight Foreign Associates of the French Academy of Sciences. Sadly he was never elected a Fellow of the Royal Society of London, which was still obsessed with the concept of 'pure' science and did not recognise the immense advances being made in applied science in the 'real' world outside London.

Although Black was said to be of 'a gentle and pleasing countenance' and 'performed on the flute with great taste and feeling' he was another who never married. In his later years he grew frail but lived carefully. He gave his last lectures in 1797 and died peacefully at table in November 1799, holding steadily in his hand the cup from which he was about to drink. He looked so peaceful that his servant thought he was sleeping and left him, only discovering on his return that he was dead. James Hutton, the geologist, was Black's closest friend and fittingly Black was buried in Greyfriars Churchyard in Edinburgh alongside Hutton.

## Black's Legacy

In scientific terms, Black left an impressive legacy through his discovery of carbon dioxide, the concepts of specific and latent heat, in the application of scientific method which he taught his students, and the need to carry out meticulous experiments measuring results accurately at all stages. He believed that scientific discoveries should be for the benefit of mankind and that the true benefit of science came not from the development of elegant theories for publication in the learned papers but in the solution of the practical problems faced by the world. It is no overstatement to say that his discovery of latent heat was fundamental to the development by James Watt of the more efficient steam engines which powered the Industrial Revolution and placed Britain at the forefront of the developed world.

**Further Reading**
J.G. Crowther, *Scientists of the Industrial Revolution*

**Online Resources**
http://www.chem.gla.ac.uk/~alanc/dept/black.htm

## Mary Somerville
### 1780 – 1872

### The 'Queen of Science'

Mary Somerville was an exceptional woman, famous both as a scientist and as a writer on science. Through her writing she brought science out of the dusty labs and into the daylight of popular perception at a time when science was definitely not on the curriculum for the well-bred young lady. Denied as a girl the opportunity of a formal scientific education, she taught herself, secretly studying mathematical works banned by her father to protect her from the dangerous notions he thought they might arouse in his impressionable young daughter.

Aware of the injustice of a world which denied opportunities to women, Somerville wrote that as a young woman she was 'intensely ambitious to excel in something, for I felt in my own breast that women were capable of taking a higher place in creation than that assigned to them in my early days.'

The fact that as a woman she could earn the respect of her peers in a scientific world dominated by men is itself a tribute to the new openness of the Enlightenment when individuals were judged on their ability and on the quality of their work and recognition was not be denied because of a lack of formal academic qualifications or because of gender.

It was with justification that Mary Somerville was described in her obituary as the 'Queen of Science.'

### Personal Life

Born Mary Fairfax on Boxing Day 1780 in the manse in Jedburgh, the house of her aunt who confusingly also was a Somerville (married to Dr. Thomas Somerville). Mary would later marry their son and therefore 'was born in the house of my future husband – a rather singular coincidence.'

Her mother was on her way back from London after seeing her husband, Admiral Sir William George Fairfax, set sail for a series of voyages which meant

that he would not see his young daughter
until she was eight years old.

Somerville shared this absence of a father
during her formative years with many
other Enlightenment figures. It gave her
the freedom to develop into a healthy, free-
thinking young girl as she roamed the Fife
coast near the small fishing village of
Burntisland where she was raised. It also
meant that her upbringing was occasionally
unorthodox; her uncle Thomas, an officer
in the Indian Army, broadened her
knowledge in appropriate army fashion by
teaching the little girl to swear, a skill
which she would occasionally use to
outraged effect. Mary acknowledged her
skill in the first draft of her autobiography,
*Personal Recollections from Early Life to*

Mary Somerville
*detail, see: colour plate 5*

*Old Age*, but it was deleted by her daughter in deference to Victorian sensibilities.

All good things come to an eventual end and upon his return home her father
declared to her mother, 'This kind of life will never do, Mary must at least know
how to write and keep accounts' – the key accomplishments perceived necessary
for a young girl. Thus Somerville began a more orthodox education at Miss
Primrose's, a small private school in Musselburgh. She was 'utterly wretched' after
the freedom of Burntisland, studying her lessons 'enclosed in stiff stays with a
steel busk in front, while, above my frock, bands drew my shoulders back till the
shoulder-blades met, then a steel rod, with a semi-circle which went under the
chin, was clasped to the steel busk in my stays' This barbaric procedure was
presumably intended to give her the deportment of a young lady although she
was in her own words 'perfectly straight and well-made.' She returned home after
only twelve months to resume her ramblings by the seashore, spending many hours
at night at her bedroom window 'studying the stars by the aid of the celestial globe.'

When she was thirteen she spent a summer at the house of her uncle, Dr.
Somerville, at the manse in Jedburgh and was delighted when he responded to
her thirst for knowledge by teaching her Latin, suggesting they read Virgil
together for an hour before breakfast, but, curiously, it was not from her uncle
but while reading a magazine that she discovered her interest in mathematics. The
magazine included a number of mathematical puzzles including a page covered
with letters – chiefly 'x' and 'y' – which she was told was 'a kind of Arithmetic,
they call it Algebra.'

Her mother took her to Edinburgh to learn the attainments of a young lady
and she was given instruction in music and in art which she studied under
Alexander Nasmyth, the celebrated landscape painter who was himself a key figure

in the Enlightenment. It was in her art classes that Naysmith explained the mathematical concept of perspective, recommending that she should study *Euclid's Elements of Geometry*, 'the foundation not only of perspective, but of astronomy and all mechanical science.' As soon as Mary returned home she persuaded her brother to purchase a copy of *Euclid* and a textbook on algebra so that she could curl up cosily under the bedclothes with some light reading.

This study of mathematics was of great concern to her father who thought such unnatural studies might perturb her mind, injuring 'the tender female frame.' Mary, however, continued her studies, reading secretly by candlelight in her bedroom until she was betrayed by a servant who noticed that each morning her candle would be burnt down to the wick.

Returning to Edinburgh she was busy; art classes with Nasmyth, piano practice, dancing until all hours and then rising early to study algebra or read the classics. With her father struggling to support the small household on a niggardly pension, convention eventually triumphed and at the age of twenty-three this high-spirited and attractive young woman married her distant cousin Captain Samuel Greig, who was serving in the Russian navy and had met Mary when he arrived in the Firth of Forth on a Russian ship and was entertained at Burntisland.

They set up home in Greig's 'exceedingly small and ill ventilated' bachelor house. Predictably and regrettably Greig did not approve of the scientific interests of his new young wife and occupied her instead in giving birth to the two children the couple had in their three years of marriage before he died in 1807.

### Maturity as a Mathematician

As a young widow Mary now had a small inheritance which gave her the freedom to return to her true love of mathematics and she settled down to master Newton's *Principia*, possibly the most influential book on mathematics ever written. This work had been given almost hallowed status in Britain and as a result the science of mathematics had developed little since its publication; in contrast, in France and Germany there had been major advances in mathematics.

Somerville's growing mathematical skill had led her to winning the prize in a mathematical competition organised by William Wallace, Professor of Mathematics at Edinburgh University, and he took her under his wing. Wallace recommended to her a reading list including a number of mathematical books by the leading French mathematicians, demonstrating the openness to new ideas of the Edinburgh intellectual establishment. One recommendation was *Mécanique Céleste*, a ground-breaking work on the mathematics of cosmology by Pierre La Place, which in five volumes explored such concepts as to whether the solar system was inherently stable and whether distant stars obeyed the same gravitation laws as the solar system.

In 1812, Somerville's growing reputation as a mathematician was put 'on hold' when, undaunted by experience, she married a second time, her cousin Dr. William Somerville, who after medical service in the Army in South Africa had been appointed as head of the Army Medical Department in Scotland. She would give birth to another four children.

Jedburgh is not far from Abbotsford and the Somervilles were friendly with Sir Walter Scott. Somerville would attend supper parties at Abbotsford presided over 'with great glee' by Scott. There she also met Adam Fergusson who 'would sing the Laird of Cockpen and other comic songs.'

Dr. Somerville was an 'enlightened' husband and positively encouraged his young wife to pursue her interest in science and mathematics. His appointment in 1816 as a member of the Army Medical Board necessitated they move to a house in Hanover Square in London; on their way to London they stopped for a day in Birmingham to visit the works of Boulton and Watt, seeing engines which 'although beautifully smooth, showed a power that was almost fearful.' She later wrote in her Recollections that she 'had lived to see this all but omnipotent instrument change the locomotion of the whole civilized world by sea and by land.'

The move to London and the increased exposure it gave to the 'great and the good' of the scientific establishment proved invaluable in the development of Somerville's scientific career. Soon after their arrival, Professor Wallace arranged for Mary and William Somerville to visit Sir William Herschel's observatory near Slough. William Herschel was the famous astronomer who in 1781 had discovered Uranus, the first planet to be discovered using a telescope. His sister, Caroline Herschel, who was herself no mean astronomer and had discovered eight comets, would in 1835 become the first woman to be elected an Honorary Fellow of the Royal Astronomical Society. Somerville would be the second when she was elected later the same year, again as an Honorary Fellow - it would not be until 1916 that the Society accepted women on the same basis as men. Somerville would later become a close friend of William's son, John Herschel.

Somerville earned a reputation for her mathematical skills, not through published work but through discussions she would have at intimate dinners and gatherings attended by the leading scientists and mathematicians of the day. On her first visit to Paris in 1817, she was introduced to leading French scientists and mathematicians, including La Place who would later say that only three women fully understood his work – Mary Somerville, Caroline Hershel and 'a Mrs. Greig of whom I know nothing.' (Greig was Mary's name by her first marriage.) She also visited the Paris Observatory.

The Somervilles were interested in mineralogy, putting together a small collection, and would hold dinner parties where scientific matters were discussed. One night they had been in the garden until 2.00 a.m. inspecting the heavens with a telescope, when they noticed the light was still burning in the house of a friend and neighbour, Dr. Young. The good doctor answered the door in a state of great excitement. He had recently received a papyrus from Egypt which contained not only a record of the reigns of the Ptolemys but also a configuration of the state of the heavens at the time allowing accurate dating for the first times. Dr. Young had earlier interpreted the Rosetta stone allowing the hieroglyphic writing of the Egyptians to be at last deciphered.

They also visited the Cambridge mathematician Charles Babbage while he was constructing his 'difference engine.' A model was built in 1991 to his original designs and was found to work correctly to a greater number of decimal places than the modern pocket calculator. He also designed an 'analytical engine' attached to a 'printer;' his analytical engine was designed to be programmable and is widely recognised as a forerunner of the computer.

The appointment of Dr. Somerville as Physician to the Royal Hospital in Chelsea necessitated a move from Hanover Square to 'a government house in a very dreary and unhealthy situation, far from all our friends.' This followed shortly on the sad death of their eldest daughter after a long illness and the loss of 'almost the whole of our fortune, through the dishonesty of a person in whom we had the greatest confidence.' The time had come for a fundamental change in her life.

## On the Mechanism of the Heavens

One other of the 'great and good' whom Somerville met was Henry Brougham, the eccentric reformist Scots lawyer who had moved to London to enter politics, eventually becoming Lord Chancellor and passionately involved in the passing of the Reform Act of 1832. Brougham was interested in the spread of scientific knowledge and in 1827 he approached Dr. Somerville with the request that his wife might translate the *Mécanique Céleste of La Place* in a form aimed towards a general rather than exclusively scientific audience. The work would occupy all the time Somerville could spare.

The result, published in 1831 as On the Mechanism of the Heavens, far exceeded Brougham's expectations and made Somerville famous. She declared, 'I translated La Place's work from algebra into common language' but in fairness she did much more than just translate La Place's book, building upon his ideas to give her own vision of the cosmos, the central theme of the book being an attempt to provide a mathematical understanding of the universe.

Her other major works were *On the Connexion of the Physical Sciences* (1834), *Physical Geography* (1848), and *Molecular and Microscopic Science* (1869 – published remarkably when Somerville was eighty-nine years old). They all were written with clarity and enthusiasm – and a lack of complex mathematics - which made her work popular with a much wider audience than the scientific establishment.

In *Connexion* she dealt not just with the cosmos but also all aspects of physics, including light, sound and electricity; there would be nine editions before her death, each time updated to include the latest scientific discoveries.

*Molecular and Microscopic Science* addressed new ideas about the formation of matter from atoms and molecules, as well as the new science of spectroscopic analysis of light whereby the composition of a compound could be analysed in microscopic detail. To her great satisfaction this technique could also be used to determine the composition of the sun and stars, proving that the same fundamental elements which made our world were present throughout the universe.

## Cosmology

Despite the scientific breadth of her writing, Somerville's main interest remained as a cosmologist. The science of astronomy developed significantly through the nineteenth century, impelled by the twin drivers of enhanced mathematical techniques which encouraged theoretical advances and the improvement in telescopes and astronomical practices which enabled those theories to be tested by observation, the exercise of reason supported by experience fundamental to the Enlightenment.

One of the questions to be answered was whether the laws of gravity as developed by Newton were unique to the solar system or whether they had universal application throughout the universe. Newton's inverse square law of gravitational attraction states that each body attracts every other body with a force directly proportional to the product of their masses and inversely proportional to the square of the distances between them with a body such as the Earth considered as a point mass with the mass concentrated at its centre. William Herschel had long before discovered 'pairs' of distant stars that appeared to be connected. If the law of gravity pertained then these stars should be in elliptical orbit about each other. Proof required the identification of other pairs of stars and then meticulous observation over a considerable period of time to track their orbits.

Somerville's growing reputation led to her being invited to take part in these astronomical observations at private observatories. She became a close friend of John Herschel and worked with him on the mathematics of star pairs and also at his observatory with its large reflecting telescope. In 1830 Herschel successfully computed the gravitational field of a pair of stars, demonstrating that Newton's law of gravity did in fact apply throughout not just the solar system but the universe, work he subsequently repeated with additional pairs.

## 'Astronomical Dust,' Neptune and the Composition of Light

A discovery, made when a comet had approached close to the earth, had shown that comets were composed largely of gaseous material; this was derived from the observation that the passing of the comet had no appreciable effect upon the seas and the tides and therefore exercised insignificant gravitational force. The comet must therefore be virtually 'weightless' and could not be composed of solid matter as previously thought. Improved telescopes enabled astronomers to investigate star clusters and nebulae; nebulae were originally thought also to be star clusters but proved to be composed not of stars but clouds of astronomical dust, the birth material of future celestial bodies to be formed through gravitational attraction.

In her second book Somerville discussed the phenomena of this 'astronomical dust' evidenced through observations of comets and the aurora borealis but adopted the common consensus that this was connected to the 'ether,' a mythical gas thought to permeate space and through which light travelled. Ether was thought to account for the irregular orbit of Uranus which did not exactly follow the path predicated by Newton's Law, but in fact this irregularity in its orbit was caused by the gravitational pull of an as yet undiscovered planet, Neptune. In 1846 the Cambridge mathematician John Couch Adams correctly predicted both the existence and the location of the planet using mathematics, later admitting to Dr. Somerville that his discovery had been stimulated by reading Somerville's suggestion in Connexions that the irregularities in the orbit of Uranus 'may reveal the existence, nay, even the mass and orbit of a body placed for ever beyond the sphere of vision.'

Somerville covered other scientific disciplines in her books, particularly addressing the composition of light – a field in which she carried out a significant amount of original research. In *Connexion*, she explained the existence of what we now call infrared and ultraviolet light which appear at either end of the visible spectrum, a phenomenon which had been discovered by William Herschel and others. She carried out a number of experiments with light and believed, correctly, that the 'rays (which) exist in the dark space beyond the extreme violet' were in fact part of the same ray which produced light in the visible part of the spectrum.

## Italy

In 1838 Dr. Somerville had a severe attack of jaundice from which he nearly died and as a result had to relinquish his post at the Chelsea Hospital. The Somervilles decided to move abroad and from 1840 were based in Italy where he recovered. From then on Somerville conducted her affairs from Italy, writing long letters about scientific matters to John Herschel and others, thereby staying in touch with scientific advances and continuing to write. After Dr. Somerville died in 1860 at the age of eighty-nine – the Italian air obviously suited him – Mary Somerville continued to live and write in Italy.

Unfortunately, she was unable to utilise the advantages of living under the clear Italian skies by obtaining access to an observatory, such employment being considered inappropriate for a lady, but she did witness *Il Risorgimento*, the creation of a new Italian state freed from the control of the Austrian Empire, a cause she enthusiastically supported, watching from the balcony of her house in Florence as Victor Emmanuel entered the city in triumph.

She moved then to Naples and in 1867 was able to watch from her house the volcanic eruption of Vesuvius, describing the ceaseless 'fearful roaring and thundering' and watching a stream of lava 'more than a mile in width and thirty feet deep' overwhelming the fields and houses in the plain below. There was a further eruption in 1872 when she was awakened by her daughter to watch 'Vesuvius in splendid eruption.' Despite her deafness Somerville could hear the thunderous noise of the volcano as the sky darkened with the cloud of black ash gushing forth so that 'neither land, sea, nor sky was visible.' The rivers of molten lava destroyed all in their path and the clouds of ash killed the vines and crops which had escaped the lava. Many were killed in the eruption including fifty or so who had recklessly approached the volcano and were literally swallowed alive when a new crater opened beneath their feet; in Somerville's evocative words they were 'scorched to death by the fiery vapours which eddied from the fearful chasm.'

Mary Somerville died twelve years after her husband at an even more remarkable ninety-two, just one year after the death of her beloved friend and collaborator Sir John Herschel. She faced death with the same courage she'd faced life, writing in her autobiography that 'The Blue Peter has long been flying at my foremast ... and now that I am in my ninety-second year I must soon accept the signal for sailing.'

## Somerville's Legacy

Although Somerville's writings gained her fame during her lifetime, her ongoing legacy is probably better expressed by the impact she made as a pioneering woman in a world which up to then had been almost exclusively male and in widening the opportunities for education for women of ability. She did indeed prove 'that women were capable of taking a higher place in creation than that (at the time) assigned to them.'

Today perhaps her most significant legacy is Somerville College, the Oxford College for Women which was named after her in 1879. She is also one of the few women to have a crater on the Moon named in her honour – an appropriate recognition given her work in cosmology.

But perhaps the most telling tribute in her lifetime was that when her book On the *Mechanism of the Heavens* was first published, a Cambridge professor, William Whewell, not only wrote to congratulate her upon her work but introduced it into the syllabus for his mathematics students thereby making it the first scientific work written by a woman to be used as a textbook in a British University. Mary Somerville considered this 'the highest honour I ever received.'

**Further Reading**
Allan Chapman, *Mary Somerville and the World of Science*
Mary Somerville, ed. Martha Somerville, *Personal Recollections from Early Life to Old Age*

Online Resources
http://www.agnesscott.edu/lriddle/women/somer.htm

'HEAD OF INVENTION' Eduardo Paolozzi - 1989; Butler's Wharf, London
photo: Thomas Haywood

inscribed: "Though human genius in it's various inventions with
various instruments may answer the same end, it will
never find an invention more beautiful or more simple or
direct than nature because in her inventions nothing
is lacking and nothing superfluous."

# Inventors
# &
# Innovators

# INVENTORS & INNOVATORS

**James Watt**
*INVENTOR OF THE STEAM ENGINE*

**William Murdoch**
*MAN WHO MADE NIGHT INTO DAY*

**William Symington**
*BUILDER OF THE FIRST STEAM-POWERED BOAT*

**Charles Macintosh**
*CHEMIST AND INVENTOR OF THE 'MACKINTOSH'*

**Robert Thomson**
*INVENTOR OF THE PNEUMATIC TYRE*

**William Thomson, Lord Kelvin**
*SCIENTIST AND INVENTOR*

**James Clerk Maxwell**
*PHYSICIST WHO UNCOVERED THE MYSTERIES*
*OF ELECTRICITY AND MAGNETISM*

**Alexander Graham Bell**
*INVENTOR OF THE TELEPHONE &*
*FRIEND OF HELEN KELLER AND THE BLIND*

**John Logie Baird**
*INVENTOR OF TELEVISION*

**Robert Watson-Watt**
*INVENTOR OF RADAR*

## Part 2 • Inventors & Innovators

### Watching the Kettle

There are common threads which run through the lives of the great thinkers of the Enlightenment, in particular a belief in the power of reason, whether in an attempt to understand the motivation of men as in the works of David Hume or in its application to uncover the secrets of chemistry through the scientific experiments of Joseph Black.

All had benefited from the excellent education available in Scotland at the time, not least from the Scottish universities, which were receptive to new ideas and not hidebound by blinkered tradition as were the ancient English universities – Adam Smith was especially scathing of his experience at Oxford.

All too believed in the virtues of hard work and in the philosophy of self-betterment. All were prepared to challenge existing beliefs, basing that challenge on experience and on the exercise of reason.

And most remained unmarried...

For many, the Scottish Enlightenment is defined by the great philosophers and thinkers of the eighteenth century whose lives we have just sampled, arguably the greatest amongst a number of remarkable men of intellect in Scotland at that time who have left their impact upon the world. It was indeed a remarkable achievement for a country whose identity had all but disappeared and whose economy had been virtually bankrupted.

If taken in isolation their contributions would be a remarkable testament to the flourishing of thought in Scotland at the time, but other countries, particularly France, had similar outpourings of philosophical thought.

What is perhaps unique to the Scottish Enlightenment is that it was not confined to the philosophical sciences; the same openness and receptiveness to new ideas is also seen in the art, literature and architecture of the time.

But firstly the sciences; Joseph Black was unusual as a scientist at that time because of his belief in the application of science to everyday life. Black's belief in the merits of applied science was directly reflected in the work of James Watt, who famously watched the steam rising from a kettle as a small boy and applied the theories of Black to improve the efficiency of the steam engine. Black's teachings would lead to the development of a tradition of scientific thought and invention among Scots which lasted long beyond the Age of Enlightenment.

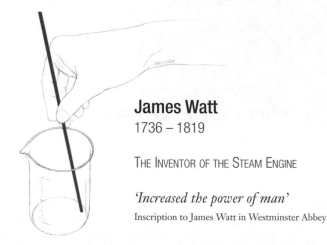

## James Watt
1736 – 1819

THE INVENTOR OF THE STEAM ENGINE

*'Increased the power of man'*
Inscription to James Watt in Westminster Abbey

Strictly speaking, James Watt did not invent the steam engine. Nor is it true that when he was a wee boy his grandmother scolded him for sitting for hours in the kitchen watching the kettle boil and measuring the steam coming out of the spout, thus receiving the inspiration which led to the development of the steam engine – but it makes a good tale.

The steam engine was in fact invented by Thomas Newcomen in 1712 and steam engines were widely used to pump flood water out of the tin mines in Cornwall well before the time of James Watt. Watt however was the engineering genius who dramatically improved the efficiency of the engine and by doing so provided the motive force which powered the Industrial Revolution.

### Childhood in Greenock

James Watt was born in 1736 in the port of Greenock, still then a small village set on a beach on the banks of the Clyde. He was named after his father, who had a marine business in Greenock as a shipwright and a general merchant. Watt's parents had five children but as was only too usual at the time, he alone survived to adulthood; three of his siblings died in infancy and his brother John died while on a voyage to America in one of his father's ships.

Watt himself was a sickly boy, suffering regularly from headaches, probably migraines, which continued to trouble him all his life. He was first taught at home by his mother and when he at last went to school he found it difficult to cope with the rough and tumble of the other boys, being often bullied. He showed particular talent at mathematics and was a great admirer of John Napier of Merchiston, who had developed in1614 the theory of logarithms. Napier described his ideas in the rather magnificently named *Mirifici Logarithmorum Canonis Descriptio* or *Description of the Marvellous Canon of Logarithms*, which in turn gave Newton the tools he needed to develop his theory of gravity and paved the way for the great

James Eckford Lauder, 'James Watt and the Steam Engine: the Dawn of the Nineteenth Century'
Scottish National Portrait Gallery, Edinburgh  *see: colour plate 6*

advances by Watt and other engineers many years later. Napier had an amazingly fertile mind; he also developed a calculating machine using rods, which was known rather endearingly as 'Napier's bones.' At home, Watt enjoyed playing with the tools — the compasses, telescopes and navigational instruments — that his father used in his business. When he left school he worked in his father's workshop, learning the elements of metal working. It was his father's wish that he should follow him into the family marine business, but when business affairs took a turn for the worse, Watt had to look further afield for a formal training in order to use the skills that he had developed.

### Training as an Engineer

Watt therefore went at the age of eighteen to nearby Glasgow to learn the trade of an instrument maker. He found the instruction he was receiving limited and so set off by horseback on the twelve-day ride to London to continue his learning there.

London then was a dangerous place. Not only were there thieves and pickpockets but there was always the danger of being seized by a press gang. Britain was at war, as usual against the French, and men were often recruited into the navy against their will; a young man might have a drop too much to drink one night and wake up the next morning to find himself on board a ship, serving in the king's navy!

Watt worked for a year as an apprentice to an instrument maker before the long hours told on his weak frame and he went back home to recover from illness and rebuild his strength. Then he returned to Glasgow, where he set up business as 'mathematical instrument maker to the university,' selling instruments such as quadrants and microscopes and repairing them as needed. He enjoyed the company and the respect of the professors and would fill his spare time by making musical instruments: fiddles, flutes and even an organ for his friend, Joseph Black. A few years later he married Black's cousin, Margaret Miller.

So his life might have continued, hardworking, reasonably prosperous but unremarkable, but for a lucky accident.

## Development of the Steam Engine

In 1764 Watt was given by a professor at the university a model of a Newcomen steam engine which needed repairing. Newcomen, who was from Dartmouth in Devon, had developed his steam engine for use in coal and tin mines where it was used to pump out flood water. Watt was surprised to find that although the model was in true proportion to a full-scale Newcomen engine he could not make it work properly as the boiler could not supply enough steam to make it run. Watt approached the problem as an engineer and quickly realised the design was very inefficient as a large amount of the steam and heat produced was being wasted.

Steam engines work on the principle that when water is boiled and turned into steam the volume of steam created is much greater than that of the original water; this increase in volume is used to drive a piston.

The Newcomen engine featured a piston which was connected by a chain to one end of a 'rocking' beam with the other end of the beam connected to a pump. The piston was tightly contained within a vertical cylinder and as the temperature rose, the steam expanded and moved the piston up the cylinder. To return the piston to its starting point, Newcomen cooled the steam in the cylinder by injecting cold water, condensing the steam and by reducing the pressure, allowing the piston to fall back under gravity. As the piston fell it pulled one end of the beam down powering the pump attached to the other end. Then the whole process repeated. It was the partial vacuum caused by the condensation of the steam to water which powered the pump, not the expansion caused by the injection of the steam.

Watt proved by experiment that when water is boiled at atmospheric pressure, the steam produced occupies eighteen hundred times as great a volume as the original water. Watt was surprised at the large amount of cold water needed to condense the steam and conversely how hot the relatively small weight of steam made the water. He discovered to his amazement that steam can raise six times its own weight of water to boiling point. Joseph Black explained that this was due to the 'latent heat' in the steam, the enormous amount of heat required to change a liquid into a vapour or given up when a vapour turns back to a liquid, a concept which Black had discovered only three years earlier. Newcomen's engine was therefore very inefficient, as all the energy which was used to heat the water into steam was wasted when the cold water was injected to condense the steam back to water and the cylinder cooled; as Black explained, the latent heat in the steam was lost. Watt realised it would be much more efficient if the cylinder could be kept all the time at the temperature of steam. But how then could the steam be condensed back to water?

Watt discovered the solution when walking one spring day on Glasgow Green, as he later explained:

> *I had gone to take a walk on a fine Sabbath afternoon. I had entered the Green ... when the idea came to my mind that as steam was an elastic body (that is, it expands to fill the space available) it would rush into a vacuum and if a communication was made between the cylinder and an exhaust vessel it would rush into it and might be condensed there without cooling the cylinder... I had not walked further than the golf house when the whole thing was arranged in my mind.*

Put more simply, his idea was to use a separate chamber to condense the steam, thus keeping the cylinder itself hot; condensing the steam into water would provide a partial vacuum which on the next piston stroke would suck the next batch of steam from the cylinder. He also developed the idea of closing both ends of the cylinder and using the pressure of the steam to force the piston back, rather than relying on atmospheric pressure, thus significantly increasing the power produced by the engine. Watt tried out his ideas in his workshop, further improving his engine by putting lagging around the cylinder to conserve the heat. It worked brilliantly. He explained his idea to Joseph Black, who at once saw the possibilities. Watt now needed the funds to translate his ideas into an engine which could work and be sold.

### How to Produce a Working Engine?

Black introduced Watt to John Roebuck of the nearby Carron Iron Works. Roebuck was troubled by repeated flooding of the mines which produced his coal and had found the Newcomen engines inefficient at powering the pumps. He agreed to provide the money needed to enable Watt to develop his ideas. But the development took much longer than originally thought as Watt wrestled with the engineering challenges of transferring a working model to a full-size engine which could be produced on a commercial basis. Meanwhile he needed money to live on – as he wrote 'I have a wife and children and I see myself going gray without having any settled way of providing for them' - and so he took a job as surveyor on a new canal intended to bring coal into the city of Glasgow, further delaying work on the engine. Then disaster struck: Roebuck became bankrupt.

There was no more money for Watt's engine. Worse was to follow. Watt's wife Margaret died in 1773, leaving him with two little bairns to bring up. He was in complete despair.

## Boulton and Watt

Matthew Boulton was a successful manufacturer with a factory in Soho, Birmingham, where he made watch chains, sword hilts, medals and the like with machines powered by water. He was friends with Roebuck, from whom he had learned of Watt's ideas, and he realised the potential of Watt's invention. Boulton had already met with Watt in Birmingham and they had immediately struck up a friendship through their mutual respect. Boulton now agreed to provide the funds needed to finish the development of Watt's engine.

In 1775 Watt moved to Birmingham with his two children. It was to be the most fertile period of his life, although he was still plagued by severe headaches. Matthew Boulton wrote that he would see Watt 'suffer under the most acute sick headaches, sitting by the fireside for hours together, with his head leaning on his elbow and scarcely able to give utterance to his thoughts.'

There was a great difference between producing a working model of a steam engine and producing a full-scale engine whose design was sufficiently robust for it to be manufactured in quantity and sufficiently reliable to give regular use. One of Watt's problems was producing a cylinder that was straight, perfectly circular and sufficiently well finished to provide a tight seal with the piston. An iron master called John Wilkinson used his experience in making the iron barrels for guns to solve the problem. These likewise had to be perfectly round in bore, straight and smooth, and he had achieved this by boring them with a cutting tool which rotated around a firmly fixed central shaft so that the inside of the barrel was perfectly cylindrical.

John Wilkinson bought one of the first engines to power the bellows at his iron works; it was immediately successful. Boulton and Watt's business now took off, with most of the early engines being sold to mines to power the pumps used to pump out water. The engines were sold on a royalty basis, with continuing payments being made by the mill owner based on the saving in the purchases of coal that could be achieved by using the more efficient Boulton and Watt engine. This was a clever concept but would inevitably in time lead to arguments with the mine owners as to the actual savings achieved.

## Improving the Steam Engine

Boulton realised there was another big potential market in selling engines to power textile mills, but to do so there was one further technical step to take. The early steam engines only drove pistons in a linear movement, but to power mills a rotating output would be needed. The trick was to convert linear movement to a rotating movement which could be used to drive a wheel.

This was solved by the invention of William Murdoch, a young Scotsman who had joined the firm of Boulton and Watt in 1777 and who had been moved two years later to Cornwall to provide engineering support for the steam engines used in the Cornish tin mines – and to take over the job of persuading the Cornish mine owners to pay their bills. Murdoch devised a method to change the output of the engine from a reciprocating to a rotating motion using a 'sun' and a 'planet.' The 'planet' was a cogged wheel fixed to a connecting rod which was driven by the piston of the engine; the 'planet' was fixed and did not itself rotate. As the connecting rod moved up and down the 'planet' rotated around the 'sun', also a cogged wheel, causing the 'sun' to rotate; the rotating motion of the 'sun' could then be transferred to a driving wheel which delivered the power by a system of belts or gears.

This opened up a huge new market for the steam engine which could now be used in the mills. Watt again employed the concept of charging a royalty based on the savings achieved, but this time there was the problem that the engine was replacing not a less efficient engine as with the mines, but horses which had been used to drive the mills. To arrive at the value to the mill owner Watt had to compare the saving in 'horses' and to measure this he invented the concept of 'horsepower.' He calculated that one horse walking in a circular track of twenty-four feet diameter would complete two and a half turns a minute with a pull of one hundred and eighty pounds, thus calculating as a 'standard' the power of one horse, leading to the convention whereby steam engines were rated in terms of their 'horsepower.'

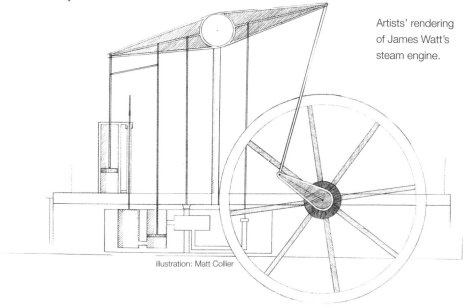

Artists' rendering of James Watt's steam engine.

illustration: Matt Collier

One of the first uses of a Watt rotating engine was in the Albion flour mill, financed largely by Boulton as a show piece, with milling machinery designed by John Rennie and built by Boulton and Watt. Steam power was used not just for milling but also for unloading the wheat from the barges in which it arrived, hoisting the sacks of wheat and sifting the flour. At the time of its completion in 1788 the mill was a 'state of the art' facility but just three years later it was tragically destroyed by fire, possibly arson. Watt introduced several other major technical advances to his engines. The first, in 1788, was a governor to control engine speed, one of the first examples of a 'feedback' control system. The governor consisted of two balls mounted on a hinged frame, which rotated around a spindle driven by the engine. As the speed of the engine increased, the spindle rotated faster and the balls moved outwards by centrifugal force, raising the frame and through a system of levers, reducing the amount of steam entering the cylinder and hence the speed of the engine; they likewise increased the flow if the speed fell.

Watt also developed a steam pressure gauge to measure the pressure in the boiler and a meter to record the number of strokes delivered by the engine – an innovation resented by the Cornish engine minders who felt he was spying on them - before the meter they could sometimes stop the engine and slip away for a quiet drink but now the time they worked was being recorded.

A safety gauge was also added which 'spilt' steam if the pressure in the cylinder rose too high. With these and other innovations Watt made his steam engines much more efficient in their use of power than any others available. Orders for Boulton and Watt engines came from all over the world, for all sorts of applications, and workers had to be trained to high standards to meet the technical demands of manufacturing the Watt engines. Wherever power was needed, Watt's engine could supply it. Boulton and Watt's patents were extended by Parliament so that the firm had a virtual monopoly on the production of steam engines, and by the time of his retirement in 1800 at the age of sixty-four, Watt had become a very wealthy man.


### Life Was Not Just Steam Engines...


Watt's inventions had not been limited to the steam engine. In order to deal with the many business letters he received, he invented the first 'copier,' the only significant piece of office machinery until the invention of the typewriter more than a hundred years later.

Boulton himself had added to his factories a mint for producing coins. Hand-produced coins were very rough and so counterfeiting was common; it was said that by the mid 1750s half the coins in circulation were forgeries. Boulton produced his coins by steam-driven presses to such a degree of accuracy that the farthing, one quarter of a penny, weighed exactly one quarter of an ounce and could be used for checking weights. As part of his sales pitch, Boulton emphasised the quality and cleanliness of his works. He proudly pointed out that the workmen wore white overalls and were required to wash once a week.

Socially, Watt enjoyed the company of other original men of science. He had been introduced by Boulton to the prestigious Lunar Society, a gathering of thinkers, inventors and engineers who met once a month on the Monday nearest the full moon – this was so that the moon could light the way home for its members, who were, perhaps not surprisingly, called the 'Lunatics'. Other members included Joseph Wedgwood of the well-known pottery firm, Joseph Priestley, who discovered oxygen, William Murdoch and other famous visitors including the astronomer Sir William Herschel. It was an exciting group of original thinkers whose ideas were fundamental to the birth of the Industrial Revolution.

In 1819, at a remarkable eighty-three years old, Watt died. He had been the recipient of many well-deserved honours. He was made a Fellow of the Royal Society of Edinburgh, a Fellow of the Royal Society of London, an Honorary Doctor of Law at the University of Glasgow and a Foreign Associate of the French Academy of Sciences. In 1824 a statue was erected in his honour in Westminster Abbey. After his death, his and Matthew Boulton's sons took over the running of their fathers' firm.

## Watt's Legacy

As one might expect, the Enlightenment in Glasgow took a more pragmatic route than its intellectual Edinburgh neighbour. An engineer could be just as much a part of the Enlightenment as a scientist and equally regarded. James Watt was such a practical member of the Enlightenment and with Joseph Black was one of the first to apply science to the practical benefit of mankind.

Watt originated the concept of horsepower as a measure of the power output of his engines, and his name now lives on in the 'watt,' adopted as a standard measurement of power or work done per unit of time (in electricity a watt is a standard unit of electrical power equal to one ampere of current flowing over a voltage difference of one volt).

Unquestionably the single most important invention of the Industrial Revolution, Watt's steam engine provided the power which drove the machinery of the new factories and leading to the development of the industrialised society in which we now live. Without Watt's steam engine the age of the railway would not have happened; typically, he foresaw this possible use of his steam engines in a patent application in 1784.

**Further Reading**
H.W.Dickinson, *James Watt: Craftsman and Engineer*

**Online Resources**
University of Strathclyde
http://scienceonstreets.phys.strath.ac.uk/new/James_Watt.html

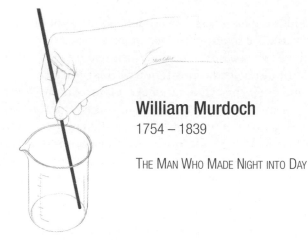

## William Murdoch
1754 – 1839

THE MAN WHO MADE NIGHT INTO DAY

William Murdoch was an inspired engineer who did not receive in his lifetime the recognition his inventions deserved. His place is unique in industrial history as the man who introduced gas lighting, bringing light to a nocturnal world that was, until then, dimly lit by flickering candle or sputtering oil lamp. He also produced the first model of a steam carriage, a small tricycle with a steam engine driving the wheels through a piston.

### Family and Childhood

The Murdoch family had been successful millers at Bello Corn Mill near Lugar in Ayrshire for generations. William Murdoch's father, John, followed the family tradition and became a miller, but only after he had first served in the Royal Artillery and fought in the campaign in Flanders.

In 1747 John married Anna Bruce, who claimed Robert the Bruce as one of her ancestors and therefore said she had 'royal blood.' They had seven children, of whom William was the third; two died in infancy.

John Murdoch was himself an inventive man. He introduced many engineering improvements to the mill, including using bevel gears made from cast iron, the first time cast iron had been used for this purpose and pre-dating Boulton and Watt by twenty years.

He also designed and built himself a wooden tricycle powered by levers driving an axle through a ratchet, sixty years before Kirkpatrick MacMillan built his bicycle. William Murdoch and his friends would ride 'Murdoch's horse,' as it was called, on the tracks near the mill. In an atmosphere of experiment and innovation, he learned at an early age to use his father's tools. As a small boy he used to spend hours in a small sandstone cave down by the river where he would carry out his experiments, playing with the effects of steam, boiling a kettle over an open fire, and apparently even with gas, which he obtained by burning coal. The coal used to heat Ayrshire homes at the time was called 'cannel coal'; it was obtained from the local mines and as it burned it created a black tar which, if also lit, would burn as coal gas, giving a spitting flame. Cannel coal was sometimes used to give extra light on dark winter evenings.

At the age of twenty-three, Murdoch decided he wanted to become an engineer but there was little opportunity in Ayrshire, so he walked to Birmingham to the famed works of Boulton and Watt, a stroll of some two hundred and fifty miles.

## Boulton and Watt

When Murdoch arrived at Boulton and Watt it is said he was interviewed by Matthew Boulton himself. Boulton watched as the young man nervously twiddled his smart circular stove pipe hat – so nervously that he dropped it. It made a strange sound when it fell and Boulton asked what it was made of. 'Timber,' replied Murdoch nervously, 'I turned it myself on a lathe.' Boulton was so impressed with the quality of his workmanship that he employed him on the spot. It is one of those stories which if not true, should be!

Within two years Murdoch had learned enough to be sent to Scotland to help with the installation of one of the new steam engines. The joints in the piping leaked and Murdoch was given instructions on how to cure the problem. While he was in Scotland he modified the engine to improve its performance giving an early indication of his fertile mind.

## Cornwall

Boulton soon recognised the worth of his new employee. Many of the early steam engines had been sold in Cornwall where the miners proved difficult customers; they would complain about the performance of the engine and refuse to pay the ongoing royalties based on performance which Boulton and Watt charged for the engine. He sent Murdoch to Cornwall to sort out the problems.

Murdoch had a simple but effective way to get the respect of the troublesome miners. When he was confronted by a miner who refused to pay he decided there was only one thing to do; he took off his shirt and offered to fight the disputing man. After beating him he put his shirt back on; there was no trouble thereafter.

The Cornishmen soon realised that Murdoch was not just a bruiser but a very talented engineer. If the engine broke down, there was immediately a danger that the mine would be flooded and it had to be repaired as soon as possible. Time and again Murdoch would arrive at the mine and get the engine working – just in time.

Murdoch gained even more favour with the locals when he married a young Cornish girl, Ann Paynter. Sadly, Ann died in childbirth after they had been married just five years, leaving two small boys. Murdoch, working long hours, was unable to care for them, so the boys were sent off to Scotland to live with their grandfather.

Murdoch was responsible for many improvements in the manufacturing design and quality of the Watt steam engine during this period, but his major contribution was to invent the 'sun and planet' system. The new engine was sold widely in industry and in the mills, replacing the water power previously used. He also developed the D-slide valve, which greatly simplified engine design, as well as the worm gear and the oscillating cylinder engine.

He felt, probably with justification, that his value to the firm was not being recognised in either his pay or his position. He was being paid a niggardly guinea (twenty-one shillings) a week but when he asked for an increase Watt turned him down. It is sad that although Watt recognised the engineering abilities of his young assistant he would not give him the reward or promotion he deserved.

## The Steam Carriage

In 1782 memories of 'Murdoch's horse' inspired Murdoch to wonder whether such a machine could be powered by steam. At the time the wheel had only a 'passive' role in transport, used for carts or wagons, with the motive power provided by horses or men. The idea of providing a source of power to drive the wheels had not then occurred to anyone, although to us today it seems obvious.

Within two years Murdoch had built his first model of a locomotive; it had three wheels, like his father's tricycle, was just nineteen inches (roughly fifty centimetres) long, and was powered by steam. To drive the wheels Murdoch used the piston of the engine to drive a crank shaft on the rear axle through a connecting rod.

One dark night on a narrow lane leading to Redruth church, Murdoch was trying out his new toy when the tricycle gained speed and left him far behind. He was alarmed to hear the startled cries of the local vicar, who had been walking quietly home through the gathering dusk when this unearthly body, lit by glowing coals, had suddenly come puffing and snorting at him out of the darkness.

Later, Murdoch fitted gas jets to light his vehicle, which he tried out on the roads around Redruth at night. He was very excited by his invention, realising the potential of steam-powered locomotion. He wanted to take out a patent to protect against it being copied by others, but to his great regret he was unable to interest either Matthew Boulton or James Watt. Watt even went so far as to write that Murdoch *'should do as we do and apply himself to the business in hand.'* Watt also revealingly wrote, in an early example of the 'not invented here' syndrome, that he *'did not like a scheme of mine, which I had revolved in my mind for years and hoped at some favourable time to bring to perfection, should be wrested from me.'* Whatever might have been his reasons, Watt refused to agree to advance the money Murdoch needed to develop his ideas although he did take out a protective patent.

Matthew Boulton was slightly more encouraging, giving Murdoch one hundred pounds to carry out his experiments and offering him the possibility of a partnership in an enterprise to market his ideas, but hedged with such conditions that Murdoch had no reasonable prospect of clearing the hurdle; Murdoch was required within just one year to make a locomotive which could carry three people together with their luggage and four hours' worth of coal at a speed of four miles an hour. Murdoch was not completely discouraged by this lack of support. He carried on working on his ideas and built a second, more powerful model with a slightly increased cylinder diameter, which he showed to a number of visitors, including the young Cornish engineer Richard Trevithick. Two years later Murdoch stopped work on his models and so it was Trevithick who some dozen years later built the first practical steam carriage and Trevithick rather than Murdoch who got the glory, and surprisingly the successful businessman Boulton and the brilliant engineer Watt had together missed the historic opportunity they had been offered by their inspired young engineer.

Murdoch did not confine his inventive mind to steam. He developed a system using compressed air to ring the bells in his house, an idea later adopted by Sir Walter Scott for his house at Abbotsford. He also designed a system to transfer packets and letters through a system of tubes by extracting air using a pump, a system still in use in some shops through the 1960s, and developed a method for producing dyes. His greatest invention, however, was still to come.


## Gas Lighting

Murdoch had memories from his childhood of primitive lighting from the gas given off by burning coal and he decided to experiment. A charming story says that he was quietly smoking a pipe one evening when he took a piece of burning coal from the fire and placed it in the bowl of his pipe. He then sealed the bowl and set light to the gas being emitted through the stem of the pipe. Whether true or not, Murdoch certainly found the time to experiment with various ways of making gas, using peat, wood and different types of coal.

He would heat the coal in a closed retort or 'oven', carefully controlling the amount of air entering the retort. A gas would be given off which he could carry a distance through a system of piping. One day a young boy was watching Murdoch in his workshop when the great man asked him to run and get a thimble. When the boy returned, Murdoch pierced the thimble with a number of small holes and connected it to his gas piping. He then lit the gas coming out of the small holes in the thimble and produced a light. He had made the first gas mantle. Murdoch realised the gas had to be 'clean' and he devised a process to 'wash' the gas.

On dark nights he would venture out with an apparatus not dissimilar to a set of bagpipes, with a bladder connected to a pipe. The bladder held the gas and Murdoch lit the mantle at the end of the pipe to light his way. Sometime between 1792 and 1794 he rigged up a system to light his house using gas piped from coal burnt in a retort located some twenty metres away. He installed iron piping in his house to carry the gas and pierced the pipes at intervals for the burners which provided the light.

Murdoch took his ideas to Boulton and Watt, but again they did not recognise the opportunity he was giving them and refused to take out the patent which would have protected his ideas, preferring to concentrate on their 'true' business of making steam engines. Murdoch realised that Watt's patents only had a few more years to run and he felt the company should have a new product for the future, but the directors did not share his vision.

After becoming disillusioned with the lack of support he received, he returned home to Scotland. However, in 1798 he rejoined Boulton and Watt when they made him manager of their works in Birmingham. There he continued to develop his ideas for gas lighting, providing a public display to celebrate the Peace of Amiens in 1802 by illuminating the works with more than two thousand six hundred gas lights.

Gas lighting had arrived! Within a few years it was being installed in homes, shops and factories; even towns were being lit by gas, and Murdoch was busy producing gas burners. Sadly, yet again the firm of Boulton and Watt, by now managed by the sons of the founders, failed to capitalise on his ideas and it was left to others to supply the growing market for the small-scale gas plants required to light houses, shops and small businesses. Unprotected by patent, Murdoch's invention was exploited by others and Murdoch himself received scant financial reward from his brilliant innovation.

## Later Years

In 1808 Murdoch was awarded by the Royal Society the Rumford Gold Medal for 'the most important or useful discovery … in heat and light' but he was never made a Fellow of either the Royal Society of London or the Royal Society of Edinburgh, at both of which Watt had membership; was Watt perhaps content that Murdoch's genius be left in the shadows? Faithfully serving Boulton and Watt until 1830, at the age of seventy-six, Murdoch most certainly enjoyed a well-earned retirement until his death nine years later.

**Further Reading**
Janet Thomson, *The Scot who Lit the World*

**Online Resources**
www.williammurdoch.com

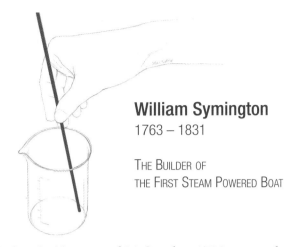

## William Symington
1763 – 1831

THE BUILDER OF
THE FIRST STEAM POWERED BOAT

The *Edinburgh Advertiser* of 24 October 1788 reported:

> *the result of an experiment no less curious than new. On the 14th inst.*
> *a Boat was put in motion by a Steam Engine upon Mr. Miller of*
> *Dalswinton's piece of water at that place. It answered Mr. Miller's*
> *expectations fully and offered great pleasure to the Spectators.*

With this understatement, the maiden voyage of the first steam-powered vessel
was recorded on Dalswinton Loch. William Symington was its designer.

### Childhood

Symington's parents lived in Leadhills, a Lanarkshire village where his father
worked as superintendent of the local mining company. The people of Leadhills
were bent on self-improvement in best Enlightenment tradition. The miners in
1741 had opened one of the first subscription libraries in Scotland, which they
named the Allan Ramsay Library in honour of the poet.

Symington was taught Latin and Greek at the local school and was encouraged
to read widely to broaden his knowledge as his father wanted him to go into the
Church of Scotland to train as a minister. Symington however had different ideas.
He wanted to be an engineer and so started work at the local Wanlockhead mine,
where his older brother George was the engineer.

### Wanlockhead: Working as a Mine Engineer

Wanlockhead and the nearby village of Leadhills had been the centre of a
mining industry since the early seventeenth century. The name of the village gives
the clue: the material mined was lead ore. From earliest times the mines at

Wanlockhead had been subject to regular flooding when the winter rains washed through the rocks and into the mine workings. Pumps powered by water were used to remove the floodwater from the workings.

By 1779 the company was working a new and rich vein of ore, the Margaret mine, which had been discovered when a tunnel, or drainage adit, had been driven through the hills south of the village to bring water in to power the pumps. As the tunnel was driven through the hills it cut through a rich vein of lead ore. At first the lead could be mined by taking the ore from above the water level in the tunnel, but as the mines were dug deeper it became essential to pump water from a depth of more than fifty-five metres below the level of the adit. It was not practical to use water power which would require a giant water wheel buried deep in the earth. The manager, Gilbert Meason, wondered if the solution might be to use one of the new-fangled steam engines.

He knew that there were Newcomen engines working in the coal mines around Edinburgh, but these were reported to be very inefficient and to use an immense amount of coal to generate the necessary power. Wanlochhead was a long way from the coal mines and the coal would have to be transported a long distance by cart to the mine, making it costly. It would be better if an engine using less coal could be found. Meason had learned of the experiments of James Watt and of his new, much more efficient steam engine. He met with Watt in Edinburgh and explained his problem and Watt agreed to provide an engine, the first to be supplied in Scotland from the Soho works of his partner Matthew Boulton.

In the early days of the manufacture of steam engines they were supplied to the customer in parts and assembled on-site. Symington worked as an apprentice to his older brother George, who was the engineer at the mine, on erecting the new engine until William Murdoch, Boulton and Watt's engineer, arrived in 1779 to sort out the last few problems and put the engine into service.

To begin with it was all sunshine; Watt wrote when the engine had been installed 'May it prosper and discover new riches.' He did not however specify whose riches. Boulton and Watt used to charge a royalty for the use of their engine, based on one-third of the savings in coal as compared with that used by a Newcomen engine, but in this case there was no Newcomen engine to compare to. Meason, not unreasonably, objected to the high royalty being levied and his relationship with Watt soured. Soon however he ordered a further, more powerful engine from Watt; he had looked for another supplier but the Watt engine was technically far and away the best.


## Symington's Steam Engine

Symington had learned a lot from his experience in building, commissioning and running the two Boulton and Watt engines and he must also have seen the more primitive Newcomen engines used in the coalfields in Fife. Although the

Watt engine was very advanced, it did have problems associated with its sophistication. The piston fitted tightly within the cylinder to prevent wasteful leakage of steam but there was no way of lubricating the piston and the cylinder cover had to be repeatedly removed for service. There was also the problem of leaks; all the joints had to be kept tight and the valves precisely adjusted. The Boulton and Watt engineers handed the engines over in perfect working order but all too often the local engineers could not maintain them to the required standard. Watt's complaint has often been repeated: 'We can make good engines but cannot make good men … to keep their engines in order.'

Symington sought to develop an engine which would match the technical advantages of the Watt engine while retaining the simplicity of the old Newcomen ones. In 1786 he built a prototype by modifying the Watt engine and in 1787 he filed for a patent. At this time Symington also worked on his ideas for a steam-driven carriage, producing in 1786 a model which he managed to run on the carpet of Gilbert Meason's house in Edinburgh. Symington wanted to obtain backing to produce a full-sized version but was unable to raise the funds needed. Symington's work on the Watt engines and the prototype steam carriage had so impressed Meason that he sponsored him to attend Edinburgh University, where he studied anatomy, surgery and chemistry under some of the finest scientific minds of the time, including the great Joseph Black. This theoretical education qualified him for his profession as an engineer, but in truth he probably learned more from his practical experience of working at the mines, learning about hydraulics, the strength of metals and the mysteries of the new steam engines.

## The Trial on Dalswinton Loch

Patrick Miller was a wealthy banker who owned a stake in the Carron Ironworks, the company that had made the parts for Symington's engine. Miller was interested in warfare and had invented a short-range large-bore cannon which he called the 'carronade.' Naval warfare also interested Miller. He believed in the revolutionary new tactic of destroying an enemy fleet by sailing across their battle lines and firing all your guns while they were unable to fire back, (a tactic Admiral Nelson would successfully use at the Battle of Trafalgar). But what, Miller mused, if there were no wind? How could you then break the enemy lines? Would it be possible to power ships so that they could attack even when there was no wind?

In 1786 Miller built a trimaran, a three-hulled boat, which he named the *Edinburgh*. It was powered by two paddles mounted between the hulls, the paddles themselves were powered by men turning cranks by hand. In 1787 he launched a further design, a catamaran or twin-hulled boat, with the paddles again driven by sailors, this time pushing on capstans. Surprisingly this idea was quite successful; in a trial race against a Customs House wherry over the six miles from the Isle of Incholm to Leith, Miller's boat triumphed by a few minutes.

This proved that boats could be driven by paddle wheels, but surely there was a better way to power them than by using men pushing capstans? Miller knew of Symington and his work on steam engines. Perhaps steam was the answer? In 1787 Miller instructed Symington to build a small steam engine that could be fitted to a boat on Dalswinton Loch.

Symington built a two-cylinder engine, each cylinder having a bore of four inches and a stroke of eighteen inches. It would, he calculated, give the same power as *one man rowing.* The power was delivered to the paddle wheels using a chain drive designed so that the wheels would continually rotate. The boat itself was twenty-five feet (seven-and-a-half metres) long with twin hulls. There were two paddle wheels, which were set in line between the two hulls. Symington fitted his steam engine in the hull and designed the drive linking the engine to the paddle wheels; all was ready for the trial.

The trial was well attended; among those watching were Alexander Nasmyth and Robert Burns, who was a tenant of Patrick Miller at Ellisland Farm, an example of how the different strands of the Enlightenment overlapped.

Although the first trial was considered a success it is probable the engine needed manual help from the crew as it was in truth underpowered for the task, but Miller was encouraged and ordered a new engine from Symington to power a steam boat on the Forth and Clyde Canal. Symington realised much more power was needed to meet the inefficiencies of the drive system. His new engine would be nearly thirty times more powerful than his first.

The trial of this second boat took place in December 1789. The engine worked satisfactorily, but this time the boat was overpowered and the paddle wheels began to break up. Miller started to lose patience.

By Boxing Day the paddle wheels had been strengthened and the boat was ready for a second trial. This time all went well, with the boat reaching a speed of seven miles an hour. For Symington however it was too late: Miller had become impatient over the time the project was taking and was not there to see the trial. He had moved on to other things. The possibility of powering a boat by steam had been demonstrated, but with no one to move it ahead, Symington returned to building steam engines.

## The *Charlotte Dundas*

More correctly, Symington worked not as an engine builder but as a designer, earning fees for his designs. He sold the concept for an engine to his customer – the coal mine or mill – who would then order the necessary parts from Carron Ironworks. The engine itself was assembled on site. From 1789 to 1806, Carron produced parts for sixty-one steam engines, of which just under half (twenty-nine) were for Symington designs, mostly for use in Scotland, but with a few for England and some for Jamaica, where they were used to power sugar mills.

In later years however business decreased, with orders down to just two engines a year. The design of the Symington engine had become outdated and neither Carron nor Symington had responded to the changed world. Engines were no longer 'one-offs' put together on-site, but were designed and built in factories such as the Soho works of Boulton and Watt, where design could be improved and quality and cost controlled. But Symington had not yet finished as a designer and builder of steamships. Over the years some attempts had been made to use steam to power ships in conjunction with sails but none had been a complete success.

The Forth and Clyde Canal had been completed in 1790, connecting the Rivers Forth and Clyde and enabling boats to cross from east to west across the country. It was a large canal, taking boats as large as nineteen feet in the beam (six metres wide) and sixty-eight feet (twenty-one metres) long.

Lord Dundas was Governor of the Forth and Clyde Navigation Company. He had coal works in Fife and a soda works on the Clyde and needed to be able to transport coal to his works. The canal worked perfectly – but only if the wind was in the right direction! Dundas wanted a steam-powered tug to pull the barges through even against the wind. In 1800 Symington was given an order to build a steam engine to be installed in a boat for use as a tug on the Forth and Clyde Canal.

The boat, called the *Charlotte Dundas* after Lord Dundas's eldest daughter, was launched in March 1801 and the engine was fitted a few months later. The tug, powered by twin paddle wheels, successfully towed boats on the River Forth but was less successful on the canal. It was again underpowered and the wash from the paddles damaged the canal's banks; it also proved difficult to control the barges being towed around the twists and bends of the canal. (Although this first boat was eventually scrapped, it was the inspiration for a succession of Clyde paddle steamers from the *Columba* to the *Waverley*, which later famously sailed 'doon the watter.' This line of boats only ended when the screw propeller was invented.)

A second boat, confusingly also called the '*Charlotte Dundas*,' was built. This had a more powerful engine, but one of unproven design. This time Symington used a horizontal cylinder driving a single stern-mounted paddle. This kept the weight low in the hull, and the power generated could be applied more easily to drive the paddle.

The first trial was in January 1803 along the Forth and Clyde Canal. The *Charlotte Dundas* steamed majestically along the canal and then returned with a sloop in tow. While a success, there was still a problem in matching the power of the steam engine with the paddle wheels. Symington changed the gearing and in March the tug towed two sloops eighteen miles to Port Dundas in just over two hours against a strong headwind.

Symington had successfully shown that a steam engine could propel a boat through water both swiftly and safely. The second *Charlotte Dundas* was the first vessel propelled by steam alone that was designed not as an experiment but actually to do a job. At last Symington had achieved success, but tragically it was too late: his patron Lord Dundas had died just two weeks before the trial. The concept of steam-powered ships had been proven but money wasn't forthcoming.

### Henry Bell and the *Comet:*
### The First Commercial Service Using a Steam-Powered Vessel

Henry Bell was a not-very-successful builder based in Glasgow. When business grew slack he decided to build a hotel at the developing resort of Helensburgh to take advantage of the new fashion for sea bathing. Rather unimaginatively, he called his hotel 'The Baths.'

He was perhaps ahead of his time and he found it hard to attract enough guests. One of the problems was the long and hard road journey from Glasgow. The only alternative was an unpredictable boat trip. A steam-powered boat, thought Bell, would enable the boat to travel whatever the wind and tide.

Bell decided to have a steamboat built to be called the *Comet*. Powered by both sail and steam, with four great paddles placed in pairs, one behind the other on each side of the hull, she was launched in August 1812. With the first voyage a success, Bell started a regular service from Glasgow to Greenock from where Bell's guests would be taken on by ferry as at the time there was no pier at Helensburgh where the *Comet* could dock. Bell advertised his service in the *Glasgow Chronicle*:

THE STEAMBOAT 'COMET'
BETWEEN GLASGOW, GREENOCK AND HELENSBURGH
FOR PASSENGERS ONLY
THE SUBSCRIBER, HAVING AT MUCH EXPENSE,
FITTED UP A HANDSOME VESSEL
TO PLY UPON THE RIVER CLYDE FROM GLASGOW,
TO SAIL BY THE POWER OF WIND AND STEAM.
THE TERMS ARE FOR THE PRESENT FIXED AT FOUR SHILLINGS
FOR THE BEST CABIN AND THREE SHILLINGS FOR THE SECOND.

This was the first steam-powered passenger service, but it was not a commercial success and so Bell took his ship through the canal to the Firth of Forth, where he started running excursions. The *Comet* continued in service until 1820, when she sank off the Western Isles.

Symington must have been furious to see someone else profiting from his idea of a vessel powered by steam. Worse was to come. By 1814 there were no fewer than ten Steam-Powered vessels on the Clyde alone. Steam had finally arrived and the Clyde became the centre of a great shipbuilding industry. But for Symington there was neither glory nor profit; the debts he had incurred in developing his ideas broke him financially and he died in poverty in 1831.

**Further Reading**
W.S. Harvey and G. Downs-Rose, *William Symington: Inventor and Engine Builder*

**Online Resources**
Undiscovered Scotland
http://www.undiscoveredscotland.co.uk/usbiography/s/williamsymington.html

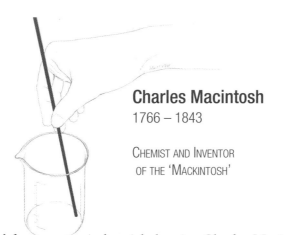

## Charles Macintosh
1766 – 1843

CHEMIST AND INVENTOR
OF THE 'MACKINTOSH'

First and foremost an industrial chemist, Charles Macintosh was responsible for a number of discoveries and new products, many of which transformed the way we live today. Some inventions transcend their inventor, whose name becomes forever associated with them, ensuring eponymous immortality. The Hoover* is one example and surely another is the 'Mackintosh' (with, for some unknown reason, the addition of a 'k').

*W.H. 'Boss' Hoover did not strictly invent the vacuum cleaner. A janitor named James Spangler suffered from asthma, which he thought was due to dust from the carpet sweeper he used. He thus produced the first prototype of an 'electric suction sweeper' from a soap box, electric motor, broom handle and pillow case. He showed one of his first machines to his cousin Susan Hoover; her husband saw it, recognised the potential and bought the patent. If he had not, the Hoover might have been the Spangler!

## Growing Up In Glasgow

Charles Macintosh's interest in chemistry did not appear out of the blue. His father, George Macintosh, was himself an industrialist specialising in the production of dyes. You could say dyes were in young Charles's blood.

Macintosh was born in Glasgow on 29 December 1766, just in time to welcome in the new year although it is doubtful he played much active part in the celebrations. His formal education began at Glasgow Grammar School, where he became fluent in Latin before moving to a school at Catterick Bridge in Yorkshire.

Unusually, he did not go to university (although later in his life he did attend university courses), but went straight into work in the 'counting house' or office of a Mr Glasford, a merchant in Glasgow. He soon joined his father's firm, which manufactured dyes and chemicals, principally 'cudbear.'

## Cudbear

The Macintosh family firm prospered from the manufacture of dyestuffs for the dyeing of cloth. One of their products was cudbear, which was used to dye woollen and silk cloth. A purple dye extracted from a specific type of lichen found in the Highlands, cudbear was the first dye to be invented in modern times. It had been discovered in 1758 by a Scot, Dr Cuthbert Gordon, who had patented the production process: the lichen is first boiled in a solution of ammonium carbonate; the resultant mixture is then cooled; ammonia is added; and after being kept damp for three weeks, the lichen is dried and ground to a powder. It is this powder which is called cudbear.

The Macintosh firm had acquired the rights to the process and jealously guarded its secrecy. Accordingly, they built a ten-foot (three-metre) high wall around their plant and employed only Gaelic-speaking Highlanders so nobody would be able to learn the secrets of the production process through loose talk by their employees.

One of the key secrets in the production was the quality of the ammonia used in the process, and one of Charles Macintosh's first actions at the company was to secure adequate supplies. The source he selected was urine.

In those days there were no toilets as such and people from all strata of society used chamber pots. A feature of evenings in cities such as Glasgow and Edinburgh was the disposal of the contents of these chamber pots, thrown out of the windows with a cry of '*gardez-loo!*'

What a waste of a good source of ammonia! Macintosh realised the value of the urine which was just being thrown away and employed a number of men in Glasgow to collect it, paying them one penny for each gallon they brought him. Each collector had with him a hydrometer so that he could measure the specific gravity of the urine he collected in order to avoid being fobbed off with 'watered-down' urine! The urine was then heated at the plant and the ammonia was distilled off. According to the amount of ammonia used in the process and the resultant acidity of the mixture, the colour of the dye produced varied from beautiful shades of pink through red and purple to blue. (Litmus paper, used in chemistry to determine the acidity of a solution by changing its colour to blue or red in the presence of alkaline or acid, is simply paper stained with cudbear).

Charles Macintosh

Cudbear became a great commercial success requiring the supply of more than two hundred and fifty tons of lichen a year and soon supplies from the Highlands became exhausted; to meet demand the Macintosh firm had to import lichen from Norway and Sweden, and even the Canary Islands. Fashion built the family's fortune, but in time it also closed the business as people turned from bright colours to greys and blacks. The Macintosh cudbear factory closed in 1852.

## Alum

A new product was needed. Alum had been used for many years as a 'mordant' to fix the colouring of dyes. It was imported to Britain for that purpose in the Middle Ages, and Pliny records in his *Natural History* that it was used to fix dyes in Roman times. A light-coloured version was used to fix bright colours and a dark version for black or dark colours.

While alum was not new, it had never been produced on an industrial scale. Macintosh knew of a seam of aluminous shale near Glasgow and noticed that the waste from coal mining was decomposed by air to give a surface 'bloom' of iron and alum. He wondered if by treating the waste with alkali it would be possible to extract the alum. The process worked and Macintosh built the first alum plant in Scotland. The alum produced was used not just for fixing dyes but also for tanning hides and hardening tallow – rendered animal fat used to make soap and tallow candles, which were a cheaper alternative to wax candles.

## Chlorine

His next venture was chlorine which had been discovered in 1774 by a Swedish chemist, Scheele; eleven years later a French scientist, Berthellot, demonstrated its bleaching powers to James Watt. On his return to England, Watt told his father-in-law, who became the first person in Britain to use chlorine as a bleaching agent. But chlorine did not prove instantly acceptable due to its strong smell. Macintosh addressed himself to the problem. In conjunction with Charles Tennant of Glasgow, who was manufacturing chlorine as a bleaching agent, he produced and patented in 1799 'bleaching powder,' chloride of lime, which was produced by passing lime through liquid chlorine. It was an instant success and made Charles Tennant one of the largest chemical manufacturing companies in Britain. Macintosh took no profit from the discovery and withdrew from the project in 1814. He had, however, stumbled on another use for the chemical. In 1804 he had written to the War Office in London to suggest that chlorine might be effective as a disinfectant in stopping the spread of infection and in the treatment of wounds; this was forty years before its first use in a hospital, the Vienna General Hospital, where (in 1847) it was used as a 'germicide' to prevent the spread of puerperal fever in the maternity ward. Macintosh was well ahead of his time. It was not until as late as 1850 that John Snow was recommending the use of chlorine to disinfect the water supply after a bad outbreak of cholera in London. At the time it was thought that infection was carried by the 'miasma' or smell of 'bad air.' Snow later deduced by analysis that the outbreak was concentrated among people who drew their water from a pump in Broad Street; when the pump was disabled the outbreak declined.

This was the first example of the use of epidemiology, the study of epidemics. Much later it was discovered that the public well had been dug just three feet (one metre) from a cesspit in which a baby's nappy containing faeces infected with cholera had been deposited.

### The Eponymous Raincoat: The 'Mackintosh'

The Macintosh Company was using a lot of ammonia in its manufacturing processes and Macintosh was continually looking for new sources of supply. Tar was one possibility.

The introduction of gas lighting in the streets and houses of Britain's cities had created a problem: the gas was produced from coal and it was not clear what to do with the waste from this production; the manufacturers of gas were becoming buried under a pile of coal tar. In London the residue was carelessly thrown into the River Thames, in Edinburgh into the Firth of Forth, and in Glasgow it was dumped in disused quarries and coal pits. The amount of waste product produced was beginning to threaten the viability of the infant gas industry.

Macintosh entered into a contract to take the waste coal tar from the works of the Glasgow Gas Company. He managed to extract the ammonia and by distilling the tar to produce pitch. As a by-product of this process he also produced naptha. Still seeking new challenges for his fertile mind to solve, rubber was the next to catch Macintosh's attention. Rubber comes from the juice of a South American tree and was known to the Aztecs. It did not reach Europe until the Spanish conquered South America and it had remained a curiosity since, its only use as a pencil eraser. Nobody had managed to find a solvent which would dissolve the rubber and widen its potential uses.

Rubber in its natural form is a milky liquid which coagulates on exposure to air and Macintosh found that the resultant sticky 'gum' could be dissolved in naptha to produce a waterproof 'rubber varnish', the consistency of which he could vary by altering the amount of naptha. With this 'varnish' it became possible to manufacture rubber gloves and tubing for hospital use, but Macintosh had another goal: he wondered whether it would be possible to use the flexibility of rubber to produce waterproof clothing.

He dissolved the rubber in naptha and then placed the sticky gum between two pieces of cloth, thus 'glueing' them together. When the naptha had evaporated the rubber 'cemented' the two sheets of cloth together and created a sheet that was impervious to both water and air. This was the breakthrough; waterproof cloth had been invented. Mackintosh patented waterproofing in 1822 and formed a new company to manufacture waterproof capes and cloaks, and even inflatable pillows and beds. The company prospered and made Macintosh a wealthy man. He had just one concern: the introduction of rail travel. With the coming of the railways and of travel inside a carriage instead of on horseback or the outside of coaches, would there remain any need for waterproof coats? With the British weather he need not have worried.

He received a number of awards during his lifetime and in 1823 was elected a Fellow of the Royal Society. He continued inventing until the end, devising a way of using carbon gases to convert malleable iron into steel more economically and working with James Nielson to produce high-quality cast iron. He died in Glasgow in 1843 at the age of seventy-seven. His wife Mary, whom he had married in 1790, died just a few months after her husband.

## The Macintosh Legacy

Despite the variety and extent of the discoveries Charles Macintosh made during his life, his immortality will be assured through his development of a method of dissolving rubber and producing waterproof clothing. Rubber pillows, gloves, tubing, mattresses and beds are just some of the items that resulted from this discovery, but every time it is raining and you put on your mackintosh you will in a small way be remembering a remarkable man.

**Further Reading**
George Macintosh, *Biographical Memoir of the Late Charles Macintosh FRS*

**Online Resources**
University of Strathclyde
http://scienceonstreets.phys.strath.ac.uk/new/Charles_MacIntosh.html

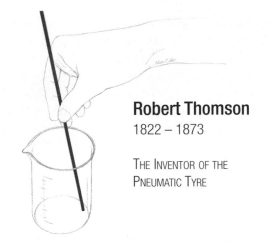

## Robert Thomson
1822 – 1873

THE INVENTOR OF THE
PNEUMATIC TYRE

*If a man write a better book, preach a better sermon, or make a better*
*mouse-trap than his neighbour, tho' he build his house in the woods, the*
*world will make a beaten path to his door.'*
—Ralph Waldo Emerson

Common knowledge has it that John Boyd Dunlop invented the pneumatic tyre. But was he the true inventor? He was a Scottish veterinary surgeon who gave his name to the eponymous Dunlop Pneumatic Tyre Company Limited, but there's more to the story.

The pneumatic tyre was certainly 'reinvented' by Dunlop, but the original pneumatic tyre, or as he called it the 'aerial wheel,' had been invented some years earlier by a relatively obscure Scot named Robert William Thomson, a self-taught engineer who became an inveterate but now largely unrecognised inventor.

Contrary to the edict of Emerson, it is arguable that the world will only beat a path to the 'maker of the best mouse-trap' if the world is ready for the mouse-trap. It is certainly possible to invent a product ahead of time, which was Thomson's misfortune that the world was not ready for the pneumatic tyre. It would need the invention of the bicycle, also by a Scot, to create the market for his aerial wheel.

### Birth and Early Days

Thomson was born in Stonehouse in 1822, the eleventh of twelve children, and life would never be easy with so many siblings to order him about. His father was a local mill owner but he had ambitions for his son and, as with many families of the time, wanted him to have a career in the church. However, young Thompson had difficulty learning the requisite Latin, and therefore left school at the age of fourteen. In desperation, his parents decided to send the boy to America, in the care of a merchant–uncle who lived in Charleston, South Carolina. This presented a new problem: Thomson did not want to be a merchant; he had a fertile and inventive mind and he wished to become an engineer. After two years he returned home, and decided in the true spirit of The Enlightenment that he needed to educate himself properly — in mathematics, chemistry, electricity and astronomy.

Robert Thomson

## The Inventions of a Fertile Mind

Soon, his father recognised his seventeen year old son's talent and determination, and built him a small workshop where Thomson could practice his skills. The young engineer would disappear there for hours. These were the days before washing machines and tumble driers, and washing would be dried by passing it through a mangle: a system of rollers which squeezed the water out of the washed clothes. One of Thomson's first projects was to redesign his mother's mangle so that the wet clothing could be put through the rollers in either direction. He also designed things like a ribbon saw, but perhaps his greatest achievement at the time was to build the first prototype of his elliptic rotary steam engine, an idea to which he would return.

Thomson took an engineering apprenticeship in Aberdeen, working for a period for the eminent Scots engineer Robert Stevenson and then for a firm of civil engineers in Edinburgh where he was employed on a demolition contract. Thomson thought that the explosive charges could be ignited by electricity more safely than by the traditional method of 'lighting the fuse and running' and he used this technique when later employed as an engineer supervising the blasting of chalk cliffs for the construction of a railway line. His invention would save many lives which would otherwise have been lost in mining accidents.

## The Railway 'Mania'

The first 'proper' railway, running from Liverpool to Manchester, opened in 1830 and proved highly successful in transporting both passengers and freight — the precursor of the railway boom. Although the economy was depressed in the late 1830s, by the mid 1840s the economy was growing again and with the new growth came optimism.

To build a railway, all that was required was an Act of Parliament with few checks on the viability of the project or the probity of the promoters. Joint stock companies were formed almost daily to fund ever more harebrained projects so that in 1846 alone as many as two hundred and seventy-two Acts of Parliament were passed authorising the construction of nine thousand five hundred miles of railway, almost as much in that one year as the entire modern UK railway network of eleven thousand miles.

Thomson was attracted by the opportunities this presented and moved to London at the age of twenty-two to set up business on his own as a railway engineer, taking premises in Adam Street just off the Strand. He intended to take advantage of the demand for railway engineers caused by the 'railway mania' and was immediately employed surveying for a new line to be built in the eastern counties of England.

Unfortunately, his timing was less than perfect. The boom didn't last. Rising interest rates, bankruptcies and the exposure of fraudulent schemes brought about the collapse of many of the projects and destroyed the savings of gullible investors. Nevertheless, it is remarkable that over six thousand miles of railway were laid as a result of 1844-6 schemes. Thomson moved on.


## The 'Aerial Wheel'

Many inventions are born of necessity, the need to solve a problem, but others are inspired with the inventor creating a completely novel concept. The idea of the pneumatic tyre, essentially an inflated tube fixed around the rim of a wheel, was one of these inspired ideas.

Travel on Britain's roads in the eighteenth and early nineteenth century had been revolutionised by John McAdam's development of 'macadamization.' A network of mail and passenger coach services had spread across the roads of the country but journeys were still a painful experience for the traveller.

Typically, the wheels of a coach would be solid, constructed of wooden spokes slotted into a wooden felloe, or rim, which in itself was protected by an iron 'tyre' which had been heated and shrunk on to the wooden rim and provided the wearing surface in contact with the road. The wheels would react to every bump on the road, painfully jolting and jarring the passengers.

What was needed was a method whereby the traveller could be 'cushioned' from these jolts. The solution proved to be a cushion of air, the pneumatic tyre, and it was a Scot, Robert Thomson, who provided the answer.

Thomson was quite clear as to the purpose of his invention. In his patent application (No:10990 submitted in December 1845) he stated that 'The nature of my said Invention consists in the application of elastic bearings round the tires (sic) of the wheels of carriages, for the purpose of lessening the power required to draw the carriages, rendering their motion easier and diminishing the noise they make when in motion.' His objectives were clear, to smooth and quieten the ride and to improve the efficiency. He called his invention the 'Aerial wheel.'

Thomson had very specific instructions as to how his patent could be implemented. He wrote that it would consist of 'a hollow belt, composed of some air- and water-tight material, such as caoutchouc (rubber) or gutta percha, (inflated) with air, whereby the wheels will in every part of their revolution present a cushion of air to the ground or rail or track on which they run,' in essence describing the pneumatic tyre as we use it today.

His reference to rail is a 'nod' to his profession as a railway engineer and refers to the wooden rails in use at the time, effectively wooden planks which provided the 'rails' upon which the iron-shod wheels of the carriages ran whilst a vertical wooden 'guide rail' kept the carriage on the track. Thomson also wrote that the use of his aerial tyres might 'enable steam carriages to run on common roads, with great advantages for carrying passengers and goods,' a concept well ahead of his time.

Thomson specified the material that could be used, proposing that the pneumatic tube should 'be made of a single thickness of rubber or gutta percha' which would be 'sulphurised' (we now say vulcanised) and then 'enclosed in a canvas cover.' The tyre he suggested should be inflated with air 'as being more suitable than anything else for the purpose' but that as an alternative, some elastic material such as sponge could be used so that the tyre when inflated 'would be less likely to be cut by concussion between the tire (sic) of the wheel and the roadway.'

In 1849, to test his ideas, Thomson made some aerial wheels with outer covers of rubberised canvas and fitted them to a brougham, a light two seat four-wheeled horse drawn carriage of the type which had been invented for the Scottish Lord Chancellor, Henry Brougham. Thomson carried out his tests in Regents Park in London, measuring the amount of force or effort required to pull the brougham with his new aerial wheels as compared with that required with conventional wheels.

The results were startling. There were efficiency savings of nearly forty percent when the tests were carried out on macadamised roads and a breathtaking seventy per cent when the carriage was on newly-laid broken flints. The Mechanic's Magazine reported in March 1849 on the tests, confirming the savings in the force required to propel the brougham and commenting on the silence, comfort and easy running of the carriage on its aerial wheels.

Thomson's aerial wheel had passed its test with flying colours. The stage was set for the pneumatic tyre, only nothing happened. No industrialist came along to develop the aerial wheel as a product, the idea was just too far ahead of its time.


## Java


Thomson's fertile mind had not remained idle and in 1849 he had taken out a patent for a 'self filling' pen, essentially the fountain pen, which he exhibited at the Great Exhibition of 1851, but by 1852 he had realised that the boom days for a railway engineer in Britain were over and left for Java to work as an engineer designing and installing machinery for use on the sugar plantations.

Prohibited by the Dutch from erecting a crane by the dockside in case at night it should provide a hazard for the natives, Thomson designed a portable steam crane which relied on the boiler to provide a counterweight and could safely be removed each night. This was manufactured in England and proved a successful product being sold worldwide. He also designed a successful hydraulic dry dock but in 1862 at the age of forty, he retired from Java and returned to make a new home in Edinburgh.

## Edinburgh

Retirement and increasing ill health, which would in time confine him to a couch, did not stop Thomson from inventing. He returned to his earlier ideas for a rotary steam engine, taking out a number of patents for improvements in maintaining and applying motive power, for the construction of steam boilers and for improvements in steam gauges. He also revisited his ideas for rubber tyres. While designing a traction engine to power the transport of sugar canes in Java, he tackled the problem of creating an interface between the rigidity of the drive and the variations in the 'road' surface; this he solved by using solid rubber 'tyres' five inches (twelve centimetres) thick.

These tyres were not fixed to the wheel but relied on the corrugations on their inner surface to provide friction, allowing the flexibility inherent in the thick rubber tyre to absorb the stresses caused by the impact of variations in the road surface on the rigid drive to the wheel. The rubber tyre distributed the weight of the traction engine over a greater surface area giving the added benefits of improving grip especially in the wet and of preventing damage to the surface of the road.

Thomson's traction engines proved very successful and he set up to manufacture road steamers, as they were called, at his workshop in Leith. The road steamers, which weighed as much as five tons each, were designed with three wheels, two at the back and one in the front with direct vertical steering, and would be seen on the streets of Edinburgh where they would pull as many as four wagons each laden with ten tons of coal and could reach a speed of as much as twenty m.p.h. Road steamers proved a commercial success and were manufactured both by Thomson and by other manufacturers in Britain under licence and exported to a number of countries including Java, India, Canada and Australia.

The Scotsman was fulsome in its praise of the new road steamers with their rubber tyres, stating in an article in June 1870 that they heralded 'a new era in locomotion as far as our large towns and public roads are concerned' and represented 'the greatest step which had ever been made in the use of steam on common roads.' Thomson also produced a passenger version, the omnibus, which ran a service between Edinburgh and Leith. Thomson died at the relatively early age of fifty after some years of poor health.

## Thomson's Legacy

Thomson was a great engineer with an inventive mind whose ideas are largely forgotten in the history of engineering development. His tragedy was that his greatest invention, the pneumatic tyre, was invented 'too soon.' It would not be until fifteen years after Thomson had died that John Boyd Dunlop would 'reinvent' the pneumatic tyre. By this time the bicycle had become the rage and cycling clubs were being set up all over the country.

The bicycle had been invented in 1839 by Kirkpatrick Macmillan, a Scottish blacksmith. It had a smaller steerable wheel at the front with a larger wheel at the rear and as a result was known colloquially as a penny-farthing; the wheels were linked by connecting rods to treadles which were powered by the rider. The bicycle was extremely heavy and must have been hard work to ride but Macmillan would often cycle the fourteen miles from his house into Dumfries.

In 1842 Macmillan rode his bicycle from his home in Dumfriesshire to Glasgow, a journey of sixty-eight miles which took him two days. The solid wooden wheels and iron 'tyres' meant he had a rather sore backside when he arrived in Glasgow. In the Gorbals area of Glasgow he had the first recorded cycling accident, knocking down and slightly injuring a young girl who had run across his path for which he was fined the sum of five shillings.

Macmillan had demonstrated that the bicycle was a practical proposition, but he never thought to make money from his invention by patenting his idea or by manufacturing and selling bicycles, and it was therefore some time before others copied his design and bicycles began to be made and sold in large numbers.

## An Unlikely Inventor

Dunlop was not an engineer; he was a veterinary surgeon. He had been born in 1840 in Ayrshire where his family had farmed for many generations and it had been planned that John too would be a farmer but he was a somewhat sickly child and so was sent to Edinburgh University where he qualified as a veterinary surgeon, eventually setting up practice in Belfast.

It was his ten year old son, Johnnie, who inspired Dunlop to invent the pneumatic tyre. Johnnie had a tricycle with solid wheels and he asked his father if he could devise any way to make the tricycle run faster and more smoothly over the granite setts and the tramlines of the city streets.

Just as Thomson had forty years before, Dunlop thought that an air 'cushion' might be the answer so he made a 'pneumatic tyre' for the front wheel of his son's tricycle.

Tricycles in those days did not have three wheels of equal size as they do today but one small wheel in front (of roughly ten inches or twenty-five centimetres diameter) and two huge wheels behind with a diameter of roughly a metre.

Dunlop made his wheel from a piece of elm wood which he fashioned into a disc the same size as the front wheel of the tricycle. He then made a rubber tube which he fitted over the elm 'wheel' and covered it with canvas for protection. Finally he inflated his tyre and needed to prove whether the invention worked. His method was simple. He took the front wheel off the tricycle and he bowled this and his new elm wood wheel across his backyard. The elm wood wheel with its pneumatic tyre easily out-distanced the solid wheel of the tricycle. A rather crude test compared with Thomson's experiment with a brougham – Dunlop was no engineer - but it proved the concept.

His next move was to fit the two rear wheels of Johnnie's tricycle with pneumatic tyres. He made wooden rims from strips of elm wood and fixed onto the rims the canvas cover of his tyre with the rubber inflatable tube inside. He then put the rims round the solid wheels of the tricycle.

Now it was time to test his work. Dunlop asked his young son to carry out a 'road test' and the tricycle was tried out for the first time secretly at night on 28th February 1888. The trial was interrupted by an eclipse of the moon but Johnnie went out again afterwards and reported that the pneumatic wheels greatly improved the speed and the comfort of the ride. Johnnie tried his new machine in races with his friends and was able to leave them well behind. It was not exactly 'Top Gear' but the pneumatic tyre had been re-invented.

### Dunlop exploits his 'invention' of the Pneumatic Tyre

Dunlop now needed to prove his ideas on a real bicycle in genuine competition. The first time his pneumatic tyre was tried in a competitive race was in June 1899 at the Queen's College sports in Belfast when it won all three races for which it was entered. 'There is a demon in that machine!' complained one of the spectators.

There was still much work to be done before the pneumatic tyre became a commercial success. One of the problems with Dunlop's prototype was dealing with a puncture, an all too often occurrence on the rough roads of the time. The tyre was fixed directly to the rim and the only way to remove it was to soak the casing in naptha, then patch the inner tube before rebuilding the casing onto the rim. The answer was discovered by an American, Willliam Bartlett, who was working at the time in Scotland. He fitted an upturned rim on the wheel over which the tyre was fitted. When the tyre was inflated it fitted snugly over the rim of the wheel. Another inventor, Charles Woods, developed the pneumatic valve which was so well engineered that the basic design remains in use today. The final improvement was to introduce a tread to prevent skidding on the un-metalled roads of the time.n It was time to exploit his invention.

A company was formed in 1899 which was called, rather engagingly, 'The Pneumatic Tyre and Booth's Cycle Agency Limited', changing its name in 1896 to 'The Dunlop Pneumatic Tyre Company' and in 1900 to 'The Dunlop Rubber Company Limited.'

Dunlop applied for patents to protect the design of the tyre and the valve and it was now that the original patents of Robert Thomson resurfaced. When Dunlop discovered his patents were invalid and that his 'invention' had already been invented many years before, he became disillusioned and in 1895 resigned from the position of director in the company which bore his name.

## The Future of the Pneumatic Tyre – The Motor Car and the Aeroplane

The use of the pneumatic tyre soon spread well beyond bicycles. Pneumatic tyres were already being used on horse-drawn traps and carriages but their main use would be on products just being invented, the motor car and the aeroplane.

The first road vehicles had relied on the steam engine for power but by the last decade of the nineteenth century a new source of power was becoming available, the petrol engine. These were smaller, lighter and more flexible than the heavy steam engines and made the possibility of the 'horseless carriage' for personal transport a reality. The first cars, such as the Gottlieb Daimler of 1886, really looked like a carriage from which the horse had just been unhitched – there was even provision to fit shafts for a horse if the car needed to be towed home. By the time of the Daimler-Benz of 1894 the design had improved, although it still relied on solid wheels and limited springing; the direct steering reflected every shock from the road and the solid wheels caused so much vibration at speeds much above twelve miles per hour that it threatened to shake the car to pieces.

Although the Germans had been the leaders in developing the internal combustion engine it was the French who had set to with enthusiasm to make cars with as many as two hundred firms building a car – or two – by the end of the century. It was the French too who pioneered road races with the first race taking place in 1887 over two kilometres (roughly a mile and a quarter) from Neuilly Bridge in Paris to the Bois de Boulogne. The race was 'won' by Georges Bouton who had built a car with the Comte de Dion, but the glory of victory was somewhat offset by the fact that he was the only entrant.

It was therefore perhaps natural that the pioneers of the pneumatic tyre for motor cars should also be French. Namely the Michelin brothers, who had already built a reputation for producing tyres for bicycles. They announced boldly that they would enter a car with pneumatic tyres in the Paris to Bordeaux race of 1895 which would take place over a distance of seven hundred and thirty-two miles. No manufacturer dared take the risk of this new-fangled idea so the brothers had to buy and enter their own car, a four horse-power Daimler. Sadly their car did not win but it was one of only nine cars to finish, having used the entire stock of twenty-four inner tubes to mend punctures along the way. The winning speed was a dashing fifteen m.p.h.

Strangely, the pneumatic tyre was not immediately accepted as it was considered that the solid tyres had a longer life and any attendant discomfort could be accommodated by better springs. In 1902 a motoring correspondent wrote 'The King's cars are on solid tyres and what is good enough for him is good enough for anybody' – surely sufficient reason to stay with solid tyres. Despite the king's example, by the end of the First World War pneumatic tyres had become accepted for motoring and were being fitted to the new 'cars for the people,' such as the Austin Seven, and the motor car became the major market for pneumatic tyres.

Another new market was for aeroplanes. The early aeroplanes were little more than box kites with engines and their builders used bicycle wheels for their landing gear as these were light and easily available. Pneumatic tyres were used from the beginning and as the power and speed of aeroplanes developed, special tyres were produced better able to absorb the stresses of landing.

The aerial wheel of Thomson, the pneumatic tyre of Dunlop, has now become a key component of our transport options.

**Further Reading**
Eric Tompkins: *The History of the Pneumatic Tyre*
Hephaestus Books: *Steam Road Vehicles*

**Online Resources**
Historic UK
http://www.historic-uk.com/HistoryUK/HistoryofScotland/Robert-William-Thomson/

## William Thomson, Lord Kelvin
1824 – 1907

SCIENTIST AND INVENTOR

*'The life and soul of science is in its practical application.'*
— *William Thomson*

William Thomson was a brilliant mathematician who used his theoretical skills to formulate two fundamental laws of physics. In harmony with the view of Joseph Black, Thomson believed that the benefits of science came not from some elegant discovery made within an ivory tower to be admired by a select few but from the application of scientific principles to the solution of everyday problems. Thomson was one of the most gifted scientists and inventors of the Victorian Age and applied his discoveries to advance the knowledge and use of electricity and magnetic forces, helping to design and lay the first telegraph cable across the Atlantic. Many of the items we use every day are based on the application of his discoveries.

### Early Years

Thomson was born in Belfast but moved to Glasgow at the age of eight when his father, James Thomson, also a brilliant mathematician, was appointed Professor of Mathematics at the University of Glasgow in 1832. Thomson had mathematics in his genes.

His mother had died when he was just six years old and he was brought up by his father, a strict Presbyterian whose idea of relaxation on a Sunday was to read to his children some chapters from the Old Testament in the morning and then by way of light relief some chapters from the New Testament in the evening.

In 1834 Thomson started classes at the university. He was ten years old. This was young even in those days, but his first years were more akin to schooling and real university work did not start until he was fourteen. Thomson studied natural philosophy, what we would now call physics, including mathematics and the study of heat, electricity and magnetism.

Thomson was a brilliant student, excelling in mathematics and always one of the first to offer an answer in class. The mathematics class met twice a day, once to attend lectures and again to work examples and answer oral questions. When Thomson was fifteen he was awarded a gold medal for his 'Essay on the Figure of the Earth,' a bold if incorrect attempt to deduce the age of the earth.

At seventeen he left for Cambridge University to study mathematics. The formal course did not keep him busy; he read, mainly books on mathematics, and wrote articles on mathematical problems for the *Cambridge Mathematical Journal*. Life was not all mathematics however, as by way of relaxation he also wrote papers on the theories of heat and of electricity. It may sound as if he had a less than wild time at university but in fairness, he was not just a single-minded theorist but also found time to be president of the university music society, playing the French horn, and to win the single sculls.

In his final examination the professors noted that the Senior Wrangler, as the university's leading mathematics student was known, and Thomson, the Second Wrangler, had provided virtually identical solutions to a mathematical problem. Was there any wrongdoing, they enquired? The Senior Wrangler explained in expiation that he had read the solution in the *Mathematical Journal*. The examining professors then asked Thomson how he had found the solution. *'I wrote the article,'* he replied!

## Professor of Natural Philosophy, Glasgow University

Within a few years of leaving university Thomson had published theoretical papers on heat and electricity, and in 1846, at the age of twenty-two he was appointed a Professor at Glasgow University, a position he held for a remarkable fifty-three years. When he took up the post he was amazed at the state of the apparatus with which he was supposed to teach the scientists of the future. It was archaic and worm-eaten, mostly more than fifty years old, with some parts even older. Thomson protested and was awarded the princely sum of one hundred pounds for its replacement, but was warned that he should not expect such generosity each year. There was no provision for experimental work and so Thomson fitted out a laboratory in an old wine cellar, sadly emptied of its earlier contents.

Thomson brought physics alive in his lectures. He stood in the lecture theatre at a table and was surrounded by instruments of various kinds. From the ceiling hung a pendulum, a twelve-pound cannon ball suspended on a thirty-foot (ten-metre) steel wire. One of his favourite experiments was to request students to calculate the velocity of a bullet by measuring the effect of its impact on the pendulum. A rifle was carefully loaded and sighted. The students waited in anticipation, those on the front bench somewhat nervously, until Thomson fired the rifle. The deviation of the pendulum from the impact was measured, and given the masses of the bullet and the pendulum the students were asked to calculate the velocity. The calculations proved less entertaining than the experiment.

Strangely, in his early years as many as two-thirds of his students went on to study theology; there was none of the later specialisation separating arts and science as it was felt that the study of philosophy, sciences and mathematics all contributed to a rounded education.

Thomson continued his research and in 1848 his studies of thermodynamics led him to propose an 'absolute' scale of temperature whose zero, known as absolute zero, is the lowest possible temperature, never in practice achievable. This scale became known as the Kelvin scale after the title of the peerage he was later granted. In 1851 he was elected a Fellow of the prestigious Royal Society of Edinburgh.

William Thomson, Lord Kelvin
with his ships' compass

## The Laws of Thermodynamics

Thomson sensibly had his students assist in the practical studies needed to support his theoretical work. Experimentation was very basic. There were no standard measurements of such things as electrical resistance, so any measurement had to be qualified by reference to a specific sample; for example a particular piece of copper wire in the experimenter's possession. It was therefore almost impossible for one experimenter to replicate another's results. Thomson would later head a committee which introduced standard measurements.

His great work during this period was to expound in two lectures to the Royal Society between 1851 and 1854 the first and second laws of thermodynamics. Later a third law was added.

The first law states that energy can neither be created nor destroyed. It can only change form. In any process the total energy within the universe remains the same. Energy is not lost; it is merely transferred into work or into other forms of energy. Work and heat are effectively interchangeable, both requiring energy, with heat a by-product of work.

The second law states that heat will flow spontaneously from a region of higher temperature to a region of lower temperature but not the other way; or in a more general form that in a thermodynamic system pressure, density and temperature tend over time towards uniformity as this equilibrium state has a higher probability than any other. A third law states that as temperature approaches absolute zero the entropy of a system, the amount of available thermal energy, approaches a constant minimum.

Thomson demonstrated the laws with examples from mechanics, heat, magnetism and electricity, and this is the work for which he is most famous.

## The Practical Application of Science

Thomson believed strongly that the principles of science should be applied to solving problems in the 'real world,' or as he wrote, 'the life and soul of science is in its practical application.' As part of his research work, Thomson had developed a number of laboratory instruments for measurements in electricity. He now used his talents on a much larger scale.

He was asked to advise on a plan to lay a copper cable under the Atlantic to enable signals to be sent by telegraph from Britain to America and back. The problem was the distance: the longer the cable, the slower the transmission of signals. Thomson calculated that the time taken to pass a signal would depend on the resistance of the copper and the total capacity of the system, and that to achieve the best results it would be necessary to use the purest copper for the cable in order to give the least resistance. The first transatlantic cable was laid in 1858 by USS *Niagara* and HMS *Agamemnon*. The intention was for the two vessels to meet in mid-Atlantic, for the cable to be spliced, or joined, and then for the ships to sail back to their respective countries, laying the cable as they went. It was a complex task requiring the manufacture of a huge length of cable made from the purest copper, its stowage onboard ship, very precise navigation and the invention of a method of laying the cable.

The transmission of signals was achieved, but sadly ceased just a month after the cable had been laid. Thomson was asked to investigate. He concluded the cable had been damaged, probably because it had been imperfectly made and because the strain through laying had been excessive. These lessons learned, a second cable was successfully laid in 1865 by Brunel's *Great Eastern*, using to advantage its dual propulsion system, a combination of screw and paddles, to give stability to the ship during the laying of the cable, the screw being used to drive the ship forward while the paddles were driven astern. During this process Thomson realised the inefficiencies of existing marine compasses and devised a new and more accurate compass which became widely used in the merchant fleet and the world's navies. He also devised an improved method for sounding depths.

One of the problems encountered with the finished cable was the time taken for the receiver to respond to the tiny current transmitted. The cable and its laying had cost half a million pounds, an immense sum for the times, and it was essential it paid its way. Speeding the time of transmission was vital if the project were to become commercially viable. Transmission of signals was based on the Morse system of dots and dashes. Thomson invented a very sensitive mirror galvanometer which reacted more quickly to these signals. For his services to the project Thomson was awarded a knighthood.

## The Age of the Earth

Since his student years Thomson had been interested in the earth and its geology and for twenty-one years served as President of the Geological Society of Glasgow. In 1868 he delivered a paper 'On Geological Time' in which he took issue with the ideas of James Hutton, in particular that there was no evidence of either a beginning or an end of the earth. In fairness, Hutton had not said there was no beginning, only that 'we find no vestige of a beginning – no prospect of an end.'

Thomson attempted to estimate the age of the earth in three different ways. He first theorised that the earth contains a store of energy which is being slowly reduced by the offsetting friction resulting from its rotation, thereby gradually reducing the rate of rotation. He then calculated how much the rotation of the earth had slowed over time, estimating it had slowed approximately twenty seconds in every one hundred years. Next he had to calculate a starting position; he knew that the earth, which is not a perfect sphere but 'bulges' around the equator, had been shaped by centrifugal forces caused by its spinning on its axis, and he calculated the centrifugal force required to give the earth its current shape, and from this deduced the speed of rotation of the earth at its formation. By comparing this with the current speed of rotation and applying his yardstick of a reduction of twenty seconds every hundred years, he was able to deduce the age of the earth. His estimate from these calculations was that the earth was approximately one hundred million years old. It was a brave attempt.

As a second method he tried to estimate the age of the solar system by calculating the loss of energy from the sun as it gave off heat. Conveniently, this also gave an age of fifty to one hundred million years.

His third method was to estimate the earth's rate of cooling from an initial molten state. Again he arrived at an estimate of one hundred million years, or more correctly given the margin of error, between twenty and two hundred million years.

Thomson therefore estimated the age of the earth at one hundred million years and held that this contradicted the theories of Hutton and other geologists that an 'immeasurably long time' must have elapsed for the changes in the surface of the earth and the development of its plant and animal life to have taken place.

It was all very clever, but sadly, also very wrong. The present best estimate of the age of the earth is between four and a half and five billion years, a lot longer than the one hundred million years Thomson had proposed. Hutton had been vindicated.

## His Last Years

Much of Thomson's later life was spent in research on electricity and magnetism. He was interested in methods of generating electricity and in the prospects for lighting by electricity; his house was the first in Britain to be lit by electricity. He was fascinated by the Niagara Falls and the possibility of using their immense power to generate electricity.

He had become a wealthy man through the formation of a company, Kelvin and White, which employed two hundred technicians manufacturing instruments for electrical and optical measurement, telegraphic equipment and aids for navigation (deriving from his experience in laying the transatlantic cable).

In 1892 he was awarded a peerage, taking the title Lord Kelvin of Largs. In 1899, at the venerable age of seventy-five, he resigned from his professorship of the Chair of Natural Philosophy, not to retire, but in order to have more time to carry out his researches. He died in 1907.

## Thomson's Legacy

Thomson is remembered for his scientific work and discoveries and in particular for the laws of thermodynamics. During his life he wrote an impressive three hundred scientific papers. He made his name by his discoveries but he made his fortune by their practical application. He showed that it is not just pure science which is important; its main benefit is in its successful application.

**Further Reading**
Andrew Gray, *Lord Kelvin: An Account of his Scientific Life and Work*

**Online Resources**
Bartelby
http://www.bartleby.com/30/1003.html
University of St Andrews
http://www-history.mcs.st-andrews.ac.uk/Biographies/Thomson.html

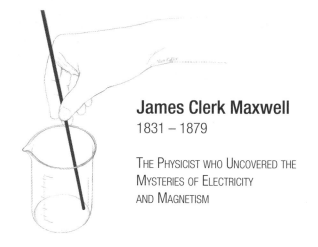

## James Clerk Maxwell
### 1831 – 1879

THE PHYSICIST WHO UNCOVERED THE
MYSTERIES OF ELECTRICITY
AND MAGNETISM

A young Scots boy from Galloway became the leading physicist of his day and one of the greatest of all time by unravelling the link between electricity and magnetism. This paved the way for many of the great inventions of the nineteenth and twentieth centuries, such as the telephone, radio, television, radar and even the mobile phone.

Scientists had been searching for years to find the secret of the relationship between electricity and magnetism, which Maxwell revealed with one flash of brilliance. Maxwell proposed the revolutionary idea that magnetic forces were similar to those of electricity so that an electric current would always be accompanied by a magnetic field and that conversely a varying magnetic field would create an electric current. He also recognised that an electric current could exist in any medium, even in empty space. Movement of a magnet or a change in electrical current would cause a ripple of energy to spread out from the source, just as a ripple spreads on a pond when a stone is thrown into it. He even calculated the speed of the waves produced, which he determined would move at the speed of light.

Light, magnetism and electricity were united in one overarching theory.

Maxwell's discovery of the laws of electromagnetism has been described as 'the most significant event of the nineteenth century.' Albert Einstein, no mean physicist himself, considered that Maxwell produced 'the most profound and the most fruitful [research] that physics had experienced since the time of Newton.' Who was James Clerk Maxwell, this largely unrecognised man of genius?

### Boyhood

James Clerk Maxwell was the son of a well-to-do Edinburgh lawyer, John, and his wife Frances. Their first child, a daughter named Elizabeth, died in infancy and they doted on their surviving son James, born in June 1831 at their home in

Edinburgh. Soon after, his father gave up the law and the family moved to Galloway. Much of Maxwell's childhood was spent there, roaming the hills of the family estate at Glenlair, which was all that remained of the wealthy lands that once belonged to the mighty Maxwell clan, most of which had been lost by John Maxwell's grandfather in unsuccessful mining investments.

The true family name was Clerk, the 'Maxwell' having been added upon marriage. The Clerk family themselves had famous forbears. An earlier John Clerk had written a textbook on naval tactics which was used successfully by Nelson at the Battle of Trafalgar – the more remarkable because John Clerk had never himself been to sea. All that now remained to John of the family's sea-faring history was a set of bagpipes which, according to tradition, his sea-captain father had used as buoyancy to keep himself afloat when his ship had sunk!

Unlike many of his country friends, Maxwell did not develop a passion for hunting and fishing, but preferred his own company as he tramped about the countryside, observing the world all around him and asking his father continual questions.

Maxwell did not attend school but was taught by his mother at home. After Frances died when he was just nine, a tutor was brought in to teach him. The tutor selected proved a strange choice for a boy as intelligent as the young Maxwell as his tutor was himself only sixteen. Not surprisingly, he did not recognise Maxwell's potential, thinking him 'stupid' and often giving him the benefit of a thrashing with his belt.

This did not do a lot for Maxwell's confidence and when he eventually went to school at Edinburgh Academy, he found it difficult to hold his own with the other boys. They would mock his country ways, his broad Galloway accent and his strange clothes; he wore a loose tweed tunic with a frilly collar and square-toed shoes with brass buckles, all very different from the elegant clothes which were worn by the sons of genteel Edinburgh folk. They nicknamed him 'Dafty.'

Later in his school years Maxwell gained in confidence, and his natural brilliance, particularly in mathematics, began to shine through. He was just fourteen when he published his first paper on mathematics, '*On the Description of Oval Curves, and Those Having a Plurality of Foci,*' a rather forbidding title for an elegant discourse on the mathematical equations which defined ellipses, or ovals.

In simple terms, Maxwell was describing the various geometric figures you can draw using a piece of string, two pins and a pencil. The simplest, with string and one pin as a focal point, is a circle. With the string tied to two pins, or focal points, the pencil will trace an ellipse, or oval shape; mathematically the shape of an ellipse can therefore be defined by the equation 'the sum of the distances of any point on the circumference of the ellipse (as traced by the pencil) from each of the two focal points is constant,' in practice, equal to the length of the string.

Maxwell discovered that by increasing the number of focal points you could derive a whole family of figures. It was a remarkable piece of work, particularly for one so young; young enough that one of his professors read the paper for him.

The only other person to have proposed a similar approach table had been the famous French mathematician and philosopher Descartes – but Maxwell's solution was much more elegant.

## University

Maxwell went on to higher education at Edinburgh University. His father intended him to become a lawyer; after all, at the time science could not be considered a career, but rather a diverting hobby, for a gentleman. Maxwell had different ideas. Mathematics and science were his interests.

At Edinburgh he published two papers on mathematics, achieving such success that he was accepted at nineteen for

Scottish Physicist James Clerk Maxwell

Trinity College, Cambridge, the college of the great seventeenth-century mathematician and physicist Sir Isaac Newton. Here Maxwell distinguished himself to such a degree that his tutor considered him 'the most extraordinary man he had met in his whole experience' – fulsome praise when it is realised that among his other students was William Thomson, later Lord Kelvin. Like Thomson, Maxwell was a great mathematician, but also like Thomson he did not win the coveted title of Senior Wrangler, or top mathematician in the university, but had to content himself with the title of Second Wrangler.

## The Nature of Colour

While at Cambridge Maxwell began his research into colour. How did people 'see' different colours? An English doctor, Thomas Young, had proposed that the eye had three different types of receptor, each sensitive to just one colour, and that the brain combined the messages it received from these three receptors to create one 'perceived' colour but how could it be proved?

Maxwell set out to create a 'colour library' by spinning discs with varying combinations of colours. He was surprised to discover that mixing the three primary colours of the artist's palette, red, yellow and blue did not give the white he expected; similarly mixing blue and yellow gave a dull pink, not green. The reason, explained by Basil Mahon in his biography of Maxwell, is the difference between 'adding' and 'subtracting' colours. When an artist mixes colours on a palette the colour seen is subtractive, that not absorbed by the coloured pigments. Maxwell through his spinning discs was adding colours and for this the three primary colours were blue, green and red. By plotting these colours as the three points of a triangle he could define any colour by varying the proportion of each primary colour, defined by its distance from each side of the triangle. White was at the centre of the triangle as the product of an equal amount of blue, green and red. This is known as Maxwell's triangle and the combination of different proportions of Maxwell's three primary colours to create 'perceived' colours forms the basis of colour television today.

Maxwell also discovered that people who were colour blind and could not distinguish between green and blue lacked red-sensitive receptors.

### Electricity and Magnetism

At the same time Maxwell produced the first of his papers on magnetism and electricity; papers which would give him enduring fame. The discovery of magnetism is attributed to the Greek philosopher, Thales, who lived in the sixth century B.C. and is credited with first recording the magnetic properties of lodestone, a naturally magnetised form of the mineral magnetite. Lodestone is found in the Mediterranean islands and the name magnetite may be derived from the ancient Greek city of Magnesia. The magnetic properties of lodestone were also known to the Chinese who used lodestone in the twelfth century to provide the magnets used for early navigation, an expertise which only reached Europe three centuries later when it led to the great explosion in European exploration; the word 'lodestone' is Middle English for 'leading stone.'

In the early seventeenth century an Englishman, William Gilbert, had written a scientific treatise on magnetism, *De Magnete*, and proposed the idea that the Earth itself was one huge magnet with a north and south pole. He made magnets from lodestone and realised that they aligned themselves along a north-south axis and that the 'north' pole of one magnet would attract the south pole of another magnet but repel the north pole.

The next breakthrough came from another English scientist, Michael Faraday, who recognised the relationship between magnetism and electricity by demonstrating that when a copper wire was exposed to a change in magnetic field an electric current would be induced.

As a result of the experimental work of Faraday and others, the four main features of electricity and magnetism had been demonstrated but there was no underlying theory explaining these effects. These features are:

> • electric charges attract or repel each other with a force which is inversely proportional to the square of the distance they are apart; like charges repel while unlike charges attract.

- the poles, or ends, of a magnet also attract or repel but always come paired, with one end of the magnet the 'north' pole and the other the 'south' pole. A 'north' pole attracts a 'south' pole but repels another 'north.'

- passing an electric current through a wire creates a circular magnetic field around the wire. The direction of the magnetic field is dependent on the direction of the current.
- if a magnet is passed through a loop of wire it induces an electric current.

The accepted wisdom of the time was that the effects of magnetism derived from 'points' of force which were located at each end of the magnet. Faraday believed differently; he thought there were lines of force which extended from the magnets throughout space, much as Newton had believed of gravity. Faraday could demonstrate this using iron filings which if placed on a piece of paper around a magnet would produce beautiful curved lines reflecting the lines of force, tightly packed near the pole where the force is strongest and more spread out and away from the poles.

Maxwell was entranced by Faraday's work but wanted to uncover the underlying science by expressing these experimental discoveries through mathematical equations. To do this he considered the lines of flow of the force as a liquid; the strength of the magnetic field would be represented by the density of the liquid with a higher density corresponding to a stronger magnetic field while the direction of the magnetic flow corresponded to the direction of flow of the liquid. It is the difference in pressure which causes a liquid to flow and Maxwell reasoned that the flow of electric current must similarly be caused by a difference in the electric potential or the voltage.

Using the analogy of the flow of a liquid, Maxwell could now express Faraday's 'lines of force' by mathematically defined magnetic fields and he published his findings in a paper he entitled *On Faraday's Lines of Force*, graciously acknowledging Faraday's pioneering experimental work.

Maxwell would later extend his theory to explain electromagnetism, the current induced in a loop of wire by passing a magnet through it.

### Maxwell Broadens his Interests

Trinity offered Maxwell a fellowship but he turned it down in order to return to Scotland. Instead he accepted the position of Professor of Natural Philosophy at Marischal College, Aberdeen. Life as a professor in Scotland was very different from the elegant and leisurely life of a Cambridge don; true, there were daily lectures and weekly tests, but there was the compensation of a long summer break from May to October during which he could return to the family estate in Glenlair which he had owned since the death of his father in 1856.

During the summers Maxwell carried out research and one of his projects was to investigate the rings around Saturn. Were these solid, liquid or composed of a vast number of small particles? This was the challenge which had been set by St John's College, Cambridge, which had offered the Adams prize to the first person who could correctly answer the question. Through lengthy and convoluted mathematical calculations Maxwell proved that the rings were not solid but made up of millions of particles and thereby won the prize. The challenge had proved so complex that no one else could provide an answer and it would not be until the 1980s, a century later, when the Voyager satellites flew past Saturn, that it was confirmed that Maxwell was indeed right and that Saturn's rings had exactly the structure which he had predicted mathematically all those years before.

Maxwell was nothing if not eclectic in his interests. The Swiss physicist Daniel Bernoulli, famous for the Bernoulli effect which explains how aeroplanes fly, had proposed that gases consist of an immense number of molecules moving in all directions and that it is their impact on a surface which gives the impression of pressure and the energy of their motion which gives the sensation of heat. But there was a problem. Why, if all these molecules are moving at a speed of several hundred metres per second, does it take so long for a smell to be diffused throughout a room, for example when a bottle of perfume is opened? Should it not be instantaneous?

Maxwell put his powerful mathematical brain to work on the problem. He realised it must be because each molecule can only travel an infinitely small distance in any one direction before it hits another molecule and changes direction. But how could he express this mathematically? He developed a new concept, a statistical law, to explain the motion of molecules, defining their motion with reference to three axes but confining his calculations not to any one individual molecule but instead to the proportion of molecules which have velocities within any given range. This breakthrough is called 'Maxwell's distribution of molecular velocities.' The resultant graph of velocities is the typical 'bell' curve given by what statisticians call a 'normal distribution.' The greater the temperature, the greater the average speed of the molecules and the flatter the 'bell.' This use of statistical methods was a breakthrough in physics.

In between this pioneering work Maxwell also found time to court and marry Katherine Dewar, the daughter of the principal of Marischal College. This did not, however, do him any good when in 1860 the College merged with King's College to form Aberdeen University - prior to the merger Aberdeen had housed two of Scotland's five universities - when Maxwell was surprisingly not chosen for the position of professor in the new combined university and abruptly left without a job.

## Maxwell's Theories of Electromagnetism

But not for long. Maxwell was soon snapped up by King's College, London, where he was appointed Professor of Natural Philosophy. During his five years at King's Maxwell had his most fruitful period of research, as it was here that he finally developed the formulae linking electricity and magnetism, expressing his ideas in four elegant equations now known as Maxwell's equations.

But first he wanted to demonstrate his work on colour in a lecture to the Royal Society. By now he was using a 'colour box' instead of the rather cumbersome rotating discs, but even this was unsuitable for a large audience. Then he decided to create a 'colour' photograph which he could project onto a screen. The technique of projecting photographs in black and white was well known but Maxwell wanted to create colour. To do this he took three identical photographs of a piece of tartan ribbon, using first a red filter, then green and then blue. He then projected the three photographs onto a screen using the same three filters. There on the screen was a picture of the tartan ribbon in all its colours. Maxwell had created the first colour photographic image.

In 1865 he decided he had had enough of London and resigned his professorship to return to Glenlair. He wanted time to look after and enjoy the estate but also to complete his masterpiece, *A Treatise on Electricity and Magnetism*, which was published in 1873.

This work comprised a thousand pages of closely reasoned scientific theories encompassing the whole field of electricity and magnetism. In this book Maxwell recognised the link between magnetism and electricity and expressed the experimental findings of Faraday and others in a series of elegant mathematical equations which encapsulated the fundamental laws of electromagnetism, that an electric current would always induce a magnetic field and that conversely a varying magnetic field would always induce an electric current. He took his thinking even further forward, predicting the existence of electromagnetic waves which could be of varying length, a prediction which led in time to the discovery of radio waves, radar and X-rays. He also predicted that the emission of electromagnetic waves would cause sunlight to exert a radiation pressure on the earth, a fact that was not experimentally proven until twenty years after his death.

This book is recognised as one of the greatest scientific works in the history of physics, second only to the *Principia* of the great Isaac Newton, still in print today.

## Cavendish Professor at the University of Cambridge

In 1871 Maxwell was approached by Cambridge University which had been given a great sum of money to build a new scientific laboratory and wanted an eminent professor to set up and head the new facility. This was to be called the Cavendish Laboratory in memory of the great scientist Sir Henry Cavendish, the great uncle of the Duke of Devonshire, who was providing the funds. Maxwell's first task was to design the building. He then set about encouraging and inspiring his students with their research. He proved an inspirational leader.

Cavendish had been a strange, unlovable man who lived as a recluse and addressed his staff only through written notes, but he had been a great, if largely unrecognised, scientist. Maxwell undertook the task of editing and publishing his papers and discovered to his amazement that Cavendish had discovered many of the fundamental electrical laws many years before researchers such as Ohm and Coulomb who had received the credit for the discoveries. Cavendish had just not bothered to publish! Maxwell's account of the discoveries of Cavendish was published in 1879, just before his own death. Sadly it occupied the last years of Maxwell's life and therefore denied him any further major creative discoveries of his own.

Maxwell suffered from stomach pains and in 1879 was diagnosed with stomach cancer, the same disease that had killed his mother. His health worsened rapidly and he died in Cambridge in November 1879. He was buried beside his mother and father in a churchyard near his beloved Glenlair. He was only forty-eight years old.

## Maxwell's Legacy

Undoubtedly his finest legacy is his contribution to the understanding of physics and in particular of electricity and magnetism. His work has provided the basis for many of the inventions, such as radio, television and the telephone, which today we take for granted as a part of daily life.

Maxwell's time as head of the Cavendish set a standard which led in later years to the Laboratory being at the centre of many outstanding developments in physics, including the discovery of the electron and the unravelling of DNA, the code that defines life itself.

Maxwell was not just a fine scientist but was also in every sense a gentleman. In his last months his doctor in Glenlair wrote, 'He is one of the best men I have ever met, and a greater merit than his scientific achievements is his being ... a most perfect example of a Christian Gentleman;' a well suited epitaph.

**Further Reading**
Basil Mahon, *The Man who Changed Everything*

**Online Resources**
James Clerk Maxwell Foundation
http://www.clerkmaxwellfoundation.org/html/who_was_maxwell_.html

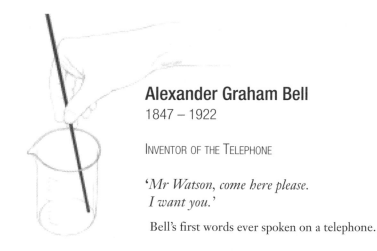

## Alexander Graham Bell
### 1847 – 1922

<small>INVENTOR OF THE TELEPHONE</small>

*'Mr Watson, come here please.*
*I want you.'*

Bell's first words ever spoken on a telephone.

Alexander Graham Bell fell in love with a girl who was deaf. While trying to invent a machine to help the deaf to hear, he suddenly realised that if he could make 'a current of electricity vary in intensity precisely as the air varies in density during the production of sound,' he would be able to transmit speech by telegraph.

He did, and the telephone was invented.

Bell himself was proudest not of his invention of the telephone but of his work with the deaf. In the words of Helen Keller, he 'taught the deaf to speak.'

### Childhood in Scotland

Bell was born in Edinburgh in 1847 but left Scotland when a young man to live in the United States of America. His father, Alexander Melville Bell, taught elocution, the art of speaking clearly and properly, in Edinburgh. He was well respected, teaching both privately and as a lecturer at Edinburgh University. He too had an inventive mind. In his developmental work he was confronted with the problem of how to teach people to speak when they were themselves deaf. How could you let them 'hear' the words being spoken? To this end he invented a system of 'visible speech' which used symbols to represent the different

<small>Corbis Images</small>

words and letters. He knew that speech was created by using the lips, tongue, mouth and throat to produce different sounds. The problem was to codify these in one overall system of speech.

The family was intimately interested in the problems of deafness; Bell's mother Eliza herself was deaf, although she managed to overcome her infirmity, even becoming a successful pianist. She could hear herself play by reversing her ear tube, holding the wide mouth piece next to the strings on the soundboard of the piano and placing the narrow end in her ear. The sound made by the piano strings was funnelled through the ear tube. People who wished to speak to her would similarly speak into the mouthpiece of the ear tube.

Bell was very close to his mother. She taught him at home, not only to read and write but also to play the piano. In order for them to communicate she taught him a special finger 'alphabet,' where the letters were 'spelt out' by different positions of the speaker's hand on the open palm of the listener's.

When he was eleven Bell started at the Royal High School, marking the occasion by adding his middle name to become Alexander Graham Bell. He did not do especially well at school and his father felt he needed a 'push start.' Accordingly, when he was fifteen he was sent to live with his grandfather, who was a Professor of Elocution at the University of London.

## Becoming a Teacher

His grandfather quickly took the young Bell in hand. He first had a tailor dress him 'properly' with suit and tie, top hat, gloves and cane. Bell was then given books to read to broaden his mind and was taught elocution: how precisely to pronounce his words. Bell would also sit with his grandfather while he taught his students and helped them with their speech problems.

Elocution was certainly in his blood and it is not surprising that he too decided to become a teacher of speech and music. He found a post in Elgin.

Bell's father had by now perfected his system of 'visible speech', which he published in 1867. The system used a total of thirty-four symbols with different parts of each explaining the shape of the tongue, lips, throat and mouth needed to create a particular sound; by using the system any word or sound could be replicated – even words in a foreign language. Bell worked with his father to help to publicise the system. During demonstrations Bell would leave the room and his father would write a word or sound on a blackboard in visible speech; when Bell re-entered he would read the symbols and replicate the sound as if by magic; once to his own surprise he found himself replicating the sound made when sawing wood.

In 1865 Bell's grandfather died and his father moved to London to take over his work, with Bell in tow. While in London however Bell was threatened by tuberculosis, or TB, a disease caused by bacteria infecting the lungs. Before the days of antibiotics it was usually fatal; it had already killed his two brothers.

The family was advised to move to Canada to get Bell away from the cold, damp climate of Britain. They arrived by ship in 1870 and the healthy air of Canada certainly suited the young Bell, whose health immediately began to improve. He now needed to find a job.

## Boston

Alexander Graham Bell was twenty-five when he was appointed Professor of Vocal Physiology at Boston University, where he was to spread the use of 'visible speech' in the teaching of the deaf. One of his students was a young deaf girl, Mabel Hubbard; this was the girl he was later to marry.

In addition to his teaching Bell continued to experiment with the nature of sound, dissecting a human ear to see how it worked. He invented a machine called a 'phonautograph' by which he could trace the patterns made by sounds, recording onto coated glass plates the movements of a needle which traced the vibrations of a membrane caused by speaking into a mouthpiece. Bell reasoned that if the sound made by talking could move a needle there must be other things it could power.

When Bell was at Mabel Hubbard's house he entertained her family by playing the piano. He showed how a piano could 'sing' in response to a sound. *'What is the use of this?'* asked Mabel's father. Bell explained that by sending messages with a different pitch, as many as ten telegraph messages could be sent at the same time over one telegraph wire, massively reducing the cost. Bell called his idea an 'harmonic' telegraph and Gardiner Hubbard, Mabel's father, agreed to provide the funds to develop the idea. The Bell Patent Association was formed.

But Bell was not convinced that the telegraph was the answer. A person sending a message by telegraph could only use Morse code. Bell did not want to transmit just dots and dashes; he wanted to transmit real speech.

## The Invention of the Telephone

He remembered the tracings of speech he had made using his phonautograph and realised that these could never be transmitted by the harsh on/off signals of the telegraph. He had to be able to transmit the smooth patterns of speech. He realised that electricity was the way, but how could he reflect in the flow of current the small changes that speech created in the density of air? Then he had his moment of inspiration: he would mimic the way the ear works, whereby changes in density are reflected by movements in the ear drum, which in turn vibrate the small delicate bones within the ear. A magnet could produce exactly the right kind of undulating current, which he could create by mounting the magnet on a membrane set to vibrate with changes in air density, just as in the human ear. That was the breakthrough in concept but it was not so easy to create in practice.

Thomas Watson was the man required; he specialised in helping inventors with their developments. Bell paid him a visit, and subsequently during the winter of 1874 Bell and Watson worked away in Watson's workshop and by early 1875 they felt they had advanced enough to file a patent on the harmonic telegraph.

Bell went to Washington and there he met the seventy-seven-year-old physicist Joseph Henry, who was the head of the famous Smithsonian Institute. Bell showed him his idea for the harmonic telegraph, but Henry was not impressed. Rather nervously Bell explained to the eminent scientist his idea for the telephone and admitted he was having difficulties completing the development because he had no knowledge of electricity. The scientist's response was immediate. '*Get it!*' he said. Bell later stated that if it had not been for the support expressed by Henry he probably would not have persevered with his work on the telephone.

By now Bell had expressed his love for Mabel and life began to get complicated. Bell wanted to continue with his work teaching the deaf but Mabel's father believed that if he did then none of his inventions would ever be finished and others would beat him to success. Gardner believed it was the telegraph that would make their fortunes – after all, who would want to talk on an instrument like a telephone? He told Bell brutally, 'either give up your teaching or give up Mabel and inventing!' Fortunately, Mabel was strong enough to resist her father and on her eighteenth birthday in November 1875 she accepted Bell's proposal of marriage.

Now Bell had a target. If he was to marry he needed money and he had to finish his invention. On 14 February 1876 he filed an application for a patent for a 'magneto-electric' telephone. He was only just in time. Within hours his great rival Elisha Gray filed his own patent, but he was too late. Bell had got there first.

Now he had to make his invention work. His idea was nothing like the telephone we know today. The caller spoke into a cone-shaped mouthpiece which vibrated a membrane placed across the bottom of the cone, which itself was placed in a tray of a weak acid solution. A needle on the bottom of the membrane moved up and down in the acid, changing the current as it moved. The current then travelled along a wire to the receiver, where a reed vibrated, repeating the sounds made by the caller. Using this crude device on 9 March 1876, Bell spoke the first words ever to be transmitted by telephone: his request to his assistant, who was in the basement, to join him: 'Mr Watson, come here please. I want you.'

## The Fight for Acceptance

The President of the United States summed up the general reaction: 'That's an amazing invention, but who would ever want to use one of them?'

Bell publicised his ideas as his father had done, by giving public demonstrations of their use. Watson, although in a building some miles away, was heard to answer questions asked him by Bell in front of an invited audience. Bell even demonstrated his telephone in front of Queen Victoria, who found it 'most extraordinary.' A telephone was installed between Buckingham Palace and Osborne House, the Queen's residence on the Isle of Wight. Gradually, the telephone began to be seen not just as a clever toy but as a useful instrument. Now, Bell had to struggle to protect his invention, fighting many expensive legal battles as others tried to copy his ideas. In fact, he fought more than 600 cases to protect his patents. The most famous of these was against Western Union, a giant telegraph company, which by trying to launch its own competing telephone justified Bell's belief that the future lay with his invention, not with the telegraph.


## Once an Inventor…

The Bell Company grew hugely in size to become the Bell Telephone Company of America, making Bell a very rich man. Bell himself did not have much to do with the actual running of the company; that was 'business.' He carried on inventing.

When President Garfield was assassinated, Bell used the principle of his telephone to form a crude metal detector and tried to locate the assassin's bullet in the dying president's body. Unfortunately he failed, perhaps because his 'metal detector' was confused by the metal of the hospital bed.

He also invented a 'graphophone' to record voices and music; a needle was connected to a diaphragm and as it moved made an impression on a wax cylinder, thus improving on Thomas Edison's earlier invention of the 'phonograph', which had used metal foil as the recording medium.

Bell was excited by the prospect of flight and experimented with specially constructed kites, running with them across the fields near his home as he tried to find the best design. This proved to be a tetrahedron, a four-sided structure all of whose sides are made of equal triangles. With a kite made out of thirteen hundred tetrahedral units he was able to lift a man into the air. Could his idea be made into a flying machine, powered by an engine and carrying a man with the ability to steer the contraption?

This time it was Bell who was beaten to the invention. On 17 December 1903 Wilbur and Orville Wright achieved the first powered flight of an aeroplane, but Bell continued working on his ideas and eventually in 1908 produced an aeroplane which flew, carrying four people.

Bell and his wife took a holiday to Italy and while there met Enrico Forlanini, who had invented a hydrofoil. A hydrofoil is a boat built with 'wings' underwater which as it moves forward lifts it clear of the water, reducing resistance and enabling it to reach great speeds. Hydrofoils also give a smooth ride as they ride above the waves and the foils smooth out their effects. Bell was amazed as they sped across the surface of Lake Maggiore. This was the future.

He decided he would build his own hydrofoil. As his ideas developed the hydrofoils became bigger and in 1919 he built a huge hydrofoil boat more than sixty feet (twenty metres) long and shaped like a torpedo. This was driven across the water by two aircraft propellers powered by two huge engines and set a speed record of just over seventy miles an hour; a record which lasted for more than ten years. But sadly Bell never got to experience personally the exhilaration of his boat's speed himself as his health was deteriorating.

Bell believed everyone should have the benefit of access to knowledge about their world. He saved *Science* magazine when it got into financial difficulties and founded *The National Geographic Magazine*.

## Work with the Deaf

Bell never forgot his true passion, helping the deaf to speak. His mother as well as his wife was deaf, and many of his deaf students had become close friends. 'Who can picture the isolation of their lives,' he asked, 'being in the midst of a crowd of happy beings with whom [they] can not communicate and who can not communicate with [them]?' He was conscious of the loneliness of the deaf, isolated in their world of silence.

He believed that deaf children should be taught in the wider community, not shut away in special schools, and supported this belief by founding a school where deaf children were taught the special skills they needed but spent their play and social time with children who could hear. Bell's most famous patient was Helen Keller.

## Helen Keller

*The only thing worse than being blind is having sight, but no vision.' –H.K.*

Born in Alabama in 1880, Keller was a normal, cheerful little girl until at about eighteen months old, she contracted a severe illness diagnosed at the time by her doctor as 'an acute congestion of the stomach and the brain,' leaving the little girl totally blind and deaf, and isolated from the world around her.

Her mother, Kate Keller, encouraged by Doctor Marigold — a Charles Dickens short story where he details a deaf and blind woman who'd been taught to communicate with the world beyond her 'prison' — believed that her daughter, too, could learn to communicate. Mrs Keller approached Dr Chisholm, an ear, nose and throat specialist for advice. He immediately recommended she should contact Alexander Graham Bell.

When Bell met Keller she was six years old, and angry with a world with which she could not communicate. He took the troubled girl on his knee and instantly calmed her with his gentleness. Bell recognised a courage and intelligence of the little girl, and was confident he could help his small patient, and reassured her distraught parents he thought she could be taught to communicate, if he could only find the right teacher. He chose Anne Sullivan, only twenty years old and herself visually impaired, who would end up working with Keller for nearly fifty years.

In 1887 Sullivan moved into the Keller house, and immediately began patiently teaching Helen to 'talk' by spelling words through her fingers into Keller's hand. She began by spelling the word d-o-l-l, while pressing into Keller's other hand the doll which she had brought her as a present.

It was exhausting work. Helen Keller could not grasp the idea that each object had a specific name which her teacher was spelling out with her fingers. She would become angry and frustrated, once even breaking the doll. Then one day, the miracle happened. W-A-T-E-R! She suddenly realised the association between the letters Sullivan was spelling out in her one

Helen Keller with
Annie Sullivan

hand, and a cool liquid flowing over the other. Excited, Keller now wanted to know the names of all the objects and sensations she could possibly feel, almost overwhelming her young teacher.

The next year Keller and Sullivan joined an Institute for the Blind where Keller learned to read using the special raised letters of the Braille alphabet, designed especially to enable blind people to read by using the sense of touch. When Keller was eight she'd progressed enough to be able to write a letter to her mentor; 'Dear Mr. Bell, I am glad to write you a letter…. I can read stories in my book.'

Six years later they moved to a School for the Deaf where Keller eventually learned to speak by placing her fingers on the lip and mouths of speakers and copying them, much as in the early phonic experiments of Bell and his father.

In 1893 Bell took Keller and Sullivan to visit Niagara Falls, NY and Keller was able to sense the massive power of the water, writing to her mother that she could hardly believe that 'it was water that I felt rushing and plunging with impetuous fury at my feet.' At this time she wrote a poem, 'Autumn,' which she dedicated 'For Dr Bell. With dearest Love.'

Helen Keller, graduate

Keller eventually gained admission to Radcliff college from where she graduated in 1904 with honours, the first deaf and blind person to gain an academic degree. Keller learned how to 'hear' people by pressing her finger tips gently against their lips and progressed to become a world famous author and speaker, lecturing on disabilities but also becoming much more, a passionate suffragette, pacifist and socialist. Keller wrote in her autobiography, *Helen Keller – Rebel Lives*, words which resonate today:

'The few own the many because they possess the means of livelihood of all… The country is governed for the richest, for the corporations, the bankers, the land speculators, and for the exploiters of labor [sic]… The majority of mankind is ground down by industrial oppression in order that the small remnant may live at ease.'

Keller was a member of the Socialist Party and helped in the formation of the American Civil Liberties Union. Her teacher Annie Sullivan introduced Keller to Christianity and Keller is reported to have said, memorably, 'I always knew He was there but I didn't know His name.'

Keller died in 1968, her last years blighted by a succession of strokes. She had written 'Death is no more than passing from one room into another. But there's a difference for me, you know. Because in that other room I shall be able to see.'

Alexander Bell and Helen Keller had become lifelong friends and she never forgot her mentor, dedicating the book she wrote about her life to 'Alexander Graham Bell. Who has taught the deaf to speak and enabled the listening ear to hear.' Her life was featured in a film 'The Miracle Worker.'

## Inventor: Teacher

Bell died in August 1922, aged seventy-five. His simple coffin bore the words 'INVENTOR: TEACHER' and at the time of his burial, all the telephones in Canada and the United States were silent for a minute as a mark of respect.

Alexander Graham Bell with his
friend, Helen Keller.

**Further Reading**
Mary Kay Carson, *Alexander Graham Bell: Giving Voice to the World*

**Online Resources**
Alexander Graham Bell Organization
http://www.alexandergrahambell.org/

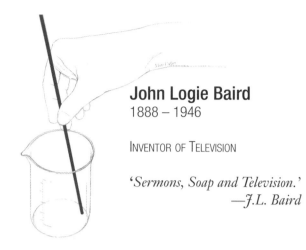

## John Logie Baird
1888 – 1946

INVENTOR OF TELEVISION

'*Sermons, Soap and Television.*'
—*J.L. Baird*

John Logie Baird was a 'lad of pairts', interested in any money-making scheme he could devise from artificial diamonds to soap. He became obsessed with the challenge of transmitting pictures by wireless and invented the first television, although he achieved this by mechanical means rather than the electronics on which modern televisions are based.

### Childhood in Helensburgh

Baird was born at 'the Lodge' in Helensburgh in August 1888. His father was a minister but had been able to buy a substantial house from the dowry he received through a shrewd marriage to the niece of a wealthy Glasgow shipbuilder. The house had originally been built for a lady whose ambition had been to have the largest dining room in Helensburgh; having built her house and achieved this ambition, she died. History does not record whether she had used her dining room. Baird was a sickly child but long absences from school meant that he read widely and from his early youth he was inventive. In those days houses in Scotland were lit by gas and the telephone was virtually unknown, but by the time he was thirteen Baird had installed electric lighting in the family home using a second-hand engine to drive a dynamo to generate the electricity and using accumulators made out of lead plates packed into jam jars and surrounded by sulphuric acid to store the electricity produced. It worked for as long as Baird gave it his attention. One night when he was distracted, the lights went out and in the darkness his father fell down the unlit stairs. Newfangled electric lighting was promptly banned and gas lighting was brought back in!

Baird also built a private telephone exchange so that he could telephone his friends. He installed the exchange in a wooden box in his bedroom with overhead wires running to the houses of his friends. One stormy night a cabbie who was sitting high on the box of his carriage failed to see the wires in the darkness and was pulled from his seat and thrown into the gutter. The cabbie knocked angrily at the doors of the offices of the Telephone Company to complain; the wires were traced to Baird's house and another venture was abruptly terminated.

After leaving school Baird enrolled in the Royal Technology College in Glasgow where he studied electrical engineering and at twenty-five he moved on to Glasgow University. Determined to make his fortune, he spent all his spare time on various harebrained money-making ideas.

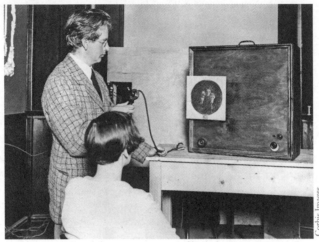

John Logie Baird demonstrates one of his television inventions.

### 'Lad of pairts'

When the First World War began in 1914, Baird was declared unfit for military duty and went instead to work at a power station. There he decided to make diamonds, perhaps inspired by a story by H.G. Wells. Diamonds are made naturally from carbon which has been exposed to immense pressure and temperature. Baird tried to replicate this by passing the current from the power station through wires to a carbon rod embedded in concrete. At midnight he threw the switch. A huge electrical current passed through the rod, there was an immense bang, a cloud of steam, all the belts came off the generators and the mains supply crashed. Baird just managed to restore order before the chief engineer arrived, but his days at the power station were numbered – and there were no diamonds.

His next idea was inspired by a personal problem; he always had cold feet. He bought pairs of socks, sprinkled them with absorbent borax powder and marketed them as 'The Baird Undersock' with the slogan 'medicated, soft and absorbent, worn under the sock they keep your feet warm in winter and cool in summer.' His marketing ideas were ahead of his time. He employed women wearing sandwich boards to advertise his product and they were often photographed for the local papers, giving him free advertising. He asked his friends to call at the shops which stocked his product to enquire after the 'Baird Undersock' to stimulate awareness and create an apparent demand. Unfortunately an illness destroyed his flourishing business, but he managed to make more money in twelve months than in twelve years at the power station. Nonetheless, it was time to move on.

## The West Indies

Baird suffered from recurring chest infections and thought the West Indies would be better for his health – and a place where he could make his fortune.

He came up with yet another scheme to make money, this time by producing jams and chutneys. The island teemed with tropical fruits: oranges, mangoes and guavas. The challenge was to package the jams in such a way that they could be shipped back to England without going mouldy. Baird studied endlessly all the cookery books he could find until his plans were ready. He set up his jam factory in a brushwood hut, placed all the chopped-up fruit in a huge copper wash tub and lit a fire beneath. The pot was filled with sugar and oranges and was soon bubbling away. Sweet-scented clouds rose into the air. The jam was an instant success, but rather sooner than Baird would have wished. A plague of insects were attracted by the sweet smells; perishing in the steam, they all fell into the jam. It was ruined. Baird salvaged what he could and returned to England, sadder and wiser but no richer.

## Back to England

How was he to make his fortune? Baird saw an advertisement offering a bulk supply of cheap soap and decided this was his opportunity to 'clean up.' He ordered a ton of 'twin-tablet double-wrapped pale yellow soap' and started selling it as 'Baird's Speedy Cleaner.' Business boomed. The secret was the price; Baird had scoured Europe to find the cheapest supply of soap.

It was not only cheap but also rather harsh and Baird was once confronted by an angry mother who displayed her baby's raw bottom to show its effect. In vain Baird protested his soap was intended for cleaning floors, not babies!

This venture was brought to a sudden end by a new competitor, George Hutchinson, who introduced the even cheaper 'Hutchinson's Rapid Washer.' Baird became seriously ill and eventually had to sell his shares and resigned from his company. It is not recorded whether Hutchinson's Rapid Washer was any kinder to babies' bottoms.

All his life Baird had suffered from chest infections. Thin and wasted after his illness he decided sea air would provide a cure and moved to Hastings on the south coast of England.

## The First Television

The idea of transmitting pictures by wireless had been around for some time and Baird became obsessed. Baird wrote in his memoirs that the idea came to him while he was walking on the cliffs near Hastings. Baird chose a mechanical system, probably because he had few resources and had to beg or borrow the bits he needed for his apparatus, but also perhaps because he was not an electronic engineer and did not fully understand electronics. He would also have argued that a mechanical system was simpler and that a result could be achieved more quickly, but in the event it turned out to be a short-sighted decision. His first apparatus was made from cardboard, tin, a powerful electric lamp and lenses from cycle lamps. The discs were cut out using scissors and put together using glue and sealing wax. He added a light-sensitive selenium cell, batteries, neon lamps and an electric motor and using this basic apparatus he achieved in 1923 the first transmission of a picture by wireless; a picture of a cardboard cross. Television was born.

The system which Baird had developed worked as follows. The object to be televised was lit by a strong floodlight. The image was then scanned through a spinning cardboard disc, which had a spiral pattern of twenty small holes one-thirty-second of an inch in diameter. This transmitting disc spun at two hundred revolutions a minute. Behind this was a further disc cut with slots which rotated ten times as fast in the opposite direction. The picture was thereby 'chopped' into small pulses which could be captured by the selenium light-sensitive cell, producing a varying electrical current.

The picture was displayed by amplifying the current and then passing it to a copper brush mounted on an arm rotating at the same speed as the transmitting disc. As it rotated the brush made electrical contact with twenty tiny electrical bulbs arranged in a 'picture frame', each of which corresponded with one of the holes in the transmitting disc. As the brush made contact the bulb lit up in sympathy with the part of the image which had been scanned by the corresponding hole in the transmitting disc.

By October 1925 Baird had developed his system to the extent that he could show pictures of Stooky Bill, the head of a ventriloquist's dummy, not only clearly but with tone. Excitedly he grabbed his office boy, William Taynton, and placed him in front of the apparatus. William became the first person in the world to be televised, but his only response to this moment of fame was to complain about the heat from the floodlight.

## The Public Launch of Television

In January 1926 Baird demonstrated his system to a number of scientists of the Royal Institution. By now he had moved on from the idea of flood lighting the object to be scanned, uncomfortably hot for the subject, and replaced it with a 'flying spot' using lenses set in the transmitting disc to focus the light. The picture was chopped into thirty lines; crude compared with the six hundred and twenty-five lines of the modern TV. In 1928 Baird transmitted pictures with this primitive apparatus across the Atlantic and even to a ship in the mid-Atlantic ocean. Baird took the concept much further; by scanning infrared rays instead of light he was able to produce a picture from darkness, a system he called 'noctavision,' and by using red, green and blue filters in the discs he could reproduce colour.

Baird was now at the peak of his fame. In 1930 he showed television on a 'big screen,' five feet wide and two feet high (one and a half metres by just over half a metre) which consisted of over two thousand electric bulbs behind a sheet of ground glass. In 1932 to great popular acclaim, televised the Derby.

## The Beginning of the End

This was to be the height of his success. Perhaps he had spent too much of his energy on eye-catching ideas and not enough on improving the basic system, but he was one man fighting the resources of the big corporations.

In 1929 the BBC had started broadcasting trial television using the Baird system, but it was not very successful. All that could be filmed at any one time was the head and shoulders of an actor who could not move out of shot. The picture was displayed on a tiny two by two-and-half inch screen (five by six centimetres) and had an orange hue caused by the neon light. If the speed of the discs got out of kilter the picture would move rapidly up and down. With all these difficulties the transmission of a play was to say the least challenging.

By 1932 other systems using electronic rather than mechanical means had been developed, particularly by Marconi, who used a cathode ray scanning system which gave much greater clarity. In a head-to-head trial with Baird the BBC chose the Marconi system. That marked the end of the Baird system. Technology had triumphed and although Baird did experiment with cathode ray tubes during the war years it was too late. Baird died in 1946.

## Baird's Legacy

Baird was the first person to demonstrate the transmission of pictures by wireless, but his mechanical system could not compete with the flexibility of electronics; television today has little connection with Baird's pioneering work, but his determination earns him his unique place in history.

**Further Reading**
Antony Kamm and Malcolm Baird, *John Logie Baird*

**Online Resources**
The Museum of Broadcast Communications
http://www.museum.tv/eotvsection.php?entrycode=bairdjohnl

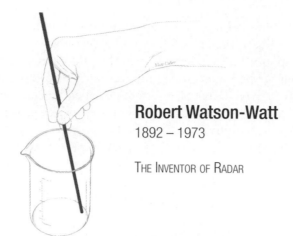

## Robert Watson-Watt
1892 – 1973

THE INVENTOR OF RADAR

So it wasn't eating carrots! The invention of radar meant that Royal Air Force pilots flying during the Battle of Britain in the Second World War could 'see' German aircraft as easily at night as during the day.

This was a critical advantage which helped the Royal Air Force to win the Battle of Britain and by maintaining control of the skies over Britain to deter Hitler from his planned invasion. The invention of radar may not have won the war, but it almost certainly was a key factor in avoiding defeat after the withdrawal of British forces from Dunkirk. Robert Watson-Watt was the man who invented radar and helped develop a chain of radar stations along the south and east coasts of Britain in the 1930s, providing that key defensive advantage.

### Early Years

Robert Alexander Watson-Watt was born in Brechin in Angus in 1892. His father was a skilled cabinet maker and claimed descent from the famous engineer James Watt. Robert would later add the hyphen to emphasise his pride in his descent from two distinguished Scots families, the Watsons and the Watts. Young Watson-Watt had a solitary childhood; one of his favourite games was to lay out his father's screws and nails as soldiers in armies and 'march' them across the bench. His father encouraged him to use his hands and with a typical Scots' belief in self-improvement to apply himself to reading, writing and the use of numbers.

Watson-Watt admitted later that his mother spoilt him – what caring mother does not spoil her son? When he was four he had what he described sixty years later in his autobiography as the most desolating moment of his life. At the wedding of his uncle he was promised the sugar swan with outstretched wings which stood on top of the wedding cake; he carefully placed it on the window-sill for safekeeping, but later, when he was being undressed for bed, the swan had gone. Not too bad a life if that was the worst he could remember...

Watson-Watt went to school in Brechin, gaining a scholarship to Brechin High School. He excelled at mathematics and science, which he thought of not as learning but as fun; he tolerated history and geography but could not see the point of learning Latin – what use was Latin to a scientist? At the age of sixteen he complained to his headmaster, saying respectfully, *'I don't want any more Latin.'* The headmaster was surprised; Latin was, he explained, the language

Sir Robert Watson-Watt

of learning and Watson-Watt as a scholar should not only be learning Latin but also Greek so that he could read the thoughts of the ancient philosophers in their original language. 'Why can't I read them in translation?' asked Watson-Watt, not unreasonably. 'I want to learn German, the language of scientists and engineers.' He got his way.

He then won a bursary to Dundee University College, by then a part of the University of St Andrews, but specialising in training students for practical disciplines such as medicine and law, and more relevantly, to Watson-Watt, engineering and German. Watson-Watt was that awesome example of a student who is both gifted and diligent. In his first year he won both the physics and chemistry prizes and in his second was asked to join the teaching staff as an assistant, despite still being a student himself. In this role he became involved with the prestigious British Association for the Advancement of Science, which held its annual meetings at Dundee. There Watson-Watt met many of the famous scientists of the time and it was through these contacts that he developed his interest in radio-telegraphy, the broadcasting of telephone messages around the world.

Watson-Watt asked his professor, the soft-spoken Professor Peddie from the Orkney Islands, if he approved of the thought of his applying to the Post Office to work on radio-telegraphy. The professor pointed out that the entrance exams were hard but, wishing to help his gifted student, agreed to give him private coaching. Watson-Watt used his practical skills to build himself a primitive radio transmitter and was delighted when he picked up signals being transmitted from the Eiffel Tower in Paris.

Life had a lighter side. Watson-Watt was introduced to the lovely Margaret Robinson, a good swimmer, a good golfer and most importantly, a good shot – Watson-Watt had taken up shooting as a pastime. They enjoyed going out together, walking, cycling and the opera, but marriage was out of the question; Watson-Watt was just a poor if ambitious student. All went well until the late summer of 1914 when the First World War broke out. Watson-Watt agonised; should he enlist? Again he turned to Professor Peddie for advice. 'What use do you think you would be marching about with a rifle?' was the professor's verdict. 'You have a fine scientific brain. Use it!'

## The First World War

Robert Watson-Watt applied to the War Office to offer to help with the war effort, but while he waited for a reply he continued with his work at Dundee becoming involved in chemical engineering. A new drug, novocaine, had been discovered which if injected into the body would give local relief from pain. The drug was being produced in small batches in the university laboratories, but the demand was to produce much greater quantities for use in the military hospitals and Watson-Watt was asked to help in the design of a small factory to produce novocaine on an industrial scale.

In 1915 he received a letter – it had only taken a year for the War Office to appreciate that a gifted engineer with knowledge of radio might be able to help the war effort – asking him to go not as he had expected to the War Office but to the Meteorological Office. Here Dr Napier Shaw opened by explaining to Watson-Watt the valuable role the Royal Flying Corps was playing in the war by flying over the enemy lines to obtain information as to troop numbers and movements and to warn of likely attacks. There was a difficulty. The planes they were flying were still primitive and they suffered many losses not just from enemy fire but also from bad weather, particularly from thunderstorms where there was the danger of the fragile planes being struck by lightning. The need was to forecast better the possibility of thunderstorms in order to save unnecessary loss of life. So Robert Watson-Watt became a weather man.

He joined the weather station at Farnborough in Hampshire. It is hard in these days of instant weather forecasts – even if they are sometimes of doubtful accuracy – to appreciate that there was no national weather forecasting at the time, indeed, little forecasting at all. The causes of changing weather patterns were barely understood.

How could thunderstorms be forecast? As a radio 'hack' Watson-Watt was aware of 'crackle' as a background to radio and knew that it was caused by lightning. Would it be possible to identify from this crackle the distance and direction of the storm which created it? The task was immense; it had been estimated that at any time all over the world there were as many as one hundred flashes of lightning every second. Measuring the distance of a thunderstorm was perhaps not too difficult; its direction was the problem. This was a challenge for a radio engineer and Watson-Watt was well qualified to meet it. First, he had to carry out his daily weather forecasting duties. The work was painstaking. Every day hydrogen-filled balloons were launched into the air to measure the speed of the wind at different altitudes. Watson-Watt and a colleague realised it was necessary to calibrate the rate of rise of the balloons in still air if meaningful measurements were to be obtained, but where could this be done? The Royal Albert Hall in London provided the answer and the two of them set off to London with their balloons and cylinders of hydrogen gas to carry out their measurements as the balloons rose majestically to the roof – surely one of the most unusual performances ever to take place in this great building.

Back at the weather station, balloons were launched each day and their speed and rate of rise were measured. It was time-absorbing and meticulous work, but it was not Watson-Watt's real interest. He wanted to be able to detect the direction of the radio waves which crackled in his earphones. In July 1916, he managed to find the time to marry Margaret and they set up their first home in a wooden hut provided as married quarters by the War Office – not perhaps the romantic love-nest of which she had been dreaming!

## The Development of a Radio Wave Detection Finder

Faced with the problem of determining the direction of the storm, he had the idea of building a sensitive radio receiver with aerials which revolved in a circle. When the aerial was in line with the source, the signal would be at its loudest; when at right angles there would be no signal at all. This was fine apart from one drawback: the flash of lightning was not continuous; how then could you make sure the aerial was facing in the right direction at the right time?

Watson-Watt now had the stroke of genius which would eventually lead to the invention of radar. He knew of the existence of the cathode ray tube, effectively a glass tube from which the air or gas had largely been evacuated and which had two electrodes, one at each end. When an electric current was applied to one electrode, the cathode, a ray would pass from it to the electrode at the far end and if this ray were focused onto a chemically coated screen, the chemical would glow, but for Watson-Watt's requirements, there was one other critical advantage. If a coil of wire were wrapped around the tube at the point where the rays impinged on the screen even small changes in current through the coil would show on the screen as blips.

He reasoned that if an aerial was moved around in a circle, and was connected to the coil, then the snaps and crackles from the lightning would show on the screen as traces. A series of these impulses coming from a storm would show on the screen in linear fashion, indicating both the direction and the movement of the storm. This could be the solution he needed. It was easier to think up the idea than to make it work, but in December 1915 his team were able to spot a thunderstorm which they estimated was in the area of Selsey Bill. The next day it was indeed confirmed that there had been a thunderstorm there. The recordings were extended to twelve other weather stations and by plotting lines from the signals received, it was possible to pinpoint the source of the storm. Progress was, however, depressingly slow.


## The Development of Radar

By the end of the First World War Watson-Watt was becoming discouraged; he had worked on the problem for many years but still the work was no more than experimental. He was approached to represent the Air Ministry on a committee which had been set up by the new Department of Scientific and Industrial Research to carry out research into the problem of 'atmospherics' in radio communication, he was keen to accept. It was long, hard work. He needed more records of atmospherics but how could these be obtained? He then had a brainwave; he explained to his wife that he would ask radio listeners around the country to record any loud atmospherics heard on their radio. 'But you will need them to record an accurate time'. his wife objected, 'you cannot expect every radio listener to have an absolutely accurate clock.' Watson-Watt explained his idea: he would ask the listeners to record the word said on the radio at the time of the atmospherics interference. With the co-operation of the BBC he would thus know exactly when it took place. The first trial took place with twenty-one selected listeners around the country armed with the script of a talk being given on the radio. They were asked to underline the words being spoken when atmospheric 'crackle' occurred. The experiment was so successful that it was repeated with listeners as far away as Fez in Morocco, thereby discovering that the crackles could relate to events not just 'next door' but thousands of miles away.

This painstaking recording of atmospherics using improved cathode ray tubes continued for many years until in the second half of the 1930s when the threat of war again loomed. Watson-Watt was approached by Sir Henry Tizzard, the chairman of the committee responsible for air defence, who asked whether it would be possible to create a 'death ray' that could be used to destroy an approaching enemy aircraft. Watson-Watt explained this was not practical because the speed of the aircraft meant it would pass through the beam of any such ray too quickly for there to be any effect.

Then Watson-Watt had a new thought: could his recorders detect and identify the source and direction not just of the atmospherics caused by storms but objects – such as approaching enemy aircraft?

In a report entitled 'Detection and Location of Aircraft by Radio Methods' which he submitted to the Air Ministry in February 1935, Watson-Watt set out his ideas for a 'radio detection and ranging' system, later abbreviated to Radar, which would not only detect enemy aeroplanes but identify their range, speed and course. He suggested sending out radio waves to see if they would be 'bounced back' from the wings and fuselage of an aeroplane, just as light is reflected from a mirror, and then displaying the 'bounced-back' waves enlarged on a cathode ray tube to give both the direction and the range of the approaching aircraft.

Stanley Baldwin, the Prime Minister, had said pessimistically that 'the bombers would always get through' because it would be impossible to have enough fighters to provide cover night and day around the whole of Britain's coastline. Had Watson-Watt found the solution – to direct the scarce fighters only to those areas where they were needed?

In 1935 Watson-Watt was asked by Air Chief Marshal Sir Hugh Dowding if he could present a demonstration of his ideas. He proposed using the radio station at Daventry as the source of the radio beam and then by experiment to discover whether he could detect on a screen the presence of an aircraft flying through the beam. On the day of the experiment the signal from the radio station was reduced to the size of a pinhead while they listened to the drone of the aeroplane flying towards them on its steady course. As the aeroplane drew closer a line appeared on the screen, reaching a length of almost one inch (two and a half centimetres) before the plane flew away and the line grew smaller again. Watson-Watt heaved a great sigh of relief. It had worked.

## The Installation of Radar Stations around the Coast

The challenge now was to transform the idea from an experimental concept into a reliable tool which would help win the war. Watson-Watt worked hard with his team to improve the reliability and range of his system, eventually being able to detect aircraft as far as fifty miles away.

He had proved the concept and a year later approval was given for a chain of stations to be built around the south-east coast of Britain, the sector seen to be most at risk from enemy aircraft attack.

There were problems to be resolved. Once the trace picked up a British fighter which had not notified its presence but fortunately was not shot down. Watson-Watt realised that it was not enough just to recognise the presence of an aeroplane; the system had to be able to distinguish between a friendly fighter and an enemy bomber. He invented a method enabling him not only to detect a signal but to identify its source.

Watson-Watt's brain was racing. Were there other uses for his ideas? Would it be possible, he wondered, to build receiving units so small they could be mounted in a fighter aircraft, which would then be able to 'spot' enemy aircraft a long distance away and in any conditions, even in thick fog or at night? This would later give rise to the 'carrots' story. The Air Ministry was keen to hide the existence of radar and so attributed the success of one of their ace fighter pilots, John 'Cat's Eyes' Cunningham, who was credited with twenty kills of enemy planes, nineteen of which were at night, to the fact that he had been fed for years on an intensive diet of carrots to improve his night vision.

Another thought occurred to him. If aircraft were fitted with a radio-location or radar set, could this be used to guide a pilot back after a mission, perhaps in thick fog, using signals from the ground? By steering his aircraft along a beam emitted from the ground, the pilot could make a blind approach and land safely. The concept of radar was extended to the Navy; after all, if one could detect an aircraft fifty miles away it should be relatively easy to detect with a high degree of accuracy the direction and range of a warship. This dramatically improved the accuracy of naval gunnery.

All of this activity created an immense demand for radio location sets. As many as twenty-five thousand radio sets were needed for the ground-based receiving stations for anti-aircraft guns and for the fighter aircraft. The amount of work to be done was immense and it was not completed until 1940. Watson-Watt used to say it was just as well that Hitler had not invaded in the autumn of 1939 as the air defences then were far from ready.

## The Battle of Britain

In August 1940 Watson-Watt and his team were watching their sets when they noticed a big build-up of aircraft in France, more than one hundred miles away. Two formations took off from Amiens followed by further formations from Dieppe and Cherbourg. The phoney war was over. The Royal Air Force stations were warned and by the time the German aircraft crossed the coast British fighters had been scrambled and were waiting for them. The attack was repulsed. This became the pattern for the Battle of Britain whereby the RAF pilots flying long spells by day and night kept supremacy of the skies and prevented the threatened invasion of German forces.

Initially only the south-east was protected by radar, with important naval and industrial ports such as Plymouth and Glasgow left unprotected, but the defensive radar screen was rapidly expanded so that by 1941 the whole of the country was covered.

The use of radar by the British Navy was also important in improving intelligence of the movements of German cruisers and the accuracy of gunnery. In 1943 the German battle cruiser Scharnhorst had escaped from the Baltic and was devastating British shipping. British naval vessels bravely attacked and destroyed the Scharnhorst – but it was radar that had disclosed her position.

The Americans had been informed of the development of radar and took up the idea with enthusiasm. However, any system is only as good as its users. In December 1941, the Japanese launched a surprise attack on the American fleet in Pearl Harbour, which had the effect of bringing the United States into the war. The approaching Japanese aircraft had been detected on radar, but the Americans refused to believe that such a devastating attack could take place without warning and took no action until it was too late. Watson-Watt himself flew to America at the end of 1941 to advise them on the construction of a chain of radar stations, firstly on the Pacific coast to guard against a further Japanese attack, and then on the Atlantic seaboard. For this he was awarded the US Medal of Merit, the highest honour which can be bestowed on a civilian.

Although the existence of radar was kept a closely guarded secret during the war the contribution of Watson-Watt to the war, effort was duly recognised when he was knighted by King George VI in 1942.

## After the War

After the end of the War, improvements in radar continued, now principally for peaceful purposes such as air traffic control, the prevention of collisions at sea and, less popularly, the police speed gun. The concept of radar was also used by the scientists at the British radio telescope at Jodrell Bank to track the movements of the furthest stars, thus expanding our knowledge of the universe.

Regrettably, the intense effort and long hours spent by Watson-Watt in developing radar had their effect on his marriage and he and Margaret separated in 1948, later divorcing. Watson-Watt married again in 1952; his new wife was Canadian and they moved to Canada where he died in 1973.

## Watson-Watt's Legacy

The invention of radar made an invaluable contribution to the Battle of Britain and the eventual defeat of Germany in the Second World War. For this alone he deserves every honour he received. In peace, radar has made an incalculable contribution to safety, particularly in shipping and flying, where it has enabled the rapid growth of air services and helped to maintain a high safety record despite the increasingly crowded skies.

We owe an immense debt to a man who worked long and laboriously for many years before bringing his ideas to their successful conclusion.

**Further Reading**
John Rowland, *The Radar Man*

**Online Resources**
Sir Robert Watson-Watt Society of Brechin
http://www.watsonwatt.org

'FARADAY' Eduardo Paolozzi - 2000
University of Birmingham
photo: Thomas Haywood

inscribed:
'Here between the hither and the further shore
While time is withdrawn, consider the future
And the past with an equal mind.'

from T.S.Eliot's *Dry Savages,* highlighting the purpose
of a university education -
'to travel, listen, think and change.'

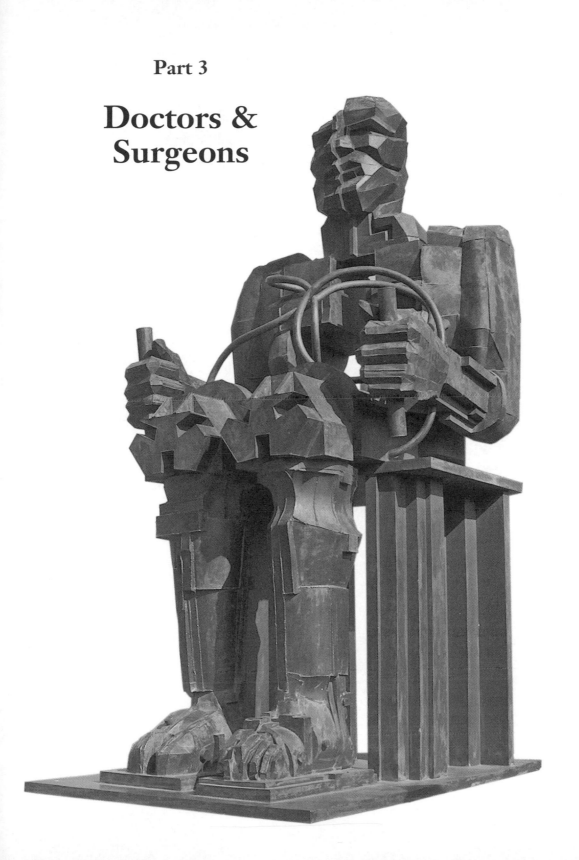

# Part 3

# Doctors &
# Surgeons

Matt Collier

## DOCTORS & SURGEONS

**James Young Simpson**
*THE MAN WHO TOOK THE PAIN FROM SURGERY*

**Joseph Lister**
*THE WORLD'S GREATEST SURGEON*

**Ronald Ross**
*THE MAN WHO UNRAVELLED THE SECRETS OF MALARIA*

**Elsie Inglis**
*THE STORY OF A MODERN WOMAN*

**Alexander Fleming**
*THE MAN WHO CURED INFECTION*

## Part 3 • Doctors & Surgeons

### The 'Science of Man'

The lives of some of these scientists and inventors, certainly Robert Watson-Watt, John Logie Baird, Alexander Graham Bell and, arguably, James Clerk Maxwell and William Thomson, do not fit strictly within the period of the Scottish Enlightenment which is usually taken to refer to the eighteenth century. However the common themes of a good education, a determination through the exercise of reason and application to determine the solution to a problem, be it a scientific concept or a practical invention, and the Calvinist conviction as to the rewards of hard effort are apparent in all their lives and consistent with the principles which define the Enlightenment.

The Enlightenment philosophers in their study of man had concentrated upon his "soul", questioning what it is that motivates a man's actions and what it is that drives his moral judgements, but the Enlightenment encompassed a similar study of man's "body" through the development of medicine.

Scotland had earned a reputation in medicine as long ago as the Middle Ages with the Beaton family, in Gaelic MacBheathadh, who had for many generations served the MacLeods and the MacDonalds and had developed a reputation for their knowledge, but the medicine they practised was still quite primitive.

By the eighteenth century medicine was still based on the principles set out in the teachings of Hippocrates in the 4th century B.C. as recorded and preserved by Arab physicians. Disease was thought to be caused by an imbalance in the four 'humours' of the body, blood, phlegm, yellow bile and black bile. Treatment consisted of cleansing the body of the out of balance humour by often brutal purges or blood letting, and then restoring overall health by the administration of herbal cures.

The death of Charles II is typical of the suffering caused by well-intended doctors. In 1685 Charles endured a lingering death, probably of kidney failure. During his last painful days, the doctors carried out no fewer than fifty different treatments intended to purge the out-of-balance humours, including the letting of blood, emetics and the application of red-hot irons. The poor king, who must have suffered terribly in his last few days, rallied briefly to apologise for taking so long to die.

With the Enlightenment in 1726 came a new era in Scottish medicine. The School of Medicine at Edinburgh University was founded, and in 1741 the Royal Infirmary was built as a teaching hospital. Before the formation of the School of Medicine the traditional route for the training of a physician in Scotland would start with a degree from a Scottish university, followed by medical training on the Continent, usually at the Medical School at Leyden such as with Alexander Monro who lived from 1697–1767.

## The Monros and the School of Medicine in Edinburgh

Monro, known later as Monro *primus*, started his education in medicine by working as a young man with his father, John, himself a surgeon, in treating the men wounded at the Battle of Sherrifmuir. More conventionally, he then attended medical school in London, Paris and Leyden before becoming the first Professor of Anatomy at Edinburgh when the Medical School was established in 1726; his father John Monro had been conveniently one of the instigators of the School.

Monro *primus* was responsible for the rapid expansion of the School which expanded from sixty or so anatomy students when he started to around two hundred by 1756. In appropriate Monro fashion he was then succeeded by his son, known of course as Alexander Monro *secundus* (1733-1817), and in due course by Alexander Monro *tertius* (1773-1859). There is a possibly apocryphal story that the last incumbent "blew" the tradition; he used to read his lectures from notes but unfortunately referred to "his time in Leyden" – were they his notes or those of his grandfather?

The advent of hospitals allowed extended examination of patients by a number of doctors and the emphasis on observation, recording and rational deduction implicit in the spirit of the Enlightenment together with a willingness to exchange ideas through discourse or through publication helped in the development of medical knowledge. Detailed post mortem examination of diseased corpses brought about the realisation that disease originated in the organs of the body and this insight even extended to the causation of disease with the celebrated physician Mathew Baillie realising for example that cirrhosis of the liver was caused by *'a long habit of drinking spirituous liquors.'* The increasing skill in diagnosis was not accompanied by improved treatment which still relied extensively on herbal cures. As Baillie wrote *'I know better, perhaps than any other man, from my knowledge of anatomy how to discover disease but when I have done so I don't know better how to cure it.'* This hiatus would not materially change until the advent of penicillin in the twentieth century.

Alexander Monro had given the Edinburgh Medical School a fine start and it was soon recognised as one of the leading medical schools not just in Britain but in Europe. This was enhanced when William Cullen was appointed as Professor of Physic in 1766. William Cullen himself had originally taught at Glasgow where one of his pupils had been Joseph Black. Black followed him to Edinburgh and the contribution of these two would be a key factor in the further development of the reputation of Edinburgh through the quality both of their teaching and of their research, in which was emphasised the importance of observation and deduction.

Edinburgh followed a more inclusive medical training than some of the older institutions so that its graduates would have experience both in the diagnosis and in the treatment of illness with "clinical rounds" for students introduced in 1750. In contrast, students at Oxford or Cambridge were taught just to observe and diagnose; touching the patient was regarded as definitely below their dignity and would be left to the others while any surgery was the responsibility of the barber-surgeons.

Scottish medical education became regarded as the best in Europe so that from 1800 to 1850 a remarkable ninety-five percent of medical graduates in Britain had graduated from a Scottish university. Edinburgh became a centre of excellence in the teaching of medicine, attracting students from England, Ireland and the Americas, comfortably outnumbering those from Scotland.

## The Hunters

William and John Hunter were two brothers who were born in Lanarkshire and who spread the gospel of Scottish medicine, both in due course moving to London.

William studied medicine at the University of Glasgow under Willam Cullen before going to London in 1740 where he studied under another Scot, William Smellie, developing there his interest in obstetrics. His life's work was to improve the quality and safety of childbirth and he investigated the bodies of women who had died in childbirth to try to determine the cause and to improve procedures, achieving such a high reputation that he became in due course the Physician to

Queen Charlotte. He wrote a number of books and formed a museum to contain his collection of anatomical specimens and his library of rare books.

John Hunter was a late starter. He had a professed distaste for books and left school at the age of thirteen, moving at the age of twenty to London where he worked as a dissection assistant to his brother. He rapidly demonstrated his abilities and became one of the leading surgeons of his time, in 1768 becoming Surgeon at St. George's Hospital. He specialised in dentistry and in the study of anatomy and was one of the first to study the development of the child within the womb and to realise that the blood supplies of the mother and the foetus are separate. He founded a museum for his collection of more than five hundred different species of plant and animals which now form part of the Hunter Museum at the Royal College of Surgeons in London.

Coincidentally, it would be obstetrics which much later James Young Simpson would make his speciality, although it would be in the use of anaesthetics that he became famous.

**Further Reading**
David Hamilton, *The Healers: a History of Medicine in Scotland*
Helen Dingwall et al, *Scottish Medicine: an Illustrated History*

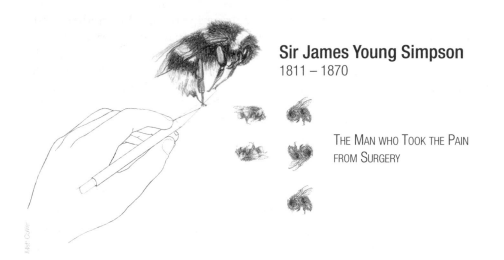

# Sir James Young Simpson
## 1811 – 1870

THE MAN WHO TOOK THE PAIN FROM SURGERY

*'Thank God for James Young Simpson's discovery of chloroform'*
— Plaque on the wall of St Giles' Cathedral in Edinburgh

James Simpson was an obstetrician – a doctor specialising in childbirth – who became appalled at the suffering experienced by mothers while giving birth. His philosophy in medicine was expressed in his teaching to his students whom he told, 'Your aim is as far as possible to alleviate human suffering and lengthen our human existence,' and so when he heard from Boston in 1846 of the first use of ether as an anaesthetic, he was keen to experiment with the use of anaesthetics. As a result of his experiments, he pioneered the use of chloroform as an anaesthetic greatly easing the pain of childbirth. Its use was extended into surgery, relieving patients from pain and freeing the surgeon from the need to operate with brutal urgency to minimise the trauma to the patient.

## Early Life

Simpson was born in 1811. His grandfather, Alexander Simpson, was a farrier and a self-taught healer of animals and people. Bloodletting was his favoured treatment for most ills, but in a nod to his grandson's future career in obstetrics, he did have a remedy to relieve the pains of childbirth which consisted of the application of a potion of white onions dissolved in oil to the mother's stomach – a method of treatment which has strangely gone out of fashion. Through his hard work Alexander became a tenant farmer, farming three hundred acres on the estates of Lord Hopetoun, an enlightened landlord and one of the founding members of the Honourable Society of Improvers.

His father was David Simpson, a baker in Bathgate, and his mother, Mary Jarvey, was descended from the Huguenots (the family name was Gervais), French Protestants who had fled from France to Scotland following persecution by the Catholics. James was their seventh son, born on the seventh of June, and the villagers, to whom seven was a lucky number, foretold good fortune for the young babe. Curiously, David Simpson's bakery business, which had been going steadily from bad to worse, did indeed take a turn for the better after his son's birth, but that might be because he handed over the business side of the operation to his canny Huguenot wife.

Simpson, who was the youngest of eight children, one girl and seven boys, was very close to his mother and was heartbroken when she died when he was just nine years old. His father was a somewhat happy-go-lucky character and it was Simpson's mother who both taught him and inspired him with the thought that he could one day achieve greatness.

He used to recall when he was a young boy he entered the house to find her darning a big hole in his stocking. 'My Jamie,' she said, 'when your mother's away [dead] you will remember that she was a great darner.' He did, and many years later he founded a prize at a school in his old village for the best darning. After his mother's death his sister, Mary, became a 'second mother' to the youngster.

## A Student at Edinburgh University

Simpson did well at school and so when he was fourteen it was decided he should go to university. As the family was very poor, his brothers generously offered to support him through his years of study. Simpson was a lonely lad at university, only cheered by the letters and parcels he received from his sister. He took lodgings with two other boys from Bathgate, who were studying medicine and encouraged by their example, Simpson decided that he too would become a doctor. He found the studies difficult after the village school, but won a bursary of £10 a year in his second year which helped with the finances; this was less remarkable when it is realised that to be eligible for the bursary you had to bear the surname of either its founder, Stewart, or his wife, who had conveniently been a Simpson before she married.

His lecturer in anatomy was the notorious Robert Knox. Knox had been finding it difficult to obtain enough cadavers upon which his students could practise dissection until a couple of Irish men, Burke and Hare, came to his aid. They had a lodger who had died of natural causes; after an appropriate period of mourning they realised there might be a market for the body and sold it to Knox for dissection.

Discovering the profit to be made on medical cadavers, but finding themselves without any more conveniently expired lodgers, they decided to increase supply by providing their own source of fresh corpses. They embarked on a series of murders, suffocating their victims so as to leave no marks. Any residual evidence of the crime was conveniently covered up by the students' subsequent dissections. When they were eventually caught, Hare turned King's evidence – confirming the principle that there is no honour among thieves – and was spared; Burke was convicted on Hare's evidence and hanged. It seems appropriate that his body was itself then given to an anatomy class for dissection.

Although there was no proof that Knox was aware of the crimes, the anger of the mob spread to him when they were uncovered; his house was attacked and his effigy was burnt in the streets. Simpson's other tutors were more conventional.

## A Medical Practitioner

After qualifying as a doctor, Simpson practised as a house surgeon when he was first exposed to the brutality of surgery without anaesthetics. Little attention was paid to cleanliness or to the suffering of the patient. The surgeon had to operate with great speed in order to avoid his patient dying on the operating table from trauma, the shock to the body's system caused by the operation. The surgeon had time only to cut out the infection or amputate the diseased limb; there was no opportunity to investigate first or to tie up blood vessels. Meanwhile the patient, screaming in agony, was held down on the table by three or four powerful pairs of arms. Often the patient would die from the shock, or still more often, from post operative infection of the wound.

Sir James Young Simpson

Surgery was very brutal and witnessing the suffering and pain affected Simpson so badly he thought about giving up medicine. He persevered however and qualified when he was twenty-one, opening a general medical practice in Edinburgh. He always remained aware of the pain suffered by patients during surgery and while a house surgeon in Leith he wrote, 'cannot something be done to render the patient unconscious while under acute pain?'

Despite this success as a general practitioner, Simpson's main interest was in obstetrics, and when in 1839 the position of Professor of Midwifery at Edinburgh became available he applied. The Chair of Midwifery in Edinburgh had been established as long ago as 1726 – the first of its kind in Britain, possibly the world.

Two objections were raised: his youth – he was just twenty-eight years old – and that he was unmarried. Simpson could deal with the second objection more easily than the first. He disappeared from Edinburgh for a couple of weeks and journeyed to Liverpool where he proposed to and married Miss Jessie Grindlay. He returned triumphantly to Edinburgh as a married man; that objection was overcome. It is only fair to point out that it was not quite such a whirlwind courtship – James first met Jessie four years prior and had been courting her by letter.

The contest for the post was keenly fought. Simpson himself spent more than five hundred pounds, a huge sum for the time, in printing and circulating his testimonials. Despite his youth, he was appointed Professor, but only by the narrowest of margins: seventeen votes against the sixteen for his opponent.

## Professor of Midwifery

Simpson had an imposing appearance, with an exceptionally large head crowned by a thick mane of long hair. (A post mortem examination discovered that his head measured twenty-two inches / fifty-five centimeters around and thirteen inches / thirty-two centimeters from ear to ear). He was a gifted teacher whose lectures soon became very popular, with students crowding in to hear him. His classes in midwifery were the largest in the medical school and Simpson soon became wealthy and moved into a fine house in an exclusive part of Edinburgh.

He also developed a very exclusive list of patients; duchesses and princesses sought his advice. With his success he could have lived a prosperous but unremarkable life had he not become concerned with the pain suffered by women during childbirth. He searched desperately for ways to ease their pain.

One method he investigated was hypnosis, or mesmerism as it was then known, after its famous practitioner, Mesmer. In hypnosis the patients are lulled into a trance-like state by the hypnotist, making them susceptible to suggestion – for example that they are feeling no pain. Simpson found that he had the gift of hypnosis and he experimented on patients to try to ease their suffering. He also performed hypnosis as a party trick. At one dinner party he hypnotised the lady sitting next to him and forbad her to speak until he released her from the trance. All would have been fine if he had not then been called unexpectedly from the table. When he returned he found the lady very angry and still unable to speak; she vented her anger in a note she had written him!

Simpson also researched the past, believing that drugs had been used to dull pain by the ancient Greeks and Egyptians and later by the Arabs.

## The Discovery of Anaesthesia

Anaesthesia is the use of a drug to induce sleep and ease pain, principally from surgery; modern anaesthetic agents also relax the muscles.

Many years before, the famous chemist Sir Humphrey Davy had noticed that inhalation of the gas nitrous oxide, known popularly as 'laughing gas,' could ease pain. A dentist in America experimented with the use of laughing gas on his patients and found that he could pull out a tooth without the patient feeling pain. This was a breakthrough; nitrous oxide is still in use today. But the search was on to find a better anaesthetic. In 1846 Simpson learned of experiments which had been carried out by a dentist called Morton in Boston who was trying different substances to see if he could find one that would act as an anaesthetic. On 30 September Morton tried breathing the fumes of ether, bravely experimenting first on himself. He successfully put himself to 'sleep' for ten minutes before fortunately waking up.

Morton then tried ether on a patient who had arrived at his door begging to have his bad tooth removed but exclaiming that he was afraid of the pain. 'Can you not mesmerise me?' he asked. 'I can do better than that,' replied Morton, who extracted the tooth after having first administered ether to put the patient to sleep. The patient showed no signs of pain but neither did he wake up after surgery; Morton panicked – had he killed him? He threw a glass of water at his patient who fortunately did then wake up. 'When will you extract my tooth?' the patient asked. 'It is all over,', exclaimed Morton, showing him the diseased tooth. The extraction had been carried out with the patient unconscious and pain free .

Morton had the imagination to realise that his discovery was not limited to dentistry but also could be used in surgery. On 16 th October an operation to remove a tumour was scheduled at the Massachusetts General Hospital; Morton decided to try anaesthetising the patient with ether. The operation took place in the surgical theatre with an audience of senior doctors. The patient was administered ether and emitted no sound or movement during the entire operation. Anaesthesia had arrived and Morton had become the first anaesthetist.

## Simpson Discovers Chloroform

Simpson discussed the use of ether with Robert Liston, another Scot, who had been one of the first surgeons in Britain to use it in an operation he had carried out at University College Hospital. Simpson realised the use of ether could be extended to obstetrics and in January 1847, he used ether for the first time on a woman who was giving birth in Edinburgh.

It was a great success, but Simpson was not satisfied. Ether had a pronounced and disagreeable smell and its use could harm the lining of the nose. Was there a better anaesthetic? Like Morton before him, Simpson experimented with a variety of different substances, which he inhaled at his house at Queen Street in Edinburgh, using himself as the guinea pig, either alone or with his friends and fellow experimenters Dr George Keith and Dr Mathews Duncan.

One day Simpson received from a chemist in Liverpool a sample of chloroform with the suggestion that he might like to try it as a possible anaesthetic. He and his two colleagues met together in the evening of 4 November and as was their habit, set down to their task of inhaling a number of different substances, but with no success. At last Simpson came to the phial containing chloroform. Without much expectation he passed tumblers to his fellow experimenters and they all began to breathe in the fumes. The effect was almost instantaneous. They immediately become bright and cheerful, chatting merrily away until suddenly they crashed to the floor, fully anaesthetised.

On wakening, Simpson found himself lying prostrate on the floor. His first reaction was 'this is far stronger and better than ether!' He then looked about him and realised Dr Duncan was also on the floor, fast asleep under a chair and snoring loudly, and that Dr Keith was lying prostrate under the dining table! Simpson's wife and their other guests were understandably somewhat alarmed. One lady said she would never forget the look on Dr Keith's face when he eventually recovered consciousness. Simpson himself was euphoric. Chloroform as an anaesthetic had arrived. The party went on into the early hours as Simpson celebrated his discovery and others tried the 'magical' chloroform.

Chloroform became an instant success. The first baby to be born to a mother given chloroform was named 'Anaesthesia' as a mark of the historic event but what she thought of her name when she grew up is not recorded. Chloroform was soon being used not just in childbirth, but in surgery too. The effect was remarkable. Not only was the suffering of the patient greatly relieved but the surgeon was no longer under such incredible pressure to work as fast as possible. He now had the luxury of time; he could examine the form of the cut he needed to make and tie off the patient's blood vessels to obtain a clearer view. The outcome of surgery was massively improved.

### The Use of Chloroform as an Anaesthetic Becomes Accepted

Strangely, despite its obvious benefits, the use of chloroform did meet some resistance. Some people, probably all men, felt that its use was *'against Nature'*; some churchmen even believed it was against the teachings of the Church, that it was divine will that women should bear the pain of giving birth. Others believed even more bizarrely that in surgery the cold touch of the steel of the surgeon's knife was a benefit to the patient – though how the patient could register this exquisite delight while nearly unconscious from pain is certainly a debatable.

Simpson fought his cause both with the numbers – the successful cases where chloroform had been used – and with religion, matching biblical quote with biblical quote. After all, had not God put Adam into a deep sleep before removing his rib to create Eve? What was good enough for God was surely good enough for man; or was it that Adam was a man 'giving birth', not a woman?

The turning point came in 1853. Queen Victoria, the mother by then of seven children and presumably therefore thoroughly experienced in these matters, chose to give birth to her eighth baby, Prince Leopold, using chloroform. As her physician wrote rather austerely, 'Her Majesty was greatly pleased and has never had a better recovery.' From the Queen's physician, this was a ringing endorsement and the use of chloroform had been given the seal of royal approval.

## Recognition

Simpson received a number of honours in recognition of his work, including the Freedom of the City of Edinburgh and an honorary degree from Oxford. He was knighted in 1866, the first doctor in Scotland to be made a baronet for services to medicine. Despite all his success he did not follow the path of others and seek greater fame and fortune in London, but continued to care for his patients in Edinburgh. Simpson was not just a great man; he was a good man. He would travel vast distances to see his patients and would often allow them to rest at his house. If a patient could afford to pay he would receive a bill, but if he was poor then Simpson would charge no fee. His work put a great strain upon his body; he was often rising at the crack of dawn to visit a patient or waiting on a cold and draughty station platform late at night for the train home.

The honours he received could not compensate him for the tragedies of his personal life, losing his cherished daughter Maggie when she was just four years old and another daughter, Mary, in infancy. In 1866 he lost his son David after he had just qualified as a doctor and whom Simpson had hoped might succeed him as Professor of Midwifery, then his oldest surviving daughter Jessie, and finally his other son Jamie, who had long suffered from skin disease and progressive loss of sight. The grief and the physical stresses of his work shortened his life and he began to suffer crushing chest pains caused by angina. He said of his knighthood, 'I felt this baronetcy such a bauble [when] in health and now when sick and heartsore [I know for certain] what a bauble it is.'

He died in 1870, aged just fifty-nine years. His wife Jessie died six weeks later. For some years she had retreated into herself, her life spent in the study of religious tracts enlivened by the odd recreational sniff of chloroform; ironically it was probably the excessive inhalation of chloroform which killed her.

William Gladstone, then prime minister, announced the death to the House of Commons, saying 'Sir James Simpson's death is a grievous loss to the nation; it is truly a national concern.' Simpson was buried, not in Westminster Abbey as was proposed, but as he wished in a graveyard in Edinburgh next to the bodies of his predeceased children. The site was well chosen; to the south was the castle, to the north the Firth of Forth and in the distance the Ochil Hills, the views he had loved throughout life.

## Sir James Young Simpson's Legacy

Simpson's belief in the importance of the medical profession is best summed up in his own words:

> *Other pursuits become insignificant in their objects when placed in contrast with ours. The agriculturist bestows all his professional care on the rearing of crops and cattle; the merchant spends his energies and attention on his goods and his commissions; the engineer upon his iron-wheels and rails; the sailor upon his ships and freights; the banker upon his bills and his bonds; and the manufacturer upon his spindles [spinning cotton] and their products.'*

> But what are these, he asked, *'in comparison with the inestimable value and importance of the very lives of these fellowmen who everywhere move and breathe and speak and act around us? What are any, or what are all these objects when contrasted with the most precious and valued gift of God – human life? And what would not the greatest and most successful followers of such varied callings give out of their own professional stores for the restoration of health and for the prolongation of life … [if] menaced by the dreaded and blighting finger of disease?*

Simpson's scientific and methodical evaluation of the various possible anaesthetics was in the best Enlightenment tradition, and his introduction of chloroform as an anaesthetic was a breakthrough in the relief of pain. Although modern anaesthetic agents have been developed since the days of chloroform, every patient having a surgical operation and every mother giving birth owes an immense debt to the pioneering work of Sir James Young Simpson.

The tribute in Westminster Abbey sums up the debt owed him by the world:

> *To whose genius and benevolence*
> *The world owes the blessings derived*
> *From the use of chloroform for*
> *The relief of suffering.*
> *LAUS DEO.*

**Further Reading**
H. Laing Gordon, *Sir James Young Simpson and Chloroform*
Morrice McCrae, *Simpson: The Turbulent Life of a Medical Pioneer*

**Online Resources**
National Center for Biotechnology Information, U.S. National Library of Medicine
http://www.ncbi.nlm.nih.gov/pmc/articles/PMC1721404/pdf/v086p0F207.pdf

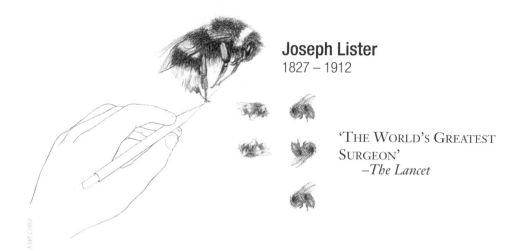

# Joseph Lister
1827 – 1912

'THE WORLD'S GREATEST
SURGEON'
–*The Lancet*

Joseph Lister was born on 5 April 1827, in the village of Upton in Essex of Yorkshire stock. Although not a Scot, he became Professor of Surgery in both Glasgow and Edinburgh and it was while working in Scotland that he produced his groundbreaking ideas on reducing the incidence of infection following surgery.

Lister's introduction of antiseptic procedures was fundamental to the improvement of the outcome of surgery and has saved the lives of literally hundreds of thousands of people who would otherwise have died from infections.

## Boyhood

The roots of the Lister family were in Yorkshire but his great grandfather had moved to London to make his fortune. Lister's father, also a Joseph, was a successful businessman and scientist who specialised in optics and helped to perfect the achromatic lens which became the basis of the modern microscope.

His was a Quaker family, and as such, they lived their lives according to the word and spirit of the Gospel. Quakerism was more than a religion; it was a way of life. Horse racing, betting and games of chance were banned as 'immoral' and pastimes like dancing, listening to music and reading novels were forbidden as 'superficial'.

Banned from such superficial pleasures the young boy followed his interest in natural history. His ambition even as a young boy was to become a surgeon and he would practice by dissecting fish, frogs and small animals to reveal their skeletons. He was sent to a Quaker school and then to University College in London; Oxford and Cambridge would not then accept Quakers!

His years at university were not happy. University College was in those days a drab and charmless institution and Lister lived a lonely life in a lodging house far from his family. He became reserved, with few friends and little to do outside the routine of classes and studying. He first took a general degree, studying classics and natural philosophy in addition to anatomy and chemistry, but then had an attack of smallpox which, coupled with the heavy programme of his studies, led to a nervous breakdown. He did not move on to medical school until 1849.

## Studies at Medical School

Charing Cross Hospital was his choice and it was here that he first experienced surgery. Surgery was still a brutal process although the recent introduction of anaesthesia had eased the surgeon's work and given him more precious time. No longer were successful operations measured by the minute.

Anaesthesia was first used in London at University College Hospital where Lister watched an operation performed by Dr Liston a few days after he had learned of the successful operation in America when ether was first used as an anaesthetic.

Although ether brought relief from pain during the actual surgery it did nothing to prevent the deaths caused by infection after surgery. Lister would remember for many years the sight and smell of rotting flesh after surgery and at this time one in three patients who had an amputation would later die of infection.

In 1852 Lister was admitted to the prestigious Royal College of Surgeons. He asked his professor how best he should advance his knowledge as a surgeon and was advised to go to Edinburgh for a month or so and then to the Continent. Lister went to Edinburgh as suggested, but not just for a month; he stayed in Scotland for more than twenty-five years and it was there he did his greatest work.

## Scotland

In 1854 Lister was appointed house surgeon at the Royal Infirmary, Edinburgh, under Professor Syme, a colourful but irascible Scot who was at the time one of the leading surgeons in Britain. Syme and Lister respected each other's abilities and Lister became a regular visitor at Syme's house in Edinburgh, not just to converse with the learned professor but also to meet with his charming eldest daughter Agnes whom he married in 1856.

In addition to his surgical duties Lister was carrying out research, first into the process of inflammation, disproving by detailed experimentation the then accepted theories, and then into the clotting, or coagulation, of blood. Clotting is the process whereby bleeding stops; without clotting the patient would bleed to death. Lister realised it only took place where the blood vessels had become inflamed and that this must in some way lead to the blood coagulating.

His reputation as both surgeon and researcher was growing and in 1860 he was appointed Professor of Surgery at the University of Glasgow, and in 1861 as Surgeon to the Royal Infirmary, Glasgow. Lister was a success both as teacher and surgeon, but he believed his true destiny lay in research.

## The Cure of the 'Hospital Disease'

Since his earliest days as a surgeon, Lister had been distressed by the high level of mortality after surgery through postoperative infection. Now that he was personally responsible for the surgical wards at the Infirmary he noticed that the infection of wounds after surgery was becoming more common. He also observed that a patient's wound was more likely to become infected if his bed was next to that of another patient whose wound was already infected, especially if the beds were close together. Somehow the infection was being transmitted.

Hygiene in those days was very rudimentary. People rarely washed and even more rarely bathed. In hospitals, surgeons and nurses would move from one patient to another, dressing their open wounds, without first washing their hands. The surgeon would take pride in wearing a blood-soaked frock coat during an operation; the more the coat was soaked in blood, the greater the surgeon's perceived experience. Infection, gangrene (putrefaction of the flesh) and blood poisoning, the so-called 'hospital diseases', were ever present in a surgical ward of the time. Hospitals became 'infected' and there was no remedy. New buildings fared no better. Within just two years of opening the brand-new surgical building of the Glasgow Royal Infirmary had become infected.

In an attempt to prevent the spread of infection throughout the wards, Lister instituted a regimen of strict cleanliness. Braving the ridicule of his colleagues, he insisted that doctors and nurses must wash their hands both before and after treating a patient and that dressings on wounds be regularly changed, but despite these improvements in hygiene there was little improvement in outcomes. 'Hospital infection' remained rampant. Lister was at a loss. He was a most careful surgeon but even so his patients were dying of infections. What was causing it? What else could he do?

At heart, Lister was a scientist. He observed, he noted, he reasoned and he drew conclusions. One fact he noticed was that a patient with a compound fracture was much more likely to end up with an infected wound than a patient with a simple (single) fracture. Why was this? After all, a fracture is a fracture. He realised that there was a difference: with a simple fracture the skin is unbroken but in the case of a compound fracture it is broken. Was this the cause? Was the open wound becoming infected through exposure to the air in the hospital? This was a revolutionary thought. After all, how could air be infected?

Louis Pasteur provided the answer. Pasteur was a brilliant French scientist who in 1856 was asked by the owner of a local distillery for help with a problem. The distillery produced alcohol from sugar beet but something had gone wrong with the process and lactic acid was forming in the vats during the fermentation and ruining the alcohol. Pasteur observed the production closely: the pressing of the beet, the addition of yeast and the process of fermentation, examining samples from each stage with his microscope. He discovered that fermentation was caused by living organisms, a combination of yeast and bacteria, and that different types of fermentation – of alcohol, lactic acid or vinegar, for example – were caused by different bacteria. Pasteur realised there must be an impurity present in the vats which was fermenting the beet to lactic acid and he showed how this could be effectively eliminated.

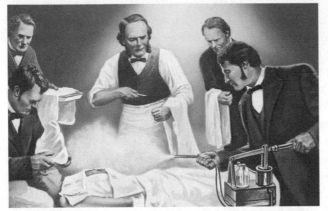

Illustration of Joseph Lister Using Carbolic Spray During Surgery

The distillery owner was delighted but Pasteur was unsatisfied. Where did these bacteria come from? At the time many people, even scientists, believed in 'spontaneous generation,' that maggots, for one example, were magically self-generated in rotting meat. In the seventeenth century one pioneer scientist had even proposed a 'recipe' for making mice. The concept of spontaneous generation had largely been disproved by experiment and now Pasteur proved that even the primitive bacteria he had discovered did not spontaneously self-generate but derived from a parent.

Pasteur had discovered that fermentation was caused by bacteria but now he discovered that there were micro-organisms everywhere; even the air, assumed pure, was full of germs. If these germs entered a receptive medium, say a fermenting liquid in an open jar, then they not only survived but rapidly multiplied and the liquid became infected and putrid. If the same liquid were placed in a sealed jar then no infection would take place, proving the germs were in the air itself. Pasteur found that the only way he could prevent the growth of these micro-organisms was by heating the solution to 60°C, a process now called pasteurisation. Heating the solution to 100°C killed the germs completely, in a process now called sterilisation.

Lister read of Pasteur's findings with amazement. At last he understood where the infections had come from: germs in the air. This was fine, but what was the solution? After all, he could hardly heat a patient to 60°C. He needed to find a substance to sterilise the germs.

Some time before he had read of a problem in Carlisle where the town's sewage had been emptied into streams which had then been diverted to irrigate the fields; the problem was not just the stench, though that was bad enough, but that cattle were becoming infected from parasites in the untreated sewage. The people of Carlisle had discovered that adding a little carbolic acid not only destroyed the parasites so that the cattle remained healthy but also got rid of the awful smell. If carbolic acid could destroy the parasites in sewage, could it destroy the germs which were infecting his patients' wounds? The only way to find out was by experiment. He would use carbolic acid to try to destroy the germs which otherwise might infect a wound after surgery. Very properly he decided only to experiment with his new treatment on patients who had a compound fracture, those patients whom he knew from his observation were most at risk from post-operative infection.

Now he had to wait for a suitable patient. It was not until August 1865 that the opportunity to carry out his experiment occurred when he was asked to operate on a young boy who had suffered a compound fracture of the leg after he had been knocked down in the street by a cart. His wound from the operation was about an inch wide and several inches deep. Lister carefully dressed it after the operation with a piece of gauze soaked in carbolic acid and left it untouched for four days. When he removed the gauze and inspected the wound it was completely free of infection. Diluted carbolic acid was then applied daily with each new dressing and after six weeks the boy was completely healed. There had been no infection.

Over the next year or so, Lister repeated his treatment on a number of patients until he was confident that his treatment was preventing postoperative infection. Then he was ready to publish his results and in 1867 wrote an article in *The Lancet*, the principal medical journal, setting out his findings.

Lister did not get the reaction he expected. His revolutionary treatment was largely ignored by his colleagues. Some asked what was so new about the use of carbolic acid. Others ridiculed the idea that the air could be full of germs: 'We are asked to believe that the air is full of vicious agents constantly ready to attack us,' wrote one. The English surgeons just did not understand the breakthrough Lister had achieved in medical knowledge, that infections were caused by germs and were not an inevitable outcome of surgery. One of the few to support him was his former mentor, Professor Syme of Edinburgh.

## The Implementation of Antisepsis

On the Continent the reaction was much more positive. Eminent surgeons came from as far as Copenhagen to learn directly from Lister how to treat wounds. Lister himself, although hurt by the rejection of his colleagues, knew that he was right. He continued to experiment, to improve on his treatment and to try other antiseptics other than carbolic acid. He implemented a programme of antisepsis, using carbolic acid to destroy germs and prevent infection and applying a regimen of hygiene throughout the ward to prevent cross-infection between patients.

His ward at the Royal Infirmary, once riddled by the hospital disease, became almost free of postoperative infection, whilst those of his colleagues who did not practice antisepsis remained as disease-ridden as ever. Rather tactlessly, Lister pointed this out in a paper 'On the Effects of the Antiseptic System of Treatment upon the Salubrity [by which he meant healthiness] of a Surgical Hospital,' which drew a parallel between the outcomes for his patients with the use of antiseptic procedures and the less successful outcomes for the patients of his colleagues.

In 1869 Syme had a stroke and resigned from his Professorship at Edinburgh University. A group of young students wrote to Lister urging him to apply for the vacant professorship. They wrote, 'Your method of Antiseptic Treatment constitutes a well-marked epoch in the history of British Surgery and will result in lasting glory to the Profession and unspeakable benefit to mankind.' They understood far better than their elders just what Lister had achieved.

Edinburgh had been for many years the leading medical school in Britain and Lister realised that the prestige of being professor would aid the acceptance of his ideas. He applied and was accepted. Now at the height of his powers, forty-two years old, tall, distinguished in a smart frock coat and confident Lister delivered his introductory address to an audience which included the frail but still immensely respected Professor Syme. He presented his 'germ' theory, paying appropriate respect to the pioneering work of Pasteur, and demonstrated by example that urine kept in open-ended flasks became putrid whereas in closed-end flasks it remained clear. He reasoned that the germs must have entered the open-ended flask from the air and then multiplied. He asked his audience to draw their own conclusion from the facts he presented. 'Do not let any authority shake your confidence in the knowledge so obtained,' he encouraged. Surgeons came from around the world to study Lister's ideas, but the majority of English surgeons remained sceptical. In 1871 Lister addressed a meeting of the British Medical Association where he forcefully asserted that those who dismissed his experimental proof were 'doubters' who cannot 'have enjoyed the advantages of sufficient education in either science or logic' – quite blunt for the time. Lister had realised that germs were not only found in the air; they were everywhere, on the hands of medical staff, on dressings, on a patient's bedding; and wherever they were found, they must be destroyed.

## A Move to London

Lister inspired the affection and respect of his students. He was a kind and considerate man who treated both patients and staff with respect. Once, while on a ward round, he found a small girl who was crying bitterly; one of the legs of her little rag doll had fallen off. Without a word Lister sat on her bed and sewed the leg back on for her. His most famous patient was Queen Victoria, who needed an operation to remove an abscess on her arm. The Queen's verdict was that he had 'most pleasantly performed a most disagreeable duty.'

There was therefore much regret when in 1877 at the end of his course of lectures he announced that he would be leaving Edinburgh to become Professor of Clinical Surgery at King's College Hospital in London.

At the age of fifty Lister was a famous surgeon when he returned to London, famous but still controversial. He had left Edinburgh, the most prestigious medical school in Britain, for the comparatively second rate King's. Why? It could only have been because he wanted to convince the doubters in London. He owed it to all the patients who were still dying unnecessarily from postoperative infections.

It proved an unhappy move at first. The English students to whom he now lectured did not share the inquiring minds and receptiveness to new ideas of his students in Edinburgh; they found his lectures 'boring' and deserted in droves. They did not want to learn about antisepsis; they just wanted to be coached through their exams. The nursing staff were also reluctant to accept the ideas of this upstart and some of his fellow surgeons were scathing in their criticism; one mocked his ideas by demanding the 'operating theatre door be quickly closed in case one of Mr Lister's germs creeps in.'

Gradually Lister won over the doubters. Surgery could now be carried out on parts of the body such as the abdomen which before would have been a death sentence for the patient. At long last Lister began to receive the honour and recognition his ideas had long deserved. He was made a baronet, Sir Joseph Lister, and in 1897 became Lord Lister. He was awarded honorary degrees by the universities of Oxford and Cambridge, the universities which as a Quaker he had been unable to attend. In 1898 he was given the Freedom of the City of Edinburgh.

At the age of 65 he retired as professor of the medical school; one of his first acts after this was to attend the celebration of Pasteur's 70th birthday in Paris. The two great men, who'd together done so much to fight infection, embraced in mutual regard. Shortly afterwards his beloved wife Agnes died, who had shared actively in all his research work. Lister was heartbroken, but lived on, suffering from increasingly ill heath for another twenty lonely years. He died in 1912.

## Lister's Legacy

Lister's great work, carried out during his years in Scotland, and the discoveries he made have revolutionised hospital practice and surgery. Many patients lived who previously would have died from postoperative infection. Surgeons could carry out operations which previously would have meant certain death for the patient. Despite these achievements, it was only in death that he at last received full recognition of his genius from his profession when *The Lancet* described him as 'the world's greatest surgeon.'

**Further Reading**
Laurence Farmer, *Master Surgeon: A Biography of Joseph Lister*

**Online Resources**
University of Adelaide
http://ebooks.adelaide.edu.au/l/lister/joseph/index.html

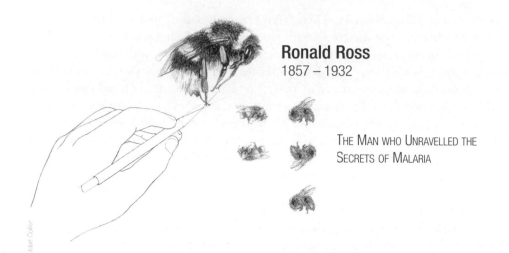

**Ronald Ross**
1857 – 1932

THE MAN WHO UNRAVELLED THE
SECRETS OF MALARIA

You may know the feeling: lying awake sweating in some tropical country, covered by just a sheet, when you hear the whining buzz of a mosquito. And then it stops and you know that somewhere on your body the mosquito is feasting on your blood. For most of us that just means an itchy bite when we wake up but for others it can be more serious. Mosquitoes carry the parasite which causes malaria, a disease which causes fever and can be fatal. Indeed, as many as a million people still die each year from malaria, out of the estimated two to three hundred million cases worldwide. Of those who die, ninety per cent live in Sub-Saharan Africa and many are children.

It was the work of one man, Ronald Ross, which revealed the link between malaria and mosquitoes. A Scot by ancestry, Ross was born in India and spent a large part of his life there. He lived long after the Enlightenment but embodied to the full the core principle of the use of experiment and reason to find the truth.

## Childhood in India

Ronald Ross was born in Almora in the Himalayas in 1857. His father, General Sir Campbell Grant Ross, served in the Indian Army, one of many Scots who went overseas in the service of the Empire. The family would regularly go into the hills in the summer to avoid the blazing heat of the plains. Usually his father would stay behind but when Ross was five years old his father had a bout of fever – malaria – from which he suffered regularly. It was felt he might benefit from a few weeks spent in the cool, clean air of the Himalayas.

They travelled by bullock cart, rumbling and racketing over the stony track. The journey took a number of days and each night they would camp in tents. Ahead of them were the giant mountains of the Himalayas, their summits snow-covered and their flanks carpeted by the bright colours of rhododendrons. When they arrived at the bungalow, Ross played with their pet leopard cub while his father lay groaning on a bed, his body wracked with fever. Ross was already aware of the ever-present threat of malaria. He realised that the accepted preventative measure, quinine, was ineffective as people who took it still suffered from the disease. He was sad to see his father suffering – surely there must be some cure?

When Ross was eight years old he was sent back to England for school. Both his father and his paternal grandfather were soldiers and Ross's ambition at that time was to join the army. He left Calcutta by boat, excited at the thought of a new country but unaware that he would not see India again for many years.

## School and Medical College

The voyage to England was made on a sailing ship and took four months as the Suez Canal had not yet been opened and the ship had to sail around the Cape of Good Hope on its homeward voyage. The separation from his family, typical of the time, was complete.

Ross stayed with his uncle and aunt in Ryde on the Isle of Wight where he also went to school. The school was tiny – Ross's class consisted of just himself and a young girl – and it was the first time he had received any formal education.

It was two years before he saw his parents again, when his father and mother came home on leave, spending a couple of months on the Isle of Wight with their young son.

When Ross was twelve he moved on to boarding school where his particular interest was natural history. He kept lizards and frogs as pets in the school greenhouse; for a time he even had a snake, until the headmaster found out and banished it. His interests were broad and he started painting water colours and writing verse, practices he continued throughout his life.

At seventeen it was time for Ross to choose a profession. His father had spent most of his military service in India and thought India would be ideal for his son. He was therefore horrified when Ross announced that he wanted to be a painter. 'That's not a real job,' exclaimed his father, 'you must train as a doctor and join the Indian Medical Service.'

Obediently, Ross entered training at St Bartholomew's Hospital, studying anatomy and physiology and assisting in surgery where he learned of the work of Lister and became convinced of the benefits of antisepsis. He was not keen on studying but managed to pass his exams to become a Member of the Royal College of Surgeons through some judicious last-minute selective cramming. He tried the same technique in the exams for the Indian Medical Service but his luck this time failed him and when the examiner asked him questions on poisons, a part of the syllabus he had left untouched, he lapsed into an embarrassed silence. Unsurprisingly he failed. His father was not best pleased!

## The Indian Medical Service

Ross decided to take a year out to work as a ship's surgeon. Life onboard ship, he reasoned, would give him plenty of time to study for his retake. He joined the *Alsatia*, a steamship working on the Atlantic crossing. He learned to deal with all sorts of emergencies. The most memorable was when the ship was being lashed by a severe Atlantic gale. She was hailed by a man holding onto the rail of a small tramp steamer which had come alongside. *'Have you a doctor?'* he shouted. *'We have a badly injured man on board.'* A small boat was launched into the storm-tossed seas and Ross climbed gingerly into it. They rowed through the wild seas towards the other ship where Ross was hauled aboard. He examined the patient and realised his arm had been badly crushed. He would have to amputate, cutting off the arm above the elbow. He had brought surgical instruments and chloroform, but a small cabin lit by a hurricane lamp swinging wildly with the rolling of the ship was far removed from the clinical operating theatres of St Bartholomew's. After successfully completing the operation and tying up the arteries, he then had to face the terrifying row back to the *Alsatia*. He had certainly earned his reward – a glass of whisky.

On his second attempt he passed the entrance exam to the Indian Medical Service with honours. He was sent on a three-month course in military medicine and surgery, where the students were taught about hygiene and sanitation – but strangely, as he later realised, not bacteriology. He would soon discover that one of the major problems facing him in India was malaria but even though a French surgeon, Charles Laveran, had recently discovered that malaria was caused by the presence of a parasite in the patient's blood – although no one knew its source – the students were left in ignorance.

In 1881, at the age of twenty-four, Ross returned to India on a troop ship. He was posted to the Military Hospital in Madras and billeted in the comfortable confines of a hotel surrounded by verandas and tree-shaded lawns. Most of the cases Ross had to deal with were soldiers who had malaria, but the only treatment he could offer was to prescribe quinine.

Later, in 1883 he became Acting Garrison Surgeon at Bangalore, sharing a bungalow with another officer. It was peaceful except for the high-pitched buzz of the mosquitoes which kept him awake at night. One evening while standing by his window, he noticed outside a tub full of water with a strange cloud on its surface. When he went outside to investigate he discovered that what he had thought was a mist was in fact a huge swarm of mosquitoes and realised that the little specks on the surface were probably mosquito grubs. He tipped the water on the ground and for the first time slept without the irritating buzz of mosquitoes. Were the mosquitoes breeding in the stagnant water? The next morning when he announced his discovery to his fellow officers his revelation was greeted by an unimpressed silence. By 1888, after five years' service, was given a year's furlough, or leave, in Britain. He used his time well, obtaining a Diploma in Public Health and in 1889 getting married. He also managed to have a novel called *Child of Ocean* published. He was certainly a man of many interests: painter, writer, polo player, violinist, fisherman and sailor. But had he actually achieved much with his life? He was not sure.

## Uncovering the Secrets of Malaria

On his return to India, Ross, who had recognised the toll exacted by malaria and the consequent recurrent debilitating fevers, resolved to carry out some serious medical research. Other interests he put aside. Surely prevention could be possible?

It had been observed that malaria occurred near swamps and stagnant water – the word 'malaria' comes from the medieval Latin '*mala aria*' or 'bad air' – and one theory was that the disease came from breathing the foul swamp air. Another was that malaria emanated from the water, possibly water contaminated by mosquitoes. Ross determined to discover the truth.

He was appointed Staff-Surgeon at Bangalore. He worked all day at the hospital and in his spare time continued his research. He used his training in bacteriology to examine the blood of patients infected with malaria in order to see if he could detect the malarial 'parasite' with his powerful new microscope.

It was not until 1895, after he had returned again from England, leaving his wife and young children there, that Ross began to make progress. He had discovered that there were little black granules in the red blood corpuscles of malaria sufferers. These black granules grew within the red corpuscles until the corpuscles split and the infection spread. These were the parasites Laveran had detected. He had also detected wispy flagella but did not know the role these played.

Ross now knew for certain that malaria was caused by parasites in the blood of the victim – he had seen them under his microscope. He had also injected healthy people with infected blood from malaria sufferers and could reproduce the symptoms. The parasites were definitely the source but how did they enter the blood in the first place? He suspected the culprit was the mosquito.

To us now it seems obvious but for Ross the problem needed many years of patient study. In England he had met Dr Patrick Manson, an authority on tropical diseases who encouraged Ross in his search for a connection between mosquitoes and malaria. Ross meticulously sent Manson regular reports of all his work, more than one hundred and ten letters in total, which have been preserved and form a valuable research archive.

The mosquito was the suspect but the problem was how to study its behaviour. To the amazement of his fellow officers Ross began breeding mosquitoes,. His somewhat unorthodox procedure was to introduce a mosquito under the mosquito netting of an infected volunteer and wait for it to bite; all too often it would not.

The patient had to lie still while the mosquito bit and then engorged itself with human blood. Ross, standing ready, would capture the mosquito and by squeezing its stomach with tweezers extract the blood. He then inspected the sample under a microscope to see whether he could trace the malarial parasite. He got his first perfect specimen of blood ingested by a mosquito from an extremely 'patient' patient who allowed the insect to suck for an amazing twenty minutes without once swatting or even disturbing it.

Ross observed that the parasites took the form of crescents in a patient's blood but spheres in the blood in a mosquito – somehow the mosquito was 'transforming' the parasite. He realised there were several different types of mosquito and not all were carriers. He asked to be transferred to a district where malaria was prevalent, and then trekked into the jungle to catch specimens of the malarial mosquitoes which he christened 'dapple-winged.'

In 1897 he succeeded in identifying plasmodia, malarial parasites, in the bodies of these mosquitoes, more properly called *Anopheles* mosquitoes, which had been fed with blood from infected patients. While he was dissecting the stomach of a mosquito under his microscope, a procedure he had carried out a thousand times before, he was astonished to find a perfectly circular body in the stomach of the mosquito, filled with a cluster of black granules: new parasites.

This was his 'eureka' moment! At last he understood the whole process: the crescents were the 'mother' cells and the flagella the 'fathers'; when they were joined they produced the spherical cells, called 'zygotes,' which were a fresh generation of parasites. These spores did not need to 'mate'; when in the red corpuscles of human blood they would split to infect more and more cells.

He now needed to discover how the mosquito infected the patient. It was proving difficult – perhaps unsurprisingly – to find enough human volunteers and Ross decided to work instead with birds, studying avian malaria. He managed to identify the parasite responsible for avian malaria and found that it was located in the salivary glands of the mosquito. He then managed to infect caged birds by exposing them to the bite of the mosquito. He had thus proved categorically that it was the bite of the mosquito which transferred the parasite from the mosquito to its victim.

He discovered that it was only the females which carried the parasite. They had a taste for blood and when they fed on the blood of an infected person they ingested the parasite, which they turned into spores; when they fed again in seven or so days the spore was injected into the victim through the salivary gland, thus spreading the infection. The male *Anopheles* mosquito on the other hand was a far less dangerous fellow, a vegetarian who fed harmlessly on the fluids from succulent plants. The female was indeed more deadly than the male!

He wrote of his findings to Patrick Manson who presented them at a meeting of the British Medical Association in Edinburgh in July 1898. It proved to be a sensation. The secrets of malaria and its causes were at last revealed. Ross's work now moved towards the eradication of malaria. He knew that malarial mosquitoes bred in stagnant water and that therefore the goal was to eradicate stagnant water, all the pools and puddles where the mosquitoes bred. This task he left to the Indian government.

## Later Years

Ross had practised as a doctor in the Indian Medical Service for nearly twenty years but in truth his interest had not been in doctoring but in research. Now that his research was successfully completed, he realised that although India had been a place of great discovery it was time for Ross and his family to move on.

Manson wanted to create a school of tropical medicine in Great Britain. Liverpool was chosen for the site and in 1899 Ross was appointed to the new Liverpool School of Tropical Medicine where he stayed for the next twelve years.

He worked not just as a lecturer but as a researcher. His first task was to visit Sierra Leone, known picturesquely, but sadly accurately, as 'the White Man's Grave' because of the prevalence of tropical diseases, principally malaria. The place abounded with mosquitoes, particularly after the rainy season when they bred in the stagnant pools.

He knew that eradication of the breeding grounds would provide the answer and returned home leaving the governor with the task, but when he revisited four years later he found little had been done. He hired a group of workmen and cleared the ground of all the cans and bottles which littered the area – on inspection many proved to be the homes of mosquito grubs – and cleared or covered the puddles. Tragically his improvements would not last long as the country soon reverted to its previous practices after his departure and the mosquitoes bred again.

He repeated the exercise in the area around the Suez Canal – this had been free of mosquitoes until the digging of the canal in 1877 had produced pools of stagnant fresh water which were the breeding areas for the mosquito – then the Panama Canal where he saved the lives of many involved in its construction, and then Spain and Cyprus. His expertise was in constant demand, but people still seemed unable to grasp the simple lesson of his discovery, that the breeding grounds of the mosquito should be eradicated. Nonetheless his reputation in scientific circles was of the highest order.

In 1902 he received the ultimate award, the Nobel Prize for Medicine, as well as many other awards and honorary degrees. He was knighted in 1911.

In the First World War he contributed his skills to the prevention of malaria among the forces fighting in Egypt and Greece, but sadly one of his two sons, Ronald Campbell Ross, was killed in the war and afterwards Ross lost some of his zest for life. He was a devoted father and was proud that some music he had composed many years before was played at the weddings of his daughters.

He spent his last years writing his memoirs which were published in 1923. In the same year the Ross Institute and Hospital for Tropical Diseases, later to become the London School of Hygiene and Tropical Medicine, was founded in London. It opened in 1926 with Ross as its Head, but after a year he retired. In 1931 his wife died. Exhausted by all his efforts Ross died the next year, appropriately enough at the Ross Institute.

## Ross's Legacy

Robert Ross was not born in Scotland and did not have the benefits of a Scottish education, but what he did have was the determination that hard work and meticulous research would solve the problem he devoted his life to solving, the same conviction which had motivated the great figures of the Enlightenment.

His work on the link between mosquitoes and malaria and on the eradication of the breeding grounds of mosquitoes has been of incalculable benefit to mankind.

Ross was more than a research scientist; he was a multi-talented man, a writer, a musician and a painter, and he penned the following lines to commemorate his success in defeating malaria:

> *This day relenting God*
> *Hath placed within my hand*
> *A wondrous thing: and God*
> *Be praised. At his command*
> *Seeking his secret deeds,*
> *With tears and toiling breath,*
> *I find thy cunning seeds,*
> *O million-murdering Death.*
> *I know this little thing*
> *A myriad men will save*
> *O Death where is thy sting?*
> *Thy victory, O Grave?*

**Further Reading**
John Rowland, *The Mosquito Man: The Story of Ronald Ross*

**Online Resources**
Centers for Disease Control and Prevention
http://www.cdc.gov/malaria/about/history/ross.html

**Elsie Inglis**
1864 – 1917

THE STORY OF A
MODERN WOMAN*

*The title of an unpublished novel
found in Dr Elsie Inglis's papers
after her death.*

While Elsie Inglis lived long after the Enlightenment, her exceptional achievement was built on Enlightenment principles and values. She qualified as a doctor – remarkable in the days when the main aim of a young lady was still to 'make a good match' – and founded the Scottish Women's Hospitals which provided battlefield hospitals staffed solely by women and by their example not only improved the quality of battlefield care but also significantly advanced the cause of female equality.

She owed her determination to eschew the conventional in part to her parents who were certainly enlightened in their views of the education of young ladies, believing, unusually for the time, that a daughter was entitled to just as good an education as a son and should not just be taught the skills of sewing, piano playing and conversation which in a Jane Austen novel would attract the 'right' husband. They also imbued her with a strong religious belief and a confidence that with such belief anything can be achieved.

Inglis fully justified their conviction. Her self-confident determination helped to bring about a dramatic change in the role of women in medicine and in society.

### Youth in India

Scottish by birth, Inglis's father, John Forbes David Inglis, served in the Indian Civil Service. Like Ronald Ross's father and many other Scots, he had gone to serve in the Empire and would complete thirty-six years of service in India with just one period of home leave. Her mother, Harriet, was eighteen when she married John whom she met at a dance; he was immediately attracted to the fresh young girl in a white muslin dress with large purple flowers. In 1858 John had his one furlough when he and his young wife made the hazardous four-month journey in a bullock cart from Lahore to Calcutta with their infant children to catch the ship for a further four month's voyage to England. During this time the Indian Mutiny broke out and John chose to leave his young family in England until the troubles were over. Five years of separation passed before Harriet and the children returned to India.

DR. ELSIE INGLIS, 1916
Dr Elsie Inglis

Wellcome Library, London

A year after Harriet's return Elsie Inglis was born, in a hill station in the Himalayas. Like other British families, the Inglis family lived in the plains during the winter but retired to the relative coolness of the hills for the summer.

Inglis spent her first twelve years in India. She had happy memories of her summers in the hills when her father would visit and the times when after a reading from the Scriptures and prayers with her mother - and a breakfast cup of cocoa – father and daughter would go off on long walks together. She was her father's special favourite.

At an early age Inglis showed her inclination towards medicine when after spots had been laboriously painted on the faces, arms and legs of their toys she declared to her young siblings that their dolls, forty or so, had caught measles. The embryonic doctor found a cure and gradually the spots were wiped clean and the dolls recovered.

In 1876 the family moved to Tasmania before returning to Scotland in 1878 and settling in Edinburgh. Inglis was again showing signs of her eventual career – her mother wrote that on the long voyage home from Tasmania she 'found occupation for herself in helping to nurse sick children.'

### Medical Training in Edinburgh

For four years Inglis attended the rather splendidly titled Edinburgh Institution for the Education of Young Ladies, a prestigious school for girls located in Charlotte Square, before embarking on her career in medicine. With her father's support she enrolled as a medical student in 1886, just a year after her mother's death, at the new Edinburgh School of Medicine for Women founded by Dr Sophia Jex-Blake, the pioneer of medical education for women in Scotland.

In 1869 Jex-Blake had applied for medical training at Edinburgh by enrolling for courses in botany and natural history. Her application was considered by the University Senate and approved, making Edinburgh the first medical school in Britain to accept women, but the achievement was short-lived. The decision had hardly won universal acceptance. The anatomy professor gave his opinion that the presence of women would affect discipline, would 'repulse' men and would inhibit the teaching of anatomy and requested the Senate to make arrangements for separate classes for women. The Senate weakly agreed. The female students took legal action to compel the Senate to apply their original ruling and won their case, only to be overturned on appeal. The time for women had not yet come. Jex-Blake eventually graduated in Switzerland, but she returned to Edinburgh to practise and to advance the claims of women by founding her school.

In 1886 the College of Physicians and Surgeons of Edinburgh gave way and allowed the teaching of women – but not at the Royal Infirmary. Women were to be taught at Leith Hospital. It was not until 1889 that women were given equal rights and status with men in the study of medicine. Progress was slow. In 1881 there had been just four female doctors practising in the whole of Scotland, but even by the start of the twentieth century this had only risen to thirty. It was the demand for doctors in the First World War which finally advanced the cause of women but still more years would pass before there was anything close to true equality of opportunity.

After three years at the School Inglis was outraged when two students were dismissed by Jex-Blake for supporting a fellow student who had been accused of dishonourable conduct when she had successfully appealed to the examiner after being wrongly failed in an examination. Inglis believed the real issue was whether women should have the same rights to appeal against injustice as men. Outraged by this perceived injustice, she left the School and with her father's help she set up the Edinburgh Medical College for Women.

Inglis completed her own medical studies at the Glasgow Royal Infirmary and then headed down to London where she was appalled by the standard of care for women. She joined the New Hospital for Women which would later become the Elizabeth Garrett Anderson Hospital for Women.


## Healthcare – and Votes – for Women


Inglis returned to Edinburgh just in time to help nurse her father in the last few weeks before he died. She was very close to her father and it would be some years before she got over his death.

She decided more must be done for the medical care and teaching of women in Scotland. What was needed, she determined, was a hospital run by women for women. Accordingly, in 1901 in partnership with Dr Jessie MacGregor, a friend from her time at the School, she set up the Hospice, a small maternity hospital for women in the High Street in Edinburgh with a dispensary and out-patients department. Inglis secured further qualifications as a Lecturer in Midwifery and in Gynaecology so that she could teach classes of young medical students and nurses, thus transforming the Hospice into a specialised teaching hospital for maternity. Aware of the problems of those who could not afford the high cost of medical care, Inglis would offer free treatment, even sometimes providing lodging in her house for poor patients. Inglis was very moved by the women she treated. One female patient she had visited and ordered to bed, instead remained up because her husband had come home drunk and taken the bed. As a doctor Inglis's proposed remedy was simple, albeit unorthodox: 'He ought to be horse-whipped.'

In 1907 she was offered the position of senior consultant at the Bruntsfield Hospital for Women. By now she was unquestionably Edinburgh's leading female doctor. In 1911 the Hospice was merged with the Bruntsfield and it was decided that the Bruntsfield would handle medical and surgical cases while the Hospice looked after maternity cases and child welfare. This was a sensible solution for Inglis, who in 1911 proudly showed Queen Mary around the new surgical unit on her visit to Edinburgh.

Inglis believed that women would never receive equal treatment until they obtained an equal say at the ballot box. For some years she had been a supporter of the suffragette movement, speaking and lecturing at their meetings. There were a number of different suffragette movements in Scotland and in 1909 they were united under the umbrella of one foundation. Inglis was a co-founder and Honorary Secretary of the new Scottish Federation of Women's Suffrage Societies and in her new role travelled extensively over Scotland speaking to the various suffragette organisations.

### First World War: Serbia

When war broke out in August 1914 Inglis realised the role which women could play in the provision of medical care and so formed the Scottish Women's Hospital Committee. She proposed setting up medical units, staffed solely by women, to provide medical help at the battlefront. Needless to say, the reactionaries at the British War Office turned down the proposal, but the French were more open-minded and in December 1914, the first Scottish Women's army hospital was set up with two hundred beds in the medieval abbey of Royaumont, not far from Paris.

In January 1915 a second medical team set sail for Serbia, which in 1915 was in a poor state. The Austrians had departed after their defeat in October 1914, leaving behind vast numbers of Austrian and Serbian casualties. Typhus was rampant. In April the doctor in charge of the hospital set up by the Scottish Women's Committee fell ill with diphtheria and Inglis herself went out to take charge.

Until her departure all her time and energies had been devoted to the creation of the Scottish Women's Hospitals. Inglis was not just an idealist but a true professional who demanded the highest standards from her staff. She was a fair employer but could be a wee bit of a tyrant if she felt standards had slipped.

At the time that Inglis arrived in Serbia the Scottish Women's Hospital unit was running three hospitals; a surgical unit to deal with battlefield injuries, a special unit dealing with the typhus outbreak and the third a general unit – a total of five hundred and seventy beds for which they were hopelessly under resourced. She threw herself into the work with enthusiasm, enjoying the opportunity of carrying out surgery on adult men, an opportunity denied her before. She also found the time to help set up three more Scottish Women's Hospitals in Serbia. The main problems they faced were sanitation and water. In one hospital the raw sewage would drain through holes in the floor of the ward to a ditch beneath and thence to a cesspit which required regular emptying – if not emptied the sewage would rapidly back up. The supply of fresh, clean water was a constant problem as their hospitals used much more than comparable Serbian units. Water was often only available by bringing it in carts.

Serbia was of key strategic importance during the war because it formed a key link in the railway between Germany and Turkey, which if opened would enable the rapid movement of men and materials between the two armies. Despite its strategic importance no British troops had been sent to help the Serbs who were fearful of an expected invasion by German and Austrian troops. The Scottish Women's Hospitals took steps to deal with the anticipated heavy casualties.

At the end of September 1915, the invasion came. The Bulgarians joined the Central Powers and a huge army of four hundred thousand invaded, rapidly overrunning Serbia. Inglis vowed the hospital staff would stay, writing home that 'As long as the Serbians fight, we'll stick to them.'

Most of the staff of the Scottish Women's Hospitals were evacuated to a new hospital set up near the place where the Serbs had successfully resisted invasion in 1914, but this time the forces against them were too great. Again they had to retreat, shipping the wounded out on crowded trains or bullock carts. The fall of Serbia became inevitable and the remnants of the Serbian army withdrew through snow and blizzards over the mountains of Montenegro and Albania. Conditions were dreadful and more than one hundred thousand soldiers and civilians died, including one of the Scottish nurses.

Inglis and a few of her staff remained behind to look after the Serbian casualties, eventually being taken prisoner by the invading German forces. Her hospital was commandeered by the Germans for the German wounded and she and her remaining colleagues were taken to work at the prisoner of war hospital. The winter was bitterly cold and there was little food and what there was did not amount to much: black bread and bean soup.

In December a number of the staff took an offer of repatriation, but Inglis and a few others stayed on – there were still patients for whom they had to care. In February 1916 Inglis and her last remaining colleagues were taken under armed guard to Vienna and they were only released and allowed to return home on the diplomatic intervention of the United States.

Elsie Inglis had learned to love and admire the Serbs and she vowed that she would return after the war to help them set up hospitals. In April 1916 she was awarded the Order of the White Eagle by the Serbs in gratitude for her heroic efforts.

### First World War: Russia

Inglis was home in Edinburgh for six months. Undeterred by her harrowing experiences, she worked tirelessly to expand the work of the Scottish Women's Hospitals, helping to raise funds for a hospital in Russia to work with a Free Serbian division fighting with the Russians. In August 1916 she went to Russia to set up a field hospital for the Serbs. When Inglis and her team arrived in Odessa they learned that the news was bad; the Serbs had lost ten thousand men in fierce fighting and there were only four thousand survivors. There was a huge demand for medical supplies to treat the wounded. Inglis left the wounded to the care of the Red Cross and with her unit moved on up to the Front where they joined the Russians. They had no sooner reached the Front than the Germans advanced. The Russian forces were soon under attack and, suffering further heavy losses, had to retreat. The medical team carried their baggage on carts through a night sky lit by the bursts of heavy artillery fire, transporting the sick to the trains. The retreat lasted for four days. They had to retreat three further times, each time setting up temporary hospitals to treat the wounded. Inglis herself worked tirelessly and with unquenchable faith; one of the Russian soldiers she had helped said, 'She was loved amongst us as a queen and respected as a saint.'

After a bitter winter came the upheaval of the Russian Revolution. Inglis was worried about the fate of the remnants of the Serbian regiment in the chaos of a Russia embroiled in the turmoil of revolt. Despite deteriorating health she bombarded the Foreign Office in London with telegrams and in October, largely as a result of her efforts, she received notice that her beloved Serbs would be sent to England. Inglis cabled her reply: 'On our way home. Everything satisfactory, and all well except me.'

This was a massive understatement. Inglis had driven herself too hard. Her health had declined badly and she was dying from cancer. She raced through the wintry countryside on unheated trains with the barest minimum of food in hopes of getting to Archangel before the ice set in and ships would not be able to leave.

The voyage home was harsh. There were violent storms, the convoy was scattered and there was an ever present danger of icebergs. She arrived in Newcastle on 23 November accompanied by the medical unit and the Serbian division. She bravely summoned up the strength to say farewell to the Serbian officers, her friends. She had fulfilled her mission and exhausted, died three days later. She remained resolute in her faith to the end. Her work on earth might be complete but as she said to her niece, 'It is grand to think of beginning a new work over there.' She lied in state at St Giles' Cathedral before being buried in Edinburgh.

### Votes for Women

As a result not just of the suffragette movement but also of the contribution made by women to the war effort, attitudes to equality had changed and in the

1918 Representation of the People's Act, women over the age of thirty were given the vote. However, the majority of the young women who had served in the war or worked in the munitions factories were still disenfranchised. Not until the 1928 Act did women achieve the right to vote at twenty-one.

## Inglis's Legacy

Dr Elsie Inglis was instrumental in advancing the cause of women, both in the medical profession and in society at large. She demonstrated an immense determination to succeed and fought hard to give the very best medical care to her patients in the most intolerable conditions. She had founded a hospital for women and the Hospice would in time be renamed the Elsie Inglis Memorial Hospital, which name it kept for just over fifty years until 1988. Her name now lives on in the Elsie Inglis maternity ward in the Western General.

If one of the tenets of the Enlightenment was that women should be treated equally with men and given the same opportunities, then Elsie Inglis through the force of her personality had advanced their cause immeasurably. Although she did not live to see enfranchisement for women enacted, she was aware that the bill giving the vote to women had passed its second reading in the House of Commons and was on the way to the statute book before she died .

The Scottish Women's Committee sent more than one thousand female doctors, nurses and orderlies to the war zones and there were eventually fourteen hospital units working in France, Serbia, Corsica, Salonika, Romania, Russia and Malta. These were run to the high standards demanded by Inglis and had a better record of preventing death through infection than the traditional military hospitals. Winston Churchill asserted that she and her nurses would 'shine in history.' *The Scotsman* wrote:

> *In Serbia and elsewhere, Scotland is associated with the work of Dr Elsie Inglis and her colleagues on the battlefield and behind the lines, where they tended the wounded and helped succour the helpless. Dr Inglis was not only the intrepid and inspiring leader on the actual scene of the work; her enthusiasm, energy, and experience were to a large extent the motive power which has created a vast organisation, of which, as a voluntary effort and an expression of humanity, any country might be proud.*

**Further Reading**
Leah Leneham, *Elsie Inglis: Founder of Battlefront Hospitals Run Entirely by Women*
Eva Shaw McLaren, *Elsie Inglis: The Woman with the Torch*

**Online Resources**
Education Scotland
http://www.educationscotland.gov.uk/scotlandshistory/20thand21stcenturies/elsieinglis/index.asp

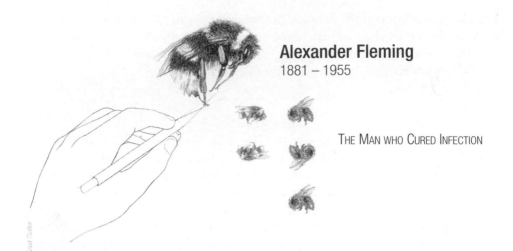

## Alexander Fleming
1881 – 1955

THE MAN WHO CURED INFECTION

The necessary conditions for scientific discovery are painstaking experiment, careful observation and meticulous measurement assessed by a mind which is receptive and unprejudiced. Before penicillin, infection was a great killer. The work of Lister – showing the need for cleanliness and antiseptic procedures to avoid the spread of infection – had done much to prevent surgical wounds from becoming infected, but if gangrene set in there was little a doctor could do but amputate the infected flesh. Wounds suffered in battle often became infected by the filth of the battlefield and would then usually prove fatal so that deaths from disease often far outnumbered the deaths from enemy action.

Doctors could diagnose illnesses such as pneumonia but they had no cure to offer and the world was searching for a cure for infection.

Alexander Fleming, a Scottish farmer's son, changed all that, providing a cure and bringing about a revolution in medicine, not through some inspired insight but by painstaking experiment and careful observation.

### Becoming a Doctor

Fleming was born in 1881 at Lochfield Farm, four miles north of Darvel, a little town set in an Ayrshire valley. The farm where Fleming grew up was in the hills, sheltered from the north winds by a ridge, with rough pasture and heather covered moors beyond and reached by a narrow track that climbed steeply from the river valley below.

Fleming was a common name in the area; it came originally from the Flemish settlers who had fled from Flanders to Scotland to avoid persecution by the Catholics and had set up in Ayrshire originally as weavers or lacemakers.

His father, Hugh Fleming, was a farmer, as his father had been before him, and he leased his farm from the Earl of Loudon. Hugh had four children by his

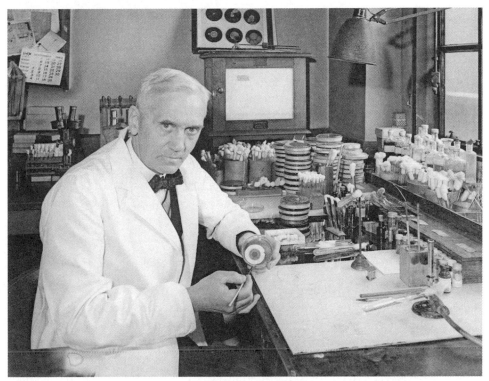

Alexander Fleming in his laboratory

firstwife and then after her death a further four by his second wife, Grace, who was Alexander's mother.

As a young boy Fleming helped on the farm and roamed the moors. Daily life meant fetching water in a bucket from the spring, feeding the animals and milking the cows. In spring there was lambing, then in May it was time to cut peat and lay the slabs out to dry for later use as fuel. In summer there was haymaking. Living conditions were very different from those today; there was no piped water, no bathroom and no indoor toilet; lighting was by paraffin lamp and the farm was heated by burning the sweet-smelling peat.

Hugh worried about his sons. His eldest, also called Hugh, would take over the farm, and the second boy, Tom, was a clever lad who had won a place at Glasgow University as a medical student and would become a doctor. But what would be the future for his three youngest boys? Fleming was just seven years old when his father died. He had started his education at the Loudon Moor School where he learned to 'read, write, spell and count.' He loved 'that wee school up the hill, that's where they really taught you something!' At the age of ten he moved to the village school at Darvel and with his brother walked the four miles there and back each day – not for him being dropped off by his mother in her four by four! When he was fourteen he went to London to join his elder brother Tom, who had by then qualified as a doctor, and went to the Polytechnic School in Regent Street.

When Fleming left school he worked briefly as a clerk earning the princely sum of tuppence halfpenny (roughly one new penny!) an hour, but he did not enjoy the work and so when the Boer War started in 1899 he joined up as a soldier in the London Scottish Rifle Regiment. He did not serve in the war but became a very good rifle shot. At the age of twenty he had a stroke of luck. His uncle died, leaving him the then sizeable sum of two hundred and fifty pounds. Tom persuaded him to use the money to study to become a doctor. There was a problem; he did not have the necessary entrance exams. Fleming took lessons in the evening and despite the fact he had not studied for many years passed all the sixteen subjects he needed, coming second overall in the exams set by the College of Preceptors. With such a success he could pick his medical school and he chose St Mary's Hospital; because he 'had once played water polo against them!'

## St Mary's Hospital

Although there had been great strides forward in the previous fifty years, medicine was still quite primitive when Fleming started his studies.

One major step was the first glimmering of understanding about vaccination. Edward Jenner had shown in 1796 that inoculating with cowpox gave protection against smallpox but had not understood why. Pasteur, the famous French scientist, discovered that different diseases were caused by specific bacteria which are single-cell organisms that replicate by dividing; they come in two main types, rod-shaped bacilli and round-shaped cocci. Cocci again come in two main types: those which grow in clusters like a bunch of grapes, called staphylococci, and those which grow in chains called streptococci.

Pasteur also discovered that by inoculation of a 'dead' sample of a natural organism he could provide a 'natural' immunity from a future infection by the same organism as the body had created its own defences. He called this process vaccination and his immunising agents vaccines in recognition of Jenner's earlier work. By the time Fleming entered medical training, doctors had begun to identify the different bacteria which caused specific illnesses – pneumococcus caused pneumonia, for example – but were still a long way from finding cures.

Fleming entered St Mary's as a medical student in October 1901 and qualified as a doctor five years later, having won nearly every prize on offer. He was offered a job by St Mary's – it is said so they could keep him in their rifle team – and he joined the new Inoculation Department which had been set up by Almoth Wright.

## Vaccination

Wright was an amazing man; he was fluent in at least four languages, could quote large tracts of poetry and was qualified as both a doctor and a lawyer. In case that was not enough he had also passed the exams for the Civil Service.

Wright was fascinated by the concept of vaccination and believed it would provide a cure for all infections. He had first become a Professor in the Army Medical Service at the time of the Boer War. Typhoid was a severe problem and Wright recommended that all the soldiers who were going to South Africa to fight the Boers should be vaccinated against the disease. When he was unable to persuade the War Office to accept his advice, he left the army in disgust. Then he joined St Mary's as Professor and set up the Inoculation Department to research and produce vaccines. Intelligent, arrogant and certain in his opinions: this was the man for whom Fleming would work.

Wright understood that vaccination stimulated the natural defences of the body to provide a cure for bacterial diseases and believed that vaccination could be the cure for all diseases. He set out to prove his ideas in a process of trial and error. His team would try to identify a particular organism, grow it in a culture, kill it and then use the dead bacteria as a vaccine, often testing the dose on themselves. Wright realised that the process worked through stimulating white blood cells to 'swallow' the bacteria. Fleming became an enthusiastic supporter of his ideas and the Inoculation Department grew within the hospital, making and selling vaccines and treating patients. Vaccine therapy was the new 'wonder' treatment – there was, after all, nothing else on offer.

With the outbreak of the First World War, Almoth Wright was sent to France to set up a laboratory and he took Fleming with him. There Fleming saw at first hand how little doctors could do to deal with the spread of infectious diseases. Antiseptic was used to control infection but in practice often made it worse and Fleming realised this was because the antiseptic was killing the white cells which 'ate' the bacteria. It was as a result of Fleming's work that Wright recommended that antiseptics should not be used and that instead the wound should be carefully cleaned, washed with a salt solution and then bound with a sterile dressing and this change in procedure brought some benefits.

## The Discovery of Penicillin

After the war Fleming returned to England and St Mary's to work again in the Inoculation Department. Some years later, in 1928, he made his great discovery. Fleming was painstaking in the experiments he carried out, but the discovery came not as a result of a planned series of experiments but by accident.

Bacteria was grown in special containers called petri dishes, flat circular dishes about ten centimetres across and three deep with a glass lid. In the dish was placed the sterile jelly or agar used to grow the bacteria. Then a small amount of the sample, for example the pus from a boil, was put on the surface of the agar and the lid was closed. After a few days the bacteria would grow and could then be examined under a microscope.

If the lid was taken off there was always a danger that the sample would become spoilt by contact with other bacteria. Fleming was not a tidy worker and would leave used petri dishes lying around his laboratory, sometimes for weeks. He always looked carefully at the old dishes and one day he noticed that one had become spoiled by a greenish mould; he also noticed that the area around where the mould had grown was free of bacteria. Somehow the mould had killed the bacteria.

Fleming showed his discovery to Wright who showed little interest. He believed the cure for infection which they were seeking would come from vaccines, not from some strange mould.

Fleming called the mould 'penicillin' and by experiment proved that it would kill many different types of bacteria. Ironically his main interest in penicillin was not as a potential cure for infections but as an agent that would kill bacteria and enable him to produce purer vaccines. Penicillin was kept alive but its true potential was not yet realised. This would require the input of others and would come from Oxford.

### Oxford: Howard Florey and Ernest Chain

In 1939 Howard Florey, a Professor at Oxford University, and Ernest Chain, a German Jew who had come to Britain to avoid the Nazi horrors, were working on a cure for infection. They read the papers Fleming had written ten years before describing penicillin and decided to investigate. Using a sample of penicillin mould they managed to crystallise penicillin as a brown powder. Florey then proved, as Fleming had done before, that penicillin would destroy bacteria but did not harm living tissues. Florey then took his tests further.

He carried out the tests which Fleming had not: he tried penicillin on patients, or more correctly on mice. Eight white mice were injected with a fatal dose of virulent streptococci bacteria and of these, four were injected with penicillin. The four mice which had not been given penicillin died, the four which had been given penicillin lived. The experiment was repeated the next day with the same results.

These successes encouraged Florey to try penicillin on humans. In February 1941 a programme of giving penicillin to selected patients who had apparently hopeless cases of infection was begun. The results were amazing. Patients who had no hope of a cure were recovering. Florey realised that penicillin could be the wonder cure for infection, the discovery of which had been the holy grail of medicine for so many years.

He wanted to carry out more trials but the problem was getting hold of sufficient penicillin. Florey needed help. Because of the war there were no resources available in Britain to develop penicillin and so he enlisted the support of the big chemical companies in the United States which were soon producing penicillin on a large scale. The era of the antibiotic had arrived.

Florey and Chain had completed the work begun by Fleming. The discovery depended as much on his original observation as on their painstaking experiments. All three were knighted for their work and they shared the Nobel Prize for Medicine in 1945. Fleming died in 1955.

## Fleming's Legacy

It was Fleming's chance look at an old petri dish, his observation that the green mould growing on the surface had killed the bacteria around it and his realisation of what that meant which were crucial in the initial discovery of penicillin, an antibiotic which would in time bring millions a cure from infection. But penicillin's true value might never have been realised without the vital work of Florey and Chain. That they shared the Nobel Prize is a fair reflection of the contribution all three men made.

**Further Reading**
Gwyn Macfarlane, *Alexander Fleming: The Man and the Myth*

**Online Resources**
Nobel Prize Site
http://www.nobelprize.org/nobel_prizes/medicine/laureates/1945/fleming-bio.html

'A MAXIMA AD MINIMA' (From the Greatest to the Least)
Eduardo Paolozzi - 1998
Kew Gardens, Londo

# Poets & Writers

# POETS & WRITERS

**Robert Fergusson**
*ILL-FATED GENIUS*

**Robert Burns**
*SCOTLAND'S NATIONAL BARD*

**James Hogg**
*THE ETTRICK SHEPHERD*

**Sir Walter Scott**
*POET AND NOVELIST WHOSE STORIES AWAKENED INTEREST
IN SCOTLAND'S COLOURFUL HISTORY*

**Thomas Carlyle**
*PHILOSOPHER AND HISTORIAN*

**Robert Louis Stevenson**
*NOVELIST, TRAVEL WRITER AND POET*

**John Buchan**
*NOVELIST TO GOVERNOR-GENERAL*

# Part 4 • Poets & Writers

### Brothers in the Muse

The Enlightenment was characterised by the ideas and the writings of the prominent philosophers. The art of writing was not, however, confined to these great minds. The Enlightenment included the rich Scottish literary tradition of poets and novelists such as Robert Burns, Robert Fergusson and Sir Walter Scott, who enhanced the Enlightenment and contributed to the wealth of world literature.

It is somewhat ironic that whereas David Hume worked hard to lose his Scots accent and to write in 'standard' English as befitted a citizen of 'North Britain,' even changing his name from 'Home' to aid the English with their pronunciation, Scotland's poets were revelling in writing, not just in English but in Scots, and it is their poems in the 'Scotch tongue' which made their fame as writers.

One of the first poets of the Enlightenment to write in Scots, and an inspiration and example for both Fergusson and Burns, was Allan Ramsay, the father of the famous painter.

### Allan Ramsay the Poet (1684–1743)

Ramsay's father was born in Leadhills in Lanarkshire in 1684. When his mother died in 1700 he moved to Edinburgh to study wig-making, a useful trade in those days when no gentleman was properly dressed without his wig. Politically, Ramsay was a Jacobite supporter and soon after the Act of Union formed a society called the Easy Club whose members were sympathetic to the Jacobite Rising of 1715. He soon began writing poetry and in 1721 abandoned his trade as a wig maker and set up premises in the High Street as a bookseller and publisher, where he started the first circulating library in Britain, providing a source of books to the philosophers and thinkers who were developing the ideas of the Enlightenment. Rumours spread that he was supplying sinful works which would subvert the populace, with books being 'lent out, for an easy price, to young boyes [sic], servant weemen [sic] of the better sort, and gentlemen, and vice and obscenity dreadfully propagated.' But mysteriously when the authorities arrived at the bookshop to inspect the contents of the shelves, they found only religious tracts and holy works!

Ramsay's new career allowed him greater time to develop his burgeoning reputation as a poet and man of letters, publishing *Evergreen*, a collection of Scots poems and songs which would provide the inspiration for the Scots poems of Robert Fergusson and Robert Burns. In his son's words, his poems showed 'the power of uncultivated genius.'

He wrote a number of books of verse and also a play, *The Gentle Shepherd*, which was performed in 1725. Daringly, he then opened a theatre but this proved a step too far; he had offended the Calvinist tradition still prevalent and the theatre was forced to close. This treatment coloured his views of Calvinist thinking and he wrote a number of poems railing against what he perceived as the arrant hypocrisy of Calvinist doctrine.

Ramsay died in 1743 but through his poems he had provided the inspiration not just for Burns, but also for the 'tragic' Fergusson, described by Burns as his 'brother in the Muse.'

# Robert Fergusson
## 1750–1774

ILL-FATED GENIUS

*O thou, my elder brother in misfortune,*
*By far my elder brother in the Muse,*
*With tears I pity thy unhappy fate!*
*Why is the Bard unfitted for the world,*
*Yet has so keen a relish of its pleasures?*

—Robert Burns, 'Lines on Fergusson'

Robert Fergusson was an archetypal genius. He was well educated thanks to the belief of his parents in the virtues of a good education and in part also to receiving the benefit of a scholarship. He joined in the literary and artistic life of Edinburgh as a member of the societies which met regularly to discourse, discuss and declaim. He knew the classics, but wrote his best work in Scots in the tradition of Allan Ramsay, and he died in a madhouse at twenty four.

## The Edinburgh of Robert Fergusson

Robert Fergusson was born in Cap and Feather Close in Edinburgh on 5 September 1750. His father, William Fergusson, and his mother Elizabeth had moved to Edinburgh from Aberdeen in 1748 in search of work. William was a clerk but the jobs he found were poorly paid and the couple had to struggle to bring up their four children.

Edinburgh was a bustling, noisy, smelly medieval city centred on the High Street. The New Town was yet to be built and all the effluent of the city still drained into the Nor Loch. Life in a close would have been very basic, with many people crowded together and continuous tumult and bustle. Living in one room, the duty of the youngest every evening was to empty the chamber pot onto the street. At ten o'clock in the evening a drum would beat, the signal for households to empty their chamber pots and their slop buckets into the street with a cry of 'Gardyloo!' From there this deluge would trickle down to the Nor Loch. 'Hud yur hande' would come from the street below if someone was passing. The streets stank with the smell of the mess until the 'scavengers' swept them clean the next morning, a daily routine recorded by Fergusson in his poem 'Auld Reekie':

> On stair wi tub, or pat in hand,
> The barefoot housemaids loo to stand,
> That antrin fock may ken how snell
> Auld Reekie will at morning smell:
> Then with an inundation big as
> The burn that 'neath the Nor Loch Brig is,
> They kindly shower Edina's roses,
> To quicken and regale our noses.

Scots Glossary: AULD REEKIE/EDINBURGH - from the smoke rising from the city, which could be seen for miles; PAT/POT; LOO/LOVE; ANTRIN FOCK/DIFFERENT FOLK; KEN/KNOW; SNELL/BITTER; NOR LOCH BRIG/NOR LOCH BRIDGE; EDINA'S ROSES/THE FLOWERS OF EDINBURGH - referring to the chamber pots being emptied into the streets.

Both of Fergusson's parents believed in the need for good schooling and after six months spent at Mr Philip's private school in Niddry's Wynd he attended the Royal High School, where he learned Latin. As a child, Fergusson was sickly and often missed school through illness.

When he was eleven years old he won a 'mortification,' or bursary, for the Grammar School in Dundee. This bursary had been set up by one David Fergusson in 1695 to provide education for two poor children with the Fergusson name. A further, quite proper stipulation was that the student 'be boarded with one of the surname of Fergusson …. and, failing of that, in any honest house.'

## The University of St Andrews

At the age of fourteen Fergusson applied to have his bursary extended and moved on to continue his studies at the University of St Andrews, which was Scotland's oldest university city, but by the time Fergusson went there it had become a 'sleepy and sordid place' in which 'only ale-houses abounded.'

The main business of the city was the manufacture of golf balls, made by stuffing a great quantity of feathers into a leather case using an iron rod. The dust produced in the process often brought on chest illness and consumption in the poor workers.

The university had only around a hundred students and no great reputation for learning. Greek, Latin, mathematics, logic and philosophy were the subjects taught, to which Fergusson added the writing of humorous verses, probably to brighten his life. Scholars with bursaries had to work harder than those who paid fees but they did have one advantage: their poor food was supplemented by a ration of ale.

At university he demonstrated a good sense of humour. One of the tasks of the bursary students was to officiate at morning and evening prayers. With his melodic singing voice, Fergusson was required more often than most to rise early for the morning service, at which one task was to recount the names of those to be mentioned in prayer. Early one morning Fergusson solemnly intoned 'remember in prayer a young man, [here today], who, from the sudden effects of inebriety, there appears but small hope of recovery.' The assembly dissolved inappropriately in laughter.

At the age of fourteen Fergusson wrote at St. Andrews his earliest surviving poem entitled 'Elegy on the Death of Mr David Gregory, Professor of Mathematics', an elegy, comical yet beautiful, written in the format of the Standard Habbie, the six line elegiac stanza of Scots poetry later adopted by Burns, on the death of one of the university's professors of mathematics, David Gregory:

> *Now mourn, ye college masters a'!*
> *And fare your een a tear lat fa,*
> *Fam'd Gregory death has taken awa*
> *Without remeid;*
> *The skaith ye've met wi's nae that sma,*
> *Sin Gregory's deid.*

Scots: Een/eyes; remeid/remedy;
skaith/trouble.

Robert Fergusson
Royal Mile Edinburgh
(Annand, 2004)
photo: Thomas Haywood

At St Andrews Fergusson came under the influence of William Wilkie, the professor of natural history, and something of an eccentric, eschewing regular washing and clean bed-linen, both of which he regarded as unhealthy, even, it is said, to the extent of admonishing a hostess who proffered clean sheets. Wilkie was himself an Enlightenment figure, writing in both English and Scots, and also a farmer who put his theoretical knowledge to good use and could discuss the successful growing of turnips with his fellow farmers with the same ease with which he discussed literature with his students. Wilkie was an early mentor to Fergusson who spent two summers on his model farm in Fife making copies of the professor's lectures.

## Back to Edinburgh and the Enlightenment

Fergusson completed his studies at St Andrews in 1768. By then, his father William had died, and his mother moved to cheaper lodgings. Early the next year he spent six months on the farm of his maternal uncle, John Forbes, in Aberdeenshire but unsurprisingly this frail and unconventional eighteen-year-old and his robust and rustic farmer uncle proved incompatible, unfortunately since his uncle's support would have been invaluable during his later illness.

Fergusson returned to Edinburgh where he had to find work to support his mother and sister and so became a copyist in the Commissary Records Office, his duties being to make copies of all the documents dealing with marriage, wills and divorce at the rate of a penny a page. Fergusson must have found the repetitive work tedious but it gave him an income and time to mingle in Edinburgh society.

He became a regular and vigorous member of the vibrant Edinburgh scene, perhaps in part as a reflection of his mischievous character and partly as an antidote to the drudgery of his daily work. Much of his poetry reflects his urban life in Edinburgh, distinguishing him from the rural background which characterises the works of Burns.

Edinburgh was in a time of great change. The Age of Enlightenment, that explosion of scientific and philosophical ideas, was just beginning and the city was host to many convivial clubs and societies, often based around the local taverns, such as the Spendthrift Club, whose members were limited to spending four pence halfpenny each night, and the Odd Fellows, whose members wrote their names upside down. All combined the discussion of ideas with the imbibing of ale.

Between work and socialising Fergusson found time to pen poems, writing regularly for The Weekly Magazine, first in English but later submitting The Daft Days, the first poem in Scots to be published in the magazine. Since the Union, English had been considered the language of literature; indeed many Scots, including David Hume, had worked hard to anglicise their speech. Fergusson helped to make Scots 'respectable' again. For the rest of his life he produced works in both English and Scots, later inspiring Burns to do the same. Unlike Burns though, who was portrayed by Henry Mackenzie as the 'heaven-taught ploughman,' Fergusson had received a formal education in the Classics and was therefore as comfortable with classical allusions in his work as with Scots.

In 1772 Fergusson joined the Cape Club whose members included writers, painters and musicians who spent social evenings in conversation or playing music, fuelled by a glass of ale or porter (a dark brown bitter beer). Each member was required to come up with a name and character he must assume at all gatherings of the club; Fergusson was dubbed 'Sir Precentor.' Among other members were Alexander Runciman, the painter of historical and mythological subjects, and Henry Raeburn. This must have been an enjoyable time for Fergusson: there was plenty of good fellowship, and the opportunity to write and sing the Scots songs of which he was so fond.

A selection of his poems was published in 1773 and Fergusson that year also published Auld Reekie, the first part of a planned long poem about his city. All too rapidly, however, the flame of his talent was extinguished by illness. He began to suffer from severe depression and 'religious melancholia,' becoming psychotically obsessed with religion. He stopped meeting with his friends and confined himself at home studying the Bible. One of his last poems, 'Job, Chapter III' expresses his despair:

> *Perish the fatal day when I was born,*
> *The night with dreary darkness be forlorn;*
> concluding:
> *Why then is grateful light bestow'd on man,*
> *Whose life is darkness, all his days a span?*
> *For ere the morn return'd my sighing came,*
> *My mourning pour'd out as the mountain stream;*
> *Wild visag'd fear, with sorrow-mingled eye,*
> *And wan destruction piteous stared me nigh;*
> *For though nor rest nor safety blest my soul,*
> *New trouble came, new darkness, new controul.*

Apart from a few poems and his will, which unconventionally was written in verse, he was to write no more.

> '*LAST WILL*'
> *While sober folks, in humble prose,*
> *Estate, and goods, and gear dispose,*
> *A poet surely may disperse*
> *His moveables in doggerel verse;*
> *And fearing death my blood will fast chill,*
> *I hereby constitute my last will.*

By March of the next year his sanity had gone. He fell down a flight of stairs, badly injuring his head, and as his mother was no longer able to care for him, he was committed to the Bedlam or madhouse. Treatment was barbaric; Fergusson slept on a bed of straw in a cold cell. He received neither medical care nor any treatment.

A few days before his death he was visited by friends and walked with them in the courtyard; they promised he would soon be restored to his family and, reassured, Fergusson went calmly back to his cell. His last visitors were his mother and his sister Margaret; it was October and he said his feet were 'cold, cold.' He asked his mother to gather up the meagre bedclothes and, placing them on his feet, sit on them to provide warmth. When she rose to go he cried, 'Do not go yet, mother; do not leave me!' but the time allotted for the visit had ended and they must leave. That night, tragically alone in the darkness, Robert Fergusson died.

In an ultimate irony, just a few days after his death his mother received a sum of money from her sailor son Hary [sic] which he gave her to 'bring her laddie home,' and then almost immediately afterwards a draft from a benefactor in India, a Mr. Burnett, for one hundred pounds, enough money for her to have cared for her son at home. But the money arrived too late. Fergusson was buried in an unmarked grave in the Canongate Kirkyard where there is now outside a statue of the poet in happier times. On a visit to Edinburgh Robert Burns paid for a headstone and wrote the inscription:

> No sculptur'd marble here, nor pompous lay,
> No story'd urn nor animated bust;
> This simple stone directs pale Scotia's way.
> To pour her sorrows o'er the poet's dust.

Fergusson died aged just twenty-four years old, leaving a small body of his work – in the distress of his last months he destroyed many of his manuscripts – and dying before he could achieve the works of which he was capable, at an age at which even the great Burns had achieved little. As Burns wrote in 'Lines on Fergusson:'

> Ill-fated genius! Heaven-taught Fergusson!
> What heart that feels, and will not yield a tear,
> To think Life's sun did set, e'er well begun
> To shed its influence on thy bright career!

While we can thank Fergusson for his inspiration of Burns, it is tantalising to think what he could have achieved had his life and sanity been spared. Perhaps Scots would be celebrating on the 5th September instead of the 25th of January.

**Further Reading**
Robert Crawford, *'Heaven-Taught' Fergusson*
Alexander Grosart, *Robert Fergusson*
Robert Fergusson, *Selected Poems* ed. James Robertson

**Online Resources**
Scottish Poetry Library
http://www.scottishpoetrylibrary.org.uk/poetry/poets/robert-fergusson

## Robert Burns
### 1759–1796

SCOTLAND'S NATIONAL BARD

Robert Burns is far more than Scotland's National Bard. Wherever Scots have travelled in the world, and that means almost everywhere, the 'Immortal Memory' is toasted at Burns Suppers on the anniversary of his birth, 25 January. The proceedings commence with the *Selkirk Grace* and then the Robert Burns poem *Address to a Haggis*:

*Fair fa' your honest sonsie face,*
*Great chieftain o' the puddin' race!*
*Aboon them a' ye tak your place*
*Painch, tripe or thairm:*
*Weel are ye wordy o' a grace*
*As lang's my arm.*

Ending with a resounding:

*Auld Scotland wants nae stinking ware*
*That jaups in luggies:*
*But, if ye wishe her gratefu' prayer,*
*Gie her a Haggis!*

Scots Glossary: SONSIE/PLUMP, GOOD NATURED; PAINCH/STOMACH; THAIRM/INTESTINES; JAUPS/SPLASHES; LUGGIES/ SMALL WOODEN BOWLS.

At the end of the evening, and at weddings, dances and other celebrations, the guests join hands in a celebration of friendship and sing Burns's *Auld Lang Syne*:

> *Should auld acquaintance be forgot*
> *And never brought tae mind?*
> *Should auld acquaintance be forgot,*
> *And auld lang syne!*
> *For auld lang syne, my dear,*
> *For auld lang syne,*
> *We'll tak a cup of kindness yet*
> *For auld lang syne.*

Above all, though, Burns is remembered for his love songs and poems, some of the most beautiful in the English language and certainly the finest in Scots. *A Red, Red Rose*, perhaps the greatest love song ever written, was penned by Burns for Jean Armour, his long-suffering wife, who forgave his many indiscretions, gave him his children and loved him till the end.

> *O my Luve's like a red, red rose*
> *That's newly sprung in June,*
> *O, my Luve's like the melodie*
> *That's sweetly play'd in tune.*
> *As fair thou art, my bonnie lass,*
> *So deep in luve am I;*
> *And I will love thee still, my Dear,*
> *Till a' the seas gang dry.*
> *Till a' the seas gang dry, my Dear,*
> *And the rocks melt wi' the sun;*
> *I will love thee still, my Dear,*
> *While the sands o' life shall run.*
> *And fare thee weel, my only Luve!*
> *And fare thee weel, a while!*
> *And I will come again, my Luve,*
> *Tho' it were ten thousand mile!*

Alexander Nasmyth, Robert Burns, Scottish National Portrait Gallery

Robert Burns
*see: colour plate 22*

## An Ayrshire Lad

So who was this man, this lover, poet and leading member of the Enlightenment? William Burns, Robert's father, moved to Alloway in Ayrshire as head gardener for Dr Ferguson, and later a tenant farmer on the estate. He was a God-fearing man, not well-read but determined with true Enlightenment zeal that his children should have the very best education he could give them.

Robert's mother was Agnes Broun, the daughter of a nearby Ayrshire farmer. She was not well educated, as her mother had died when she was ten and her childhood was spent rearing her siblings, but she had an immense store of songs in Scots which she would sing to her own wee bairns. Burns remembered his mother singing to him and acknowledged the great debt he owed her for introducing him to the delight of songs; over the years he would write new words for the tunes his mother had sung to him.

His father moved when Burns was six to become a tenant farmer on a nearby property, which proved a bad decision as the land was of poor quality and William had to struggle to scrape an existence. This was an early lesson to his young son of the hardships of a tenant farmer's life.

With his brother Gilbert, Burns was sent to the local school, where the school master, an outstanding teacher named John Murdoch, himself only eighteen years old, had been personally chosen by William and some of his friends. Burns stayed there for three years, polishing his knowledge of English by reading poems and tales, memorising hymns and learning by heart passages from the Bible, which gave the young schoolboy an appreciation of the rhythm and cadence of words.

After three years spent giving the two boys an excellent rounding in literature, Murdoch moved on. They worked for the next three years on their father's farm, relying on their father for continuing education and whatever books they could lay their hands on. When Burns was twelve Murdoch returned to Ayr to teach at the burgh school. He also resumed teaching young Burns's when his commitments on the farm allowed, often having him to stay for a few weeks at a time. Burns' reading expanded under Murdoch's tuition to include the Classics; by now he was reading the works of Shakespeare as well as those of Scots writers. Burns was still working full time on the farm and the continual hard labour often left him with a dull headache, perhaps an early sign of the ill health which would later afflict him.

There were compensations. During the harvest it was the custom to pair together a man and a woman and it was while working in the fields that Burns met his first love, Nelly Kirkpatrick, for whom he composed the song *My Handsome Nell* – the first of many love songs, poems and conquests...

> *O once I lov'd a bonnie lass,*
> *An' aye I love her still,*
> *An' whilst that virtue warms my breast*
> *I'll love my handsome Nell.*

The song tells of her 'innocence and modesty':

> *'Tis this in Nelly pleases me,*
> *'Tis this enchants my soul;*
> *For absolutely in my breast*
> *She reigns without controul.*

## The Tarbolton Bachelors

In the end, William gave up the impossible fight to make a success of the farm and in 1777 the family moved to another farm near the village of Tarbolton. Burns was finding the farm work a hard drudge but still made time to indulge his passions – the lasses, poetry and songs, and drinking with his friends. Together with his brother Gilbert and some friends, all of whom were young working men, most of them farmers, he formed the Tarbolton Bachelors' Club, fashioned in the spirit of the Enlightenment as a debating club. The club met every fourth Monday night in an upstairs room in an alehouse to discuss formally, although with good humour, motions appropriate to the age, such as 'Whether the savage man or the peasant of a civilized country [is] in the most happy condition.' He also became a Mason, which was an association more acceptable to his serious God-fearing father.

The continual toil of trying to eke out a living from poor land eventually wore his father out and William Burns died in 1784, virtually destitute after a long legal struggle to protect his family from the landlord's demands. Burns was much moved by his father's struggles to keep his head financially and the fear of poverty would haunt him all his life. Burns, who had a somewhat tumultuous relationship with his father, recorded a tribute to 'the loving husband, the tender father and the generous friend' in his commonplace book, in which Burns noted poems and writings he enjoyed and also recorded scraps of his own poem, calling him 'the friend of man, to vice alone a foe.' Around this time Burns also discovered the poetry of Allan Ramsay and Robert Fergusson, both of whom had written in Scots. Burns had become discouraged with his poetry; as he wrote in 1787 to Dr John Moore, 'Rhyme, except some religious pieces which are in print, I had given up; but meeting with Fergusson's Scotch Poems, I strung anew my wildly-sounding rustic lyre with emulating vigour.' He thus paid tribute to the debt he owed to the tragic Fergusson, the 'Ill-fated Genius,' whom he described as his 'elder brother in misfortune, by far my elder brother in the Muse', and for whom he would later petition to raise money to provide a tombstone for Fergusson's unmarked grave in Edinburgh.

Robert Burns and his brother Gilbert moved the family again, this time renting a farm near Mossgiel. Burns no longer felt the restraining pressure of his father and indulged rather more freely his love of the lassies. This was, perhaps not coincidentally, one of his most productive periods as a poet.

He had an affair with Elizabeth Paton, a maid servant, and fathered a daughter, also Elizabeth. The babe was given to his ever-tolerant mother to rear, but Burns never denied the numerous children he fathered; he rather charmingly wrote of the inconvenient and one imagines unintended arrival in *A Poet's Welcome to his Love-begotten Daughter*:

> *Welcome! My bonnie sweet wee dochter*
> *Though ye came a wee unsought for!*

It was while ploughing at Mossgiel that Burns famously turned up the nest of a mouse which inspired his ode *To a Mouse, on Turning Her Up in Her Nest with the Plough*, which begins:

> *Wee, sleekit, cowrin', tim'rous beastie,*
> *O what a panic's in thy breastie;*

Life as a farmer was hard and he concludes, considering sadly his own position and prospects:

> *But, Mousie, thou art no thy lane,*
> *In proving foresight may be vain:*
> *The best laid schemes o' mice an' men*
> *Gang aft a-gley;*
> *An' lea'e us nought but grief and pain*
> *For promis'd joy.*
>
> *Still, thou art blest, compar'd wi' me!*
> *The present only toucheth thee:*
> *But, Och! I backward cast my e'e*
> *On prospects drear!*
> *An' forward, tho I canna see,*
> *I guess an' fear!*

But for Burns there was always another day, and another young girl to woo.

### Jean Armour

When Burns was twenty-six he met Jean Armour, the daughter of a master-mason and the only constant love of his life. Jean not only had striking looks but she knew and would sing *'all the ballads of Scotland.'* True to form Jean was soon with child, but Burns's offer of marriage was rejected by her father who as a Calvinist fundamentalist thought little of the morals and even less of the prospects of the struggling farmer and would-be poet.

This was a Calvinist time and Burns had to bear the mortification of attending church three Sundays in succession in penitence for his earthly sin.

Burns did not pine for long but sought consolation with Margaret Campbell, better known as 'Highland Mary.' Becoming disillusioned by the prospect of farming in the Borders, Burns had thoughts of emigrating to Jamaica. Burns and Campbell pledged mutual fidelity and in his poem he tried to persuade her to join him in Jamaica:

WILL YOU GO TO THE INDIES, MY MARY?

*Will ye go to the Indies, my Mary,*
*And leave auld Scotia's shore?*
*Will ye go to the Indies, my Mary,*
*Across the Atlantic's roar?*
*O sweet grows the lime and the orange,*
*And the apple on the pine;*
*But a' the charms o' the Indies*
*Can never equal thine.*
*O plight me your faith, my Mary,*
*And plight me your lily-white hand;*
*O plight me your faith, my Mary,*
*Before I leave Scotia's strand.*

Campbell died suddenly in the autumn before any plans could come to fruition, perhaps fortuitously for the future of Scottish poetry. Burns wrote '*Highland Mary*' in her memory; the last verse sings a sad farewell to his love:

*O pale, pale now, those rosy lips,*
*I aft have kissed sae fondly!*
*And closed for aye the sparkling glance,*
*That dwelt on me sae kindly!*
*And mould'ring now in silent dust,*
*That heart that lo'ed me dearly!*
*But still within my bosom's core*
*Shall live my Highland Mary.*

A month before Campbell's death Burns had become a father again; Jean Armour had given birth to twins, appropriately if unimaginatively given the names of Robert and Jean.

### 'Heaven-taught Ploughman'

Burns found the inspiration for his songs and poems from his tangled love life and published in July 1786 his Poems Chiefly in the Scots Dialect, a collection of thirty poems and fourteen songs and other pieces. Burns had six hundred copies printed privately and amidst the trauma from the death of his Highland Mary and the birth of his twins, rode throughout Ayrshire selling copies. The first review appeared in the Edinburgh Magazine in October 1786 and it was immediately hailed as the work of a poetic genius, encouraging Burns to borrow a pony and ride to Edinburgh where he took lodgings off the Lawnmarket.

Burns deprecated his talents to the Edinburgh literati, portraying himself as a simple uneducated farmer and disguising the knowledge of poetry, literature and the classics he had so assiduously acquired. Burns persuaded Henry Mackenzie, a lawyer, aspiring novelist and part-time literary critic to believe he had sprung full fledged upon the world as an unlettered poetic genius. Mackenzie wrote in his review, perhaps patronisingly, that readers will appreciate 'with what uncommon penetration and sagacity this Heaven-taught Ploughman, from his humble and unlettered station, has looked upon men and manners.' Burns became the toast of the drawing rooms.

At last Burns had money in his pocket, or more correctly the promise of money as the publisher was tardy in paying over the sums due. Thoughts of Jamaica were forgotten and Burns decided to use his newfound wealth to fund a tour of the country. He set off first to Duns in the Borders and then briefly to England before journeying to the Highlands, where he was feasted by a number of the lairds – and loved by some of their wives and daughters.

Regrettably, Burns did not take advantage of the situation to secure a patron; indeed he would often perversely insult – for example by ignoring an invitation to dinner – the people who might have been able to sponsor his life as a poet. So he returned to farming.

Success meant that Burns was now an acceptable match in the eyes of Jean's father. They set up home together as husband and wife on a one hundred and seventy acre farm in Ellisland in Dumfriesshire, which Burns leased from Patrick Miller of steamboat fame whom he had met while in Edinburgh. Burns had to build a farmhouse and it would be some time before Jean joined him. He missed her, writing in *'Of A' the Airts the Wind Can Blaw'*:

> *Of a' the airts the wind can blaw,*
> *I dearly like the West;*
> *For there the bony Lassie lives,*
> *The Lassie I lo'e best:*
> *There's wild-wood grow, and rivers row,*
> *And mony a hill between;*
> *But day and night my fancy's flight*
> *Is ever wi' my Jean.*

Scots: ROW/ROLL.

Jean joined him in December 1788 and bore him three more children. She also accepted into their home the child of a brief affair Burns had in 1790 with Ann Park, a young barmaid who worked at the Globe Inn in Dumfries, where Burns would sometimes stay overnight. Jean was certainly a forgiving wife.

## Burns the Exciseman

Burns was always worried by the threat of poverty and as farming was proving a hard living determined to become an Exciseman. After a long period of training and waiting, Burns was appointed but found that this too was exhausting work. He had to ride thirty or forty miles five days a week, and to complete the complicated bookkeeping required by the Excise.

Burns was not a natural exciseman; his innate sympathies lay with the people whom he saw as oppressed by the corrupt government of the Prime Minister, William Pitt, and with the extension of democracy and of power to the people later embodied in the ideals – if not the practice - of the French Revolution.

But needs must. He wrote in a letter to his friend Robert Ainslie, 'I know how the word, Exciseman, or still more opprobrious, Gauger, will sound in your ears … but a wife & child are things which have a wonderful power in blunting these kinds of sensations. Fifty pounds a year for life, & a provision for widows & orphans, you will allow, is no bad settlement for a Poet.'

Burns wrote some of his finest poetry during this period, including the *Tale of Tam o' Shanter*, who, after a drunken evening spent in a hostelry, realises he must ride home to his wife; after being tempted by a young girl in a cutty-sark, he narrowly escapes death when his horse, Meg, loses her tail to a chasing witch:

> *Now, wha this tale o' truth shall read,*
> *Ilk man and mother's son, take heed:*
> *Whene'er to drink you are inclin'd,*
> *Or cutty-sarks run in your mind,*
> *Think, ye may buy the joys o'er dear,*
> *Remember Tam o' Shanter's mare.*

Scots: CUTTY-SARK: A GIRL'S SHORT SHIFT.

When the lease on Ellisland expired in 1791, Burns gave up farming and moved his young family to Dumfries to become a full-time Exciseman. His duties were to collect tax, payable on many goods ranging from candles to claret, and to control smuggling.

Burns was once involved in the seizure of a smuggling schooner aground on the quicksands of the Solway Firth. The schooner was towed into dock and then sold together with her cargo. As an Exciseman, Burns would have received part of the proceeds. It was a strange role for him, who instinctively had more sympathy with the smugglers than with the Excise. The incident was commemorated by Burns in his song *The Deil's Awa wi' the Exciseman*.

He was becoming increasingly vocal in his radical opinions – even dangerously so in the hothouse political atmosphere of the time, with Revolutionary France just across the Channel. He still espoused the romantic Jacobite cause and wrote a song about the Act of Union and those who, encouraged by English gold, had agreed the terms. The poem *Such a Parcel of Rogues in a Nation* ends:

> *We're bought and sold for English gold,*
> *Such a parcel of rogues in a nation!*

Burns continued in his radical beliefs, writing in 1793 his famous 'Scots Wha Hae' before the battle of Bannockburn which he intended to refer not just to Scotland's historical struggle for freedom in the Wars of Independence but to *'other struggles of the same nature, not quite so ancient'* – by which he meant the overthrow of the Hanoverian monarchy.

> 'SCOTS WHA HAE'
> *Scots, wha hae wi' Wallace bled,*
> *Scots, wham Bruce has aften led,*
> *Welcome to your gory bed,*
> *Or to victorie.*
> *Now's the day and now's the hour:*
> *See the front o' battle lour!*
> *See approach proud Edward's power –*
> *Chains and slaverie!*
> *Wha will be a traitor knave?*
> *Wha can fill a coward's grave?*
> *Wha sae base as be a slave?*
> *Let him turn and flee!*
> *Wha for Scotland's King and law*
> *Freedom's sword will strongly draw,*
> *Freeman stand or freeman fa'?*
> *Let him follow me!*
> *Lay the proud usurpers low!*
> *Tyrants fall in every foe!*
> *Liberty's in every blow!*
> *Let us do or die!*

Burns was aware of the dangers of his republican views and sensibly joined the Royal Dumfries Volunteers, formed to counter the threat of French invasion, but fears of reprisals for his views did not prevent him from writing, but wisely not signing, *A Man's a Man For A' That*, a hymn to equality where, 'The honest man, tho' e'er sae poor, is king o' men for a' that.'

It was also at this time that Burns heard that a lady with whom he had been corresponding, 'Clarinda,' Mrs Agnes McLehose, was leaving to join her husband in the West Indies. Burns had a passionate but unconsummated relationship with his Clarinda; he was fascinated by elegant women whose position in society made them unattainable, but the girls he bedded usually came from a humbler background. McLehose duly went to Jamaica but sadly when she got there she learned that her husband had inconsiderately acquired in her absence a mistress and children; disillusioned she came straight back to Scotland. Her departure inspired Burns to write *Ae Fond Kiss, and Then We Sever!* which concludes:

> *Had we never lov'd so kindly,*
> *Had we never lov'd so blindly,*
> *Never met – or never parted,*
> *We had ne'er been broken-hearted.*
> *Fare thee weel, thou first and fairest!*
> *Fare thee weel, thou best and dearest!*
> *Thine be ilka joy and treasure,*
> *Peace, enjoyment, love and pleasure.*
> *Ae fond kiss, and then we sever;*
> *Ae fareweel, alas, for ever!*
> *Deep in heart-wrung tears I'll pledge thee,*
> *Warring sighs and groans I'll wage thee.*

The winter of 1794/5 was especially hard, requiring Burns to ride out through heavy snow. The nature of his work, concerns about his financial future and worries about his political writings conspired to bring Burns' health to a low ebb. In September 1795 when his four-year-old daughter Elizabeth died, Burns, although much affected by her death, was too ill with rheumatic fever to go to the funeral. By June of the next year he realised he was himself dying and tried to make appropriate farewells, telling his illegitimate daughter Betty 'to be a gude girl.'

Wasted from long illness, Burns unwisely took his doctor's advice not just to take the curative waters of the ancient well at Brow, but to walk out daily into the icy cold waters of the Firth and immerse himself there. The cure, unsurprisingly, did not save him. Robert Burns took to his bed and died a few days later on 21 July 1796. His funeral, complete with three volleys fired by the Royal Dumfries Volunteers, took place four days later. Jean could not be there; she had given birth that morning to another son. Burns, who for years had been dogged by worries about money, in death became famous.

Robert Burns contributed to world literature a unique collection of songs, poems and ballads which above all demonstrate his humanity. He is not just Scotland's National Bard – his works are read and admired throughout the world.

**Further Reading**
*The Poetical Works of Robert Burns* e Robertson
Robert Crawford, *The Bard*
Patrick Scott Hogg, *Robert Burns: The Patriot Bard*

**Online Resources**
http://www.robertburns.org/

## James Hogg
### 1770–1835

<small>THE ETTRICK SHEPHERD</small>

'I am neither a drunkard nor an idiot nor a monster of nature.' With these words James Hogg defended himself against the scurrilous depiction of him in *Blackwood's Magazine*. Indeed, James Hogg was not a drunkard, nor an idiot, nor a monster of nature but a self-taught shepherd who became a successful poet, composer of ballads and novelist, recognised as such more now than during his own lifetime. He was also the friend of Sir Walter Scott.

He was a remarkable example of how to make the most of your gifts and how much true learning can come not from school but from loving and caring parents.

### The Ettrick Valley

James Hogg was born in 1770 in a remote valley near Ettrick in Selkirkshire. His father, Robert, was a peasant farmer. When Hogg was just six years old, his father, who had been dealing in sheep, was ruined by a sharp fall in their price and the absconding of his principle debtor; all the family owned was sold at auction and his parents were turned out of their home, destitute; it was only through the kindness of a local landowner that Robert was given work as a shepherd. Hogg himself was immediately put to work; his task was to look after a few cows.

Hogg is often described as uneducated – he only attended school for six months before he had to start working as a cowherd – but this is taking a narrow view of education. He may not have learned Latin and Greek, indeed he could not even read and write until he taught himself to do so when in his teens, but he had a broad education. He would listen to his father reading from the Bible and to the minister preaching on the Sabbath and he would sit enchanted as his mother recited the stories and ballads of the Borders. She would also read from the Bible and his brother, William, recounted that James could recite the Psalms long before he could spell a word. He became a shepherd and worked for James Laidlaw, who, impressed by his ambitions, provided him with books from his library. Hogg also taught himself the fiddle, a favourite instrument of the time, which he would play at local gatherings.

## A Literary Career

After spending many long years as a young shepherd, alone in the hills but surrounded by the history and romance of the Borders, Hogg veered between trying to become a sheep farmer and developing a literary career. It must be said he did neither during his lifetime with conspicuous success. Hogg was a serial farmer, excusing the pun; whenever he had funds he would purchase a farm only for it to fail, leaving him penniless. As a poet and writer he had a similarly chequered career, only achieving full literary recognition long after his death.

He developed a taste for poetry and ballads and in his twenties started writing songs mainly for 'the lasses to sing in chorus.' He wrote in his autobiography 'a proud man I was when I first heard the rosy nymphs chaunting my uncouth strains.' With his brother, William, and William Laidlaw and Laidlaw's brother to write verses, he formed a society which they would read to each other, often travelling some distance to attend meetings.

His isolation from the literary world can be shown by the fact that Hogg had not learned of Burns until 1797, a year after Burns's death, when he heard Tam o' Shanter recited for the first time. He was much moved and resolved to follow in the footsteps of Burns; after all, as a shepherd he would have 'much more time to read and compose than any ploughman could have.' His first collection of poems, *The Mountain Bard*, was published in 1807 but received little attention.

With his epic poem, *The Queen's Wake*, he fared much better. He wrote the poem as if it had been composed by Mary, Queen of Scots. This received critical acclaim and raised awareness of the shepherd poet. As a result of this success he was selected to contribute to *Blackwood's Magazine*, which had been launched as a hard-hitting competitor to the Whig 'establishment' *Edinburgh Review*. Hogg developed a close relationship with *Blackwood's* and much of his work was first published there.

Somewhat unwisely, Hogg joined with two other writers to produce a scurrilous article they called *The Chaldee Manuscript*, a satire in biblical language on leading establishment figures. It caused uproar. One of his fellow contributors fled, the other had to issue a written apology, and Hogg's own relationship with the literary 'gentry' was greatly damaged. However, it did no harm to the circulation of the magazine.

*Blackwood's* Tory views and hard-hitting articles soon made the magazine a success. But mocked as rustic and not fitting naturally into the Edinburgh scene, Hogg increasingly found himself being excluded from the inner circle of contributors. As time passed a certain reluctance to accept his work crept in. Eventually *Blackwood's* rather cruelly lampooned him in a regular feature of the magazine which consisted of a series of imaginary conversations held in a tavern among fictional characters and the 'Ettrick Shepherd' was a thinly disguised caricature of Hogg, who was unkindly and unfairly portrayed as a wild rural simpleton who enjoyed heavy drinking. It made him a celebrity but meant he was not taken seriously by the literati.

Scott advised him not to take any action, in law or otherwise, although he realised that 'the advice to be quiet under injury is hard to flesh and blood.' The Ettrick Shepherd articles continued until Hogg's death in 1834.

### Friendship with Sir Walter Scott

In 1802 Hogg met Scott through an introduction by James Laidlaw. At the time Walter Scott was researching the ballads of the Borders for his book *Minstrelsy of the Scottish Border* and Laidlaw introduced him to Hogg because of the latter's knowledge of Border history and ballads; knowledge he had gleaned from listening to the songs of his mother and to the tales of the elders.

Somewhat surprisingly, in view of their very different backgrounds, they struck up a friendship which lasted until Scott died. Hogg described Scott as 'the best and most steady friend that I have ever had to depend on.' Scott frequently tried to persuade Hogg to strive harder, to cut and to revise, but the advice went unheeded; Hogg would boast that he never wrote a second version of his poems and admitted that when he wrote the first line of a novel 'I know not what the second is to be … I sail on without star or compass.'

The only time they fell out was when Hogg tried to retrieve his fortunes by publishing an anthology of contemporary poems, *The Poetic Mirror*, each to be contributed by a leading poet of the time; Scott, to Hogg's annoyance, refused to participate. Indeed, few of the other potential contributors fulfilled their promises and Hogg was forced to write most of the contributions himself, which he did in the style of the various poets, including pastiches of Wordsworth, Coleridge, Byron and even Scott himself:

> *Wat o' the Cleuch came down through the dale*
> *In helmet and hauberk of glistening mail;*
> *Full proudly he came on his berry-black steed.*
> *Caparisoned, belted for warrior deed.*

The poem could indeed have been written by Scott. Scott's reservation had been because he had felt it was wrong to make money through the work of others, but the two were soon reconciled. Hogg later wrote a tribute to his friend, *The Life and Manners of Sir Walter Scott*, in which he wrote that Scott 'was a good man, an anxiously kind husband; an indulgent parent, and a sincere forgiving friend.' He concluded, 'And is it not a proud boast for an old shepherd, that for thirty years he could call this man friend.'

## Songs and Poems

Hogg may have been treated somewhat disparagingly in his lifetime, but his memory and deserved reputation live on today in the works he left behind. Hogg was a romantic and many of his poems and ballads had a Jacobite flavour. One such is the lament of a Jacobite soldier, *Callum-a-Glen*:

> *Was ever old warrior of suffering so weary?*
> *Was ever the wild beast so bay'd in his den?*
> *The southron bloodhounds lie in kennels so near me,*
> *That death would be freedom to Callum-a-Glen!*
> *My sons are all slain, and my daughters have left me,*
> *No child to protect me, where once there were ten;*
> *My chief they have slain, and of stay have bereft me,*
> *And woe to the grey hairs of Callum-a-Glen!*
> *The homes of my kinsmen are blazing to heaven,*
> *The bright steep of morning has blush'd at the view;*
> *The moon has stood still on the verge of the even,*
> *To wipe from her pale cheek the tint of the dew;*
> *For the dew it lies red on the vales of Lochaber,*
> *It sprinkles the cot, and it flows in the pen;*
> *The pride of my country is fallen for ever;*
> *Death, hast thou no shaft for old Callum-a-Glen?*

He also enjoyed the company of the ladies and many of his songs were written about them. As in *'The Women Fo'k'*:

> *O sarly may I rue the day*
> *I fancied first the womenkind;*
> *For aye sinsyne I ne'er can hae*
> *Ae quiet thought or peace o' mind!*
> *They hae plagued my heart an' pleased my ee,*
> *An' teased an' flatter'd me at will,*
> *But aye, for a' their witcherye,*

*The pawky things I lo'e them still.*
*O the women fo'k! O the women fo'k!*
*But they hae been the wreck o' me;*
*O weary fa' the women fo'k,*
*For they winna let a body be!*

This song, which James Hogg claims he was 'forced to sing by ladies against my will, which too frequently happens,' continues for another three verses in the same vein and was very popular.

Another favourite was *When Maggy Gangs Awa'*, which was inspired by his hearing a young girl singing the first two lines to his little daughter, Maggy. This is the first of four verses:

*O what will a' the lads do*
*When Maggy gangs away?*
*O what will a' the lads do*
*When Maggy gangs away?*
*There's no a heart in a' the glen*
*That disna dread the day.*
*O what will a' the lads do*
*When Maggy gangs away?*

The third main theme of his ballads was his love of Scotland and the Borders. These are the first two verses of '*The Highlander's Farewell*':

*O where shall I gae seek my bread,*
*Or where shall I gae wander,*
*O where shall I gae hide my head,*
*For here I'll bide nae langer?*
*The seas may rowe, the winds may blow,*
*And swathe me round in danger,*
*But Scotland I maun now forego,*
*And roam a lonely stranger!*

*The glen that was my father's own,*
*Maun be by his forsaken;*
*The house that was my father's home*
*Is levell'd with the braken.*
*Oh hon! Oh hon! Our glory's gone,*
*Stole by a ruthless reaver –*
*Our hands are on the broad claymore,*
*But the might is broke for ever!*

## A Justified Sinner

In addition to his songs and poems Hogg wrote a number of historical and supernatural stories and three novels of which the most famous and successful is *The Private Memoirs and Confessions of a Justified Sinner*. He wrote this in 1824 when he was desperate for money. He had a young family, his farm was failing and he was no longer writing for *Blackwood's*.

The *Confessions* is a story of good and evil, casting back to the religious fundamentalism of the Calvinist sermons he had listened to in his youth, mocking the concept that moral good is necessarily the outcome of regular prayer and satirising the strict Calvinist view of predestination, by which it is determined before you are even born whether you are destined for heaven or hell, from which the logical argument follows that it does not matter how you act in life because your fate is already decided.

The book is in two parts: the first is written by the 'editor' and the second, which purports to be a manuscript found in the grave of a suicide, is written in the first person by Robert Wringham, a young man who in his life encountered and befriended a devilish figure known as Gil-Martin, his evil other self.

Robert is brought up to pray 'twice a day and seven times on Sabbath days' and is identified as one of the 'chosen,' predestined for eternal life in heaven. Thus emboldened he decides to arrange the banishment of his adoptive father's serving man, John Barnet, for no better reason than that he irritates him. Barnet is not one of the 'chosen' so in accordance with the logic of Calvinist doctrine he is banished and is predestined for eternal damnation, while the vile Robert remains predestined for heaven.

Worse follows. Robert encounters his evil alter ego, Gil-Martin, who appears to him as a friend. Gil-Martin argues that, as Robert's salvation is predestined, every act that he commits, no matter how evil, is justified and will not exclude him 'from the limits of the covenant.' Arguing thus, Gil-Martin encourages Robert to commit a number of evil crimes, including the murder of his brother, George.

Robert is eventually taken over by his evil side, believing that 'my body was at times possessed by a spirit over which it had no control, and of whose actions my body was wholly unconscious.' He attempts to flee his evil alter ego but fails. After much hardship he takes the only escape, suicide – the one crime for which 'there was no remission.' The book cruelly satirises the doctrine of predestination. It is understandably thought to have been the inspiration for *The Strange Case of Dr Jekyll and Mr Hyde* by Robert Louis Stevenson, in which good and evil are two parts of the same person and the persona of the 'good' Dr Jekyll eventually gives way entirely to the 'evil' Mr Hyde.

When first published, the novel had little impact and made even less money. *Blackwood's* virtually ignored the work by its former contributor, giving it only a cursory review, and the *Confessions* lay largely neglected for some hundred years. Today it is regarded as one of the major Scottish novels of its time.

## Hogg's Legacy

Hogg might be thought to have had an unhappy life given the lack of critical appreciation of his work: 'worn out by a life of misery,' as he wrote. He remained, however, steadfastly cheerful, declaring that 'the case has been quite the reverse … I have never known man or woman who has been so uniformly happy.'

His married life had been so content that he could scarce 'distinguish one part from another, save by some remarkably good days of fishing, shooting and curling on the ice.'

He left a collection of songs, poems and novels but perhaps his greatest legacy was the proof that a humble background is no bar to self-improvement and achievement. He may be an unlikely figure of the Enlightenment, but his acceptance by and friendship with Sir Walter Scott are tribute to the inclusiveness of a time when a man could be judged not by his parentage or schooling but on his merit and character. These merits can be identified in excerpts from an irresistible love letter to Miss Margaret Phillips, the young lady who became his wife:

> *Ah, Maggy, thou art gane away,*
> *And left me here to languish,*
> *To daunder on frae day to day,*
> *Swathed in a sort o'anguish.*
> *My mind's the aspen o' the vale,*
> *In ceaseless waving motion;*
> *'Tis like a ship without a sail,*
> *On life's unstable ocean!*
> *[...]*
> *May still thy heart be kind an' true,*
> *A' ither maids excelling,*
> *An' heaven shall shed its purest dew*
> *Around thy rural dwelling.*
> *May flow'rets spring, an' wild birds sing*
> *Around thee late an' early,*
> *An' oft to thy remembrance bring*
> *The lad that loes the dearly!*

**Further Reading**
James Hogg, *Songs by the Ettrick Shepherd*
James Hogg, *The Private Memoirs and Confessions of a Justified Sinner*
Henry Thew Stephenson, *The Ettrick Shepherd: A Biography*

**Online Resources**
Poem Hunter
http://www.poemhunter.com/james-hogg/

## Sir Walter Scott
### 1771–1832

POET AND NOVELIST WHOSE STORIES AWAKENED INTEREST
IN SCOTLAND'S COLOURFUL HISTORY

Sir Walter Scott was an inspirational figure of the Enlightenment, whose heart was in the Highlands of the Scotland he loved. At first a poet, he is now better remembered for his historical 'Waverley' novels, in which he told stories of medieval times and Scotland's past — sentiments foreshadowed by Robert Burns:

*My heart's in the Highlands, my heart is not here*
*My heart's in the Highlands a-chasing the deer;*
*A-chasing the wild deer, and following the roe,*
*My heart's in the Highlands wherever I go.*

Scott wrote twenty-seven novels; stories of adventure, gallantry and romance. But the story of his own life is nearly as colourful as those he fabricated.

### Childhood

Scott's father, also Walter, was a Writer to the Signet, a well-to-do lawyer. He lived with his wife Anne and their family, in an Edinburgh tenement, and later in a house in George Square. Poor diet and hygiene meant that although families were large in the eighteenth century the chances of children surviving through to adulthood were not good. Scott was Anne and Walter's ninth child of twelve, and six of his siblings died in infancy. At first he was a healthy baby but when he was just eighteen months old he contracted polio and lost all use of his right leg which became withered and shrunken by the illness. The distraught parents sent young Walter to live with his grandfather, Robert Scott, who had a farm in the Borders, believing that fresh air and exercise might bring about a cure.

While the stay did nothing to help his paralysis, it did shape the rest of his life.

Scott spent three happy years with his grandfather. As he went about the countryside, he heard people tell the unwritten tales of the Borders, of love both true and betrayed, of battles won and lost, and of daring raids south into England. Then sadly, his grandfather died. Next Scott was sent to Bath to 'take the waters' in another attempt to cure his lameness. He sailed from Berwick with his aunt Jenny on the twelve-day voyage to London and from there went by stagecoach to Bath. It had long been believed that the mineral-flavoured waters which came from the hot springs at Bath would cure diseases and the Romans had built a thermal bath there. By the time Scott arrived Bath had become a splendid city with smart Georgian buildings and a lively social scene. Unfortunately, the waters brought no improvement to his withered leg, but his time in Bath gave Scott a 'perfect English accent' which after the Union had become the aim of every ambitious Scot.

*Sir Henry Raeburn, Sir Walter Scott, Scottish National Portrait Gallery. Purchased with assistance from the Art Fund 1935*

Sir Walter Scott
*see: colour plate 21*

Returning to Edinburgh, Scott went to the Royal High School, where he first showed his talent as a writer. At fifteen he was ready to go to work and his father took him along to his office to train as a lawyer. There was, however, a flaw in his father's plan: Scott could not stand being caged in an office.

## A Lawyer in Edinburgh

Scott was a dutiful son and so studied law at Edinburgh University as his father wished, but as often as he could he escaped from Edinburgh to travel around Scotland, the country he had come to love so dearly. On one of his travels he met Alexander Stewart who had fought a duel with Rob Roy. This fired Scott's growing interest in the history of his country.

In 1792 Scott was called to the Bar; he could now practise as an advocate. His first case was in Jedburgh, where he defended a man accused of poaching. Somewhat to Scott's surprise the man was acquitted. Scott turned to him and said, 'You are a lucky scoundrel.' 'I'm just o' your mind,' replied the poacher, 'and as thanks I'll send you a hare in the morn!'

On a visit to the Lake District, the inspiration for the Lakeland poets, Scott met a charming young lady, Charlotte Charpentier, a refugee from revolutionary France. After a short romance they were married and set up home in Edinburgh but also kept a cottage in the Borders, on the river Esk. They had four children:

two daughters, Sophia and Anne, and two sons, Walter and Charles.

In 1799 Scott became sheriff deputy for Selkirk, which meant he had to live for four months of every year in the sheriffdom. This only increased his love for the Borders, a land of rolling hills and forests, of castles and rivers. He began to record the ballads he heard, which told the tales of the clashes that had taken place between the Scottish reivers, or raiders, and the English across the border.

### Scott the Poet

Scott enjoyed the society of the great thinkers in Edinburgh; he loved to read and had started writing. Scott's first major publication was *Minstrelsy of the Scottish Border*, a three volume collection of the popular ballads and stories he had first heard as a child. The *Minstrelsy* captured the excitement of battles fought long ago between mighty chiefs, of triumphs and disasters:

> *Now Liddlesdale has ridden a raid,*
> *But I wat they had better hae staid at home*
> *For Michael o' Winfield he is dead*
> *And Jock o' the Side is prisoner ta'en*

In 1805 he published the first major work of his own, an epic poem called *The Lay of the Last Minstrel*, in which the aged Minstrel tells a story of love and chivalry set in the Borders. Scott himself was a minstrel, singing of Border chivalry:

> *The way was long, the wind was cold,*
> *The Minstrel was infirm and old;*
> *His wither'd cheek and tresses grey,*
> *Seem'd to have known a better day.*
> *The harp, his sole remaining joy,*
> *Was carried by an orphan boy.*
> *The last of all the Bards was he,*
> *Who sung of Border chivalry*

*The Lay of the Last Minstrel* sold an amazing forty-four thousand copies and made Scott famous. He had created a romantic history with fierce warriors and beautiful maidens, battles and stormy seas, all set within the landscape of Scotland.

His next work was a narrative poem, *Marmion*, an historical romance telling the story of the death of the flower of Scotland's chivalry on the battlefield of Flodden. Scott received an advance of one thousand guineas for *Marmion*, the first time a literary advance had been paid, and it was another runaway success.

An exemplary stanza from *Marmion*:

> *O, young Lochinvar is come out of the west,*
> *Through all the wide Border his steed was the best.*
> *So faithful in love, and so dauntless in war,*
> *There never was a knight like the young Lochinvar.*

Scott's third great poem was *The Lady of the Lake,* in which James V travels in disguise around his kingdom. (The device of a hero in disguise whose identity is only disclosed in the later stages of the story appears again in a number of Scott's novels.) Disguised, James is welcomed as a traveller and encouraged to relax:

> *Soldier rest, thy warfare o'er,*
> *Sleep the sleep that knows no breaking*
> *Dream of battlefields no more,*
> *Days of danger, nights of waking*

The Lady of the Lake was another success, encouraging people to visit the Trossachs to see the 'mountains that like giants stand' and opening up the Highlands to visitors. But it was to be Scott's last major poem. He had read Childe Harold and recognised the genius of Byron's poetry: a genius he felt he could not match. As Scott admitted, 'Byron has beaten me.'

## Abbotsford

By now Scott was a prosperous man. He had his legal work and he was earning large sums from his writing. He invested some of his earnings in 1805 by taking a one-third financial stake in his publisher, Ballantyne's, which then merged with Constable, the publisher of the *Edinburgh Review*. This meant he could add to the money he earned from writing his books the profits made from publishing them. Scott kept his involvement secret – perhaps he did not consider it quite 'proper' to be involved in 'trade' – but this investment would in time nearly break him financially. To quote *Marmion*:

> *O what a tangled web we weave*
> *When first we practise to deceive!*

But that was still in the future. Scott was ambitious and decided to create an estate in the Borders. He spent an outrageous four thousand guineas to procure a one hundred and ten acre farm on the banks of the Tweed. He borrowed the money for the purchase, perhaps unwisely securing the loan against future earnings from his writing. Scott was not content with owning a farm. He wanted to become a laird and to create an estate suitable for his position. He thus bought another thirteen hundred acres and built there a mansion with a great drawing room, a palatial dining room, a conservatory, a library which he would fill with twenty thousand books, a study and an armoury. He furnished it throughout with antiques, including Rob Roy's broadsword, a crucifix which had belonged to Mary Queen of Scots and that essential of any Scots collection, a lock of the hair of Bonnie Prince Charlie. He named his estate Abbotsford.

He also introduced all sorts of new-fangled ideas. He was a shareholder in the Edinburgh Oil and Gas Company and was one of the first to introduce gas lighting into a private house. As daylight faded in the evenings a screw was turned and gas light from three splendid chandeliers bathed the dining room. Scott had a poor sense of smell and so did not notice the stench of gas that pervaded the house. The harsh gaslight was also rather unkind to the complexions of his older lady guests!

He was also proud of the pneumatic system he installed in order to summon his servants. The pressure created by pushing down a piston was transferred pneumatically to the servants' quarters where it expelled a piece of wood from a tube which struck a bell alerting the servants to their master's call.

Abbotsford was an expensive venture which Scott had financed by pledging his future earnings against borrowings. He needed to earn some money.

## The Waverley Novels

Scott decided to finish a novel he had had in mind for some time. It would tell the story of Bonnie Prince Charlie and the Forty-Five Jacobite rising, but unusually it would be told not by a Jacobite Scot but by an Englishman called Edward Waverley. In the novel Waverley is an officer in the government army who is sent north to help put down the rising but instead crosses over to join the Jacobites and fight with Bonnie Prince Charlie against his old comrades. Interestingly, Scott published *Waverley* anonymously, perhaps because writing novels was not then considered 'respectable' for someone with Scott's position in society. *Waverley*, the first of the Waverley series of novels, was published in 1814 and met with immediate success, and in good time. Scott's publishers were losing money heavily and urgently needed the cash from the book's sales.

Scott felt he had earned a holiday and set off with Robert Stevenson of lighthouse fame on a voyage around Scotland inspecting lighthouses. They travelled by yacht, fortified by fresh herring, bannocks and whisky, sailing from Arbroath via Aberdeen to the Orkneys and then back down the west coast, calling at Skye and visiting Staffa, and finally reaching the Clyde. Scott put the trip to good use in a poem, *The Lord of the Isles*.

Scott was now writing feverishly, publishing in 1815 *Guy Mannering*, a novel set in the Borders – thought by many to be his best – and *The Antiquary*; then in 1816 *The Black Dwarf*, a tale set in the time of Queen Anne, and *Old Mortality*; in

1817 *Rob Roy*, the story of the Jacobean outlaw; and the next year *The Heart of Midlothian*, set in Edinburgh. In *The Heart of Midlothian* a young woman cannot bring herself to lie to save her sister from being hanged for a crime she did not commit. The sister is eventually saved from hanging, but on the way home the woman sees another prisoner, Madge, on the scaffold and only then realises the fate that had been in store for her sister. Madge's song on the eve of her death, when she is 'married' to her grave, is simple but moving:

> *Proud Maisie is in the wood,*
> *Walking so early;*
> *Sweet Robin sits on the bush,*
> *Singing so rarely.*
> *'Tell me, thou bonny bird,*
> *When shall I marry me?'*
> *When six braw gentlemen*
> *Kirkward shall carry ye.'*
> *'Who makes the bridal bed,*
> *Birdie, say truly?'*
> *'The grey haired sexton,*
> *That delves the grave duly.'*
> *'The glow worm o'er grave and stone*
> *Shall light thee steady.*
> *The owl from the steeple sing,*
> *Welcome, proud lady.'*

More books followed: *The Legend of Montrose*, *The Bride of Lammermoor*, *Ivanhoe*, *Kenilworth*, and later *Quentin Durward*, *Redgauntlet* and *The Talisman*.

But Scott's interests and influence now reached far beyond his fame as an author.

## The Honours of Scotland

The Honours of Scotland, comprising the Sword of State, the Sceptre of James V and the silver Mace of the Treasurer of Scotland, had been locked away since the sceptre had last been used – to 'touch' the Act of Union and so bring it into force. Scott had befriended the Prince of Wales, a fat and lecherous drunkard who lived on cherry brandy and little else, and persuaded him that he should restore to Scotland her pride and her history. He suggested the Prince make a start with the Honours of Scotland, which were reputed to be stored in an old chest in Edinburgh Castle. Scott asked for and was granted the right to find and open the chest. In 1818 a small group stood before a sealed chamber inside the castle, wondering what they would uncover within. The grille was removed and inside stood a dusty chest secured by great iron padlocks. There was a moment of doubt, but when the chest was opened the Honours were there, covered with a cloth, just as they had been placed more than a hundred years earlier. It was a triumph for Scott, who had become 'the most famous man in Scotland.' His fame was recognised with a baronetcy, and he became Sir Walter.

## George IV Visits Edinburgh

When in 1822 the former Prince of Wales, now King, was to visit Scotland for the first time, it was perhaps only natural that Scott was chosen to mastermind the visit. On 14 August the royal yacht was towed into the port of Leith and onboard went Scott and a party of dignitaries to greet the King. 'Ah!' exclaimed the King, 'Walter Scott. The man I most wanted to see!'

The King went ashore the next day and was escorted by a procession through streets crowded with cheering onlookers to Holyrood Palace. Two days later a reception was held in his honour. Scott had decided to make the Highlands his theme and everyone was dressed in tartan. The King himself, fat and scarlet-faced, barely able to walk, was dressed in a kilt which sagged beneath his enormous belly; underneath his kilt the King wore flesh-coloured stockings to cover his podgy knees. Ironically, the King, the great nephew of the Duke of Cumberland who had butchered the Highlanders at Culloden, was now wearing the 'banned' tartan, dressed almost as a Highlander. Scott by this action embraced the Jacobite tradition and helped revive the wearing of the tartan, now so closely associated with Scotland. A few days later the King took part in a grand procession up the Royal Mile to the castle, where a royal salute was fired. The jollifications ended with the King attending a play, an adaptation of Scott's *Rob Roy*.

## Ruin!

It seemed that everything Scott touched turned to glory, but in 1826 disaster struck. There was a panic on the London Stock Exchange and shares plummeted. Scott was already in debt to Constable, owing them ten thousand pounds borrowed against books yet to be written. But worse was to come. Constable's London agents went bankrupt, losing the huge sum of three hundred thousand pounds and bringing down with them both Constable and Ballantyne's, in which Scott had a substantial investment. Scott was left owing the huge sum of one hundred and thirty thousand pounds; his only assets were Abbotsford, his house in Edinburgh – and his pen. Scott had to make a choice.

If Ballantyne's declared themselves insolvent, he would lose everything, including his beloved Abbotsford, but could start afresh free from debts. Instead he pledged to repay all the monies owing. He would do this through his writing. By this time he was fifty-five years old and not in the best of health, but he set to, writing furiously. He wrote a number of novels, perhaps unsurprisingly not among his best, writing every day from early in the morning until late at night.

He also wrote a massive nine-volume *Life of Napoleon Buonaparte* and was threatened with a duel by a French general who felt he had been unfairly slandered! Scott armed himself with a pistol from his armoury at Abbotsford but fortunately the general, who was a crack shot, never appeared. Scott then wrote for his grandson a four-volume history of Scotland, published as *Tales of a Grandfather*. As he said, 'I will make if possible a book that a child will understand yet a man will feel some temptation to peruse should he chance to take it up.'

After years spent 'chained' to his writing desk, Scott had done it! He had earned enough to pay off his debts in full. To celebrate he set off with his daughter Anne to tour Italy. But the effort had taken its toll. Scott was exhausted. He struggled back to Scotland and reached Abbotsford, where, tired out by his efforts, he died.

The funeral procession took his coffin from Abbotsford, the horses pausing at the place now known as Scott's View, as they had done so often during his life, before proceeding to his burial place set in the ruins of Dryburgh Abbey by the banks of the Tweed, which had formed such an important part of his life. During his lifetime Scott had become a towering figure in Scotland and this is recognised in the prominent statues to him in Princes Street in Edinburgh and George Square in Glasgow.

Sir Walter Scott invented the historical novel. His writing may not be in accord with current tastes, perhaps a reflection on those tastes, but reading the works of Scott is an essential part of a rounded literary education. More than anyone, he was responsible for popularising the romance of the Highlands: the way of life, the stories and the tartan. Many of the features which today make Scotland so popular a place to visit, both for tourists and for Scots coming home to seek their roots, derive from the enthusiasm created by the writings of Scott, summed up in his words from *The Lay of the Last Minstrel*:

> *Breathes there the man, with soul so dead,*
> *Who never to himself has said,*
> *This is my own, my native land!*
> *Whose heart hath ne'er within him burn'd,*
> *As home his footsteps he hath turn'd*
> *From wandering on a foreign strand!*

**Further Reading**
Sir Walter Scott, *The Waverley Novels*
A.N. Wilson, *A Life of Walter Scott*

**Online Resources**
Edinburgh University Digital Library
http://www.walterscott.lib.ed.ac.uk/

## Thomas Carlyle
1795–1881

PHILOSOPHER AND HISTORIAN

*'A well-written life is almost as rare as a well-spent one.'*

Carlyle should know. He wrote a number of 'Lives' and was the leading historian of his age. He had a high regard for his own work and a healthy contempt for that of his contemporaries.

The great minds of the Enlightenment had died by the time Carlyle was born, however he demonstrated the Enlightenment virtues of self-belief and desire for self-improvement. He further exhibited these qualities through his craving for literary fame, which runs as a thread through the lives of the Enlightenment figures.

He was, particularly during the middle part of his life, the leading intellectual and moral force in Britain, expressing through his ideas the strong tenets of religious belief which sprang from his Calvinist upbringing. J.A. Froude, his biographer, wrote of Carlyle that for him 'God's existence was not an arguable possibility … but an awful reality to which the fate of nations, the fate of each individual man bore perpetual witness.' It was this certainty which he directed to the moral issues of his time.

His beliefs were in some ways ahead of his time. He thought that life had more to offer than mere economic success, a conviction which resonates with us today. He could not tolerate insincerity in politics – a view which smacks of idealism in today's political world, where a sincere politician is seen as an implicit contradiction – and he believed that philanthropy should be tempered by good sense. Who could quarrel with such ideas?

In history he believed that great men were not just the creatures of their age but were themselves creators of history; as he wrote, 'No great man lives in vain. The history of the world is but the biography of great men.' Carlyle was one of the first of the leading Scottish intellectuals to feel constrained by the Scottish scene and to move to London to fulfil his ambitions, but he always remained true to the core values of his Scottish upbringing.

## Ecclefechan

Carlyle was born in Ecclefechan in Dumfriesshire in 1795. The Carlyles claimed to have come from the English town of, self-evidently, Carlisle, during the reign of King David II. The churchyard of Ecclefechan is sprinkled with family graves.

Carlyle's father, James, was a stonemason, one of five brothers who were known, probably with justification, as the 'five fighting masons.' Carlyle's mother was Margaret. He was the eldest of five sons – there were also five daughters, so James must have found time for activities other than fighting! James had strong moral and religious principles, and a violent temper to accompany them.

Carlyle respected and was proud of his father and of his natural, if untutored knowledge and wit. While Carlyle was still a boy, James moved the family to a farm at Mainhill near Lockerbie, where he worked so hard that, despite the poor quality of the land, he left on his death in 1832, the surprising amount of one thousand pounds to the family.

The young Carlyle read voraciously, encouraged by his mother, who had ambitions for him to join the Church. His formal schooling began at the parish school before he went at the age of ten to Annan Academy, where he was unhappy, mocked by the other boys for his moods and his unboyish habit of bursting into tears. He left, however, with a good grasp of Latin and French, a taste of history and some algebra. He had also made contact with Edward Irving, who would prove a lifelong friend and mentor.

In 1809 he attended Edinburgh University, famously walking there from Ecclefechan, and there encountered for the first time the works of Isaac Newton. He gained distinction in Mathematics.

## 'Grant Me that I May Attain to Literary Fame'

Carlyle believed he was destined for greatness, but for now greatness would have to wait: he first needed to earn a living. After university he became a schoolmaster, teaching mathematics in his old school in Annan. He spent his vacations at the family farm in Mainhill and there taught himself German. Later he moved on to teach at Kirkcaldy, where he was reunited with Irving.

Carlyle did not believe he was destined to be a teacher all his life, declaring arrogantly that 'it were better to perish than to continue school mastering,' and in 1819 decided to return to Edinburgh, which still shone as a place of literary elegance, even if its light had somewhat dimmed. He tried private tutoring, teaching mathematics and studying the law, without finding his true vocation. He had always been a writer, but now he began to write professionally, contributing sixteen entries for the new Edinburgh Encyclopedia, in the section from M to N, 'Lady Montagu to Northumberland,' and reading extensively the works of Goethe and Schiller.

It was at this time that he had his 'Road to Damascus' moment, somewhat prosaically on Leith Walk, when he realised that his soul could be free to think and that hard work would mean that his efforts would not always be thwarted by an 'Everlasting No.'

In 1822 he completed the translation of a work on geometry and in 1823, the *London Magazine* began to serialise his *Life of Schiller*, which was subsequently published as a book two years later. After being translated into German, this book received praise from Goethe. He was beginning to receive the fame he sought.

In 1821 Carlyle had been introduced by Irving to one of his students, the talented and beautiful Jane Welsh, who was the daughter of a Haddington surgeon, and he began a long correspondence with her, wooing her unconventionally through a mix of literary criticism and sarcastic witticisms. Despite her initial view of her suitor as 'uncouth and ungainly' she responded to his persistence and they married in 1826. Two years later they set up home on an isolated farm at Craigenputtock which she inherited and where they lived until 1834.

It was not a happy time for the young bride. Carlyle would spend his days absorbed in his books and his writing, leaving her to endure a lonely life. Carlyle was not an easy man. He had an acerbic wit and few friends; those he had trod carefully to avoid becoming the target of the barbed witicisms to which he was ever prone.

During this period Carlyle wrote a number of articles on German literature, including two essays on Goethe, but his main project was an extraordinary book titled *Sartor Resartus*. This was part fantasy, part spiritual and part autobiographical, written in a fresh and vivid style, and set out Carlyle's philosophy of life. Carlyle was disheartened by the difficulty in obtaining a publisher; it first saw light of day in the form of magazine extracts and was not published in book form until 1838. The reaction of the magazine's subscribers could not have helped his mood either: 'It is a heap of clotted nonsense,' wrote one angry reader, whilst another complained, 'Stop that stuff or stop my paper!' It was somewhat better received in America, where the editors wrote (possibly with some bias since they had already paid for the rights) that 'the author makes ample amends for the occasional eccentricity of his genius not only by frequent bursts of pure splendour, but by the wit and sense which never fail him.'

## Carlyle Succumbs to the Call of London

Sadly, Carlyle believed that the glorious days of the Scottish Enlightenment had passed. He became unable to find sufficient intellectual challenge in Scotland, and when Irving suggested he move to London he responded positively.

The Carlyles moved in 1834, to set up a permanent home in Cheyne Row, Chelsea, where Carlyle concentrated upon his literary career. His first project was to write a major history of the French Revolution. He was initially helped by John Stuart Mill, who had himself planned such a work but abandoned the project when Carlyle showed interest, generously giving him the works of reference he had collected. After Carlyle had sent Mill the draft of the first volume, however, he carelessly

*Thomas Carlyle by Daniel Maclise*

left it lying around and one of his servants used it as scrap paper to light the fire; it took Carlyle six months to rewrite.

*The French Revolution: a History* was finally completed in 1837. It was history portrayed as drama. At last Carlyle's reputation was made, if not his finances; these only improved after the death of Jane's mother, who left them an annuity.

Carlyle soon developed a glittering list of friends attracted by his intellect and brilliant conversation. He was almost as quick to lose them, however, as they recoiled from his caustic criticism; those he insulted included Shelley, Byron, Keats, Balzac, Victor Hugo and Charles Lamb – it was a distinguished group. His dismissal of Gibbon was typical: 'With all his swagger and bombast, no man ever gave a more futile account of human beings than he has of the Decline and Fall of the Roman Empire.'

Jane was a staunch supporter during this period, although she did complain 'let no woman who values peace of soul ever marry an author!' She was herself a remarkable lady, intellectually gifted and able to express herself forcefully both in conversation and in writing. Neither she nor Thomas suffered fools gladly. Although their house in Chelsea gave the Carlyles access to the literati of London, they both missed the quiet of their home in Scotland and were troubled by the street noise at night, so much so that they built a special sound-proof room on the top floor of their house.

## Carlyle's Growing Reputation as a Historian

His next major work was a biography of Oliver Cromwell. This took him four years to complete and was published in 1845, cementing Carlyle's growing reputation as one of the leading historians of his time. A few years later he journeyed north to see his mother for the last time; she had recorded his success with all the pride a mother should show. She died on Christmas Day, 1853.

What should his next project be? After considerable deliberation he decided to write the definitive biography of Frederick the Great. He travelled extensively in Germany to research his subject and to see the scenes of the major events in his subject's life. The book soon developed a momentum of its own, stretching beyond the narrative of events which had marked *The French Revolution* or a straightforward biography such as Cromwell, to become in effect, a history of Germany and its part in European history through the eighteenth century.

*History of Friedrich II. of Prussia: Frederick the Great*, comprised six volumes and took seven years to write, which took their toll on the relationship between husband and wife. 'That tremendous book,' she wrote, 'made prolonged and entire devastation of any satisfactory semblance of home life or home happiness.' But when it was finished she was as loyal as ever; in a letter to Thomas she wrote 'Oh, my dear, what a magnificent book this is going to be, the best of all your books, forcible, clear and sparkling as the French Revolution, compact and finished as Cromwell.'

She was a good judge; the first two thousand copies soon sold out, and then the next thousand. The book was translated into German and rapidly became the required reading of historians in Germany. Carlyle's fame was fully established. Scotland had been slow to recognise the growing fame of her son, but now, belatedly made amends by inviting Carlyle to become Rector of Edinburgh University in 1866.

Jane had sacrificed her own considerable talent and potential for her husband, but her indomitable spirit was now breaking and she began complaining of chest pains. Thomas was in Edinburgh in April, 1866, when she died from heart failure whilst driving in her carriage in Hyde Park. It was perhaps only with her death that Thomas Carlyle realised the depth of quality of his wife. He composed her epitaph:

> *In her bright existence she had more sorrows than are common, but also a soft invincibility, a capacity of discernment, and a noble loyalty of heart which are rare. For forty years she was the true and loving help-mate of her husband, and by act and word unweariedly forwarded him as none else could in all of worth that he did or attempted. She died at London, 21st April, 1866, suddenly snatched from him, and the light of his life as if gone out.*

One can only hope that in whatever place she lay she could hear his words.

## Life After the Death of His Wife

Carlyle never fully recovered from Jane's death. He wrote his Reminiscences, in which he attractively portrays his early life and pays tribute to his wife.

He lived for another fifteen years, increasingly involving himself in politics and deriving benefit from his discrete gifts of charity. Once he gave a shilling to a blind man, whose dog promptly guided him across the road to the gin shop. When a friend remonstrated with Carlyle that this was a misuse of charity, he wearily replied, 'Poor fellow. I daresay he is cold and thirsty.' He had certainly mellowed.

Many of the political concepts he had advocated had come to pass: promotion by merit rather than the purse; the introduction of a Minister with responsibility for Education; the belief that ownership of land implies responsibilities as well as rights; regulation of working hours; and care for the destitute.

Carlyle died in February 1881 and as he had requested, his body was buried in the snow-covered churchyard in Ecclefechan.

## Carlyle's Legacy

In many ways the life of Thomas Carlyle was a contradiction. He was an idealist yet always ready to insult a friend with a cruel comment. He upheld courage and forbearance yet would grumble about his personal plight. He had a brilliant mind yet distrusted the findings of scientists such as Darwin. He believed in God but could not accept the membership of any Church. He believed in free trade but thought it should be enforced if necessary. He believed in strong leadership, that Might is Right, but did not explain what to do when Might was not Right. He was scornful of the rights of women but believed they should be able to study for a medical qualification. He loved his wife but made her life a torment.

Throughout, he believed that man should live by the consequences of his actions and according to the doctrine of personal responsibility – beliefs that derived from his strict upbringing in Scotland.

He believed in self-help, that effort brought reward. His philosophy was perhaps best summed up in the lines he quoted at the start of the *Latter-Day Pamphlets*. To the statement 'Well, let God mend all!' he responded, 'nay, by God, we must help Him to mend it.' Above all, he was a brilliant historian, an original thinker and a great moral force.

**Further Reading**
John Nichol, *Thomas Carlyle*

**Online Resources**
The Literature Network
http://www.online-literature.com/thomas-carlyle/

## Robert Louis Stevenson
### 1850–1894

NOVELIST, TRAVEL WRITER AND POET

*Here lies one who meant well, tried a little, failed much.*

Robert Louis Stevenson wrote these words as an epitaph for himself. This disparaging view greatly understates his achievements. Despite being seriously ill for much of his life, he wrote some of the world's greatest adventure stories, which continue today to enthral and entertain both children and adults.

### From Childhood to Marriage

Almost from birth Stevenson suffered from illness, probably tuberculosis, a disease of the lungs which was one of the most common causes of death at the time but which has now been almost eliminated from Britain by a programme of vaccination. He wrote later of his childhood of 'terrible long nights, that I lay awake, troubled continually with a hacking, exhausting cough, and praying for sleep or for morning from the bottom of my shaken little body.'

A sickly, hollow-chested child with lank hair and knobbly legs, Stevenson did not have many friends and school was an unhappy time. His father, Thomas Stevenson of the family of lighthouse engineers, wanted his son to become an engineer and join the family company, but Stevenson would have none of it. The life of a lighthouse engineer was far too uncomfortable. Instead he agreed reluctantly to study the law, but he was a dreamer. He believed himself to be made in the mould of Robert Fergusson, and like him he tasted low life in the bars and dens of Edinburgh. Often ill, his weak chest probably suffering in the cold, damp Edinburgh air, his body frequently wracked by coughs and fevers, but when well he was excellent company, full of talk and jests.

At twenty-three Stevenson became so seriously ill that his parents sent him to the south of France in the hope that the warmer climate would help his health. From there he moved north to Paris, where he lived the life of the Bohemian student; wearing a long purple cloak he would smoke opium with other students in smoke-filled bars while they talked the night away.

Robert Louis Stevenson
*see: colour plate 9*

Count Girolamo Nerli, Robert Louise Stevenson, Scottish National Portrait Gallery

Somewhat restored, he returned to Edinburgh, where to please his parents he took and passed his law examinations, although he never planned to be a lawyer. He had begun to write but he earned very little from his writing and lived off money given to him by his father.

The next time he was in France he met Fanny, an American lady eleven years older than himself, with a colourful past. When Fanny moved back to California, Stevenson decided to write a travel book and trekked through France with an obstinate donkey called Modestine, who refused to move above a snail's pace. He recorded his experiences in *Travels with a Donkey*.

Stevenson's view of marriage was not positive; he wrote that 'it is a field of battle, and not a bed of roses.' However, he could not live without Fanny and so he followed her to America, where they were later married. He was twenty-nine and Fanny forty. He acquired a wife, a grown-up stepdaughter, Belle, and a young stepson Lloyd. Fanny proved a good wife who lovingly nursed him through his recurring illnesses.

## TREASURE ISLAND

*Fifteen men on the dead man's chest*
*Yo-ho-ho, and a bottle of rum!*
*Drink and the devil had done for the rest*
*Yo-ho-ho, and a bottle of rum!*

One wet day in the Highlands, Stevenson passed the time with his stepson by telling him a story of pirates, buried treasure and adventure. He drew a map of an island with a cross to mark the buried treasure and each day would tell more of the story. *Treasure Island*, first published in weekly installments in a boys' paper called *Young Folks*, would become one of the greatest adventure stories of all time.

The story begins in the 'Admiral Benbow,' an inn kept by the parents of the hero, Jim Hawkins. Billy Bones, a mysterious stranger, lodges at the inn, and when he suddenly dies Jim finds a map of an island hidden in his sea chest. He shows the map to Squire Trelawny and Doctor Livesey, who realise it shows the place where the famous pirate Captain Flint hid his treasure. The Squire hires a ship, the *Hispaniola*, to find the treasure and takes Jim and the Doctor with him, but he little realises that most of his crew, including the one-legged cook known as Long John Silver, are themselves pirates who had before sailed with Captain Flint.

On the island Jim meets Ben Gunn, a former pirate who has lived alone on the island since he was left there by Captain Flint. Long John Silver and his crew take Jim prisoner and then set off with the map to find the treasure for themselves, but when they reach the spot marked on the map there is only an empty chest; the treasure has gone. The pirates are angry and turn against Long John Silver. He gives Jim a pistol and together they face the angry pirates until they are rescued by the Doctor, who shoots and kills one of the pirates; the others then flee.

Ben Gunn tells Jim that he moved the treasure to his cave many years ago and together they carry it back to the *Hispaniola*. Long John Silver protests he is Jim's friend and they all set sail for home. One morning they awake to find that Long John Silver has disappeared, taking with him most of the treasure. Jim, the Squire and the Doctor eventually reach home with what is left of the treasure and Jim swears he will never go treasure hunting again.

### A Child's Garden of Verses

After writing *Treasure Island* Stevenson was again seriously ill, coughing up blood and losing weight, so he and Fanny went to Davos in Switzerland to try to find a cure for his illness and to finish his new book, *A Child's Garden of Verses*. He could only write with difficulty, lying in bed in a darkened room and using his left hand to write with as his right arm was bound to his body to stop the bleeding from his lungs. Despite his illness he achieved a remarkable lightness of touch, as shown in the poem *'Bed in Summer'*:

> *In winter I get up at night*
> *And dress by yellow candle-light,*
> *In summer, quite the other way,*
> *I have to go to bed by day.*
> *I have to go to bed and see*
> *The birds still hopping on the tree,*
> *Or hear the grown-up people's feet*
> *Still going past me in the street.*
> *And does it not seem hard to you*
> *When all the sky is clear and blue,*
> *And I should like so much to play*
> *To have to go to bed by day?*

## The Strange Case of Dr Jekyll and Mr Hyde

In 1884 the couple moved to England and settled in Bournemouth where Stevenson thought the gentle sea airs of the south coast would be good for his health. There he wrote another masterpiece, *The Strange Case of Dr Jekyll and Mr Hyde*. The idea for this disturbing story came to him in a dream. He woke and feverishly wrote it down and showed his draft to Fanny. She thought it confused and that there was not enough distinction between the 'good' Dr Jekyll and the 'evil' Mr Hyde. Angered, Stevenson threw his draft on the fire but then agreed she was right. He sat down immediately to write it again.

The story tells of Dr Jekyll, who believes that man consists of two parts, one good and one evil, and takes a potion to liberate his 'other' self. This is perhaps a reflection of Stevenson's own early life in Edinburgh when he was on the one hand a gentleman but on the other a rake who visited the bars and low nightlife of the city. When Jekyll takes the potion in his laboratory he changes into Hyde, a wholly evil man who tramples without a thought over the body of a young girl he meets in the street and later brutally murders an MP, Sir Danvers Carew, beating him viciously with a heavy stick. As a result Hyde is wanted for murder and can no longer appear on the streets of London.

Jekyll tries too late to control Hyde and to redeem the evil done by his other self by doing good deeds, but the power of Hyde is now too strong and Jekyll can no longer control his other self. While in a park, in broad daylight, Jekyll feels the change coming over him and in the person of Hyde has to find a hotel room to avoid being caught. He sends to a friend, Lanyon, to go to his laboratory to find the potion for him so that he can change back.

Lanyon brings the potion to Hyde in his hotel room and watches him take it, describing how he

> put the glass to his lips and drank at one gulp. A cry followed; he reeled, staggered, clutched at the table … there came a change – he seemed to swell – his face became suddenly black, and the features seemed to melt and alter – and the next moment I had sprung to my feet and leaped back against the wall, my arm raised to shield me, my mind submerged in terror. "O God!" I screamed, and "O God!" again and again; for there before my eyes, pale and shaken, and half fainting, and groping before him with his hands, like a man restored from death – there stood Henry Jekyll!

Lanyon is, rather understandably, deeply shocked by what he has seen and dies. The supply of potion runs out and Hyde can no longer transform himself into Jekyll to avoid capture and so he takes refuge in Jekyll's laboratory. Jekyll's servant notices that a stranger (Hyde) has broken into the house and with a friend of Jekyll breaks down the door to the laboratory to find Hyde inside, dead. There is no trace of Dr Jekyll, just a letter in his hand confessing what he has done and that he and Hyde are two sides of the same person. The book was an instant success and has become a classic tale since it was first published in 1886, with over one hundred and twenty films made of the story.

Stevenson may have owed the idea of a man having two sides to his life to the strange story of Deacon Brodie, who had lived in Edinburgh in the eighteenth century. By day he was a respected cabinet maker working for the gentry at the best addresses in Edinburgh. At night he took on another persona, that of a gambler, a drunkard and a womaniser, a life he funded by robbing the houses of the gentry whom he served, employing accomplices to burgle their houses with keys he had made by using wax impressions. Inevitably, one of his accomplices was captured and turned 'king's evidence.' Brodie fled to Amsterdam but was recaptured and brought back to Edinburgh, where he was tried and found guilty. In an ultimate irony, he was hanged in 1788 at the Old Tolbooth on a gallows which as carpenter to the city he had himself designed and built.

## Kidnapped

*Kidnapped* tells the story of a young boy, David Balfour, whose parents have died and who goes to see his uncle, Ebenezer, who lives in an old tower house. Ebenezer is very careful with his money but he gives David forty guineas and tells him to fetch more from a chest at the top of the tower. David climbs the stairs of the tower in the dark and suddenly realises that not only are the stairs uneven but they suddenly stop; beyond there is nothing but a huge drop! His uncle had planned that he should fall hundreds of feet to his death.

David is tricked again by his uncle, bundled up and put on a ship to be sold into slavery. On the ship David meets up with Alan Breck, a Jacobite adventurer, and together they escape. Alan is being hunted by the 'redcoats,' the government soldiers. Together they flee through the Highlands, hiding in the heather to avoid capture by the soldiers. After many adventures they reach Ebenezer's house where David confronts his uncle with his treachery. David is given his rights to the estate and Alan Breck leaves for France.

*Kidnapped* was published as a story for boys in *Young Folks* from May to July 1886. It is an historical adventure written with pace and was a huge success. Stevenson was no longer just a famous author but at last a financial success as well!

Soon after the publication of *Dr Jekyll* and *Kidnapped*, Stevenson's father died, too ill to recognise his son. There was nothing now to keep Stevenson in Britain so he and Fanny set sail for New York, where he was given a great welcome as a famous author.

## Samoa and the South Sea Islands

The welcome may have been warm but New York was too cold for Stevenson. He needed sunshine to keep him from illness. In 1888 he and Fanny hired a luxury schooner, the ninety-five foot (thirty metre) *Casco*, and sailed out through the Golden Gate of San Francisco harbour bound for the Pacific Islands.

First they settled in Tahiti and then moved to Honolulu, where Stevenson finished *The Master of Ballantrae*. Stevenson found even Honolulu too cold and they moved on again, eventually settling in Samoa, where he at last found the warmth his body craved.

Stevenson bought an estate of four hundred acres on the slopes of Mount Vaea, reachable only by a stony track. There he built a house which he called 'Vailima,' furnished with furniture sent from Scotland, and there he spent the last five years of his life. He was reading a chapter of his unfinished *Weir of Hermiston* to Fanny one day, when he asked her, *'Do I look strange?'* Suddenly he went into a coma and died two hours later, just forty-five years old. He was buried on the summit of Mount Vaea. On his tomb were carved the words he had written many years before:

> *Under the wide and starry sky,*
> *Dig the grave and let me lie.*
> *Glad did I live and gladly die,*
> *And I laid me down with a will.*
> *This be the verse that you grave for me*
> *'Here he lies where he longed to be;*
> *Home is the sailor, home from the sea,*
> *And the hunter home from the hill.'*

Robert Louis Stevenson wrote some of the most renowned stories in British literature, whose fame and appeal have lasted to the present day. Amazingly, he wrote these vivid tales while suffering from constant illness. As he wrote to a friend, 'For fifteen years I have not had a day's real health. I have wakened sick and gone to bed weary; and I have done my work unflinchingly. I have written in bed and written out of it, written in haemorrhages, written in sickness, written torn by coughs, written when my head swam for weakness; and for so long it seems to me I have won my wager.' He had won his wager, his bet with life. His determination had prevailed. His genius had triumphed over the weakness of his body.

**Further Reading**
Claire Harman, *Robert Louis Stevenson*
Robert Louis Stevenson, *Kidnapped*
---, *The Strange Case of Dr.Jekyll and Mr.Hyde*
---, *Treasure Island*

**Online Resources**
http://www.robert-louis-stevenson.org/

## John Buchan
### 1875–1940

FROM NOVELIST TO GOVERNOR-GENERAL

*'Do what has to be done – now!'*
—Buchan

John Buchan was born many years after the Enlightenment, but the influences on his life were similar to the Enlightenment ideals and he certainly achieved great things. He was a writer of both biographies and novels, most famously the Richard Hannay stories, and he had a distinguished political career, devoting his later years to public service.

His life was ordained by his upbringing. His father was a minister in the Free Church, which had been formed in 1843, when nearly five hundred ministers of the Church of Scotland marched out of the General Assembly in protest against the rights of landowners to appoint ministers. But in reality the split was deeper, a schism between the moderates and the evangelicals. To be a Free Church minister you had to be prepared to flout the establishment to preserve your beliefs. You would also be a believer in Calvinism, perhaps a somewhat less extreme form than that of Knox, but still a world ruled by God where Good would always triumph over Evil.

This was the background to Buchan's childhood and the formative influence upon his life, but his determination he inherited from his mother, whose motto was 'Do what has to be done – now!' His mother's words would stay with him all his life; even at university he worked to a strictly controlled schedule, rising early and allocating his day to reading and writing, with some hours set aside in the afternoon for exercise, usually walking or rowing. His self-discipline and his determination he owed to his Calvinist roots.

## Childhood and University

John Buchan was born in 1875 in Perth, but his family roots were in the Border country. His grandfather, also John, had, after a period as the accountant to the City of Glasgow Bank, formed a prosperous law firm in Peebles, and bought a house appropriate to his status with twenty acres of ground. This idyll was somewhat interrupted in 1878 when the City of Glasgow Bank crashed; as a trustee of the bank his grandfather was responsible for its debts and he had to sell much of his property, only clearing his liabilities shortly before his death in 1883.

At the age of five, Buchan suffered a serious head injury when he fractured his skull falling out of a carriage. The physical scar would stay with him all his life. Buchan spent a year in bed recovering, creating a firm bond between John and his mother, Helen, who nursed him through his convalescence. Buchan's father enjoyed reading and much of his education came from listening to his father reading from the Bible or from books about the tales of the Borders.

Each summer Helen took the children to her father's farm at Broughton in the Borders. Perhaps it was there that the young boy became enraptured by the romanticism of the Border country. Buchan later wrote of the Borders that he could there enjoy 'feelings of happiness and security, of enterprise and adventure, of sadness and nostalgia.'

When Buchan was thirteen, his father's ministry was moved to the Gorbals in Glasgow; originally in the days of the wealthy Glasgow merchants the Gorbals had been a prosperous district of the city, but latterly it had become neglected and it was now the home to the poorest of Glasgow. The young Buchan was prevailed upon to take a Sunday School class and after some token religious instruction he would spin tales for the entertainment of the boys from the Gorbals, boys whom he later immortalised in *Huntingtower* as the 'Gorbal Die-Hards.'

Buchan attended Hutcheson's Grammar School, which had been formed in 1641 by the Hutcheson brothers for the education of orphan boys. The school opened its doors with a roll call of just twelve boys and epitomised the early investment in education which helped contribute to Scotland's reputation for a well-educated and highly literate population.

Already showing his literary inclinations, Buchan kept a commonplace book in which he recorded his favourite excerpts from famous works together with his own first attempts at writing.

When he was seventeen he entered Glasgow University, each day walking the four miles from home to arrive for his classes by eight o'clock and each evening walking the four miles home again. The university had some distinguished professors and Buchan studied for the broad Master of Arts, reading classics – the young Gilbert Murray was Professor of Greek – natural and moral philosophy and history, a civilised mix of subjects which together gave a well-rounded education.

He wrote a number of pieces for the university magazine, but at this time his ambition was to become a university professor. Gilbert Murray befriended Buchan, encouraging him to broaden his reading, and Buchan's first novel, *Sir Quixote of the Moors*, published in 1895 when he was nineteen, was dedicated to Murray.

## Oxford

Buchan was becoming disenchanted with what he saw as the parochialism of his father's life; he wanted a broader canvas on which to spread his talents.

After two years at Glasgow he won a scholarship to Oxford University. With an echo of Adam Smith, Buchan was not initially impressed with the quality of teaching at Oxford, but he persevered, becoming involved in student life, financing himself with a little embryonic journalism on the side, writing articles for the Glasgow *Herald* and *Blackwood's Magazine* and publishing an anthology on fishing and a collection of essays. He was a serious and committed student, working long hours and exhibiting a dedication somewhat frightening to many of his peers, whose days were rather more typically centred on parties and pleasure.

Even though he was surrounded by some of the finest brains in the world, Buchan began to make his mark. His second novel, *John Barnet of Barns*, was published while he was at university and he was appointed a reader of manuscripts by his publisher, which provided some much required cash to fund his social life. He was also asked to write a history of his college, Brasenose. He finished his time at Oxford on a high: he was awarded a First in his final classics exams and was made President of the Union in his last year, a prestigious post which often presaged a political career.

He had however one set-back – he was not granted a Fellowship of All Souls which was his ambition. He set off instead for London to study for the Bar. Writing, he thought, was not a proper job.

## The Aftermath of the Boer War

Buchan's star was in the ascendant. The Boer War between the Dutch settlers and the British colonialists in Africa was nearing its end after a bitter campaign which had matched the lightly armed but highly mobile and motivated Boer farmers against the might of the British military machine. 'Might' had eventually triumphed but only after four hundred and fifty thousand British troops had been committed to the war, and even then only after a number of military disasters which had threatened Britain's presence in South Africa. Eight thousand British troops died in battle and a further fourteen thousand from disease. Perhaps Almoth Wright had been right to suggest vaccination.

The British government wanted to restore effective colonial rule in the Transvaal and the Orange Free State, which had been devastated by the bitter war. Buchan would make an excellent candidate to help with the task, and it sounded more interesting than practising as a barrister. Buchan was shocked with what he found when he arrived in the Transvaal.

It is not always realised that the concept of concentration camps, which would later form such a tragic component of the Second World War, had originated during the Boer War, and shamefully it was the British who had invented them, although not of course, as part of a planned process of ethnic extermination.

The camps in South Africa were originally set up as 'refugee camps' to provide for the Boer families whose men folk had ridden off to war and whose homes and livelihoods had been destroyed by the war. In 1900 General Kitchener had embarked on an all-out offensive to end the war, using a scorched-earth policy to destroy the Boer farms which provided support to the Boer fighters. Farms were burnt, wells were poisoned and fields were destroyed. Tens of thousands of women and children were taken from their devastated homes and placed in these new camps.

By the end of the war there were more than one hundred and sixty thousand people housed in an estimated forty-five camps for Boer women and children and sixty-four for black Africans. Conditions in the camps were terrible; they were overcrowded, with virtually no sanitation, meagre food rations and poor hygiene. It is estimated that twenty-six thousand women and children died in these British concentration camps, compared with the less than four thousand Boer fighters who died in battle.

Buchan claimed some success in creating order out of this appalling chaos and in improving the living conditions in the camps before the women and children were returned to their homes. The British adopted a policy of resettlement after the war with the idea of introducing less belligerent settlers from Britain and Australia into South Africa in an attempt to dilute the Boer influence; the young Buchan worked on these plans, riding extensively around the country and advising on improved agricultural methods. It was with some relief, and some regret, that he returned two years later to London. He published an account of his experiences in a book in 1903.

## The Great War

Buchan had a busy life in the first decade of the twentieth century, working at the Bar, writing and developing his political contacts. He also found time to enjoy London's social life – perhaps a weekend at a country house, or oysters at Sweetings; devilled kidneys at the Savoy or a night of dancing followed by a breakfast of whitebait. It was a life of privilege far removed from his Scottish roots.

One evening at a select dinner party, he met Susan Grosvenor, related to the wealthy Westminster family. It seemed a perfect match, but not to Buchan's mother, who complained that the prospective bride was English and, even worse, couldn't sew. There is no pleasing some mothers!

They were married in 1907. It was a 'simple' wedding held at St George's, Hanover Square, the church where Grosvenor brides were traditionally married; the bride arrived in the Grosvenor coach provided by her cousin the Duke of Westminster and there were just the eight bridesmaids and a few hundred guests.

Buchan's new responsibilities meant that he needed a regular income and so he joined Nelson's as literary editor. While with Nelson's he introduced the Nelson Sixpenny Classics and then the Sevenpenny Library, which featured books such as the *Riddle of the Sands*, described by Buchan as 'the best story of adventure published in the last quarter of a century,' and the works of Mark Twain and Conan Doyle, offering these 'modern' classics to a much wider audience. He continued with his own writing, the most successful book of this period being *Prester John*, which drew on his experiences in South Africa.

When war broke out Buchan was suffering severely from a duodenal ulcer, which together with his age prevented him enlisting. His younger daughter, Alice, had had an operation and the family rented a house in Broadstairs to give her the benefits of sea air. Susan's cousins rented a house nearby, with steps leading down to a private beach. The steps, the imminent threat of war and the scare stories of German spies gave Buchan the idea for probably his most famous novel, *The Thirty-Nine Steps*, which introduced Buchan's South African hero, Richard Hannay, and was set largely in the Scottish countryside. The use of atmosphere in creating fear and tension in the reader may owe something to the 'first and greatest spy story,' the *Riddle of the Sands*.

If he could not join the war, Buchan wanted to play his part. He embarked on an ambitious project, to tell the history of the war 'as it happened.' Each volume ran to around sixty thousand words and a new one was published every three months; the total ran to an amazing one million words in twenty-four parts and kept Buchan busy for the next five years.

But even this massive undertaking did not exhaust his time or energies. In 1915 he was appointed special correspondent for *The Times* and was sent off to the Front. Soon he was recruited by the army, firstly into Intelligence, where he was responsible for propaganda, and then to the staff of General Douglas Haig, Commander-in-Chief of British Forces. He still found time to write two more novels, *Greenmantle* and *Mr Standfast*, both of which featured Hannay.

The war deeply affected Buchan. He might be writing propaganda, but he was all too conscious of the dreadful waste of life. On a personal level, his younger brother Alastair was killed in action alongside a fellow officer in April 1917. Their nurse movingly 'washed the battle-grime from their faces and smoothed their flaxen hair … [and] knowing that somewhere over the Channel hearts would break for these bright heads, before they were laid in the earth she kissed them for their mothers.'

Buchan was exhausted at the end of the war, devastated at the loss of his brother and of many of his close friends, and with many of his ideals shattered. He was ill for some time – indeed, throughout his life he had recurring bouts of illness.

## Governor-General

After the war the Buchans bought a seventeenth-century manor house in Oxfordshire where Buchan could continue his writing. He finished another Hannay book, *The Three Hostages*, then *Huntingtower* and his *History of the Great War*.

In 1925 he published *John Macnab*, the story of three successful but bored men who decided to accept the challenge of illicitly taking a stag and a salmon from each of three landed estates without getting caught. Buchan vividly evokes the Scottish countryside and the thrill of the chase. In 1927, Buchan saw the publication of *Witch Wood*, an historical novel and perhaps one of his finest works.

He had long mulled over the idea of a political career and in 1927 stood as a candidate for one of three parliamentary seats elected, not entirely in the spirit of democracy, exclusively by the graduates of the ancient Scottish Universities. His time in the House was honourable if without especial distinction, possibly because Buchan believed in logical argument, seeing a problem as an intellectual challenge rather than a point-scoring political opportunity. He was also a thoughtful, courteous and sensitive man – not, sadly, the characteristics associated with a successful politician.

Despite the political pressures he continued to write – mainly biographies, including a biography of Montrose, the introspective but charismatic leader and poet with whom he most closely identified. He also produced the definitive biography of Sir Walter Scott and biographies of Cromwell and the Emperor Augustus, a fairly eclectic selection.

In the years since the war, the main Buchan income had come from writing. He was certainly prolific: for fifteen years he had written a novel every year together with twenty full-length non-fiction works and numerous articles and essays. As this was combined with a political career and other public duties, it is possible that the quality of some of his work was not the best.

There was a contrast between his adventure stories, which Buchan himself rather disparagingly called 'shockers,' and his historical novels. In one of his books Buchan gave the recipe for writing a shocker:

> *I begin by fixing on one or two facts which have no sort of obvious connection – an old blind woman spinning in the Western Highlands, a barn in a Norwegian saeter, and a little curiosity shop in North London kept by a Jew with a dyed beard. Not much connection between the three! You invent a connection [and] the reader ... is pleased with the*

*ingenuity of the solution, for he doesn't realise that the author fixed*
*upon the solution first, and then invented a problem to suit it.*

In 1933 Buchan was appointed Lord High Commissioner to the General
Assembly of the Church of Scotland, where his duties were to give the opening
and closing addresses of the Assembly and to preside over its meetings. This gave
him all the trappings of the 'great'; he was housed at Holyrood House and, as the
King's representative, was greeted by a twenty-one gun salute. Buchan was in his
element – and at long last his mother could feel proud of him, although
characteristically she would have preferred to see him as Moderator!

In 1935 *The Thirty-Nine Steps* was made into a film directed by Alfred
Hitchcock, creating one of the 'all-time great' adventure films. The same year
Buchan was offered an even more prestigious post, that of Governor-General of
Canada. He immediately resigned his seat in the House of Commons and moved
straight to the House of Lords, taking the title Lord Tweedsmuir, and in October,
Lord and Lady Tweedsmuir set sail for Canada.

With great energy Buchan entered into his new role, as he had done in each
stage of his life. He travelled extensively through the country and cemented
relationships with his American neighbours. In 1938 he hosted a royal visit and
just one year later he signed Canada's declaration of war on Germany.

It would be one of his last official acts because six months later he died  from
an embolism following a fall. He was buried in the Oxfordshire village which had
been his home since 1920. His memoirs, *Memory-Hold-the-Door*, were published
in 1940. In this book Buchan included many portraits of his friends but regrettably
referred only briefly to his wife and to his daughter not at all.

Susan lived for a further thirty-seven years, during which she wrote a number
of historical novels. Perhaps her light could shine when she was no longer in her
husband's shadow.


### Buchan's Legacy

Above all, John Buchan was a Scot, although he spent most of his adult life
outside Scotland. He saw his role in service to the British Empire and believed
Scotland served as part of this Empire. He did not recognise the opposite side of
that coin: the disservice of the Empire to Scotland as that country's greatest talents
sought their careers outside their homeland.

Buchan enjoyed outdoor sports, fishing, walking and climbing – extensively in
Scotland, South Africa and Switzerland. He had a wide network of male friends
but was essentially a complex and private man who, although proud of his children,
found it difficult to relate closely to them or indeed to his wife. He was above all
driven by his Calvinist upbringing. A man of great learning and distinction, from
an early age Buchan imposed upon himself a disciplined routine of reading,

writing, work and leisure which would occupy him from six o'clock in the morning to ten at night. His literary work was distinguished, although he was too often merely a good storyteller rather than a great writer. His record of public service was honest but did not do full credit to his gifts.

Although by the standards of most he had a highly successful writing career and achieved the political heights of Governor-General of Canada, he did not perhaps reach the pinnacle of achievement for which as a young man he had seemed to be destined.

In a sense John Buchan was a perpetual outsider – a Scot in England but English when in Scotland. He was a man 'who had a great future behind him,' and left an immense collection of works, over a hundred books in all, histories, biographies and novels. He should be remembered above all else as a superb teller of stories whose books breathed the air of Scotland, the magic of the hills, the excitement of the stalking of a stag or the patient reward of the fisherman.

**Further Reading**
John Buchan, *John Macnab*
---, *The Richard Hannay Stories*
Andrew Lownie, *John Buchan: The Presbyterian Cavalier*

**Online Resources**
http://www.johnbuchansociety.co.uk/

**'MANUSCRIPT OF MONTE CASSINO'** (HAND, 1 of 3 pieces)

Eduardo Paolozzi - 1991

Picardy Place, Edinburgh

photo: Thomas Haywood

Paolozzi created this work as an allegory to the
manuscript for which it is named, *A Journey*.
Consisting of three pieces: a hand, ankle and foot,
the work refers to Ancient Roman sculptures on
Capitoline Hill, Rome.

# Painters

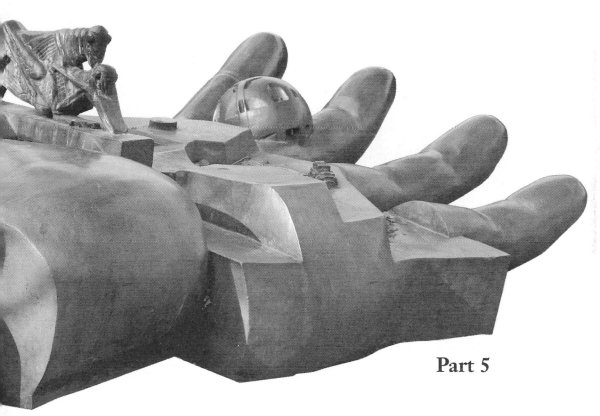

Part 5

PAINTERS

**Allan Ramsay**
ARTIST WHO HELPED TO FOUND THE SELECT SOCIETY

**Sir Henry Raeburn**
SCOTLAND'S GREATEST PORTRAIT PAINTER

**Alexander Nasmyth**
THE FATHER OF SCOTTISH LANDSCAPE ART

**Sir David Wilkie**
THE PAINTER WHO PORTRAYED EVERYDAY LIFE

# Part 5 • Painters

## The 'Select Society'

Ironically, Scotland's small population, which might have been thought a disadvantage to the development of intellectual thought and the arts, was in fact probably a benefit as all the leading members of the Enlightenment were well known to each other.

Poets, writers and artists were all a part of the close-knit society, where it was impossible to walk down an Edinburgh street for more than half an hour without tripping over an eminent philosopher. It is hard to overestimate the importance of this ability to exchange ideas with other great intellects, the benefit derived not just from input from the leading thinkers in your own discipline but the lateral input from others, the artist, the writer or the historian.

Some may take a narrow view of the Enlightenment, concentrating on the lives and works of the philosophers, but its influence was felt across a wide spectrum, reflected not just in the works of such writers as Fergusson, Burns and Scott, but equally in the world of visual art.

Scottish painters adopted a new openness, ready to embrace the art of the Renaissance and of contemporary Europe and to bring these influences into their own work. Art, the appreciation of art, and the teaching of art flourished in Scotland in the late eighteenth and early nineteenth centuries. The Royal Institution was founded in 1819 and the Royal Scottish Academy just a few years later. This resurgence in Scottish art was followed by the emergence in the late nineteenth century of the Glasgow Boys and the Scottish Colourists, Fergusson, Peploe, Hunter and Cadell.

Scottish artists were not just developing Scottish art but were intimately involved in the Enlightenment; Raeburn painted many of the leading Enlightenment figures whilst Nasmyth, a friend of Burns, was also involved with the foundation of the Royal Institution, and Allan Ramsay was famously a founding member of the Select Society.

In examining the history of the Enlightenment, it would be hard to overestimate the role of the societies, especially the Select Society, in expediting and encouraging the interplay of ideas through intellectual discourse in convivial surroundings. The roll call of the founders of the Select Society underscores the breadth of interest of its members.

Fifteen members attended its first meeting on 22 May 1754; amongst them were the painter Allan Ramsay who was the moving force behind its formation; William Robertson, the historian and principal of Edinburgh University; Adam Smith, the economist and philosopher; Lord Kames, the lawyer and philosopher; the eccentric Lord Monboddo, who more than a century before Darwin believed that man had developed from the ape, losing the tail over time, and that the orangutan was merely a form of primitive man who had survived into the present day; and of course David Hume himself.

The Select Society met on Wednesday evenings in the Advocates' Library, which would be the scene of many lively discussions. It grew fast in both influence and numbers, so that David Hume wrote of the Select Society just one year later that:

> It has grown to be a national concern. Young and old, noble and ignorable, witty and dull, laity and clergy, all the world are ambitious of a place amongst us.

Alexander Carlyle opined that the main benefit came not from the formal debates but from the *'warm suppers and excellent claret'* served afterwards, explaining

> The conversation at those convivial meetings frequently improved the members more by free conversation than the speeches in the Society. It was those meetings in particular that rubbed off all the corners … and made the literati of Edinburgh less captious and pedantic than they were elsewhere.

The Select Society lasted about ten years, in the end becoming almost too successful with as many as one hundred and thirty-five members by 1759; as Hume said to Ramsay, *'Such felicity has attended the seed you planted.'* It was a painter, Allan Ramsay, who had been instrumental in the formation of the Select Society and it is the painters to whom we now turn, beginning appropriately with Ramsay himself. Not only a first-rate portrait painter, Ramsay also participated actively in the ideas of the Enlightenment, writing treatises on affairs of public import.

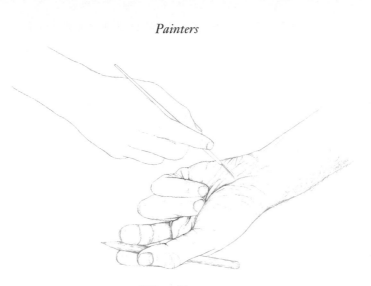

# Allan Ramsay
## 1713–1784

ARTIST WHO HELPED TO FOUND THE SELECT SOCIETY

Four great Scottish artists, Allan Ramsay, Henry Raeburn, Alexander Nasmyth and David Wilkie emerged during the Enlightenment. Their work evolved alongside the ideas being developed by the philosophers and scientists of the Enlightenment and they were receptive to new influences, enthusiastically embracing their European artistic heritage. Allan Ramsay was one of the greatest of the portrait painters of the eighteenth century, surpassed only by the younger Joshua Reynolds and his fellow Scot Henry Raeburn. The son of the poet, also Allan Ramsay, he was born into a family which was already a part of the Enlightenment. He became not only a fine artist but a key member of the Enlightenment movement, responsible with his friend David Hume, for the formation of the Select Society which would play such a pivotal role in the Enlightenment's development.

## A Burgeoning Talent

Ramsay always wanted to become a painter. Eager to learn and realising that Scotland could not give him the breadth of experience he sought, he moved at the age of twenty to London, where he studied painting under the Swedish painter Hans Hysing. He recognised that to develop his style he needed to study the Italian Masters and so travelled to Italy where he spent three years in Florence, Rome and Naples; this openness of mind to other influences and desire for improvement form a common theme among all of Scotland's finest Enlightenment painters.

In Rome he became friendly with a young landscape painter, Camillo Paderni. Some years later Paderni sent him details of the ancient frescoes which were being uncovered at Herculaneum which Ramsay had published for the Royal Society. These created great excitement, revealing artworks of a classical civilisation which had lain hidden for years *'as fresh as if they had been done a month ago.'*

During his time in Rome Ramsay was also presented to the young Prince Charles Edward, better known as 'Bonnie Prince Charlie.'

## Success as a Fashionable Portrait Painter in London

Nourished and stimulated by his time in Italy, Ramsay returned in 1738 to Britain, dividing his time between London and Edinburgh. He soon gained success as a portrait painter in a time when the taste was developing for less formal portraits. One full-length portrait of the '2nd Duke of Buccleuch,' painted in 1739, is an elegant if frank portrayal of the Duke with none of the affectation of the painting of some of his rivals, though nevertheless retaining the traditional formal pose with the left foot turned out and the weight borne on the right leg. His full-length portrait of 'John Campbell, 2nd Duke of Argyll,' a year later, presents a richly clothed portrayal again in a classical pose.

Ramsay's style was simple and robust and his portraits of men were striking. His less formal portraits, such as a sensitive depiction of 'Anne Bayne' (1743, colour plate 10) – his first wife whom he married in 1739 – were the most successful. Bayne's pose is somewhat stiff as she gazes haughtily at the onlooker, but the portrait has a charming freshness. In March 1741 Bayne gave birth to a son, whom they named Allan; sadly, he died at fourteen months, but he is remembered by a posthumous portrait which Ramsay painted to help assuage his grief. Bayne herself died in childbirth in 1743 . None of their children would survive childhood; the youngest, named Anne after her mother, died when she was ten years old.

In 1744 Ramsay painted 'Archibald Campbell, 3rd Duke of Argyll' (colour plate 11), one of his most successful early portraits. The Duke of Argyll was Robert Walpole's representative in Scotland in the 1740s and '50s and as such was one of the most powerful men in the country. He was to become an important patron for Ramsay.

In 1746 he painted 'Sir Peter Halkett Wedderburn,' sympathetically portraying his old age, and in 1747 'Dr Richard Mead,' a governor of and the medical consultant to a foundling hospital in London, depicting the doctor in a relaxed moment sitting by a table. Ramsay presented the portrait to the hospital to form a pair with an earlier 1740 portrait by Hogarth of 'Captain Thomas Coram,' the hospital's founder. Ramsay's charming portraits of ladies include 'Anne Cockburn, Lady Inglis' (1754), a study of a formidable middle-aged lady; 'Flora Macdonald' of Bonnie Prince Charlie fame (1749); and 'Rosamund Sargent' (1749).

## Return to Edinburgh

Ramsay spent the winter of 1751 in Edinburgh. He obviously spent it productively because the next year he rather scandalously married his pupil, Margaret Lindsay. The couple eloped as her parents did not approve of her marriage to an artist, who, even more unacceptably, was the son of a bookseller. Very properly, her father never forgave her and Margaret and her mother would not be reconciled until after his death.

In Edinburgh Ramsay painted a number of portraits, including one of 'David Hume' (1754, colour plate 3), rather strangely wearing a turban, and a fine one of 'Hew Dalrymple, Lord Drummore' (1754), a man who is comfortable with his authority and is shown seated informally with one arm resting on the arm of his chair. This painting demonstrates Ramsay's 'new' style with a much more relaxed and natural attitude for the sitter, a more restrained use of colour and emphasis on the play of diffused lighting. It was a very different painting from his earlier, formal portrait of Dr Richard Mead.

Allan Ramsay
*see: colour plate 12*

## The Select Society

In true Enlightenment style Ramsay also tried his hand at writing, producing a treatise on whether it was appropriate to use ridicule as a test of truth, inspired by his developing friendship with David Hume.

Ramsay also published a pamphlet concerning the case of one Elizabeth Canning, who claimed she had been abducted, robbed of her clothing and kept for four weeks in a 'house of ill repute.' As a result of her claims, a gypsy woman was found guilty of robbery and condemned to death by hanging and her employer, the keeper of the 'bawdy house,' was convicted of being an accessory to the crime, her punishment to be branded and committed to prison. Through the exercise of logic and reason Ramsay argued that the evidence given by the girl had been circumstantial and unsound, and that the verdict, based on the premise that the evidence while improbable was not impossible, was likewise unsound. His pamphlet came too late to prevent the branding but the hanging was forestalled; the complainant Elizabeth Canning was found guilty of perjury motivated by her need to explain an absence from her master's house of four weeks while she gave birth to an unwanted child. It was a dramatic demonstration of the power of reasoned argument which characterised the Enlightenment.

In 1754 Ramsay, Hume and Adam Smith founded the Select Society, which provided the core of the Enlightenment as a place for the intellectual elite of Edinburgh to meet for the interchange of ideas and for challenging discourse. It became a powerhouse of new ideas, where a proponent would receive a more rigorous examination by his peers than he would at a university. Much of the exciting new Enlightenment thinking was forged at its weekly meetings. Originally intended to have a membership limited to fifty, the Society became so popular that before long its membership topped one hundred and thirty.

Much of its strength derived from the breadth of interest of its members – philosophers, economists, lawyers, historians, writers and painters – all with their unique contributions. Its membership included in addition, Alexander Monro, the anatomist and founder of the Monro medical 'dynasty,' Lord Monboddo, the pioneering anthropologist, and the architects John and James Adam.

The Select Society and its offspring the Edinburgh Society were principal factors in the success of the ideas of the Enlightenment. The Edinburgh Society would feature particularly in the improvement of Scottish agriculture and industry.

## Italy Revisited

In the summer of 1754 Ramsay decided to revisit Italy with his new wife, together touring the archaeological sites and studying the works of the Old Masters. Although he was already a painter of international renown, Ramsay attended drawing classes in life studies at the French Academy in Rome to perfect his technique. Later they were joined in Rome by the young Robert Adam who was making his own pilgrimage to see the artistic and architectural wonders of Italy.

While Ramsay was in Italy his *'Dialogue on Taste'* was published, in which he explores his idea that there is no 'absolute' standard of taste but that it is a matter of personal liking, advancing his discussion through a fictitious conversation between a soldier, Colonel Freeman, and a conventional English aristocrat, Lord Modish. He advocates the ideas and architecture of ancient Greece over those of the Romans, whom he disparagingly calls the 'robbers of the world,' and champions  the Italian Renaissance. He also mocks the Palladian style of large private houses which he points out are modelled on the public buildings of antiquity rather than on the domestic architecture (domestic buildings were just then being uncovered at Pompeii and Herculaneum). He shared these views with Robert Adam.

## Royal Approval

Ramsay received patronage from the wealthy Earl of Bute, who secured a number of commissions for him in London, the most important of which was his portrait of 'The Prince of Wales' (1757, colour plate 13), later George III. He followed this a year later with a portrait of his patron, 'John Stuart, 3rd Earl of Bute' (1758), producing an elegant but relaxed portrayal which pays due justice to the Earl's legs, of which he was inordinately proud.

Around this time Ramsay painted a touching and intimate portrait of his second wife, 'Margaret Lindsay' (c. 1758). This picture, one of his most famous, pays tribute to her classical beauty, showing the light falling on her face and shoulders. It has a delicate naturalism, with restrained tones, subtle textures and soft feminine colours and reveals the tenderness Ramsay could evoke. By now he was a supreme colourist, probably the greatest of his generation. Margaret is portrayed arranging flowers but turning to look at her husband who has interrupted her task.

The royal introduction paid off handsomely on the Prince's succession to the throne and in 1761 Ramsay was chosen to paint the new King and Queen in their coronation robes, becoming Principal Painter to George III. This seal of royal approval marked the pinnacle of Ramsay's career, but although a prestigious position, it also meant he was required to produce a plethora of portraits of the King and Queen which were given as gifts to numerous visiting royalty and ambassadors. Useful for paying the household bills, this was artistically somewhat stifling. He employed assistants to help him meet the demanding requirements of his royal patron; one assistant alone is reputed to have painted ninety pairs of the coronation portraits and for each painting he received twenty guineas of the forty charged by Ramsay. This arrangement continued even after Ramsay's retirement from painting in 1773; it is said that on Ramsay's death, the copyist laid down his brush in relief and from thence forward would paint only animals!

Ramsay's royal commitments did not exhaust all his energies and he also painted a number of society portraits, including a series of family portraits for the private gallery of Lady Caroline Lennox.

In 1765 on a visit to Paris, Ramsay resumed his friendship with Hume, 'le bon David,' and a year later presented a portrait, 'David Hume' (1766, colour plate 14) as a gift to the eminent philosopher. A soft smile plays on Hume's lips while he contentedly and with simple dignity regards the painter, his arm appropriately resting on a pile of books. Ramsay also painted a portrait of 'Jean-Jacques Rousseau' (1766, colour plate 15), an incisive depiction of the eminent French philosopher who sought refuge with Hume in Britain because his ideas on education, religion and the form of society, were a little advanced for the French. He is somewhat unusually attired in the fur hat and fur collar of the Armenian costume he chose to wear, but the painting itself is a masterpiece of portraiture, with the light playing on his sensitive face and dark, intense eyes.

Ramsay continued with his writing and involvement in politics, publishing his *'Thoughts on the Origin and Nature of Government'* in 1769, in which he defended Britain's right to tax her American colonies. But it was not a desire to write which brought his career as a painter to a conclusion, nor indeed failing ability, but an accident caused by an attempt to increase safety awareness.

In 1773, he was appalled to read about a fire which had resulted in the death of most of a family who were unable to escape their burning house. Calling his own family and servants together, he took them up to the loft and showed them that if there was a fire downstairs they could escape over the rooftops. On his way down the ladder he slipped and, as his biographer Allan Cunningham wrote, 'he missed the step, fell and dislocated his right arm in so severe a way that it never fully recovered.'

The fall triggered a general decline in Ramsay's health and he developed rheumatic pains which were not eased by a spell 'taking the waters' in the hot springs at Buxton. Ramsay did not completely eschew art, producing some self-portraits in chalk, one of which is in the National Portrait Gallery in London, and some chalk portraits of his wife and daughter. His beloved wife Margaret died in 1782 and, with his two daughters in Jamaica, one married to the Governor, Ramsay set off with his son John on a final tour of Italy. While they explored the art and antiquities of Italy together, Ramsay's health steadily declined. On hearing that his daughters were returning to England he hurried back to see them, but the journey proved too taxing and in 1784 he died at Dover in his son's arms, without being reunited with his daughters.

## Ramsay's Legacy

Allan Ramsay was one of the earliest Scottish painters to embrace the European artistic tradition and through his father had an early involvement with the founders of the Enlightenment.

During his own lifetime his fame as a painter undoubtedly suffered from his enforced retirement, but he is now recognised as one of the greatest portrait painters, respected particularly for his draughtsmanship and his use of colour; his sensitive portrayals are true to the character of the sitter. This was important to Ramsay, who believed truth was 'not only an addition to the common stock of human knowledge but an addition to the common stock of human happiness.'

A significant participant in the Scottish Enlightenment through his painting, particularly his more sensitive personal portraits, and his writing, perhaps Ramsay's most important contribution was as co-founder and active proponent of the famous Enlightenment 'factory of ideas,' the Select Society.

**Further Reading**
Murdo Macdonald, *Scottish Art*
Alastair Smart, *Allan Ramsay: Painter, Essayist and Man of the Enlightenment*

**Online Resources**
National Galleries of Scotland
http://www.nationalgalleries.org/collection/artists-a-z/R/6240/artist_name/Allan Ramsay

# Scots Who Enlightened the World

artwork & illustrations

Thomas Carlyle was a great believer in 'heroes' and in their importance to history. He was influential in the establishment of the London National Portrait Gallery and his ideas also influenced the foundation of the Scottish National Portrait Gallery which opened in 1889, eight years after his death.

'It has always struck me that Historical Portrait Galleries far transcend in worth all other kinds of National Galleries of pictures whatever; that in fact they ought to exist ... in every country, as among the most popular and cherished national possessions,' Carlyle observed.

Special thanks are due to the National Galleries of Scotland for permission to reproduce paintings and photographs from the National Gallery of Scotland and the Scottish National Portrait Gallery and indeed to all other providers of artwork who are separately acknowledged.

**Frances Hutcheson**
Allan Ramsay, 'Frances Hutcheson' (1694–1746) oil on canvas c.1740-45
Hunterian Museum and Art Gallery, University of Glasgow

In this portrait by Allan Ramsay, Hutcheson is depicted wearing a black academic gown. As Professor of Moral Philosophy at the University of Glasgow Hutcheson proved an inspirational teacher who included among his pupils William Hunter and Adam Smith. Smith later famously described him as the 'never to be forgotten Hutcheson.'

*colour plate 1*

**Henry Home, Lord Kames**
David Martin, 'Henry Home, Lord Kames' (1696–1782) oil on canvas 1794
Scottish National Portrait Gallery, Edinburgh

This portrait was painted by David Martin twelve years after Kames' death and is presumed to be a copy of an earlier painting. The judge was famed for the biting sarcasm of his wit and some trace of this is evident in the sardonic smile playing on his lips. His parting words to his fellow judges on leaving court for the last time, 'Fare ye a' wel ye bitches,' was characteristic of his acerbic style.

**David Hume**
Allan Ramsay, David Hume (1711–1776) oil on canvas 1766
Scottish National Portrait Gallery, Edinburgh

This is Ramsay's first portrait of his friend David Hume who is depicted wearing a turban.
Ramsay and Hume were instrumental in the formation of the influential Select Society.

**James Hutton**
Sir Henry Raeburn, 'James Hutton' (1726–1797) oil on canvas c. 1776
Scottish National Portrait Gallery, Edinburgh. Purchased with the aid of
the Art Fund and the National Heritage Memorial Fund 1986.

'No vestige of a beginning – no prospect of an end...' The geologist Hutton is shown with a manuscript — perhaps his 'Theory of the Earth,' on which he is working. Geological specimens and fossils lie scattered on the table.

**Mary Somerville**
Thomas Phillips, 'Mary Fairfax, Mrs William Somerville' (1780–1872) oil on canvas 1834
Scottish National Portrait Gallery, Edinburgh

'The Queen of Science.' Thomas Phillips was an English portrait painter famous for his portrayal of men — and women — of genius. Mary Somerville was deservedly included in the distinguished company which included Brunel and Faraday.

### James Watt

James Eckford Lauder, 'James Watt and the Steam Engine: the Dawn of the Nineteenth Century' 1855. Scottish National Portrait Gallery, Edinburgh

A representation of Watt in his workshop painted after his death. James Eckford Lauder was one of a remarkable group of Scottish artists born at the beginning of the nineteenth century.

*colour plate 6*

**James Hogg**
Sir John Watson Gordon, James Hogg, (1770 - 1835) Poet;
'The Ettrick Shepherd' oil on canvas 1766
Scottish National Portrait Gallery, Edinburgh

The portrait by Sir John Watson Gordon shows a man with the sensitive face of a poet and the plaid of a shepherd. It was painted for Blackwood's Magazine to which Hogg had contributed for a number of years as 'The Ettrick Shepherd.'

*colour plate 7*

Sir David Wilkie, **'The Honours of Scotland'**, pencil and watercolour on paper 1822 Scottish National Portrait Gallery, Edinburgh

Scott was instrumental in the move to discover the Regalia of Scotland which had been stored away in safe keeping after the Act of Union. Wilkie shows the moment in 1818 when the 'Honours of Scotland,' the Mace, the Sceptre and the Sword of State, were taken from the chest in which they had been kept for over one hundred years.

*colour plate  8*

**Robert Louis Stevenson**
Count Girolamo Nerli, 'Robert Louis Stevenson' (1850–1894) oil on canvas 1892
Scottish National Portrait Gallery, Edinburgh

Count Girolamo Nerli was born in Siena and studied art in Florence. In the course of a somewhat chequered life he met Stevenson in Samoa where he painted this portrait in 1892. Stevenson, whose face betrays the ravages of continued ill-health, was a difficult and restless sitter, inspiring Fanny to remark that 'with such a sitter, the victim is the artist.

*colour plate 9*

**Anne Bayne**
Allan Ramsay, 'Anne Bayne, Mrs Allan Ramsay' oil on canvas c.1743
Scottish National Portrait Gallery, Edinburgh

A charming if slightly severe portrait of his first wife whom he had married in 1739. Ramsay utilises with effect the play of light on the face and dress of his sitter. Anne died in childbirth in 1743.

### Archibald Campbell
Allan Ramsay, 'Archibald Campbell / Mac Cailein Mòr, 3rd Duke of Argyll
(1682–1761) oil on canvas c.1744 • Scottish National Portrait Gallery, Edinburgh

The Duke of Argyll, shown in a three quarter length portrait in the rather stylised pose characteristic of the time half turned to the painter. He was one of the most important men in Scotland in the middle of the eighteenth century and would become an important patron for Ramsay.

*colour plate 11*

## Allan Ramsay
Allan Ramsay, 'Allan Ramsay' (Self-portrait) , (1713–1784)
pastel on paper c.1756 • Scottish National Portrait Gallery, Edinburgh

This self-portrait in pastel and watercolour demonstrates Ramsay's master of the medium with the pale blue of his coat subtly reflected in the soft colours of the background.

**Margaret Lindsay**
Allan Ramsay, 'The Artist's Wife: Margaret Lindsay of Evelick'
oil on canvas c.1758 • National Gallery of Scotland, Edinburgh

This painting is one of Ramsay's most sensitive and charming portraits and depicts the painter's second wife, Margaret Lindsay, with whom he had eloped in 1752. It is a sensitive and loving portrait in which the sitter turns towards the painter, her husband, who interrupts her as she is arranging the bowl of flowers. It is a remarkably tender and graceful portrayal, arguably Ramsay's finest.

**David Hume**
Allan Ramsay, David Hume (1711–1776) oil on canvas 1766
Scottish National Portrait Gallery, Edinburgh

This sensitive portrait, painted as a gift by the artist, emphasises the serenity of the philosopher, his hand resting on books in an allusion both to his learning and his published work. He is shown wearing the splendid 'uniform' he had worn as Secretary to the Military Mission in Vienna to Turin. Ramsay is reported to have replied to a remark by King George III that he thought the dress 'rather too fine,' with the quip 'I wished that posterity should see that (at least) one philosopher during your Majesty's reign had a good coat upon his back.'

**Jean-Jacques Rousseau**
Allan Ramsay, 'Jean-Jacques Rousseau' (1712–1778)
oil on canvas c.1766 • National Gallery of Scotland, Edinburgh

Rousseau had fled France in 1766 with the assistance of David Hume. This portrait was painted by Ramsay as a gift to his friend Hume a few months after Rousseau's arrival in Britain. Rousseau portrayed wearing Armenian costume. Shortly afterwards the unpredictable Rousseau broke with Hume in a bitter and unprovoked dispute.

*colour plate 15*

**Niel Gow**
Sir Henry Raeburn, 'Niel Gow' oil on canvas 1787
Scottish National Portrait Gallery, Edinburgh

This iconic portrait of the famous fiddler portrays Neil Gow as a man totally comfortable with himself and absorbed in his music. Gow wrote more than eighty tunes, many of which are still played at ceilidhs today.

Alexander
Nasmyth,
**'View of
Tantallon Castle
and the
Bass Rock'**
oil on canvas c.
1816 National
Gallery
of Scotland,
Edinburgh

A small boat is
tossed in the stormy
while the crew tries
to keep it off the
rocks. Above looms
Tantallon Castle,
impressively sited on
the cliffs overlooking
the Firth of Forth
and the Bass Rock.

The castle was built
in the mid-
fourteenth century
by William Douglas,
the first Earl of
Douglas. He had
become chief of the
Douglas by the time-
honoured expedient
of murder, in
this case
of his god-father Sir
William Douglas of
Liddlesdale.

*colour plate  23*

Alexander
Nasmyth,
**'Princes Street
with the
Commencement
of the Building
of the Royal
Institution'**
oil on canvas 1825
National Gallery
of Scotland,
Edinburgh

Royal Institution on
Princes Street
against a background
of the medieval
Old Town and
Calton Hill.

*colour plate 24*

## Chalmers Bethune Family

Sir David Wilkie, 'William Chalmers Bethune, his Wife Isobel Morison and daughter Isabella
Maxwell Morison', Purchased with the Barrogill Keith Bequest Fund, with additional funding
from the Rutherford and Laird McDougall Funds and the Cowan Smith Bequest Fund 1985
oil on canvas 1804 • National Gallery of Scotland, Edinburgh

Painted when Wilkie was nineteen years old this painting demonstrates a surprisingly mature
understanding of the dynamics of family relationships, showing the inter-relationship between
each of the family members and of each with the artist.

Sir David Wilkie, **'Pitlessie Fair'**, National Gallery of Scotland, Edinburgh • oil on canvas 1804 • Remarkable for the artist's relative immaturity, made Wilkie famous. Perhaps inspired by the 17th century Dutch school, Wilkie relied on Scottish cultural traditions for this depiction of everyday life.

Sir David Wilkie, **'Distraining for Rent'**, National Gallery of Scotland, Edinburgh • oil on canvas 1804 • This emotive painting shows a poor tenant farmer slumped at the table as he is faced with ruin by the arrival of the implacable bailiff. The assistants of the bailiff are noting down the goods they plan to seize while friends of the farmer attempt to intervene and his family wait by in despair. This painting was painted at a time when farmers were endured with pressure from the falling price of corn as cheap imports became available

after the conclusion of the Napoleonic wars while confronted by the implacable attitude of the landlords intent on collecting their rents, a conflict reflected in the bitter Parliamentary arguments over the Corn Laws. Wilkie's painting was unpopular with the landed gentry because of its implicit criticism of their behaviour.

*colour plate 27*

**Eric Liddell**
Unkown, 'British runner Eric Liddell at the Amateur Athletic Association Championships'
photograph c. 1924 • Corbis Images

Eric Liddell is pictured before his victory in the 440 yards in the AAA Championships in 1924 in one of his rare races at that distance. Although he won relatively easily, his winning time of 49.6 seconds was unexceptional and gave no hint of future Olympic glory.

*plate 30*

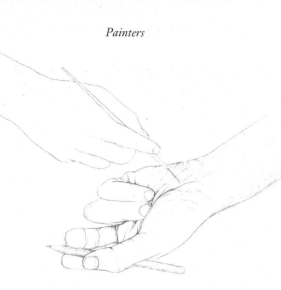

## Sir Henry Raeburn
### 1756–1823

SCOTLAND'S GREATEST PORTRAIT PAINTER

*'Nothing should divert the eye from the principal object; the face.'*
– Henry Raeburn

Henry Raeburn's renowned portraits are not just a realistic record of his subject but evoke the spirit of his sitters. A product of the Enlightenment, he achieved international fame while working for the most part in his native Scotland.

### Early Success

Raeburn was born in Stockbridge, just outside Edinburgh. His father owned a textile mill and he might have expected that his son would follow him into the trade, but he died while Raeburn was still a boy.

Educated at George Heriot's School, he exhibited there the first stirrings of his artistic ability. At fifteen he left school to become apprenticed to a goldsmith, a move reminiscent of some of the fine sculptors, artists and architects of the Italian Renaissance. As with Ramsay, Italy would become an important influence on Raeburn's art.

The goldsmith's craft was considered in Italy the best grounding for an artistic career, but Raeburn soon demonstrated a greater talent for painting the ivory in jewellery, work which required the highest dexterity and patience. From there it was perhaps natural that he should gravitate to painting miniatures, exquisite little portraits of the important people of the time. By mutual agreement his apprenticeship with the goldsmith was terminated and Raeburn started a career as a miniaturist.

Then he was introduced to David Martin, an Edinburgh portrait painter who encouraged him to expand his skills into the painting of full-size portraits. Martin, though, proved an unhelpful teacher, perhaps jealous of Raeburn's obvious talents, and Raeburn had to discover for himself the skills of the portrait painter, the preparation of colours and the use of the palette.

Preferring spontaneity in his portraits, Raeburn's talent was to elicit the individual personality of his sitter which was beginning to bring him fame and fortune: he had learned a boldness of technique, painting directly onto the canvas, giving his work an immediacy that is lacking in more stylised portraits. The methods he used in his studio have been recorded by visitors. Raeburn would first relax his sitters with conversation, then after placing them in the pose desired would withdraw to the end of the studio from whence he would regard them intently with his dark, deep eyes. Then, he would stride forward and paint directly onto the canvas without any preliminary drawing before withdrawing for another look. He painted first the forehead, the chin, nose and mouth, finding the painting of a fold of drapery more trying than a head, and with the belief that the background should not detract from the figure, preferred the half portrait. His sessions did not last longer than two hours to avoid overtaxing his sitter. His method of painting directly onto the canvas may help to explain his ability to convey the inner spirit of his sitter.

After developing intimate friendships with many of the Enlightenment figures, one of his early portraits was of 'James Hutton' (c. 1776, colour plate 4), the father of modern geology. He depicts him sitting beside a table littered with fossils and the manuscript of *Theory of the Earth*. He painted a number of Enlightenment figures, including Sir Walter Scott whom he painted twice.

Raeburn was already earning a good living as a portrait painter when at the age of twenty-two he was commissioned to paint the portrait of the young widow of John Leslie, the 11th Earl of Rothes. It proved to be a most profitable commission. She was still young, a few years older than Raeburn, comely if not beautiful, and wealthy, and they were wed within a month. As Cunningham wrote in *The Lives of the Most Eminent British Painters*, he was now in possession of '*an affectionate wife and a handsome fortune.*' He had also acquired two step-daughters. Raeburn moved his studio to his new wife's home, Deanhaugh House, where he painted for the next seven years.

Now he could afford to make the longed–for journey to Italy to see the work of the Italian masters and to expand his skills. In London he met Sir Joshua Reynolds, one of the greatest English painters of the day, receiving from him letters of introduction. After arriving in Italy he studied the portraits of the famous Italian Renaissance painters and those of the Venetian School, including Titian and Tintoretto.

## Return to Scotland

The couple returned to Scotland in 1786 and shortly thereafter Raeburn's brother William died and Raeburn inherited the family house to which they moved. The house was adjacent to Deanhaugh, enabling the development of the land about the house to meet the growing expansion of the city. Raeburn was able to indulge a burgeoning taste for architecture in the planning of the development. He extended his interests to marine architecture, designing and building models of ships which he would sail on the local water, once falling in and only with difficulty being rescued.

## Raeburn's Creative Work

Unusually, Raeburn spent most of his painting life in Edinburgh, not feeling the need to go to London to seek the valuable commissions available there. As a result, he was not as well-known internationally than he might have been but became the major figure among the Scottish artists of his time.

In 1791 he painted one of his major masterpieces, 'Sir John and Lady Clerk of Penicuik,' in which he demonstrates his mastery of his subject, expressing the relaxed intimacy of the couple, who are shown bathed in reflected light.

Another delightful painting of the time is a portrait of the musician 'Neil Gow' (1793, colour plate 16), Scotland's most famous fiddler and the composer of many reels and strathspeys. Gow is shown as an unpretentious man, relaxed and in total harmony with his instrument.

Raeburn's somewhat later painting of 'Isabella McLeod' (1798) portrays a young woman and gives a hint of her self-confidence as she sits graciously at ease with herself and with her portrait. His painting of 'Thomas Reid' (1796), now in Fyvie Castle, is a sensitive portrait of a man nearing the end of his life (it was painted in the year of Reid's death).

He also painted a number of clan chiefs dressed formally in tartan, perhaps the equivalent in paint of the romanticism of the Highlands promoted by Scott's *Waverley* novels. One such painting, 'Colonel Alasdair Macdonnell of Glengarry' (1811, colour plate 19), is typical. The portrait shows the Colonel in an elegant pose reminiscent of the portraits of Highland chiefs of earlier times. He strikes a heroic pose but the face is weak, belying the arrogance of his posture. It is not surprising to learn that Colonel Macdonnell was renowned not just for his love of donning Highland dress but as an anachronistic and sometimes violent figure who tried to live in a feudal past when the clan owed a binding loyalty to its chief.

Another fine portrait is of 'Major William Clunes' (1809, colour plate 18) who had served with distinction under Sir John Moore in the Peninsular War against France. He is depicted standing confidently beside his magnificent steed which occupies half the canvas and interestingly is shown not with its head towards the

Sir Henry Raeburn, 'Revd Dr Robert Walker Skating on Duddingston Loch' National Gallery of Scotland

Rev'd Robert Walker
*(detail) see: colour plate 17*

onlooker but facing away with its rump catching the light as if the major has just dismounted. The sky is darkened with the oncoming clouds of war.

Perhaps the painting that is most reproduced, however, (although there is now some doubt over its attribution to Raeburn) is that of 'The Reverend Robert Walker Skating on Duddingston Loch' (c.1795, colour plate 17), known more usually as 'The Skating Minister.' The Reverend had spent some of his childhood in Rotterdam, where his father was a minister of the Scots Kirk and had probably learned to skate as a youngster on the frozen Dutch canals. Besides being a Church of Scotland minister, he was also an enthusiastic member of the Edinburgh Skating Society.

## Raeburn's Honours & Legacy

In 1822 during George IV's visit to Edinburgh, Henry Raeburn was knighted, the first Scottish painter to be knighted since the Union. He was also appointed the King's Painter for Scotland but suddenly died in 1823 before he could complete his commission of a portrait of the King in Highland dress.

Henry Raeburn was a Renaissance man, trained as a goldsmith but achieving lasting fame as a portrait painter while finding time to indulge an interest in architecture and even naval design. He painted portraits of many of the leading figures of the Enlightenment together with clan chiefs and other prominent people of the time. His work was revealing but sympathetic, sharing common beliefs and values with his sitters, and forms an invaluable record of his era.

**Further Reading**
Edward Pinnngton, *Sir Henry Raeburn RA*

**Online Resources**
National Galleries of Scotland
http://www.nationalgalleries.org/collection/artists-a-z/R/4399/artist_name/Sir Henry Raeburn

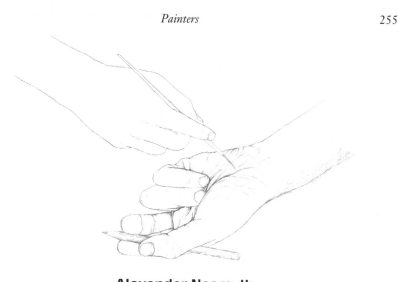

# Alexander Nasmyth
## 1758–1840

THE FATHER OF SCOTTISH LANDSCAPE ART

Alexander Nasmyth was an intimate participant of the Enlightenment and a friend of Burns. He painted the iconic portrait of Scotland's national poet but earned his reputation as a landscape painter. As the son of a master builder, building must have been in his blood; many of his landscapes include man-made structures and his interests would encompass architecture, landscape design and engineering, truly a Renaissance man.

## His Early Years

Nasmyth was born in 1758 in the Grassmarket in Edinburgh and educated at the Royal High School. His great-grandfather, Michael Naesmyth (Alexander would later drop the 'e' from the family name), had established in the late seventeenth century a firm which specialised in the design and building of houses for the landed gentry, reflecting a time when the country house had ceased to be a stronghold and had become a gracious home built to display the wealth and taste of its owner. After his death the firm continued to prosper, reaching its peak under Alexander's father, also called Michael Naesmyth. He too built a number of country houses and was also involved in the development of the New Town, building among other projects a house on the southwest corner of St. Andrew Square for David Hume. He amassed a collection of books of travel, probably the stimulus that prompted Alexander's older brother to go to sea, and also numerous volumes on architecture, including the works of Palladio, the influential Italian architect.

With the family tradition of architecture, it might have been natural for Nasmyth to join the firm, but his one desire was to paint. In 1773 he was apprenticed to the principal heraldic painter in Edinburgh and was employed in decorating the panels of the coaches of the nobility with heraldic designs. To further his artistic career he enrolled at the new Trustees' Academy, formed to provide training in the decorative trades such as cabinet making and the work of goldsmiths and coach painters but which proved to be the training ground for many an aspiring fine artist. The master, or principal, of the Academy was Alexander Runciman who, a well-known painter of historical subjects himself, favoured the award of places to embryonic artists rather than to the apprentice tradesmen preferred by the trustees.

Naysmith's skills were noticed by Allan Ramsay, who offered him a place in his London studio when he was only sixteen. Nasmyth worked on portraits for Ramsay, leaving the master to add the final touches. It is questionable though how much benefit Naysmith derived from his apprenticeship since by then Ramsay's career was in decline as he concentrated instead on the lucrative reproduction of royal portraits.

In 1778 Nasmyth returned to Edinburgh and set himself up as a portrait painter. An early patron was Patrick Miller of Dalswinton for whom he painted a family portrait. Miller was impressed with the young painter and gave Nasmyth a loan to enable him to visit Europe and study the works of the famous Italian painters of the Renaissance and Post Renaissance. Nasmyth left for Italy in December 1782 and stayed for two years, his return home hastened by thoughts of marriage. A year after his return in January 1786, he married Barbara Foulis to whom he had become engaged before his departure. Their eldest son, named Patrick after Patrick Miller, was born in 1787 and was followed in fairly quick succession by ten more children with just a short pause, possibly to catch breath, between 1793 and 1798.

## Landscape Painting

On his return to Scotland, Nasmyth initially set up as a portrait painter; in 1787 painting the iconic oval portrait of his friend Burns, but increasingly he used the skills he had learned in Italy to develop as a painter of landscapes, both rural scenes and townscapes, leaving portraiture to his good friend Raeburn who lived opposite in York Place. After 1792 Nasmyth would only paint two portraits, of Patrick Miller and another friend John Sacheouse, and two copies of the Burns oval. In a biography of his father, his son James suggested this change in direction may in part have been due to the alienation of his predominantly Tory patrons through Nasmyth's radical Whig views and his enthusiasm, shared by Burns, for the revolutionary ideas being expressed in France. It may however have just been a natural progression as his portraits had increasingly emphasised the landscape setting. His own somewhat ungallant explanation, reported by Cooksey, was that he 'preferred the ever beautiful face of nature to the faces of some of his sitters which were without charm or attraction.'

Initially, Naysmith painted his landscapes in an Italian style, but later became influenced by the Dutch Masters, learning a more naturalistic treatment of the scene, the positioning of trees, the handling of the foreground, the use of light and the treatment of water, all of which he employed in his landscapes. There was a new sense of Scottishness expressed in the writings of Scott and others and Nasmyth expressed visually the growing appreciation of Scotland's history and of the beauty of her land. Some of his landscapes such as that of 'Stirling Castle' (1827) resonate with historical allusion.

Nasmyth formed a school of landscape painting in Edinburgh and was responsible for developing many young artists, including his son Patrick, who also became a landscape painter, and his six daughters, all of whom became painters. He was modern in his outlook, encouraging his students to paint from life rather than copying the famous works of the Masters or the idealised classical landscapes of earlier years. Among his pupils was Mary Somerville in whom he awakened an interest in mathematics.

. One forceful landscape he painted is a 'View of Tantallon Castle and the Bass Rock' (1809). The castle stands stark and firm against a storm-tossed sky, a symbol of indestructibility. In the surf below, a small solid boat is being crushed against the rocks by angry seas while the crew try desperately to take down the sails.

Nasmyth typically painted country scenes, usually incorporating an architectural feature such as a house, a castle or a ruin as the main theme and many of his landscapes also featured water. He also painted a number of seascapes and townscapes including scenes of Edinburgh. His painting of 'Edinburgh with the High Street and Lawnmarket' (1824) is reminiscent of the style of David Wilkie; in it he sketches the daily life of the Lawnmarket, the women selling loaves and cabbages, the brewer's cart, the servants collecting water and the lawyers clustered about the inn.

Nasmyth was friendly with Sir Walter Scott, sharing his interest in Scotland's history, and he produced a number of illustrations for the *Waverley* novels. The development of the theatre in Scotland had long been held back by religious dogma but by the second half of the eighteenth century, it had become a popular form of entertainment and the fashion for melodrama, historical pageants and tragedies had created a demand for scene painters who could create sets with historical accuracy. Nasmyth painted scenery for Dumfries Theatre, for the Adelphi and the Theatre Royal in Edinburgh and for the Theatre Royal in Glasgow for whom James Nasmyth records he painted a 'magnificent view of the Clyde looking towards Dumbarton Rock.' The scenery for Scott's *Heart of Midlothian*, painted in 1819, was his last major commission for the theatre and comprised a total of sixteen scenes, six of which measured twenty-four feet by sixteen feet six inches (seven metres by five).

By the 1820s Naysmyth had reached the top of his profession, described in 1819 by Lockhart in Peter's Letters as the 'father of landscape painting in Scotland.' In 1822 when Raeburn was knighted by George IV, Nasmyth chaired the dinner held in Raeburn's honour, declaring that 'they loved him as a man not less than they admired him as a painter.' Nasmyth would repeat the favour a year later at a dinner given in honour of David Wilkie to mark his appointment as King's Limner for Scotland.

## The Royal Institution and Royal Scottish Academy

In 1825 Nasmyth painted a view of Edinburgh entitled 'Edinburgh from Princes Street with the Commencement of the Building of the Royal Institution' (1825). This is an historically important painting because it shows the classical New Town of Princes Street before it was defiled by modern commercialism. He depicted the start of the construction of the Royal Institution building, the North Bridge linking the New and Old Towns, and in the distance a misty Arthur's Seat. It is a busy picture recording the hustle and bustle of the street and the building work taking place on the new Royal Institution with to the right the outline of medieval Edinburgh, contrasting the 'new' Edinburgh with the 'old.'

Nasmyth was a strong supporter of the Royal Institution, or the Royal Institution for the Encouragement of the Fine Arts in Scotland, to give it its full title, which was formed in 1819 and was intended to provide a home to show the works of contemporary Scottish artists and also to exhibit the Old Masters. The Royal Institution was the first building in Edinburgh specifically designed and built as a showcase for Scottish art.

William Playfair designed the original building in 1822 in the classical style reflecting the remarkable self-confidence of its promoters, adding a new facade in 1832 to allow for expansion. His design incorporated a statue of Athene above the pediment intended as a tribute to the Parthenon, a temple of classical proportion and unmatchable beauty. His plan was changed, rather prosaically, to incorporate instead a statue of Britannia, a decision possibly motivated more by politics than art.

In 1826 the Royal Scottish Academy was established by a group of artists who rejected the perceived elitism of the Royal Institute which excluded practising artists from its decision-making in favour of a board of trustees who were described as 'a body of autocratic, aristocratic men.' In 1835 the Academy secured exhibition rights at the Royal Institution and in 1837 was granted the Royal Charter. The Academy grew fast in importance and soon became a cuckoo in the nest of the Royal Institution. Its members believed Scotland should have a National Gallery. A new building was needed and William Playfair's second art gallery on the Mound was opened to the public in 1859, housing the collections of both the Royal Scottish Academy and the National Gallery of Scotland.

Today the National Gallery of Scotland is home for Scotland's internationally respected collection of fine art from the Renaissance to the late nineteenth century, including works by such masters as Raphael and Titian; and the Impressionists such as Van Gogh, Monet, Cezanne and Degas. It is a striking collection for a nation of Scotland's size and a tribute to the foresight of its founders. In these institutions and buildings, Scotland demonstrated the growing national self-confidence and the recognition of the importance of the arts which were integral to the Enlightenment.

## Nasmyth as Architect, Landscape Designer and Engineer

It was perhaps natural given his background that Nasmyth should expand his activities into architectural design which he often illustrated with a painting. He worked as an architect for the Duke of Argyll, designing a number of buildings for Inverary, including a round cottage with a round central fire and a lighthouse in the Gothic style for the town quay, which he illustrated in a painting but which was never built. Nasmyth then worked extensively on plans and drawings for the rebuilding of Rosneath, the home of the Duke's son, the Marquis of Lorne, which had been destroyed by fire in 1802. Nasmyth was caught between the parsimony of his patron and the reckless extravagance of his patron's charming but spendthrift son until eventually, probably to his relief, another architect was appointed.

Nasmyth produced designs for Taymouth Castle and architectural and landscape outlines for Loudoun Castle in Ayrshire (the designs for the grounds were discovered many years later in an outhouse on the estate) and in 1789 he designed in St. Bernard's Well in Edinburgh, a building erected over a sulphur spring thought to possess healing powers and the design of which evoked the classical simplicity of Adam's memorial to David Hume. He also prepared a design, not used, for the Nelson Memorial (1806), a design for the layout of Calton Hill which was incorporated into the eventual plan and contributed to the design and layout of the New Town.

Nasmyth also worked for a number of patrons as a landscape consultant where he again used the medium of paint to outline his ideas. One of his patrons, the Duke of Atholl, demanded that trees be planted on an inaccessible rocky crag. He accomplished this 'impossible' task by loading a cannon with a canister containing the seeds of trees which when fired at the rock burst, scattering the seeds. In time the crag was luxuriantly clothed in trees.

The geometric side of mathematics was seen at the time as more important than the algebraic and every Scottish artist, architect or engineer had his roots in geometric design. Nasmyth had a keen interest in engineering and scientific design, helping Patrick Miller in the design for his first man-powered paddle boat. Nasmyth and his close friend Robert Burns were present at the maiden voyage on Dalswinton Lock of the later steam-powered version, bringing together

Scotland's most famous poet, her premier landscape artist, the designer William Symington and its proponent, Patrick Miller, a linking of people from different strands of life characteristic of the Enlightenment.

In 1819 he devised an arrangement for driving a ship's screw propeller in front of the rudder, a major improvement on the unwieldy paddle wheel; Brunel's *Great Britain* of 1843, the forerunner of the ill-fated *Great Eastern*, would be the first commercial steamship to incorporate a screw propeller to accompany the traditional sails and paddle wheel. His fourth son James inherited this more practical side of his father's character and designed the steam hammer which would prove a fundamental tool of the Industrial Revolution.

Alexander Nasmyth died in 1840. He was eighty-one years old and had been in good health until a few weeks before his death, completing his final painting, aptly entitled 'Going Home' (1840), just eight days before he died. He was a devoted husband and father, but sadly all but one of his children died childless as did his three grandchildren. The spark of genius which had blossomed in one man and his talented children died out in two generations.

## Nasmyth's Legacy

Like Allan Ramsay and Henry Raeburn, Nasmyth was an artist at the heart of the Enlightenment whose work developed alongside and in association with the thinkers and writers of that time. He was, however, much more than an artist; in true Enlightenment fashion he was a man of many talents, an architect, a landscape designer, an engineer, but above all, a man of independent mind.

His personal legacy can be seen in the Scottish school of landscape painters. As David Wilkie wrote to his widow on his death:

He was the founder of the landscape school of painting in Scotland, and by his taste and talent has for many years taken a lead in the patriotic aim of enriching his native land with the representations of her romantic scenery.

**Further Reading**
J.C.B.Cooksey, *Alexander Nasmyth: 1758-1840*

**Online Resources**
http://www.windsorscottish.com/pl-scotartist-anasmyth.php

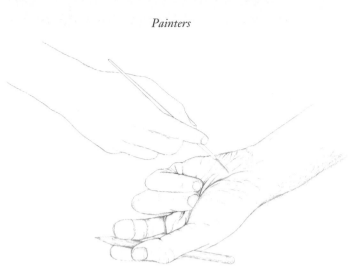

# Sir David Wilkie
## 1785–1841

THE PAINTER WHO PORTRAYED EVERYDAY LIFE

'My ambition has got beyond all bounds, and I have the vanity to hope that Scotland will one day be proud to boast of your affectionate son.' Buoyed by the response to his paintings when shown at the Royal Academy, David Wilkie wrote thus to his father. Scotland would indeed be proud of him.

The formal portrait and conventional landscape were not his chosen style. In the tradition of the Dutch painters, he wanted to show life as it was actually lived in Scotland in the early nineteenth century. This became known as 'anecdotal' or 'genre' painting and Wilkie earned fame not just in Scotland but throughout Britain for his works, founding the nineteenth-century school of genre painters. He was the first of the Enlightenment painters to feel that Scotland could not fully embrace his talents and to move permanently to London, although he never forgot his Scottish roots.

## A Student of Art

David Wilkie was born in 1785 in a small parish called Cults near Pitlessie in Fife, where his father, David, was the minister. His mother, Isabella, was the daughter of James Lister, the farmer of Pitlessie Mill. Isabella was David's third wife, the first having died of consumption within twelve months of her marriage and the second in childbirth after seventeen months – not, one would have thought, an encouraging prospect for the new bride. The life of a minister's wife was frugal, involving subsistence on a minimal stipend.

From the very first the young Wilkie, the third of their children, busied himself by drawing the people and animals around him. At school in Pitlessie he would sit apparently applying himself assiduously to the task he had been set but instead sketching portraits of his classmates. Wilkie had no early schooling in art but sketched the people and scenes he saw about him, and this was perhaps his strength as a painter. He was from the beginning a natural genre painter, sketching the sights that caught his eye, perhaps an old man or a girl milking a cow, rather than a painter of formal portraits or landscapes in the classical mould.

There were three career paths for the young ambitious Scot: the Army, the Kirk or the Law, but Wilkie chose none of these. His father had hopes he would follow him into the church but realised that his son was determined to be a painter. He was naturally concerned, for the life of a painter was hard and uncertain, but reluctantly agreed, recognising that Wilkie had shown his artistic ability from an early age.

Accordingly, Wilkie enrolled at the Trustees' Academy in Edinburgh when he was just fourteen. There was a new master, John Graham – his predecessor having been not unreasonably sacked when it was discovered the paintings in his portfolio were not his own. Graham encouraged painting from nature and introduced the use of oils and under his encouragement Wilkie prospered at the Academy. He worked hard at his art, seeking out fairs and markets where he could find country people as subjects for his drawings. He won a number of prizes before he returned home to Fife in 1804. One of his first great paintings is his family portrait, 'William Chalmers Bethune, his Wife Isobel Morison and their Daughter Isabella' (1804, colour plate 24), which explores openly the relationships linking the father, mother and daughter and between them and the artist: the father looks aggressively straight at the painter while his wife looks down lovingly at their young daughter – there is, one senses, not too much love between husband and wife. The daughter gazes openly and trustingly at the painter.

Next he painted one of his first great paintings in the genre he would make his own, 'Pitlessie Fair' (1804, colour plate 25), which evokes the drama of a bustling country fair in Fife, reminiscent in subject and style of the Dutch and Flemish schools. Wilkie visited the fair and wanted to show all its characters: shoemakers selling shoes, farmers selling ducks and hens, an old woman selling sugar-plums, even a recruiting sergeant. There are one hundred and forty separate figures shown in the painting, all engaging in the everyday life of the fair.

Wilkie's problem was how he could model all his different figures. One day in church he noticed one of his fellow churchgoers nodding gently during the sermon. He quickly took out a chalk and sketched a portrait in the leaf of his Bible. This was his answer: many of the people portrayed were based on sketches he had made of parishioners during church services. Wilkie sensibly avoided the temptation of using some of the more revealing sketches he had made of worthies slumbering deeply and contentedly through the sermon, their minds no doubt devoted to inner contemplation of the scriptures. He sold the painting in 1805 for a magnificent twenty-five guineas, which gave him enough money to move to London to study at the Royal Academy. Although he would maintain his links with Scotland, Wilkie based himself in London for the remainder of his career.

## The Royal Academy

Wilkie had a productive time at the Royal Academy, soon earning a high reputation as a painter and becoming in 1809 an Associate of the Academy when he was just twenty-four years old and two years later a Fellow. Two paintings of this period were of exceptional merit; 'The Village Politicians' (1806) and 'The Blind Fiddler' (1806). When the first was exhibited in the Royal Academy exhibition there was a daily crush of people crowding to see this exciting painting by a new artist; on a more pragmatic level, its sale helped him bridge the gap between his limited earnings and the expense of living in London. The picture represents a group of countrymen gathered to discuss current affairs in an alehouse.

'The Blind Fiddler,' which he showed at the Academy the next year, portrays an obviously poor family group listening to the fiddler. Two of the children stare enraptured while the third imitates the playing of the fiddle.

These paintings brought Wilkie fame but not fortune. He had an intrinsic problem: his paintings were very complex and although he worked at least five hours a day each piece could take from six months to a year to complete to his satisfaction and the price he could obtain was not enough to meet his needs. He received only thirty guineas for 'The Village Politicians', for example. At first he would often agree to a price for a painting in advance, which he later regretted, but he soon learned not to agree to the price until the painting was finished when it might attract a far higher sum than would have been paid unseen.

He still needed to supplement his income, so he arranged for an engraving to be made of 'The Blind Fiddler,' which enabled him to sell prints, bringing in some additional money. He also augmented his income by painting portraits, which were easier and quicker to paint and commanded a better price – although he admitted few of his female sitters were over-pleased with the results, possibly because his portraits eschewed flattery for honesty.

In 1813 he painted 'The Letter of Introduction' (colour plate 27), which shows a gauche young man uncomfortable in the presence of an older man to whom he has just handed his letter. The older man is visibly underwhelmed. It is said to have been based on Wilkie's own experience when he first went down to London.

In his paintings Wilkie showed life as he saw it, without pretension or sentimentality, not necessarily making any point or political statement as Hogarth did in his famous Cartoons, but representing the life of 'ordinary' people. 'Distraining for Rent' (colour plate 28) for example, shows a family distraught at the arrival of the indomitable rent collector. The farmer sits disconsolately at the table knowing he has not paid the rent and that his wife and children will soon be thrown on the street. The bailiff and his two assistants are on the right of the picture, noting down the property and chattels they will seize. Anxiously, friends stand by offering to intervene but the bailiff ignores them. It is a sad tale and the painting was just slightly unpopular with his wealthy London patrons with its implied criticism of the property-owning classes. Happily, he received a healthy six hundred guineas for it from the British Institution.

Wilkie had by this time become generally recognised as one of the leading painters of his time. He followed his earlier successes with 'The Village Festival' (1812), which sold for an amazing eight hundred guineas, and then with two paintings commissioned by the Prince of Wales, 'Blind Man's Buff' (1813) and 'The Penny Wedding' (1818), the latter an uncontentious painting of a rural wedding entertained by the playing of a fiddler.

Wilkie did not forget his Scottish roots and in 1817 visited Scotland, revisiting the Edinburgh of his youth and then touring the country. He accepted the hospitality of Walter Scott at Abbotsford and produced a painting of Scott and his family – the not very successful 'The Abbotsford Family' (1817), where Scott is portrayed somewhat strangely as a miller. Scott arranged for Wilkie to visit his friend Hogg, the Ettrick Shepherd, who entertained him to a breakfast of fried trout in his simple cottage, somewhat less impressive than Abbotsford. Hogg had not at first realised the identity of his guest – *'This is no' the great Mr. Wilkie?'* he asked.

In 1819 he was commissioned by the Duke of Wellington to paint 'The Chelsea Pensioners' (1822) which aroused great interest when it was first exhibited at the Academy; the painting features a pensioner, the portrait of a veteran who had fought with Wolfe reading out the news of the victory at Waterloo and a number of other veterans of different nationalities who had fought in other campaigns, all meticulous portraits from life. He also prepared a preliminary sketch for a work to be entitled 'The Preaching of Knox before the Lords of the Congregation 10th July, 1559' – not for Wilkie the pithy title! In this painting, which would not be completed until ten years later, Wilkie shows his fascination with the fiery preacher but treats the berated Mary Queen of Scots with a delicate sympathy.

## George IV's visit to Edinburgh

Wilkie was part of the group welcoming King George IV on his visit in 1822 to Edinburgh, which was orchestrated by Walter Scott. On the death of Sir Henry Raeburn, who sensibly had died before he needed to address the task, Wilkie was appointed to the position of King's Painter, or King's Limner, and was commissioned to produce a painting recording the historic first visit to Scotland of a reigning monarch for over one hundred and seventy years. It would be an important painting but was no easy task. King George IV struck a faintly ridiculous and corpulent figure in his tights and Highland dress and yet the painting must flatter his royal client.

## Italy and Spain

The necessary compromise of his artistic integrity would put a strain on his always fragile health, which was badly affected by the deaths in 1824 of both his mother, with whom he was very close, and his two elder brothers. Wilkie suffered the beginning of a breakdown and decided to go abroad to get away from the pressure, travelling for three years through Italy, where he especially admired the Sistine Chapel of Michelangelo and the works of Titian and Tintoretto, and then to Germany and Spain. The tour refreshed his art; the early influence of Dutch masters replaced by Velasquez and Murillo, and his later paintings reflected this, perhaps as a result losing some of the artistic integrity of his early genre paintings.

Revitalised, he returned to Britain in 1828 and completed his commission, which was somewhat prosaically entitled 'Reception of the King at the Entrance of Holyrood Palace'. Wilkie had sacrificed artistic integrity for flattery – but what else could he do? The King struck a manly figure in the picture, his corpulent body flatteringly slimmed and his scarlet Highland dress suitably subdued. The tights the King had worn under his kilt to disguise his podgy legs were discretely omitted! In 1836 Wilkie received his reward; he was knighted.

While he was in Italy he learned of the collapse of Hurst and Robinson, the firm who sold the prints of his pictures, a business in which he owned a large share. He was therefore sympathetic when Scott encountered his own similar financial difficulties, agreeing to produce sketches for engraving an 'omnibus' edition of the Waverley novels in 1829, and in 1842 additional sketches for the Abbotsford Edition, another example of how the different strands of the Enlightenment came together. He also drew a number of illustrations for editions of the poems and songs of Robert Burns, culminating in 'The Cottar's Saturday Night' (1837). In this later period, inspired by the example of the Italian and Spanish masters, he rejected genre painting to paint well-researched historical paintings; these he was able to produce more quickly and therefore by number they represent the greater part of his works, but perhaps they do not have the outstanding qualities or the originality of his earlier genre paintings which had been painted 'from the heart.'

In 1840 Wilkie decided to travel again, setting off rather ambitiously to tour the Middle East. He travelled through Germany and Holland and then spent four months in Turkey, where he painted his last picture, a portrait of the Viceroy of Egypt, Muhammad Ali. On his way home he was taken ill on board ship and died. He was buried at sea in the Bay of Gibraltar.

**Further Reading**
William Bayne, *Sir David Wilkie RA*

**Online Resources**
National Galleries of Scotland
http://www.nationalgalleries.org/collection/artists-a-z/W/6004/artist_name/Sir David Wilkie

'MANUSCRIPT OF MONTE CASSINO' (FOOT, 2 of 3 pieces)
Eduardo Paolozzi - 1991
Picardy Place, Edinburgh
photo: Thomas Haywood

Paolozzi created this work as an allegory to the
manuscript for which it is named, *A Journey*.
Consisting of three pieces: a hand, ankle and foot,
the work refers to Ancient Roman sculptures on
Capitoline Hill, Rome.

# Travellers
# & Explorers

## Part 6

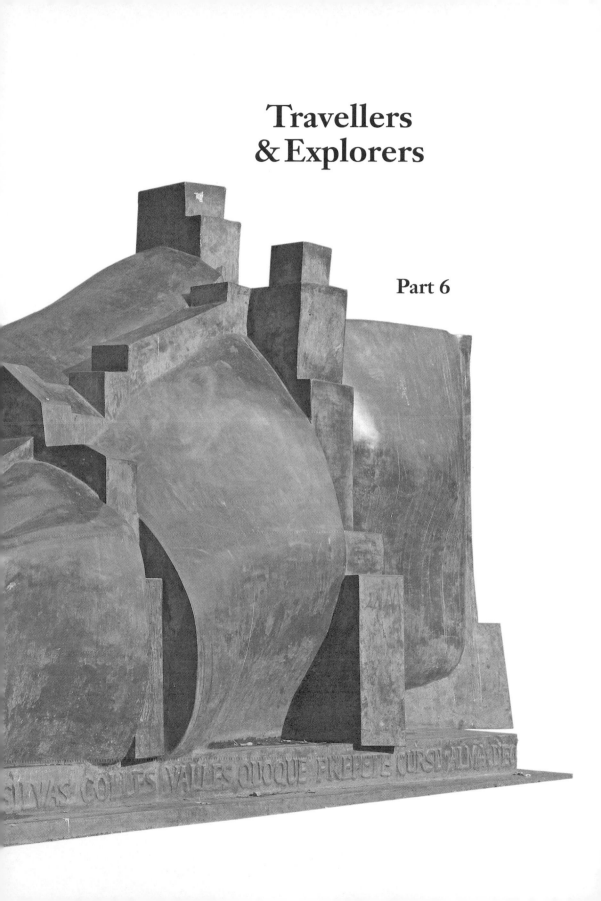

# TRAVELLERS & EXPLORERS

**Archibald Menzies**
PLANT COLLECTOR

**Mungo Park**
EXPLORER OF THE RIVER NIGER

**David Livingstone**
MISSIONARY AND EXPLORER

**Eric Liddell**
CHAMPION OF HIS FAITH

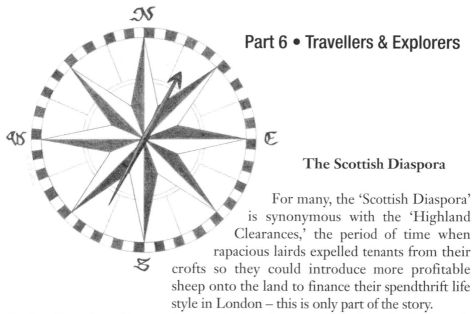

## Part 6 • Travellers & Explorers

### The Scottish Diaspora

For many, the 'Scottish Diaspora' is synonymous with the 'Highland Clearances,' the period of time when rapacious lairds expelled tenants from their crofts so they could introduce more profitable sheep onto the land to finance their spendthrift life style in London – this is only part of the story.

Scotland has a long history of outward migration, stretching from the fourteenth century, when Scots ventured to Europe as soldiers of fortune, students, merchants or traders, setting up Scottish 'colonies' in many European cities, to the economic migration of the eighteenth, nineteenth and early twentieth centuries when many Scots left their homes, attracted by the perception of greater opportunities in England, in the Americas or in the Empire.

### Early migration to Europe

Before the Union, Scottish migration was principally to Europe as soldiers or as merchants. Scottish soldiers have a long history of serving in the armies of France. In 1418 Charles VII of France formed an elite Scottish unit, the Garde Écossaise, to act as a personal bodyguard. Scots fought with Joan of Arc who, inspired by her vision, successfully led the French troops against the English until in 1430 she was burnt at the stake, agonizingly and deliberately slowly, by the English soldiers. She had been sold to the English by the Duke of Burgundy after she had bravely been the last to leave the field of battle, as her small force was surrounded by a combined force of more than six thousand English and Burgundian soldiers.

The Garde Écossaise remained the bodyguards of the French kings until they were disbanded in 1791 with the fall of the monarchy. Even this did not mark the end of Scottish involvement in the French military. One of Napoleon's generals was a Scot, Marshal Macdonald, whose father had fled to France with Bonnie Prince Charlie. Scots also served in the armies of the Swedish kings.

In medieval times Europe was seen as the place of learning and many Scots studied at the great European universities. George Buchanan, the learned tutor of James VI, studied in France becoming one of the greatest Latin scholars of his age, albeit a harsh taskmaster to his young charge. Monro Primus was one of many Scots doctors who learned their medicine in Leyden, then acknowledged to be the leading medical school in Europe.

By the end of the sixteenth century, there were enough Scots in Rome to justify the construction of the Scottish church, Sant'Andrea degli Scozzesi, and in 1717 to persuade James Stuart, the Old Pretender, to settle in Rome. It was from Rome that Bonnie Prince Charlie set off on his ill-fated attempt to recover the crowns of Scotland and England, and there is a monument to the Stuarts in St. Peter's, Rome.

Many Scots also travelled in Europe as merchants, trading with the cities of the Hanseatic League along the shores of the Baltic. By the beginning of the seventeenth century there were a reputed thirty thousand Scots in Poland, some merchants but many of them traders and pedlars. Scottish merchants helped the Polish aristocrats to market their surplus grain and these commercial skills, honed in Europe, would later prove invaluable when the Act of Union opened new markets to ambitious people from Scotland.

## The Act of Union opens the Doorway to the Empire

The Act of Union with England in 1707 accelerated the trend of outward migration, offering opportunities in England or in the countries of the Empire and providing gainful occupation for the younger sons of Scottish lairds who did not inherit the family lands.

The Empire provided a fertile market for Scottish linen, for the ships, railway engines and engineering products of the Clyde, and for the jute products of Dundee until in time these markets collapsed as production moved overseas and Scotland lost its comparative advantage in the manufacture of heavy engineering products.

Emigration increased rapidly through the late seventeenth and the eighteenth centuries with many Scots seeking their fortune in America, even going as far as New Zealand and Australia where strong pockets of Scottish settlers developed, attracted by the opportunities available.

Many Scots sought their future in India, filling many of the senior ranks within the East India Company, often acquiring great wealth along the way, or serving in the armies of the Company which by 1805 had reached more than one hundred and fifty thousand men making it one of the largest of the world's military powers. Half of the fourteen East India Company regiments were Scottish and officered by Scots. Both Ronald Ross and Elsie Inglis were born to Scots who had made their careers in India.

Another favoured destination for the ambitious Scot was the Americas where they would often take a leading role, exporting the ideas of the Enlightenment and exploiting the excellent education they had received in Scotland. A typical Scottish student would spend twice as long each day at school as his French counterpart and at the age of nine would be expected to be fluent in spoken and written Latin. Scottish universities also played their part with a broadening of teaching into new areas such as medicine, law and natural sciences and expanding so that by the early nineteenth century Scotland had more university places per thousand of its population than any other country in Europe. The high standard of basic education and the Calvinist ethos of hard work would bear fruit and Scots would often feature disproportionately in the leadership of their new communities.

Scots also migrated in large numbers to Canada, providing the majority of the management of the Hudson's Bay Company in Canada. Scots Alexander Mackenzie and Simon Fraser would be prominent in the exploration of that new country.

This mass emigration from Scotland continued even during the period of strong industrial growth in the second part of the nineteenth century and up to the First World War. During this period roughly two million Scots left Scotland, more than half of whom went to the United States; some were rural workers attracted by the availability of land, but many were skilled workers responding to the better prospects overseas. Another half million or so moved to England. This net emigration would continue through the twentieth century and has only recently turned positive through increased inward migration, principally from England and Poland. But not all emigration was voluntary.

## The Highland Clearances and the Potato Famine

Many Highlanders left Scotland not through choice but through coercion, forced to leave their homeland. Some were refugees from the Battle of Culloden who fled overseas to avoid the scourge of 'Butcher' Cumberland and many were evicted in the infamous Highland Clearances, when houses were burnt down to clear the land for the Cheviot, the 'great white sheep' which could thrive on the poor Highland pastures and would bring far more profitable rents to the Highland lairds who were struggling to find the money to finance their social life in London.

The Clearances were harsh but the depopulation of the Highlands was probably inevitable. A rapidly rising population had put strains on the food supply which could not be met through the traditional crofting system. The more enlightened lairds did attempt to re-house their dispossessed tenants by building new settlements on the coast where they could earn a living from the sea or from collecting kelp, but the crofters often lacked the necessary skills.

By the middle of the nineteenth century, potatoes had largely replaced oatmeal as the staple diet of the Highlanders, since potatoes would grow on the often poor and exposed ground and provided a crop with a greater food potential per acre. In 1846 this dependence on the potato crop badly backfired when the potato blight struck. The air was filled with the stench from the potato crop as it lay rotting in the ground and there was widespread famine.

Many of the more enlightened lairds tried to alleviate the hardship of the crofters by providing supplies of food. Relief programmes were introduced so that a crofter who worked six days a week on building roads could earn a daily ration of oatmeal for himself and his family which ensured survival but little more. Destitution was widespread and hundreds of thousands of Scots left Scotland during the years of famine, in many cases forcibly expelled from the land with their passage 'assisted' by their landlords. These were the unfortunate ones.

## Missionaries and Explorers

Many of the Scots whose lives we examine left their country for more positive reasons; some - such as John Buchan, Thomas Carlyle and David Wilkie – were attracted by the greater wealth and opportunities in England, while a number also left Scotland to take the Gospel to foreign lands or to explore the unmapped parts of the world - indeed often to do both. Among these are Archibald Menzies, Mungo Park and David Livingstone and, much later and post dating the Enlightenment, the missionary and Olympic runner Eric Liddell who was featured in the film 'Chariots of Fire.' It is these historic missionaries, travellers and explorers that we discover next.

**Further Reading**
T.M.Devine, *To the Ends of the Earth: Scotland's Diaspora*

**Online Resources**
Scottish Diaspora Tapestry
http://www.scottishdiasporatapestry.org/

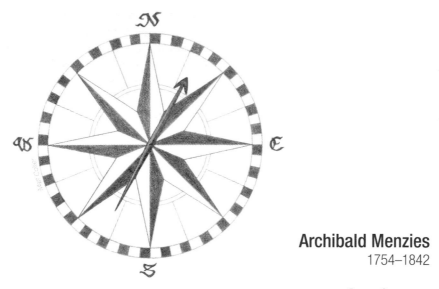

## Archibald Menzies
### 1754–1842

<small>PLANT COLLECTOR</small>

*'The red-faced man who cut off
the limbs of men and gathered grass.'*

This was the description of Archibald Menzies given by the natives of Hawaii, neatly summarising his career both as a surgeon and as a plant collector, and perhaps also his Scots skin burnt by the South Pacific sun.

Menzies' botanical discoveries helped increase mankind's store of knowledge and the reputation he earned as a botanist is a tribute not just to his innate abilities but to his determination to make the best use of them. This determination, coupled with his desire to learn and to travel, is in the best tradition of the Enlightenment .

### The History of Plant Collection

The collection of new species of plants from foreign countries started in the sixteenth and seventeenth centuries when plants such as lupins, lilies and crocuses were first introduced into Britain. Wealthy landowners brought onto their estates exotic plants and trees from faraway places, not just for their beauty and originality but as status symbols. Botanical gardens, such as those at Edinburgh and Kew, provided a scientific outlet for plant collections, which were brought into order by a method of classification developed by the Swedish botanist Linnaeus between 1735 and 1753.

Joseph Banks, the botanist who served with Captain Cook in his voyage around the world on the *Endeavour*, argued that a botanist should be included on all ships' expeditions and that examples of all new species should be brought back to the botanic gardens at Kew. Thus Kew became the home of the world's finest collections of plants and Banks himself was credited with introducing more than seven thousand new species. Botany, the collection and study of plants, had become a respected, and popular science, but how did a poor boy from Perthshire become a famous botanist?

## Learning His Trade

Menzies was born in 1754. His father was head gardner to Sir Robert Menzies. His family was Presbyterian with a strict view of religion and the importance of a good education provided at the local school, where the discipline would have been severe.

Weem was Menzies land, dominated by the formidable Castle Menzies, home of the clan chief Sir Robert Menzies. More than half the workers on the estate were Menzies, including Archibald's father, and in due course his brothers, who all worked as gardeners. Unsurprisingly Archibald showed a keen interest in plants from an early age and also became a gardener.

The Royal Botanical Garden in Edinburgh had recently moved from its old site, which was a physical garden where herbs were grown for their healing powers. On the new site a garden was developed under the direction of the Scottish botanist John Hope, where in addition to growing medicinal plants, scientific studies could be made into improving propagation and growth and exotic plants could be grown under glass. John Hope was among the leaders of Enlightenment thinking in botany.

In 1768 Menzies joined the Royal Botanical Garden as a gardener. Life was hard and he was expected to work until eight at night in the summer; for this he received a small wage and the share of a bed! He soon attracted attention as a lad with ability and a keen interest in botany. He learned the system of classification of plants developed by Linnaeus and how to pack plants to keep them alive during the long voyage home from their place of origin.

In addition to his role as Keeper of the Botanical Garden, John Hope was Professor of Medicine and Botany at the University of Edinburgh and, impressed by the young lad's attitude, he encouraged Menzies to study as a surgeon. At the time the medical profession was divided into two groups, the physicians and the surgeons: the physicians were the 'elite' while the surgeons were treated as little more than technicians, only recently separated from their origin as 'barber surgeons.' On completing his training in 1778, Menzies went to work as an assistant to a surgeon in Wales. But this was not how he wanted to spend his life; he wanted to see the world.

## A Naval Surgeon

In 1782 Menzies obtained the post of assistant surgeon on the Royal Navy ship HMS *Nonsuch*. Conditions onboard were harsh. Ships, particularly warships, were overcrowded, with men packed together below decks in cramped and damp living conditions and subsisting on meagre rations, eating meat which was often rotten and having little fresh fruit or vegetables so that the threat of scurvy was ever present. Fevers and disease could spread like wildfire.

The problem of scurvy had been long known and another Scot, James Lind, had proposed as long ago as 1747 the use of citrus fruits to prevent an outbreak. Lind was a physician and in April of that year had taken charge of twelve patients suffering from scurvy with the typical symptoms of putrid gums, spots and general weariness. With admirable scientific technique he divided them into six pairs and carried out a controlled experiment. One pair was treated with a rich diet of mutton broth, another with cider and so forth. One pair was treated with two oranges and a lemon each day and it was this pair which recovered first. Lind therefore recommended that all ships of the Royal Navy should carry citrus fruits – he recommended oranges – but perhaps predictably the advice was rejected as being far too revolutionary. It was not until 1795 that the Admiralty was finally persuaded to carry limes on all Royal Navy ships, leading to the use of the word 'limey' to describe firstly a British sailor and then more generally anyone from Britain.

On the *Nonsuch* more than fifty men died, many from scurvy, on the voyage to the West Indies, where she joined the fleet commanded by Admiral Rodney to fight the French at the Battle of the Saints near Dominica in 1782. Although the British won this battle, the losses were horrendous and Menzies would have been required to operate on wounded and screaming men while surrounded by the noise and clamour of the battle.

Many injuries, particularly in battle, would result in the need for amputation. Operations took place on chests pulled together to make a platform and covered with a sail. Dim light was provided by smoking candles and lanterns swinging with the movement of the ship. The surgeon's instruments were basic: amputation knives, saws, forceps and bone nippers. In the absence of anaesthetic to ease the pain, surgery was brutal and quick. Any delay and the shock and bleeding would kill the patient. A practised surgeon would aim to cut through the broken flesh, saw off the damaged limb and tie the arteries in not more than two minutes before the patient, probably in shock, was passed to the surgeon's mate to prepare the stump. In these grim conditions the chances of a successful outcome were slim.

## Nova Scotia

In the spring of 1784 Menzies was posted to the HMS Assistance, stationed in the port of Halifax in Nova Scotia, now a part of Canada but then British. Halifax was the last major port remaining in British hands after the revolt by the American colonists and it was crowded with refugees, who were often scantly clothed and poorly housed to face the harsh conditions of a bitter northern winter. Menzies, freed from fighting, was able to indulge his skills as a botanist. He had collected vast numbers of seeds from his time in the West Indies and found still more in Nova Scotia, all of which he sent back to his mentor in Edinburgh, John Hope. He wrote, 'I arrived here from the West Indies in the Assistance a few days ago and I am charmed with the general appearance of the country which seems to offer a most delightful prospect for botanical researches.'

Nova Scotia was covered by thick and impenetrable forest and much of Menzies' exploration was by small boat. After one trip he wrote again to Hope, 'Returned to Halifax after an expedition of five weeks in an open boat round the eastern coasts of Nova Scotia, a journey of some danger and difficulties.' He sent a parcel of seeds and specimens which he had tried to identify, expressing the wish that Hope would 'readily forgive the mistakes and freely correct the inaccuracies … when you are informed that they were examined and described with candlelight in a noisy cockpit which is my station on board.'

## The Voyage of the *Discovery*

In 1790 the British decided to sponsor a voyage of exploration in the appropriately named *Discovery* under the command of Captain George Vancouver who was charged with surveying the north-west coast of Canada and finding the north-west passage connecting the Atlantic and Pacific Oceans. Menzies had the right experience; he had already completed such a voyage, been promoted from assistant surgeon to surgeon and worked with Sir Joseph Banks on his botanical collection – so it was natural that in December 1790 he should be recommended by Banks as the ideal person to accompany the expedition as botanist. Later, he also became surgeon to the expedition.

Menzies was given clear instructions for labelling and packing the seeds he collected and for the care of plants, which were to be placed in the plant frame he took with him which took up a large portion of the ship's quarterdeck.

The *Discovery* spent five weeks at the Cape of Good Hope in South Africa before favourable winds took it to Australia, then known as New Holland, where Menzies found many new trees and flowering plants. These included five Banksias, which he named after his mentor, one specimen of which, the Banksia menziesii, with red and yellow flowers, he further named after himself. He also found a new variety of the eucalyptus tree and saw a number of birds including the rare black swan, but the only kangaroo he saw was dead.

The *Discovery* then followed the tracks of the earlier expedition of Captain Cook to Dusky Bay in New Zealand, where Menzies was enchanted with the varieties of ferns and mosses he found, and then sailed on to Hawaii.

In Hawaii the expedition was greeted by a chief, who came out to the ship in a double-hulled canoe while dressed in a fine cloak made from thousands of bright yellow feathers taken from kauai o'o birds. The birds were trapped by placing a few bright red berries on the boughs of trees covered with sticky bird lime and after the feathers had been taken the birds were freed.

Menzies formed an expedition to climb Mauna Loa, one of the two high mountains on Hawaii, whose peak was at more than four thousand metres (thirteen thousand feet) above sea level. Few plants were in flower but Menzies did discover the koa tree and a huge Hawaiian tree fern, now named after him, which grows to nearly ten

Monkey Puzzle Tree

metres. The climb was hard, first through thick vegetation and then over jagged lava, which tore apart their shoes, until they reached the snowline. Frozen with cold and without proper boots and clothing, only Menzies and two companions reached the summit, the first Europeans to do so. He measured its height by readings from a barometer which he carried with him, calibrated by simultaneous readings taken at sea level on board the ship.

In San Francisco, California, they were entertained generously by the Spanish settlers. There Menzies discovered the huge sequoia or redwood tree and was also the first scientist to record the Californian condor, a huge bird with a wingspan of more than three metres.

## The North-West Coast

The *Discovery* spent three summers surveying the north-west coast of what is now Canada. Small boats loaded with food and provisions and which could enter the narrow inlets along the coast were despatched from the mother ship. The survey was carried out using compass bearings taken every measured mile while the speed of the boat was calculated by dropping a log on a line over the side and counting the number of knots in the line as it passed astern; this is why the speed of a ship is expressed in knots. It was long and laborious work – the crew were often cold and wet and it could be two or three weeks before they could return to the ship.

They explored Puget Sound and then sailed along Queen Charlotte Sound between Vancouver Island, which they named after the captain of the expedition, and the mainland, until they reached Menzies Point, named after the botanist. The country was largely wooded, with just a few Indian settlements. Perhaps reminded of Scotland, Menzies thought the scenery was 'romantic,' but his captain found it 'gloomy and desolate' – which could also be an apt description of Scotland in the rain.

Menzies spent as much time as he could ashore, collecting plants and making sketches and paintings as a record. He found many rare plants and trees, including fairy slipper orchids, the mock orange and the western red cedar tree; in all he collected more than two hundred and fifty specimens.

The expedition set sail for home in September 1794, its tasks complete. They had surveyed more than ten thousand miles in small boats and had sailed as far north as Cook Inlet in Alaska, thought by James Cook on a previous voyage to be the entrance to the mythical north-west passage. They found there was no such passage; it was no more than an inlet from the sea. Unfortunately, nearly all the plants Menzies had so painstakingly collected were ruined by a tropical storm.

## Later Years

Menzies never got the recognition he deserved as a plant collector, partly because a shortage of funds soon forced him to return to the sea as a naval surgeon so that he did not have the time to write and publish the details of his botanical expedition. He did, however, prepare samples of the plants and seeds he had collected which he gave to fellow botanists.

He retired from the navy at the age of forty-eight to practise as a surgeon in London. There he married Janet, a fellow Scot. Their house provided a meeting place for botanists for many years, until his death at the age of eighty-eight.

## Menzies's Legacy

Menzies was typical of the Scottish Enlightenment, a boy from a poor background who benefited from a good education and went on to excel in his field, in his case botany.

He collected more than three hundred previously unknown plants, including many like the flowering currant which are common in gardens today; many more were collected as seeds. His name is remembered in more than a hundred flowering plants, but perhaps his greatest discovery was the monkey puzzle tree, that strange and ancient tree which dates back to the time of the dinosaurs and is now found in gardens across Britain.

**Further Reading**
James McCarthy, *Monkey Puzzle Man*

**Online Resources**
Undiscovered Scotland
http://www.undiscoveredscotland.co.uk/usbiography/m/archibaldmenzies.html

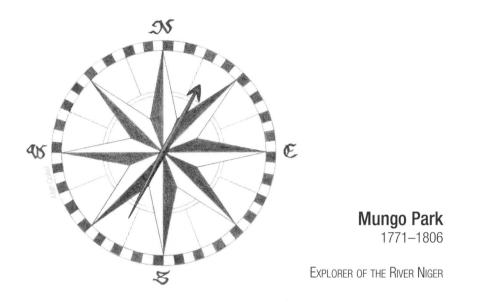

# Mungo Park
## 1771–1806

EXPLORER OF THE RIVER NIGER

*The long sought for majestic Niger, glittering in the morning sun,
as broad as the Thames.*

This was Mungo Park's description of the River Niger when he saw it on his first expedition to West Africa. Park was an explorer who led two expeditions into West Africa to pursue the course of the River Niger. He developed a deep understanding of the land and its people and wrote a book of his travels, increasing our knowledge of Africa and the Africans.

## Childhood in the Borders

Mungo Park was born at Foulshiels near Selkirk in 1771(within a few years and a few miles of two other Enlightenment figures, Sir Walter Scott and James Hogg), the middle child in a family of thirteen, of whom five died in childbirth. His father was a tenant farmer who grew cereals in the valley and had sheep and a few cattle grazing in the hills. There would also have been a good crop of potatoes, by now joining oats as the staple food of the small farmer and his family. Meat would have been a rare luxury, mutton or salt-beef eaten perhaps once a week or when guests came. Clothing too would have come from the farm, with wool spun into cloth and leather for shoes.

The farmhouse would have been the traditional but and ben, about ten metres long and three wide, with rough stone walls and a turf roof. The 'but' was the living room, where the cooking was done on an open peat fire and the smoke filled the space. There would have been a partitioned area for the box beds of the children. The 'ben' was where the parents slept and where they would greet

Corbis Images

Mungo Park

guests. This room was smarter and would have some furniture, perhaps a chest and a clock, and a desk with the family Bible.

Park's father believed in the value of a good education and for some years paid for a private tutor for his children. Park then enrolled at Selkirk Grammar School for his formal education but continued to learn from his father, listening to the ballads and tales of the Borders which he would remember all his life.

Park's father, true to form, wanted his son to go into the Church – but this was definitely not what young Mungo wanted. At the age of fourteen he became apprenticed to the local doctor, Thomas Anderson, to learn the trade. He did more than that; he also met the doctor's young daughter whom many years later he would marry.

At eighteen Park packed his bags and set off for Edinburgh University to study medicine for the next three years. At the time Edinburgh was the leading medical school in Britain, comparable in reputation with the best in Europe. The quality of the teaching was very high; Park's chemistry professor was Joseph Black and he learned anatomy and surgery from Alexander Munro *secundus*. At Edinburgh he also developed an interest in poetry, particularly in Scots, and took part in a debate arguing the relative merits of the works of Allan Ramsay and Robert Fergusson.

When he finished his medical studies, Park chose not to adopt the quiet life of the Borders but like many Scots of the time he sought a bigger arena for his talents.

## Sumatra

The young Mungo Park set off for London with his brother-in-law, Thomas Dickson, a botanist who had awakened in him an interest in natural history as they tramped through the hills of the Borders. Dickson introduced Park to the greatest botanist of the time, Sir Joseph Banks.

As he had some years earlier with Archibald Menzies, Banks proposed Park should take the position of assistant ship's surgeon on the *Worcester*, an East India ship bound for Sumatra with chests of silver to buy pepper, Sumatra's principal export.

Park collected a large number of specimens on the voyage, including eight new fish, which he recorded in sketches and watercolours. Upon his return he presented these in a paper to the prestigious Linnean Society and so impressed his mentor that Banks asked if he would lead an expedition to West Africa which was being financed by the African Association, a body formed by the members of a London dining club, to explore the River Niger from source to sea. It was a remarkable opportunity for a young man and a tribute to his skill and dedication. He was just twenty-three years old at the time.

## West Africa

His ship, the *Endeavour*, reached the coast of West Africa in June 1795 and sailed up the River Gambia to Pisania where there was a British trading post. That was to be the beginning of an amazing adventure.

The West African interior had remained largely unexplored since classical times although the Portuguese had ventured inland in their pursuit of slaves. Herodotus, the Greek geographer, had written in the fifth century BC of a great river flowing to the east; the Romans even had a name for it: the River Nigir [*sic*]. But did this river exist, and if so where was its source and to where did it flow? If its source was in the mountains south-west of Timbuktu, like the Rivers Gambia and Senegal, did it turn in on itself like those rivers and flow back into the Atlantic or did it carry on eastwards into the interior?

Mungo Park's initiation to West Africa was not auspicious. While waiting for the end of the rainy season he went down with fever, caused, it was thought, by exposure to the dew when he stayed out overnight to watch an eclipse of the moon – in fact it was almost undoubtedly malaria, but it was to be many years before Ronald Ross identified the cause of that disease.

Slavery was endemic in the country and only about one quarter of the population was free. The rest either worked as slaves or were sold to European slave traders. Park had planned to join one of these slave-trader caravans, but as they were suspicious of his motives he decided instead to journey alone. He travelled light, accompanied only by an interpreter and a boy, a horse, two asses, some beads and tobacco to trade for food, a compass, a thermometer and two pistols.

The small group headed eastwards through various small kingdoms whose religion was mainly Islam, introduced by traders from the north. When they reached the kingdom of Bondu, Park was invited to an audience with the King. Suspicious of the King's intentions, he hid some of his possessions in his hut, but he thought it prudent to wear his best blue coat for the occasion. That proved a mistake; the King admired his coat and Park had no alternative but to take it off and present it as a gift, in return receiving food and some gold.

His route took him northeast through a wilderness which he was advised to cross at night, which he did, listening to the cries of the hyenas and the howling of wild dogs. On entering the town of Joag he was summarily seized by twenty armed horsemen and told that as he had not given a present to the ruler, all his goods would be forfeited. He only managed to secure his freedom by handing over the gold he had been given. Easy come easy go.

Crossing the River Senegal into Khasso he once again had to pay tribute. This journey was proving expensive. He had planned to travel through the kingdoms of Kaarta and Bambarra until he reached the Niger, but was warned to travel north to avoid a war which was about to break out between the two. The drawback was that this northern route would take him into the country of the Moors who had a fearsome reputation as dangerous raiders. The interpreter sensibly decided it was a good time to go home, leaving Park with just his faithful boy as a travelling companion.

## Taken Prisoner by the Moors

Park had reached a village and was conversing with a group of its elders when suddenly he found himself surrounded by a party of raiding Moors, who seized him and took him to their leader, a white-bearded Arab inevitably called Ali. The Moors knew Park was a Christian and so they tortured and humiliated him, confining him in a tent with just a wild hog to keep him company. His boy was taken by Ali as his personal slave.

After a week the Moors met to decide what they should do with him; none of the options seemed attractive to Park: death, having his right hand cut off or having his eye gouged out. Fortunately no decision could be made until the arrival of Queen Fatima, a lady so fat she could only walk if supported by two slaves.

When she eventually appeared, Park waited anxiously while she decided his fate. It was now the dry season and Park suffered dreadfully from thirst, dreaming he was drinking from the clear burns of the Borders but waking to find he was a prisoner in the desert. He was not allowed to drink water from the wells in case as a Christian he defiled them but at last found succour through drinking from a cattle trough, sharing the water with two rather surprised cows.

## Escape and the River Niger

Events took a dramatic turn. The various tribes were always fighting with shifting loyalties and Ali took Park with him on one of his raids. In the confusion Park managed to escape. He was at last free but the outlook did not look too good: he had no food and nothing to buy it with; he had no water and no knowledge of where the wells were; his horse was a broken nag. However, after his experiences with the Moors, '*even the desert looked pleasant and I dreaded nothing so much as falling in with some wandering parties of Moors.*' This fear of the Moors would return to haunt his second expedition.

He was desperate for water but fortunately there was a rainstorm. He had nothing in which to collect the precious water so he spread his clothes over the ground and sucked the moisture from them; to obtain food he traded locks of his hair, seen as precious charms which would give their wearer the wisdom of the white man.

Park joined with a group who were fleeing the fighting and together they made their way southwards, stopping at villages where sometimes they were fed, sometimes sent away hungry, until they reached Segu, a city on the banks of the River Niger, where he first saw the magnificent river which was the purpose of his expedition. Segu was a major city of perhaps thirty thousand people living in four quarters, each with a mosque. The King's quarter was across the river and there was a regular ferry service manned by the King's slaves. The King would not allow him to cross the river, fearing perhaps that he was a spy – no rational person could believe that Park had travelled all that way and endured such hardship just to see a river! – but gave him cowries with which he could buy food and provided him with a guide.

Park set off east to follow the course of the Niger towards Timbuktu, a Moorish city. The rains had set in and much of the land was flooded. The journey was hard; his horse collapsed and he was incessantly bitten by mosquitoes. He had journeyed seventy-five miles eastwards along the Niger until, exhausted and fearful of again encountering the Moors, he decided to turn and head back to the coast.

Since he now realised the King had become convinced he was a spy and had given orders for him to be captured, he travelled fast avoiding Segu and taking to the hills because the main route to the coast was flooded and impassable. Weak and feverish he made his way as far as Kamaila in the land of the Mandango, but there he collapsed. His fever persisted for five weeks and left him sorely weakened.

The Mandango gave him food and shelter and he stayed with them during the winter learning their customs, knowledge which would later form the basis of the book of his travels. The following April he set off with a slave caravan for the five hundred mile trek back to the coast. The slaves were bound in groups of four with a rope around their necks. Park writes movingly of their suffering, often ill and undernourished, and of the hardships of their journey; if one fell by the wayside he or she – for many were women – was left behind to die.

## The Voyage Home

When he reached the coast Park took a berth on the first ship available, as ship's surgeon on an American slaving ship bound for the Carolinas. The slaves were kept chained in confined conditions below decks; many died from fever and there was not much he could do to ease their sufferings. The ship itself was in sorry condition and limped in to Antigua in the West Indies, where it was condemned. Twenty slaves had died on the journey and the hundred and ten left were sold to slave owners in Antigua.

In the book of his travels Park is somewhat ambivalent about the rights and wrongs of slavery. He had seen the suffering it caused and was deeply sympathetic to their hardships but had realised that slavery was an intrinsic part of African life. Perhaps he felt wary of commenting on an issue which was a political hot potato.

Park took a ship back to England, arriving in December 1797. He had been away for more than two and a half years. He reported in to Sir Joseph Banks and learned that he had become a celebrity, fêted by London society.

Soon he tired of the artificiality of society life and returned to the family farm in Scotland to write an account of his journey, *Travels into the Interior Districts of*

*Africa*, which was well received and sold widely, even being translated into French and German. The book was significant in increasing the store of knowledge of Africans and their customs, which he had gained from his enforced stay with the Mandango. During the time he was writing, he again met Allison, the daughter of Dr Thomas Anderson. She was now a lovely eighteen-year-old and Park was smitten. They were married in 1799.

Park was invited to take part in other expeditions but his romantic attachment kept him at home. The earnings from his book provided for them for a while, but the couple soon had two little babies and Park needed work. He decided to qualify as a surgeon and open a doctor's practice in Peebles. It was a hard life. Sir Walter Scott, who met Park in 1804 and became a close friend, wrote of the country doctor:

> *I have heard that the celebrated traveller Mungo Park [would] rather give preference to travelling as a discoverer in Africa than to wandering by night and day the wilds of his native land in the capacity of a country medical practitioner … His was not the heart which grudged the labour that relieved human misery … [but] there is no creature in Scotland that works harder and is more poorly requited than the country doctor, unless perhaps it may be his horse.*

## His Second Expedition

It is therefore not surprising that Park was tempted when he was contacted by Sir Joseph Banks in September 1803 and learned that the government, concerned the French were planning to increase their influence in West Africa, was financing an expedition to explore the Niger. Allison, now with a third little one, agreed, probably accepting that her husband would not be satisfied until he had completed his unfinished business in Africa. In September 1804 he bade farewell to his family and to Scotland. He would see neither again.

Park's plan was to march with his expedition, which would be made up of soldiers from the Royal African Corps, as far as Segu and then to build a boat to sail eastwards down the Niger to Timbuktoo and then to its outlet, wherever that might be. The expedition did not set sail until the end of January 1805, making their planned trek to Segu dangerously near the onset of the rainy season.

When Park arrived in Gambia he had just six weeks to make the five hundred mile trek before the rains began. With hindsight he should have delayed their departure until after the rains, but he was driven by the promises he had made.

The party made slow progress and had only journeyed half the distance when in June the rains came. Within a week dysentery and malaria had affected most of the expedition. Paths became streams and streams became impassable torrents. They were all soaked through, living and sleeping in their sodden clothing. Thieves followed the disintegrating caravan like vultures, stealing anything that came their way. After one hundred and fifteen days the tattered remnants of the expedition reached the Niger. It had taken twice as long as planned, and only twelve of the forty-four Europeans who had set out were still alive.

Mungo Park explained to the King of Segu that he planned to find a route whereby ships could reach Segu from Britain and bring trade to his country. He gave the King many presents and received permission to build his boat, joining together two canoes to create a boat which was thirteen metres long and two wide but had a very low draught suitable for the shallows they would find on their journey. The party was reduced to just five men and before the expedition departed Park wrote letters of condolence to the families of those who had died. He also completed a journal, which would prove the last report of the expedition received from Park.

Surprisingly Park did not follow his normal practice of securing letters of safe conduct and of paying tribute to the kings through whose lands he passed, a practice which had served him well on his first expedition. Instead his plan was to stay in the canoe, refusing to land to meet the kings. Worse, he decided to open fire upon any who came too close to the boat, treating it as a floating fortress. This may be because he had a terror of again being seized by the Moors, but this lack of courtesy angered the kings and set them against his expedition.

The canoe was attacked repeatedly as they sailed through the hostile territories, the small band of explorers repulsing all assaults. Hungry, ill and often menaced they journeyed many miles along the river following it from Timbuktu as it swung to the south-east and increasingly desperate to reach the point where it met the sea, but when they reached Bussa the canoe was overturned in rapids. Park and his three companions, the last remnants of the original expedition, were tossed out of the boat and drowned. They had remarkably covered one thousand miles of the river, whose total length is two and a half thousand miles. It was not until 1830 that the swampy delta through which the River Niger disgorges into the Gulf of Guinea was discovered.

## Park's Legacy

Mungo Park's main achievement was probably not geographical knowledge, but his account of the life of the Africans included in *Travels in the Interior Districts of Africa*, a classic of travel literature. He understood and treated the Africans as people, not as some inferior race – respecting their customs, honouring their kings and believing with true Enlightenment fervor that the country and the lives of its inhabitants could be vastly improved if access for trade could be obtained and better agricultural practices introduced.

**Further Reading**
Mark Duffill, *Mungo Park: West African Explorer*

**Online Resources**
http://ebooks.adelaide.edu.au/p/park/mungo/index.html

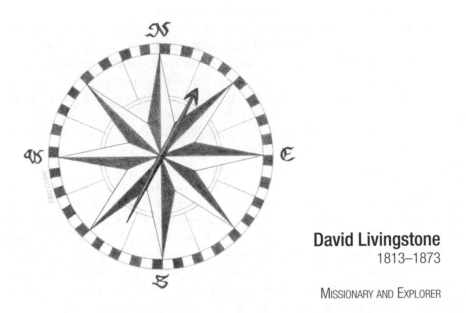

### David Livingstone
1813–1873

MISSIONARY AND EXPLORER

David Livingstone was a doctor and missionary who believed it was his destiny to bring Christianity to Africa. He was deeply opposed to the slave trade, adopting the Enlightenment belief that all men were equal but recognising that some nations had moved further along the process of 'civilization.' Why, he asked, should Africans be shipped over to America to work as slaves on the cotton plantations, with all the suffering, disease and death that entailed, if they could work in their homeland. He believed that opening up Africa to both Christianity and trade would in time bring this despicable trade in human flesh to an end and dreamed of finding a river which would provide a trade route from the heartlands of Africa to the sea, bringing the benefits of trade to the Africans. He spent much of his life exploring Africa, seeking in vain for this river and is remembered now more for his exploration than for his missionary work.

### His Early Years

David Livingstone was born on 19 March 1813 to a poor Scots family in Blantyre, a village near Glasgow. His father, Neil, was a God-fearing man who worked as a travelling tea salesman, and Livingstone lived with two brothers and two sisters in one room in Shuttle Row, a tenement building owned by a mill owner. There were no taps or baths and his mother had to work hard to keep the one-room house clean.

Livingstone was only ten years old when he went to work at the cotton mill; in those days it was common for children to work either in factories or on the land.

David Livingstone
*(detail) see: colour plate 28*

Thomas Annan, 'David Livingstone'/Scottish National Portrait Gallery

Livingstone was employed as a 'piecer,' his job to piece together the broken threads as the cotton was being spun into cloth. The work was long and hard. Children worked in the mill from six o'clock in the morning to eight at night from Monday to Saturday, with just half an hour's break for breakfast and an hour's break for lunch. As a piecer, Livingstone had to watch the cloth closely all the time, checking the threads. The foreman in the mill would beat him with a stick if he stopped watching or throw a bucket of water over him if he dozed off.

By the standards of the time the mill owner was 'enlightened' and provided schooling in the evenings after work. Livingstone would attend school from eight until ten to improve himself, believing strongly it was his duty to God to make the best of his life. Then after a night's sleep, it was back to the factory for the six o'clock start. Livingstone's father was a strict Calvinist and Sunday was given to God. The family would go to church and only after the service did he have any time to himself.

## Becoming a Missionary

Livingstone believed strongly in the existence of God and in the need to improve himself in order to better serve Him. But how was this to be? He read an appeal for people to serve as missionaries, taking the word of God to faraway lands – could this be his destiny? To us now it seems arrogant that anyone should believe that the whole world should accept the Christian faith and beliefs, but in Livingstone's time it was believed that by taking Christianity to distant places such as China and Africa the souls of the people would be saved. Livingstone made up his mind. He would train as a doctor and then go out to Africa, helping to save the people's bodies as a doctor and their souls as a missionary, and so he enrolled to study medicine at Anderson's University, Glasgow.

## Voyage to Africa

After being duly qualified as a doctor and ordained as a missionary in 1840, when he was twenty-seven years old, Livingstone boarded a ship for Africa to join the mission of a fellow Scot, Dr. Robert Moffat, who had fired his imagination with stories of Africa. He had already come a long way from the small boy working as a piecer in a cotton mill. The voyage to South Africa in the *George* was hard as the sailing brig was continually battered by fierce storms. Livingstone wrote, 'Our little vessel went reeling and staggering over the waves as if she had been drunk, our trunks perpetually breaking from their lashings, were tossed from one side of the cabin to the other [as the little ship] writhed and twisted about terribly.' He spent his time on the voyage learning Tswana, the language spoken by the tribes where he would be working. Eventually, the ship reached Cape Town.

Livingstone loved Africa. He loved the noise and the colour, the bustle and the excitement, as he made the seven-hundred mile journey by oxcart from Cape Town in the South to Dr Moffat's mission station at Kuruman. There he met Moffat's daughter, Mary, with whom he fell in love.

## Life as a Missionary

Livingstone journeyed north to Mabotsa, where he started the hard work of building a house for a mission station and it was while he was there that he was mauled by a lion. He had gone to help some Africans whose sheep had been attacked by the lion and seeing the beast sitting on a rock just thirty yards away, he fired both barrels of his gun but only succeeded in wounding it. Enraged, the lion sprang on Livingstone as he tried desperately to reload. He wrote, 'Growling horribly close to my ear, he shook me as a terrier does a rat.' Fortunately, the lion turned away from Livingstone to attack the Africans when suddenly it fell dead; the bullets had at last done their work, but Livingstone was badly wounded. 'Besides crunching the bone into splinters, he left eleven teeth wounds on the upper part of my arm.' When later asked what thoughts he had while seized by the lion he replied, laconically, 'I was thinking ..... which part of me the brute would eat first.' This experience gave Livingstone a sense that he was being saved for his destiny and a courage which would hold him in good stead in his later travels.

David and Mary married and moved up-country to a new mission station at Chonuane. It was a very hard life and they had to grow all their own crops which often failed through the lack of rain. Their children lived as simply as the Africans.

Livingstone converted the tribal chief, Chief Sechele, to Christianity. The Chief then built a house for them and a church, but unfortunately, no more of the tribe could be persuaded to convert. Chief Sechele had the answer: 'I will beat them,' he said, 'it is the only way!' Livingstone did not accept this offer of a somewhat unorthodox route to Christianity and Chief Sechele later reverted to his tribal beliefs.

Eventually, the river where they were living dried up and in the drought the crops and animals were dying. Livingstone realised he must move his mission again, further north to Kuruman, where he was faced again with the back-breaking task of creating a new home. He was so poor that he had to burn down his old house at Chonuane just to obtain nails for the new building.

Once again he set off on his exploration but this time, perhaps selfishly, accompanied by his wife Mary, who was pregnant, and their children, Robert (4),

Agnes (3) and Thomas (aged 1). This unconventional group of explorers crossed the Kalahari Desert in burning heat for days without food or water. During the expedition Mary gave birth to a little girl but sadly all the children caught a chest infection and the baby died. They were forced to return home.

## The Search for a Future for Africa

Livingstone believed his mission was not just to bring Christianity to Africa but to open up the land to trade. He wanted a place where the Africans could grow cotton and a route whereby their crops could be shipped to the coast and then exported to the world. Better he felt for the Africans to be growing their own cotton than to be captured and shipped as slaves to the Americas to grow cotton on a plantation. The slave trade was an abomination which must be ended.

To achieve his aim he needed to find a place which was free from disease and had ample water. He mounted a further expedition, this time to journey into the heart of Africa, and was amazed to find that, far from being the arid desert he had expected, it was watered and well populated. Was this the place where he could realise his dream of a prosperous Africa freed from the horrors of the slave trade?

He needed to find the great river that would allow ships to sail to the centre of the continent, to bring wealth and opportunity rather than famine and despair. He planned that his next exploration would be to find such a river.

Realising his young family were not ideal companions for such an arduous journey, he sent Mary and their children back to Britain to be looked after by the Missionary Society. They had no money and not unreasonably, Mary asked her husband how she would live in England. 'God will look after you' was his trusting but not too reassuring reply.

Livingstone set off with a party of Africans first north through the harsh desert then westwards through wet, marshy ground plagued by the tsetse fly. He took little with him, 'only a few biscuits, a few pounds of tea and sugar and twenty pounds of coffee, a rifle to shoot animals for meat, a spare set of clothes, a compass and a sextant.' In the unhealthy marsh lands everyone except one of the Africans and Livingstone himself caught malaria, but eventually the small party reached the country of the Kololo under Chief Sekeleto, where he found a warm welcome. The Kololo would be his companions on all his future journeys.

The party set off again, trekking through incessant rain and suffering recurring illness. They walked all day through the rain and slept each night in soaking wet clothes until at last they reached the coast at Loanda where there was a Portugese settlement from which captured slaves were transported to the Americas. He had seen the convoys of slaves in his travels, manacled together as they were marched to the coast; sometimes he would see the body of a woman slave who could not keep up with the relentless march and had been left to die – or whose throat had been slit to speed the process.

Since Livingstone had not discovered any river, nor any route into the heartland of Africa, he had to continue his search. He set off again, this time to cross Africa from the west coast to Mozambique on the east, facing great hardship through hunger and disease while becoming the first European to cross the continent.

He trekked along the mighty Zambesi River as it wound its way southeast from its source in the highlands of Central Africa and became the first European to see the great waterfall on the Zambesi River which he named the Victoria Falls after his queen. He determined to measure the height of the falls and paddled in a canoe to an island in the centre of the river which jutted out over the falls, then crawling to the edge he dropped a weighted rope over the mighty falls, measuring the height as three hundred and sixty feet (one hundred and ten metres). It was, he said, *the most wonderful sight I have seen in Africa.*

Could the Zambesi be the great river he had been seeking, the river which would enable ships to sail into the heartland of Africa? Would this river fulfil his destiny?


## The Zambesi Expedition

When Livingstone eventually returned to Britain he discovered he had become famous as an explorer and soon became wealthy through the publication of his book on his exploration which he called *Missionary Travels.*

He believed he had found the answer to his dream and that the Zambesi was the river which would open a path for trade and Christianity into the heart of Africa. He raised funds for another expedition, this time to explore the Zambesi from sea to source.

In 1858 Livingstone set off from the mouth of the Zambesi in a launch which he called the Ma-Robert or 'Robert's mother,' the name the Africans had given to Mary. The exploration went badly from the start. It took months to discover the true mouth of the Zambesi among all the different channels in the delta and when they did, they found that the Ma-Robert was not powerful enough to make away against the flow of the river and that she continually ran aground in the shallow waters. In 1861 Mary Livingstone left her children behind in Britain and sailed to Africa to join the expedition on the Zambesi. Within months she had died of malaria and Livingstone was devastated; he wrote to a friend, 'I cannot tell you how greatly I feel the loss. It feels as if heart and strength were taken out of me.'

After months of struggling they reached the Cabora Bassa Gorge. Livingstone explored the way ahead by land. The river ran through a narrow gorge with teeming rapids and rocks as big as houses. His dream was over. The gorge was impossible to navigate. The Zambesi was not the route from the coast to the heartland of Africa which he had hoped to find, but he did discover Lake Nyasa before he returned disappointed to England in 1864.

## The Source of the Nile

As a result of the failure of the Zambesi expedition, his reputation had fallen but the challenge of locating the true source of the River Nile remained. James Bruce (1730-1794), the flamboyant and irascible son of a Scottish laird, used the profits from the coal on his family's estates to finance expeditions, first to Abyssinia and then to Africa where he had discovered the source of the Blue Nile. He wrote:

> *It is easier to guess than to describe the situation of my mind at that moment – standing in the spot which had baffled the genius, industry and inquiry, of both ancients and moderns, for the course of near three thousand years.*

Sadly, he received little recognition for the discovery; although the Blue Nile provides the majority of the water which flows through Egypt, it is the White Nile which is longer and therefore seen as the true source. Angry and disillusioned, Bruce retired to his estates in Scotland.

Finding the true source of the Nile became the Holy Grail of African exploration. In 1855 the British explorers Richard Burton, who in disguise had famously entered the holy – and forbidden - city of Mecca, and John Hanning Speke made their first attempt to find the source of the Nile, but their expedition was abandoned when their camp was attacked by Somali bandits. During this attack Burton received the fearsome scars to his face, caused by a spear thrust deep into his skull, for which he became notorious.

They mounted a second exploration in 1857, setting off from Zanzibar and heading inland towards Lake Tanganyika. After a year trekking though forest, grassland and swamps, they reached the shores of the lake, a massive stretch of water stretching as far as the eye could see to both the north and the south. This they agreed must be the source of the Nile, but critically they were never able to find the river flowing north from the lake which would prove their claims. Running short of food, they were forced to turn for home when Burton was struck down by malaria. While he recuperated, Speke set out north with a small group of porters. To his amazement he found another vast lake which he patriotically named Lake Victoria, but critically again he did not explore around the lake either to trace the Nile flowing northwards or to confirm that no river flowed into the lake from the south; instead he relied upon the stories of the local tribes, drawing a map on the basis of what they had told him. On his return he excitedly told Burton of his discovery and that Lake Victoria must be the true source of the Nile. Burton was furious. He demanded that they trek north to confirm the claim but Speke pointed out that they had insufficient supplies of the beads and cloth they would need to buy food. Returning home was the only option. They trekked back to the coast, racked by illness and consumed by mutual hatred, then sailed back to London on separate ships and never spoke again.

Speke arrived in Britain first and, declaring that 'The Nile is settled,' claimed that he had discovered the source of the Nile; it was Lake Victoria. Burton held to their original view that the source was Lake Tanganyika. Who was right?

In 1864 a meeting was called by the Royal Geographical Society at which both Burton and Speke would present their cases for public debate and the dispute would be decided. Burton waited patiently in the hall for Speke to arrive, but he never came. Bitterly hurt by the scepticism which had greeted his claim, Speke had shot himself, accidentally or otherwise, on the day before the debate. He had gone shooting game with his cousin and had rested his rifle, which had no safety-catch, against a stone wall while he climbed over. He was shot through the heart.

The mystery remained unresolved. The President of the Society, Sir Roderick Murchison, proposed that Livingstone be given a small amount of funds to finance an expedition to return to Africa to determine finally the true source of the Nile. Livingstone arrived in Zanzibar in 1866 and from there he set out as the only European on the expedition with the support of just a few bearers.

He had two aims; first to explore the highlands to the north-east of Lake Nyasa to see if these could be the fertile lands he had spent his life seeking as a solution to Africa's poverty and second to explore Lake Tanganyika to discover whether this, rather than Lake Victoria, was the true source of the Nile. He wanted to approach Lake Tanganyika from the south to find whether it was joined to Lake Nyasa in a 'chain' of lakes which would provide a waterway through Africa.

Livingstone set off in good spirits, writing, 'Now that I am on the point of starting on another trip into Africa, I feel quite exhilarated.' The expedition proved hard; food was scarce and he was deserted by many of his men, being left with just eight. When he reached Lake Nyasa conditions worsened; the animals he relied upon shooting to provide food had moved on, and the party suffered from extreme hunger, from the burning heat and from a lack of fresh water. Livingstone became gradually weakened by starvation and with his body wasted by continued hardship, he suffered recurrent fevers and bled continually from open sores, his condition worsened by the fact that two of the bearers had absconded with his medicine chest and his precious supply of quinine.

He remained obsessed by the desire to find the source of the Nile, but now it was just his willpower which drove his emaciated body. Eventually the small party reached Lake Tanganyika where for months he lay on his bed with pneumonia, too ill to move or to write. He had arranged for supplies to be sent to Ujiji, a settlement on the far side of the lake to await his arrival, but when he eventually crossed the lake in a canoe, he found to his horror that all the medicines and food had been stolen; all that remained were eighteen bales of cloth, out of the eighty he had ordered — this cloth was vital as it gave him the means to barter for essential food supplies.

Despite all adversity he had not given up his search and, realising that the current in Lake Tanganyika flowed north, he believed this proved the lake was the long sought source of the Nile. He had heard of a great river flowing northwards from the lake and resolved to explore. Eventually he reached the Lualaba, which was indeed a great river and he optimistically claimed it as the possible source of the Nile, although in his journal he wrote, correctly, that he 'feared' that it was in fact the Congo. Weakened by illness and without the means to acquire supplies, Livingstone depended upon charity for survival and stayed for months in a village called Nyangwe on the banks of the Lualaba, watching the women as they came to market to barter their goods. There were a few Arabs present, Zanzabari Arabs who were in the market for ivory and slaves, but it was tacitly understood that the villagers would be spared from slavery. One hot and sultry day he noticed with alarm that the Arabs in the market were carrying guns. Livingstone had spent much of his time among the Manyema people whose lifestyle he had come to love and respect and he was therefore horrified when a dispute between two Arabs and an African in the market suddenly erupted into violence. The Arabs shot the men, women and children of the village as they jumped screaming into the river trying to swim to safety, but either getting shot by the Arabs or seized by voracious crocodiles. Shocked by the massacre, Livingstone wrote, 'the bloodshed ... filled me with unspeakable horror.' His report on the massacre, when it eventually reached home, would be instrumental in raising awareness in Britain of the horrors of the slave trade in East Africa.

As soon as he could, Livingstone fled the scene back to Ujiji, reaching Lake Tanganyika on 8 October 1871. His body was ravaged by starvation and sickness and his mind broken by his failure to succeed in his quest of finding the source of the Nile. Then he crossed by canoe to Ujiji to find disaster – the stores he had been expecting had been stolen. He was desperate.

## The Search for Livingstone

For a long time no news of Livingstone had reached Britain and it was feared he had died. In February 1871 an expedition under Henry Stanley, financed by the *New York Herald*, had set sail from Zanzibar to try to find the 'lost' explorer. Stanley encountered immense hardships in his journey to Ujiji, but, improbably, in November they met two white men in the middle of Africa. Stanley greeted Livingstone with the immortal words 'Dr Livingstone, I presume.' He stayed for some time with Livingstone for whom he developed both admiration and friendship and together they explored the north end of Lake Tanganyika, confirming that there was no river flowing northwards, and the lake was not, therefore, the source of the Nile. When Stanley eventually left, the two men parted on good terms. Stanley was unable to persuade the explorer to come back with him but took with him Livingstone's journal and his report of the massacre at Nyangwe.

Livingstone felt that his work was unfinished. He wanted to complete the exploration of Lake Tanganyika by exploring the southern side. For a time Livingstone lived comfortably with the supplies left by Stanley, but soon illness and bleeding returned; he would not live much longer. He reached the south side of the lake in November 1872 - and then the rains came. He wandered lost in swamps for some months, becoming increasingly frail. In the following April he was carried into a village where he received shelter, but Livingstone realised he was dying. He declared to the few who had stayed faithful to him, 'Build me a hut to die in, I am going home.' They found him one morning on his knees beside his bed, dead; true to his beliefs his last words had been spoken to God. His heart was buried under a tree in his beloved Africa, but his body was embalmed by his few remaining faithful Africans and carried for eleven months on an amazing fifteen hundred mile journey to the coast, and from there by ship to England where it was buried in Westminster Abbey.

The source of the Nile would not finally be confirmed until Stanley explored around the whole of Lake Victoria in 1875 and found the outflow at the Ripon Falls which feeds into the Nile, making Lake Victoria the source — although now somewhat pedantically it is not Lake Victoria itself, but the longest of the rivers which feed into it which is regarded as the 'true' source.

## Livingstone's Legacy

David Livingstone never achieved his aim of ending the slave trade in Africa by opening up a route for trade, nor did he succeed in converting many Africans to Christianity. He had, however, come from the poorest of backgrounds and, through determination, a compelling desire to do God's work and a belief that one should make the most of one's talents, become one of the world's greatest explorers and an inspiration to future generations of explorers and missionaries.

**Further Reading**
Martin Dugard, *Into Africa*
Andrew Ross, *David Livingstone: Mission and Empire*

**Online Resources**
Livingstone Online
http://www.livingstoneonline.ucl.ac.uk/biog/dl/bio.html

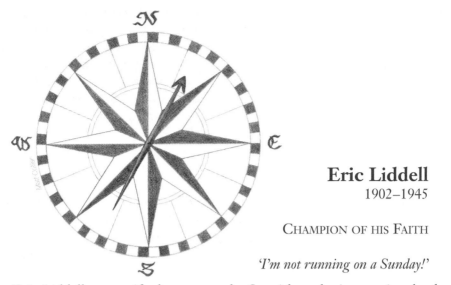

# Eric Liddell
## 1902–1945

<small>CHAMPION OF HIS FAITH</small>

*'I'm not running on a Sunday!'*

Eric Liddell was a gifted runner and a Scottish rugby international, who was given the nickname 'The Flying Scotsman' after the famous locomotive of that name. Like many during the Scottish Enlightenment, he held strong Christian beliefs and as a result gave up the chance of an Olympic gold medal because one of the heats of his chosen event, the one hundred metres, was held on a Sunday, God's day. Many years later his story was told in the film 'Chariots of Fire'.

## The Opium Wars

Liddell was born in China. His father James Liddell came from Drymen, a little village at the foot of Loch Lomond, and went to China as a missionary sent by the London Missionary Society. There he married a girl he had met back in Scotland at a church picnic named Mary, who bravely travelled to China to become his wife.

It was not an easy time to be a European in China. The great powers of Europe were eager to trade with China, buying silks and tea to gain access to the trade routes, and none more so than Britain. From the late 18th century, British merchants traded with China, using opium which was shipped from India to pay for the goods they wanted to buy. The Imperial Government of China became worried by the prevalence of opium smoking among its people and tried to put a stop to the practice by making the import of opium illegal, which became the background for the Opium Wars.

It might be thought that Britain as a 'civilised' country fought the Opium Wars to stop the use of opium as a drug. Unfortunately this was not the case. British merchants were making huge profits from their trade and Britain declared war not to stop the use of opium but to force China to continue importing it so the British could continue to trade and make profits.

For many centuries China had deliberately isolated itself from the world banning foreigners from its land and as a result, it had become technically backward. Its ships were no match for the mighty British navy and China had to sue for peace. The settlement reflected the power of the victors. Trade in opium was made legal, Hong Kong became a British colony and British settlers in China were freed from having to obey Chinese law. It was not the greatest moment in the history of the British Empire and as a result Europeans in general and the British in particular became deeply disliked by the Chinese people.

In 1900 this dislike erupted into an uprising against the Europeans in China. It was led by a secret society usually known as the Boxers but whose Chinese name was the more flamboyant 'League of Righteous and Harmonious Fists.' The Boxers captured an embassy in Beijing (known then to the British as Peking) but were soon defeated by a European expeditionary force and the victors forced China to pay huge sums of money as a penalty. This further humiliation caused riots throughout China, with over two hundred missionaries killed by the Boxers.

## Liddell's Childhood

China was dangerous for Europeans, particularly missionaries, but nonetheless where James and Mary chose to set up home. They set off straight away after their wedding to their intended destination; a mission in Mongolia, but with the country in turmoil from the Boxer Rebellion were forced to flee for their lives back to Shanghai.

Their second son was born in 1902 and christened Eric Henry. He was originally to be called 'Henry Eric' but they realised just in time that the initials H.E.L. were not really suitable for a God-fearing family. James, his father, moved to a mission in the plains in northern China where Mary joined him with the children — first, a six-hour train ride and then a forty-mile journey on a mule cart rattling across bumpy unpaved Chinese roads. The family increased with the birth of a baby girl, Jenny, and then another boy, Ernest. Eric Liddell and his brothers and sister were the only European children in the mission where they lived and spent their time playing with the Chinese children while their father ministered to the needs of the growing number of Chinese Christians.

Liddell was brought up by his missionary parents with strict Christian beliefs and these would stay with him and guide his actions throughout his life. When Liddell was five his father became seriously ill and the family went back to Drymen in Scotland so he could recover. Liddell and his elder brother Rob started at the village school, but when Liddell was not yet seven his father returned to China. The two boys were sent to a special school which had been set up in London for the sons of missionaries where Liddell first began to shine as an athlete, often with his brother as his greatest rival. He was awarded a cup for the best athlete and appointed captain of both the rugby and cricket teams. Despite this early success

Liddell remained true to his Christian upbringing, 'entirely without vanity' as his headmaster wrote. His success was not for him a cause for personal pride but an expression of the talent he had been given by God.

## Fame as a Runner

Liddell went from school to Edinburgh University in 1921, joining his brother, and soon began to make a national name for himself, both as a runner and as a rugby player. He used his outstanding speed to score tries as a wing three quarter. In his first term at university he entered two races, the one hundred yard and the two hundred and twenty yard sprints (roughly one and two hundred metres),

©Corbis Images

Eric Liddell in action

winning the first and losing the second by inches. Remarkably, his loss in the second race was the only time Liddell ever lost a race in Scotland.

It was all fairly simple in those days, you just went out and ran. Liddell was chosen to become a member of the university athletics team and trained three days a week. The athletes did not use track suits, but if it were cold, might wear an overcoat to keep warm before the race. There were no starting blocks; each sprinter carried a trowel to make a hole in the track to anchor himself.

The next year, he won the university one hundred, two hundred and twenty and four hundred and forty yard races and two titles in the Scottish championships.

He also gained fame as a rugby player, playing seven times in a Scotland shirt in the years 1922 and 1923, incredibly only once ending on the losing side. One of the victories was against Wales, when Scotland won by eleven points to eight, the first time in more than thirty years that Scotland had won in Cardiff. It is as a sprinter, however, that Liddell will best be remembered

## The 1924 Paris Olympics

Liddell mostly competed in Scotland, but in July 1923, he ran in the British Amateur Athletics Championships in London, winning both the two hundred and twenty and one hundred yard sprints. He won the hundred yards in 9.7 seconds, a new national record and only one tenth of a second outside the world record — remaining a British record for an amazing thirty-five years.

The following week, in an international match between Scotland and England, he not only won two short sprints, but also ran a memorable quarter mile (440 yards or roughly 400 metres). Shortly after the start he was jostled by another runner and went off the track onto the grass, but he gathered himself together

Eric Liddell

and, although by then, twenty yards behind the rest of the runners, he set off in pursuit. In characteristic style his fists were pumping and his head thrown back as he gradually overhauled the rest of the runners and won the race by two yards. He had in effect given all the other runners a twenty-yard start and still won.

It was natural that Liddell would be selected for the 1924 Olympic Games in Paris. He was entered for the two sprints, the 100 and 200 metres. He was one of the favourites for the 100 metres but then came the news that shattered his hopes of glory: the heats would be held on Sunday, and Liddell immediately withdrew his name. His Christian beliefs would not allow him to run on a Sunday and for those beliefs he was prepared to give up his very real chance of a gold medal.

Liddell decided to put his name down for the four hundred metres. He had hardly ever run this distance competitively and he had to change his training to meet the demands of the longer distance. His performances improved, but he was still recording times a few seconds slower than the top runners in the world during a blisteringly hot July.

On the Sunday when Liddell should have been competing in the heats of the 100 metres he was in church, preaching. Britain's place in the 100 metres was taken by his great rival, Harold Abrahams, who was very different from Liddell. Abrahams trained hard under the eyes of a professional coach and honed his running to make the most efficient use of his energy; not for him the extravagant style of Liddell, arms pumping, fists punching and head thrown back. Abrahams won his heat and then won through into the final on the Monday. He took the gold medal with a time of 10.6 seconds, cheered on by an enthusiastic Eric Liddell.

On Tuesday the heats for the 200 metres were held and both Liddell and Abrahams got through to reach the final which took place on the Wednesday, but it was won by an American, with Liddell beaten into third place and Abrahams last. Liddell had won a bronze medal but not the gold for which he had been hoping. Had he lost the chance of a gold medal? There was only the 400 metres left, a distance over which he had only raced a few times.

The heats were scheduled on Thursday; he won his in 50.2 seconds, well below the times of the established runners. He won the quarter final in 49.0 seconds and the semi-final in 48.2 seconds. Was he coming into form at the right time? Six competitors reached the final. In addition to Liddell, there were two Americans, a Swiss, a Canadian and another British runner, Guy Butler, who had already won a silver medal in the 1920 Olympics.

Before the race, Liddell was handed a note of good wishes by one of the masseurs. It read, *'He that honours me I will honour.'* It was a quotation from the Book of Samuel in the Old Testament and referred to Liddell's decision to honour

God by choosing not to run on a Sunday. The note made a big impression on him.

As was his custom, Liddell, shook hands with all his competitors before the race and then took his place in the outside lane, recognised as the most difficult since you cannot see the other runners and use their performance to judge the pace. As they were lining up there was a sudden interruption, a skirl of the pipes as the pipers of the Cameron Highlanders broke into 'Scotland the Brave!' to inspire Liddell to do his best. In those days, the 400 metres was considered a middle distance event and the runners would ease off in the back straight before sprinting to the finish. Liddell however set off like a rocket, covering the first two hundred metres in 22.2 seconds, only 0.5 seconds slower than the winning time in the two hundred metre race, and by the half way mark had built a lead of more than three metres — a stunning pace. Gradually, the American Horatio Fitch closed the gap until with fifty metres to go he had nearly reached Liddell's shoulder. Then Liddell made his supreme effort; relying on his inner strength he managed to increase his pace and open a gap. At the tape he had won by an amazing five metres. What's more, he had set a new world record of 47.6 seconds.

The stadium erupted in a great roar. Liddell was the only one who remained calm, for he had only done what he had set out to do. He left shortly after the race — after all he was due to preach on Sunday to all the Olympic competitors and he needed to write his sermon.

In a moving postscript, when another Scot, Alan Wells, won the 100 metres in the 1980 Moscow Olympics, he was asked whether he was dedicating his win to Harold Abrahams, the previous British winner of the one hundred metres. 'No,' Wells replied 'This one is for Eric Liddell.' So in a way Liddell did finally achieve his 100 metres gold.

### Becoming a Missionary in China

For all his success as an athlete, it was as a missionary that Liddell chose to devote his life. Following his Olympic success, he returned to Edinburgh, where he was greeted as a hero and received his university degree. Then he joined the Scottish Congregational Church to train as a missionary. During his year of training he travelled widely throughout Scotland, using his fame as a runner to help proclaim his Christianity. In July 1925 when he left Scotland for China a huge crowd, singing hymns, gathered at Waverley Station to wish him farewell.

China was still a troubled country. In 1911 the last emperor had been overthrown and by the time Liddell arrived, the country was split between the Nationalists under Chiang Kai-shek, who believed in a strong centralised Chinese state, and the Communists under Mao Tse-tung. The country was in turmoil as the two sides fought each other and their armies laid the countryside to waste, burning, pillaging and destroying crops.

Liddell was bound for Tientsin, a city of about a million people set on the banks of the River Haihe in the north-east of the country, which suffered from bitterly cold winters and hot humid summers. The Anglo-Chinese Christian College where he was heading was housed in an impressive building. It had been established to educate the sons of important Chinese, the future leaders, with the idea that they would then spread Christianity throughout the country.

In September Liddell started work as a science teacher. While he was not a good classroom teacher, he soon became involved in the sport of the college. He also continued running, recording some fast times and beating world-class runners, but he was overlooked for the 1928 Olympics – perhaps he was too far away from Britain to be noticed. He was greatly admired by the students for his faith expressed in the way he lived his life.

In 1934 Liddell married a Canadian nurse called Florence whose family were also missionaries in China. They had two little girls, Patricia and Heather, but Liddell was not to see much of his family because soon after they were born he was moved from Tientsin to Siaochang in a poor part of China, which had suffered badly from the bitter civil war, and for safety he left his young family behind.

## Japan Invades China

Life in Siaochang was very hard. There was little food because the crops had been destroyed by the armies. Whole families would live in one room and the people lived in fear of the soldiers returning. But then a bad situation got worse. In July 1937, after many years of sporadic fighting, the Second Sino-Japanese War started with the invasion of China by Japan. The Japanese used terror tactics to frighten the local Chinese; if Chinese fighters attacked a Japanese outpost, the Japanese soldiers would march into the nearest village and shoot all the peasants who lived there. The three-way war was bitter, as the Chinese fought the Japanese and the Nationalist Chinese fought the Communist Chinese. The Japanese occupied north-east China and it was through this dangerous country that Liddell travelled as a missionary, on foot or on his bicycle, spreading the message of Christianity and trying to avoid the Japanese soldiers.

Sometimes he would arrive at a village after a long hard journey through the parched land only to find it abandoned, all the houses burnt to the ground. For Liddell it was heartbreaking, but he never lost his faith.

It soon became too unsafe for Liddell and the other missionaries to stay. No longer did the Japanese soldiers respect the missionaries and their Christian ideals. In 1941 Liddell returned to his family in Tientsin but even there it was not safe. He booked his wife and children on a ship to Canada and said a fond goodbye, little realising he would never see them again.

Life became even more dangerous in December 1941, when Japan declared war on the United States with a surprise bombing raid on American shipping in Pearl Harbour. The Japanese strengthened their control over China and Liddell and his fellow missionaries were forced to live confined to a compound. In March 1943 all foreigners in Japanese-occupied China were immediately ordered to gather their belongings and go to an internment camp in Weihsien. Conditions in the camp were very poor, with people sleeping in dormitories with only basic toilet and washing facilities. Liddell remained a tower of strength, taking particular care of the youngsters who were incarcerated in the camp and organising games to keep the youngsters busy. He was always ready with a cheery word for his fellow inmates and many believed they owed their lives to Eric Liddell, remembering his calm and his firm Christian faith which gave them all the strength to go on. The effort took its toll on Liddell.

He began to suffer from blinding headaches and his health rapidly worsened until in February 1945, he died from a massive brain tumour. He was given a warm and rousing funeral by his fellow inmates, including a spirited rendering of his favourite hymn 'Be Still, My Soul.' It was more than two months before his wife, in Canada, learned of his death.

## Liddell's Legacy

Eric Liddell is most famous as the runner who would not run in the Olympics on a Sunday. But for all those who knew him, he was best remembered for the Christian way in which he lived his life and for the peace he gave to others. Deeply held Christian beliefs as demonstrated in the life of Liddell and the lives of many of the leading lights of the Enlightenment, such as Francis Hutcheson, may be unfashionable in this secular age, but whatever our beliefs we would all gain from a more general acceptance of the love of humanity expressed in his life.

In 1990 the Eric Liddell Centre 'dedicated to inspiring, empowering and supporting people of all ages, cultures and abilities' was set up in Edinburgh as a living memorial to this remarkable man 'Currently it supports people suffering from dementia and their carers. There is a video of Liddell running the 400 metres in the Paris Olympics on their website (www.ericliddell.org.uk).

Liddell's memory lives on. In 2008, a remarkable eighty-four years after his Olympic victory, Liddell was named as Scotland's most popular athlete in a poll conducted by *The Scotsman*. The same year official papers were released revealing that during the War, the Japanese had made a deal with the British with Churchill's approval for the exchange of a few selected prisoners. Liddell was chosen for exchange, but characteristically, he gave up his chance of repatriation to a woman in the camp who was pregnant.

**Further Reading**
John Keddie, *Running the Race*
Sally Magnusson, *The Flying Scotsman: The Story of Eric Liddell*

**Online Resources**
http://www.ericliddell.org/ericliddell/home

'MANUSCRIPT OF MONTE CASSINO' (HEEL, 3 of 3
Eduardo Paolozzi - 1991
Picardy Place, Edinburgh
photo: Thomas Haywood

Paolozzi created this work as an allegory to the
manuscript for which it is named, *A Journey*.
Consisting of three pieces: a hand, ankle and foot,
the work refers to Ancient Roman sculptures on
Capitoline Hill, Rome.

# Architects, Civil Engineers & Builders

# ARCHITECTS, CIVIL ENGINEERS & BUILDERS

**Robert Adam**
*ARCHITECT OF GEORGIAN BRITAIN*

**John Loudon McAdam**
*MACADAMISING THE ROADS OF BRITAIN*

**Thomas Telford**
*THE MAN WHO BRIDGED THE WORLD*

**John Rennie**
*DESIGNER AND BUILDER OF
BRITAIN'S CANALS*

**Robert Stevenson**
*THE FAMILY THAT BUILT
SCOTLAND'S LIGHTHOUSES*

# Part 7 • Architects, Civil Engineers & Builders

### Building a New Britain

Eric Liddell post-dated the Enlightenment by many years, but he embodied Enlightenment ideals and was self-evidently a remarkably *good* man, and there are not many of whom that can be said. His mission was to take Christianity to the Chinese and he did this in the belief that he was bringing them salvation, a moral certainty, perhaps an arrogance, which we might question in these more tolerant times.

Other Scots chose a more practical route, helping to build a new Britain. The Act of Union and the failure of the Jacobite Rising under Bonnie Prince Charlie had a profound influence on Scots. Leading figures of the Enlightenment such as David Hume identified with the new Britain, not narrowly thinking of themselves as Scots but rather as 'North Britons.' (There is, however, no evidence that the English started to think of themselves as 'South Britons') The architects, builders and civil engineers at the time of the Enlightenment similarly embraced the opportunities which came from being a part of Britain.

The Adam brothers participated in a Scottish 'renaissance,' with Robert Adam travelling extensively in Italy to see at first hand the classical works of the Romans and Renaissance masterpieces. As a result he was disparaging of the Palladian style of architecture, extensively applied at the time to the building of the country houses for the wealthy English, arguing that it was based on the formal elegance of public buildings, not on the more sensitive domestic architecture of the ancient Greeks and Romans as shown in the excavations being uncovered at Herculaneum.

Robert Adam worked as much in England as in Scotland and would have a major impact upon the architecture of Britain.

Scots influenced more than architecture. The last quarter of the eighteenth century and the first quarter of the nineteenth were dominated by three Scottish civil engineers, McAdam, Telford and Rennie, who would together have a significant impact upon Britain's infrastructure.

In Scotland itself a major transformation was also about to take place with the construction of the New Town.

## Edinburgh New Town

With the passing of the Act of Union, Scotland had lost her Parliament and Edinburgh had lost any remaining vestiges of political power. The terms of the Act had however protected the autonomy of the Church and of Scotland's legal system, and Edinburgh retained its position as the premier city of Scotland, being the site of the College of Justice and through hosting the annual meeting of the General Assembly of the Church of Scotland.

Edinburgh had not only lost its political power. While from a distance its impressive skyline, dominated by the Castle and the tall tenement blocks stretching along the High Street and down to Holyrood House, presented an imposing vista, entry to the city would reveal its rotting medieval heart.

A network of narrow wynds and closes with tenement buildings as high as ten storeys housed a densely packed population of people and animals. The smell arising from the city must have been appalling. The air would have been filled with the smoke from the thousands of coal fires which gave the city its nickname of 'Auld Reekie,' an odour blended with the stench arising from the human effluent which drained into the Nor' Loch.

The original proposals to build a New Town on the vacant land north of the city owed much to George Drummond, who was an important Edinburgh citizen during the Enlightenment and six times Lord Provost. Drummond had already played a leading role in the establishment in 1736 of the Royal Infirmary and was instrumental in the draining of the Nor' Loch, a necessary precondition to any development; in this he was responding to a poem addressed to him by Allan Ramsay, which, in an unusual form of planning application, proposed the draining of the Nor' Loch to create a space (now Princes Street Gardens) where:

> *Sweet all the Northern Springs would flow,*
> *Sweet Northern Trees and Herbs would grow,*
> *And from the Lake a Field be gain'd:*
> *Where on the Springs green Margent by the Dawn,*
> *Our Maids might wash, and blanch their Lace and Lawn.*

Drummond was also instrumental in the construction in 1763 of the North Bridge which would link the Old Town with the New and was fundamental to the realisation of his dream of a New Town, saying to Thomas Somerville:

*You are a young man, and may probably live, although I will not, to see all those fields covered with houses, forming a splendid and magnificent city. To the accomplishment of this, nothing is more necessary than the draining of the North Loch, and providing a proper access from the old town. I have never lost sight of this object since the year 1725, when I was elected Provost.*

Drummond was correct. He died in 1766, the year in which a competition was organised for the creation of a New Town on land which the City would buy to the north of the Old Town to 'enlarge and improve the City and adorn it with public buildings.' The competition was won, surprisingly, by a young unknown architect, James Craig, who would be described by Boswell as 'the ingenious architect of the New Town of Edinburgh.'

His concept consisted of a grid of three broad streets with impressive squares at each end. At a time when any sophisticated Scot thought of himself as a 'North Briton,' Craig rather cleverly played the Hanoverian card in the names he gave his streets and squares; George Street, Queen Street and Princes Street, intersected by Frederick Street and Hanover Street; St Andrews Square after Scotland's patron saint and Charlotte Square after the Queen (Craig's original intention was to name it St. George's Square after England's patron saint – a step too far?); and Rose Street and Thistle Street after the national flowers of England and Scotland.

Unusually, the New Town would not be dominated by the stately homes of the landed rich. Instead the size of the houses and the stone to be used in their construction were tightly regulated to give architectural cohesion to the development and the middle class moved rapidly in. David Hume would buy himself a plot on the northwest corner of St Andrews Square.

The New Town provided an opportunity for some fine Georgian architecture, which still gives an air of grace and elegance to the area, including the work of Scotland's finest architect, Robert Adam. Adam was responsible for a number of the buildings in the New Town, including the Register House and many of the houses around Charlotte Square.

It is to Robert Adam we now turn.

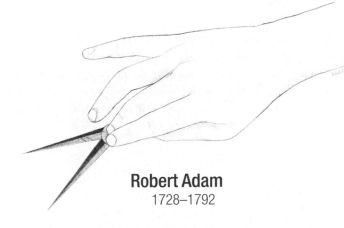

## Robert Adam
### 1728–1792

Architect of Georgian Britain

*We have not trod the path of others ... but have brought about a revolution in the art of architecture.* –Robert Adam

Robert Adam and his brothers indeed brought about a revolution in architecture. The Enlightenment flowered not just in the ideas of the philosophers and thinkers but also in the arts. One of its key features was a willingness to be open-minded and to accept new ideas. Much as Ramsay had done before him and other artists would do later, Robert Adam travelled to Italy to see the works of classical times, particularly Roman architecture, both the public buildings and the domestic architecture then being uncovered at Pompeii and Herculaneum.

While in Italy he met and befriended Allan Ramsay, a bond of different skills and ambitions with a mutual respect for the works of antiquity. Adam would put this experience to good use in his architectural designs.

### Architecture in the Eighteenth Century

In the early part of the eighteenth century. the architecture of large stately homes and of public buildings in Britain became dominated by the ideas of the Italian architect Palladio, who had worked in Vicenza in the sixteenth century and had been much influenced by a visit he had made to Rome to study classical Roman architecture. He revived the classical concepts of symmetry and proportion; the palaces he designed had severe classical porticos with columns and his villas were ruthlessly symmetrical in design.

Palladianism was brought to Britain by the English architect Inigo Jones, who had seen the works of Palladio on his visit to Italy and used his ideas for two great buildings he designed and built in the seventeenth century: the Banqueting House,

photo: Thomas Haywood

Bute House (Gaelic: Taigh Bhòid) official residence of the First Minister of Scotland

which was to be the first stage of a new, but never completed, Whitehall Palace, and the Queen's House in Greenwich.

In Scotland the first Palladian style building was the delightful Kinross House, constructed between 1685 and 1691 to the design of Sir William Bruce; the formal gardens, also designed by Bruce, stretch down to Loch Leven, with a view through the Fish Gate to Loch Leven Castle, the island fortress in which Mary Queen of Scots was imprisoned after being accused of complicity in the murder of her second husband, Lord Darnley. The Palladian model was later adopted by the Scottish architect Colin Campbell in his designs for Burlington House and Houghton Hall and Palladianism became the widely accepted style for new, stately buildings throughout Britain.

### Childhood, Study and the Grand Tour

Adam was born in Kirkcaldy in 1728, one of ten children of William and Mary Adam. His father was himself a successful architect and builder of the old Royal Infirmary in Edinburgh and of several large country houses in the Palladian style, of which the most famous is Hopetoun House near Edinburgh. He was also Master Mason to the Board of Ordnance in North Britain, a grandiose title which gave him responsibility for building throughout Scotland a series of forts to subdue the rebellious Highlanders. William also owned coal fields and a brewery, and was able therefore to profit from the provision of both inner and outer warmth.

When the family moved to Edinburgh, Adam enrolled at Edinburgh High

School to learn Latin, Latin and little else but Latin. He went to university at fifteen and there was exposed to a broader curriculum, studying among other subjects, natural philosophy, mathematics, logic and Greek. He didn't complete his university course but moved on to work in his father's office, where he rapidly showed a talent for drawing and design. William died soon after and the thriving business passed to John, William's eldest son, who took his brother as a partner in the firm. They worked together on the design and construction of Fort George, a new fort set on a promontory in Moray Firth, and completed their father's work on Hopetoun House and on Marchmont House in Berwickshire, showing an ability to add a lighter touch to the strict Palladian designs of their father.

Adam earned a substantial sum of money, so when in 1754 he learned that Charles Hope, younger brother of the Earl of Hopetoun, was planning a 'Grand Tour' of Europe he was able to take advantage of the opportunity. The Grand Tour was the goal of every wealthy young man, and Adam wanted to visit Rome to see for himself the classical buildings which had so influenced architectural ideas.

While travelling through France Adam engaged a drawing instructor, Charles-Louis Clerisseau. When they arrived in Rome, Adam was set the task of drawing, sketching and copying every monument and building they could find; Clerisseau believed that the ability to draw was fundamental to the profession of architect. As he said, 'How can you design if you cannot draw?' Adam was amazed at what he saw in Rome: the wonders of St Peters, the Pantheon, the Roman Forum and the Coliseum. He wrote that the city was 'the most glorious place in the universal world.'

In Rome, Adam took the opportunity of getting to know the wealthy young English and Scottish sons of landed families who were also making the Grand Tour — he realised they would be useful in giving him commissions in the future.

With Clerisseau, Adam visited Naples to see the villa of the Emperor Nero and then Herculaneum, the ancient Roman city which had been buried by lava after the volcanic explosion of Mount Vesuvius in AD 70 and had recently been rediscovered. There he saw Roman life as it had been lived, captured in the moment of disaster. He realised that these ancient Roman villas had light, spacious and colourful interiors far removed from the severe austerity of the Palladian style which had been modelled on the public buildings of antiquity. Adam wanted to understand the classical Roman style in its entirety.

After some time in Rome, he ventured across the Adriatic to Spalatro, modern-day Split in Croatia, where he drew and measured the ancient palace of Diocletian, publishing his sketches as *Ruins of the Palace of the Emperor Diocletian in Spalatro in Dalmatia*. The palace, with its elegant colonnades and shaded gardens, confirmed Adam's view that the ancients had designed their buildings not to impress but to delight.

He returned to England in early 1758 after four years away. Georgian Britain was prospering. The Seven Years War against France had been won and there had been decisive victories against the French in India, by Clive at the Battle of Plessey in 1757, and in Canada by Wolfe with the capture of Quebec in 1759. In 1763

France sued for peace. With its population of eleven million, Britain had beaten the twenty million French. With peace came prosperity and with prosperity came opportunity for an ambitious young architect.

## The 'Age of Adam'

Now Adam wanted to put the knowledge he had gained of classical architecture to use in designing new and graceful buildings. His cultivation of the wealthy paid off and he designed Syon House for the Duke of Northumberland, Luton Hoo for the Earl of Bute, and Kenwood for the Earl of Mansfield.

Adam created interesting interiors in a way that was new to Britain; oval rooms, rooms marked by columns and rectangular rooms with rounded ends all brought variety and excitement to his buildings. The anteroom to Syon House, for example, is marked by Roman columns of veneered marble surmounted by statues and the walls between are a very pale green. The ceiling is cream and gold and the floor is patterned with yellow, red, blue and green. He had broken with Palladian severity and realised that the use of decoration, statues and the like could greatly enhance the overall effect.

He also designed furnishings, including mirrors, light brackets, even rugs, but perhaps the most famous characteristic of Adam designs were his ceilings, decorated with curved mouldings enclosing decorative paintings. The Adam style became the fashion and at the height of their powers the Adam brothers – joined by James after he too had completed a Grand Tour, and then by younger brother William – employed more than three thousand people; stonemasons, bricklayers, plasterers, plumbers, coppersmiths and joiners.

Perhaps emboldened by all this success, they reached too far. In 1788 the brothers embarked on a massive development of a three-acre site south of the Strand in London, to be built on the mudflats alongside the Thames. Adelphi Terrace, as it was called, comprised a number of elegant town houses with river views supported on brick arches; underneath there would be vaults with access to three riverside wharves. The plan was to let these vaults to the Government Ordnance Department for warehousing. The plan was fine; the problem, rather fundamental, was that the government did not take up the lease.

The Adam brothers had already spent more than one hundred and twenty thousand pounds developing the site, a huge sum for those days, and all they had to show for it was an unfinished development. The money had run out; work was stopped and all the workmen had to be laid off. The brothers desperately needed cash. Robert and James sold all the drawings, paintings and Roman antiquities which they had painstakingly collected over the years but still could not pay off their debts. Then Adam had a brainwave; he would organise a lottery, both to sell the houses and to pay off their debts. The lottery raised an amazing two hundred thousand pounds and the brothers were back in business.

## Adam in Scotland

As the century developed Adam found work harder to obtain in England, but in 1772 he opened an office in Edinburgh and the new mood of prosperity in Scotland provided a lively market for his skills. He built Kinross County Court House, Seton House in East Lothian, and most importantly the Register House in Edinburgh. This building, with its central domed hall, said to be based upon the design of the Pantheon in Rome, was completed in 1792 after eighteen years. He also built many town houses, most famously the north side of Charlotte Square.

Perhaps his most remarkable legacy in Scotland is Culzean Castle. The Earl of Cassilis commissioned Adam to build a mock castle on his lands in Ayrshire, choosing a breathtaking cliff-top site overlooking the Firth of Clyde. The only landward approach was across a steep ravine, which Adam bridged, creating an arch to frame the entrance to the castle. Culzean has the battlements and round towers appropriate to a castle but the interior is typical Adam, with a splendid oval staircase and delightfully decorated rooms and ceilings almost feminine in their delicate use of pastel colours. It is a breathtakingly beautiful building in a stunning location. The top floor was later presented to General Eisenhower, the Allied Supreme Commander during the D-Day landings in Normandy in the Second World War, for his personal use.

Perhaps Robert Adam's greatest achievement as an architect was his work on rebuilding the University of Edinburgh, for which he designed a monumental entrance. The foundation stone was laid in 1789, but unfortunately, he died before the project was completed. Charlotte Square was also left incomplete, with Adam only accomplishing the north side before his death in 1792.

## Adam's Legacy

As a testimony of his genius, Robert Adam left not only the buildings and interiors he constructed, but two volumes of *The Works in Architecture of Robert and James Adam*, with a third volume published posthumously. The book is prefaced with an apology; that yet another work on architecture is appearing 'after so many works of this kind have been published in Italy, France and England during the last two centuries,' which is excused, disarmingly, with the expressed hope that it will be justified by 'the novelty and variety of the … design.'

**Further Reading**
Robert and James Adam, *The Works in Architecture of Robert and James Adam*, with an introduction by Henry Hope Reed

**Online Resources**
http://www.vam.ac.uk/content/articles/r/robert-adam-neo-classical-architect/

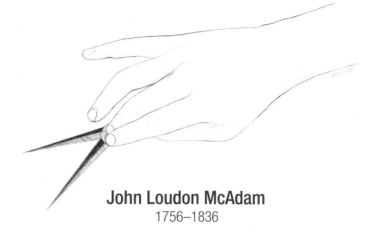

## John Loudon McAdam
### 1756–1836

MACADAMISING THE ROADS OF BRITAIN

The last people to have successfully built roads in Britain prior to the eighteenth century were the Romans, so it is hardly surprising that the road system was in poor shape. Most roads were only roads in name; they were, in fact, little more than dirt tracks which in winter became impassable morasses of mud, so that towns and villages became cut off for months.

John McAdam was the man who came to the rescue, using the exercise of reason, in best Enlightenment fashion, to invent a method of construction, 'Macadamisation,' that allowed the creation of a network of properly built roads.

### His Early Years

McAdam was born in Ayrshire in 1756, the youngest of ten children. The McAdams were a well-to-do family and sported a title, the Baron of Waterhead, given, not because of any great success in battle or service to their king, but because they were wealthy landowners who held their lands from the Crown and were required to sit in Parliament. In those days only wealthy people sat in Parliament; elections were largely a formality, and only a few men, and certainly no women, had the right to vote.

McAdam's father, also called John, was therefore Baron Waterhead. His mother was Susannah Cochran, the daughter of an impulsive inventor, Archibald Cochran, the 7th Earl of Dundonald.

At the time, tar was widely used by the navy to preserve the wooden timbers of their fighting ships and Archibald Cochran was one of the first to produce tar from coal by the process of distillation. Tar would eventually be used in the surfacing of roads in the form of 'tarmacadam,' but somewhat ironically, despite McAdam's later involvement in the tar-making business begun by his grandfather, that was not until long after his death. While McAdam was still a youngster, his father lost most of his money through the collapse of the Bank of Ayr. Although he did not become  bankrupt, the strain told and he died not long afterwards in 1770. His widow, Susannah, was left with ten children to raise.

McAdam was therefore shipped off at the age of fourteen to New York to seek his fortune. He joined his uncle, who was a merchant providing supplies to the army and navy. McAdam soon made a success of this new venture, becoming a wealthy young man. When he was twenty-two he married Gloriana, a wise choice as she was not only described as being 'a young lady of great Beauty and Merit,' but had the added attraction of being a wealthy heiress 'with a large fortune.'

Gloriana's family had played a key part in the expansion of British influence in America. Her great-great-grandfather, Matthias Nicolls, had taken part in the expedition sent by Charles II to claim the territory of New Amsterdam, then held by the Dutch. The English fleet anchored off New Amsterdam and Matthias 'persuaded' the Dutch, who had no military forces with which to resist, that they should hand the territory over to the British. The English named the city in honour of the King's younger brother, the Duke of York, and so New Amsterdam became New York without a shot being fired. Gloriana's family had since remained loyal supporters of Britain.

With a successful business and a lovely young wife, McAdam's future looked assured. But the world was changing.

These were difficult times for loyalist Britons in America. The American War of Independence was born from the refusal of the American colonists to pay taxes to the British Parliament when they had no representation in that Parliament. War broke out in 1775 and was at first a money-making opportunity for McAdam and his uncle; they adopted the Loyalist cause, believing that America should remain a British colony. But they had made the wrong choice and when the British were eventually defeated, McAdam and his young wife had to move rather fast, sailing back to Scotland and safety.

## Return to Scotland

McAdam was welcomed back and soon granted the position of Deputy Lieutenant of Ayrshire, becoming responsible for raising a band of volunteers to meet the threat of a French invasion. It was in this role that he first realised the appalling state of the country's roads; it was often impossible to move troops quickly because of their impassable state.

McAdam began to experiment with new methods of road construction on his estate at Sauchrie. He soon realised that the accepted practise of using clay or earth in their construction was doomed to failure because with heavy rains they would turn into a quagmire. What was needed was a firm foundation of stone.

## McAdam Becomes a Road Builder

After fifteen years in Scotland, McAdam moved with his family to Bristol, where he became a merchant in a business similar to that of his uncle's in America, but this time providing supplies for the British navy. He rapidly became very wealthy and decided to spend his time and energy on revisiting and developing the science of road building. The Romans had built a lasting network of roads throughout the country, but their skills and knowledge had been either forgotten or ignored.

McAdam travelled throughout the country, surveying the roads and examining their method of construction, covering more than thirty thousand miles. Through this research, he discovered the same problems he had noted many years before in Ayrshire; poorly constructed roads which were badly affected by traffic and heavy rains. The roads were terrible and the surface was dangerous.

Ironically in view of their poor condition, the amount spent to repair them was very high. The system relied on a network of turnpikes; toll houses were set up at intervals where tolls were collected from travellers to pay for upkeep. Turnpikes had originally been created in the reign of Charles II, but it was not until 1767 that they were extended throughout the kingdom. The effect of the legislation was disastrous, with turnpikes springing up all over the country; at each one a charge was levied on the traveller and his journey was interrupted. In the thirty or so miles from Ayr to Glasgow there were no fewer than ten turnpike gates, with the traveller having to stop at each. Understandably, the introduction of turnpikes was not popular. Not only was the progress of the traveller delayed but the money collected was often wasted on useless repair, or else it 'disappeared' into the pockets of the turnpike trustees. In Wales there was rioting, known popularly as the Rebecca riots because the rioters disguised themselves by dressing in women's clothes. There had to be a better way.

## Macadamisation: A Revolution in Road Building

McAdam's hard work and research did not go unnoticed. Bristol was an important port and trading centre and it was essential to the city that the roads to and from it were kept in good condition to enable easy access. In 1816 McAdam was appointed by the City of Bristol as General Surveyor, and given personal charge of the roads. This was the opportunity he had been seeking.

Rapidly McAdam got to work. In 1819 he set out the method he was using to build roads, recommending it be adopted throughout the country. He declared that roads should be built only of stone and forbade the use of earth, clay and chalk as these would absorb water, making them impassable in winter and causing them to break up in frost. He required that stone be used to a depth of ten inches (twenty-five centimetres). The stones should be no more than six ounces (one hundred and seventy grams) in weight and should pass through a two-inch (five-centimetre) ring. Before he introduced the ring as a measure he used a slightly less scientific method; a stone was too big if it did not fit in the workman's mouth! This somewhat erratic measure failed when McAdam, who had complained at the size of the stones being used on the construction of one road, discovered that not only did the foreman in charge have an exceptionally large mouth but it contained no teeth! A ring provided a more reliable measure.

No binding or surfacing was required, but the stones, ideally of granite, would be compacted by rolling and by the weight of the traffic passing over to provide a hard, smooth and solid surface which would be neither damaged by the pressure of the wheels of the carriages passing along it, nor affected by water. A road, McAdam stipulated, should be eighteen feet wide (five-and-a-half metres) and as flat as possible, with just a small rise in the middle of three inches (seven-and-a-half centimetres) to allow the water to run off to the sides. He was strongly opposed to the use of paving or of larger stones for the base course in the system proposed by his fellow Scot – and great rival – Thomas Telford.

McAdam's method was an immediate success. Three of McAdam's sons and seven of his grandsons followed him to England to become surveyors, making a total of eleven McAdams' working to create turnpike roads. Road building was truly 'macadamised' and their roads enabled a network of stagecoaches and mail coaches across the country, 'paving' the way for the eventual motor car.

John McAdam resigned from his position as Surveyor in Bristol soon after the death of his wife. He had travelled widely around the country advising the more than seventy turnpike trusts upon the improvement and maintenance of their roads. He rarely charged for the advice he gave, or even claimed his expenses, believing it was his duty to improve the roads of the kingdom, so that in his later years he was forced to petition Parliament for financial support. After a lengthy enquiry, in which the immense benefits derived from his advice were officially recognised, he was awarded the sum of four thousand pounds.

He proved resilient, marrying again at the age of seventy and returning each year to Scotland on a 'pilgrimage' to his beloved country. He died at the advanced age of eighty and was buried in his grandmother's grave to 'sleep amidst the mountains of Moffat' as he had wished.

John McAdam revolutionised road building, literally laying the foundations of today's road network and bringing the possibility of countrywide travel first by horse-drawn coach and later by car. He did not, however, invent tarmacadam, despite his family's involvement in the tar business. This was the brainwave of a County Surveyor in Nottingham in 1901 who noticed that when a barrel of tar had been spilt on a road it produced a hard, smooth and dust-free surface. He formed a company to exploit his discovery, which grew to become a major road-building and surfacing company, Tarmac.

**Further Reading**
Roy Devereux, *John Loudon McAdam*
http://www.robinsonlibrary.com/technology/highway/history/mcadam.htm

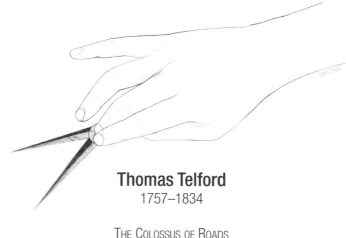

## Thomas Telford
### 1757–1834

THE COLOSSUS OF ROADS
—ROBERT SOUTHEY

The life of Thomas Telford was the classic story of the poor Scots boy made good. Born in a simple shepherd's shieling, he became perhaps the greatest of all civil engineers, building roads, canals and bridges throughout Britain. Trained as a stonemason, Telford went to Edinburgh to work on the construction of the New Town. There he saw the works of the Enlightenment architects such as Robert Adam and vowed that he, too, would produce great works.

Telford was born in August 1757 in a simple, isolated cottage built of mud with a thatched roof, set in sheep pastures in the hills north of Langholm in the Borders. His father, John, was a poor shepherd who died when he was just a few months old. The cottage was tied to John's work as a shepherd and on his death Telford's mother, Janet, was forced to move out with her wee bairn. She was given a room in a two-roomed cottage and worked on the nearby farms, milking cattle, shearing sheep and making hay according to the seasons. Life for Janet was hard and her boy grew up strong and independent and soon joined her at work in the fields.

Telford had an uncle who paid for him to attend the parish school. At fourteen he was apprenticed as a stonemason and worked with his master learning to cut and shape stone. After he had learned the skills of a stonemason, he moved to Edinburgh where the city was buzzing with activity as the new Georgian town was being built. Telford worked on the building of the New Town, where he developed a love for architecture. Then at last, fortune smiled on him.

Telford learned that one of his neighbours, Sir James Johnstone, wished to send a horse to London, and he volunteered to ride it. Armed with letters of introduction, Telford rode south to seek his fortune. In London he met Sir William Pultney; Sir William and Sir James were brothers but William had changed his name to Pultney, taking his wife's name on their marriage. His new wife was inordinately wealthy and it was a condition of receiving her immense wealth that he should adopt her family name. Any passing regrets he may have felt at losing his own name were surely assuaged by the great new estates he gained from the marriage.

## Shropshire

As a part of his new estates Sir William had acquired Shrewsbury Castle, then in an almost ruinous state, and he asked Telford to carry out its restoration. Telford not only restored the castle but improved the estate to control the flooding of the low-lying meadows, introducing levies and a drain called to this day the 'New Cut.'

Telford worked hard, rising at five o'clock and often working until late at night. His hard work did not go unnoticed and at the age of thirty he was appointed the County Surveyor for Shropshire, becoming responsible for all the roads and bridges in the county.

He built his first bridge at Montford on the River Severn; he also built bridges at Bewdley and Bridgnorth, to replace those destroyed in the floods of 1793. His graceful stone bridges are still in use today. In 1796 he built a bridge at Buildwas near the famous iron bridge at Coalbrookdale, the first iron bridge in the world. Inspired by this example, Telford also built his bridge of cast iron; he made it longer and lighter than the bridge at Coalbrookdale and its iron ribs provided a clear arch over the shipping using the River Severn below.

## The Ellesmere Canal

In the days before the railways, water was the only way goods could be transported easily around the country and there was a boom in the building of canals to link inland rivers and provide a network for the water-borne traffic. The canal-building boom was remarkable, perhaps even more so than the railway boom which followed, and huge sums of money were made by the early developers of canals. Vast quantities of earth were dug out by hand to provide the waterways and the men doing the work were known as navigators or 'navvies.' The standard of civil engineering was remarkably high as, self-evidently, the canals had to be exactly level and made completely watertight by lining them with clay.

The directors of the half-built Shrewsbury Canal had a problem. They needed to build an aqueduct to carry their new canal over the River Tern. The only known way to build an aqueduct was to construct a massive stone structure, squat and strong enough to take both the weight of the puddled clay which kept the canal watertight and the weight of the water itself. Telford's idea was revolutionary. He constructed an aqueduct of iron, making a trough of iron plates bolted together and carried by an iron frame to hold the water. It was lighter and slimmer than the traditional aqueduct yet strong enough to support the weight. As a result in 1793 he was appointed 'general agent, engineer and architect' of the new Ellesmere Canal Company, formed to construct a canal linking three rivers - the Mersey, the Dee and the Severn. Sadly, the canal was never finished and it ends ingloriously, not reaching the River Severn. But Telford did complete one of the greatest civil-engineering achievements of the time: the building of the Pontcysyllte Aqueduct by which the canal crossed the Vale of Llangollen. A cast-iron trough, twelve feet (three-and-a-half metres) wide, carries the canal over a distance of one thousand feet (three hundred metres) at a height of one hundred and twenty feet (or thirty-seven metres) above the River Dee, supported by iron arches resting on slender stone columns.

Pontcysyllte Aqueduct, Wales.

## Opening up the Highlands

At the Battle of Culloden in 1746, the Highlanders fighting for Bonnie Prince Charlie had been routed by government forces. The victorious Duke of Cumberland, known forever after as 'Butcher' Cumberland, had then marched through the Highlands, destroying the old clan system, burning houses and killing men, women and children without mercy. Although some of the lairds were later given back their lands, conditions for their people did not improve as the lairds threw them off their lands, often burning their houses to 'persuade' them to leave, and replaced them with more profitable sheep in a time known as the 'Clearances.' All this meant that the Highlands had become a wilderness devoid of people and potential employment.

Pultney and a number of others tried to bring trade back to the Highlands by creating small ports to encourage fishing and Telford advised on the design and construction of the harbours that were built at Tobermory and Ullapool. But there remained a problem: there were no roads to take the fish to market. There was also a market for beef from cattle reared in the Highlands, but the only way it could be brought to market was 'on the hoof,' the cattle and their drovers following the old drove roads and swimming any rivers in their way. A fine road system had been built in the Highlands some years before by General Wade, but it had been made for military purposes, designed to enable armies to move rapidly to deal with any uprising, not to transport goods. What was needed was a new look at the problem. When Telford was asked to report, he realised that the Highlands were dying; people were leaving by the thousand to seek new lives elsewhere. The Highlands had to be linked by road and canal with their markets in Lowland Scotland and England. What was needed, he said, was a new network of roads and a massive new canal joining the lochs of the Great Glen to link the east and west coasts. This was the time of the wars against Napoleon and such a canal would not only provide a transport network across Scotland, but also enable warships to move swiftly from one coast to the other without braving the treacherous seas to the north.

Telford spent eighteen years in the Highlands. He built more than nine hundred miles of new road, twelve hundred bridges (mostly of stone but including a delightfully graceful iron bridge over the Spey, Craigellachie Bridge, the first iron bridge to be built in Scotland) and for good measure, forty churches, mainly in the Western Isles. Telford would regularly tour the Highlands to inspect the works in person and in 1819 he was accompanied on his journey by the poet Robert Southey, who would endow his companion with the epithet of *'The Colossus of Roads.'*

Telford had a different approach to road construction from that of his contemporary McAdam. Southey described Telford's method:

> *The Plan upon which he proceeds is this, first to level and drain; then, like the Romans, to lay a solid pavement of large stones, the round or broad end downwards, as close as they can be set; the points are then broken off, and a layer of stones broken to about the size of walnuts, laid over them, so that the whole are bound together; over all a little gravel if it be at hand, but this is not essential.*

Telford was determined to ensure good drainage through a cambered surface and frequent drains and to ensure a gradient of no more than one in twenty. He relied on the iron wheels of the coaches to bed down the surface. The procedure gave good lasting roads, but was much more expensive than 'Macadamization.' Telford's main engineering achievement in Scotland was not, however, the roads and bridges that he built, but the Caledonian Canal stretching from Fort William on the west coast to Inverness on the north-east.

## The Caledonian Canal

The survey of a route for a canal linking the Atlantic with the North Sea had been initially carried out by James Watt in 1773, and then again by John Rennie in 1793. In 1801 Telford carried out a completely new survey of the whole route, travelling on rugged tracks through the hills. Of one of his journeys he wrote,

> *I passed by a very rocky and precipitous track down to the head of Loch Hourn; from Loch Hourn I travelled by a track scarcely less rugged to the top of Glen Elg and over the steep mountain of Raatachan to the top of Loch Duich.*

It was a hard ride. One of his concerns was to ensure that there was a sufficient supply of water to the summit at Loch Oich to replace the water lost each time a loch gate was opened. Eventually he presented his plans and they were accepted; the reasoning was that at the time Britain was at war with France and the canal would provide a safe route for ships to cross from the west to east coasts and back without braving the treacherous waters of the Pentland Firth and the dangers of enemy attack. This was either a very optimistic view as to the length of time it would take to build the canal or a very pessimistic view of the length of the French war.

So with the building of the canal approved, who should build it? Thomas Telford was the obvious choice.

The Great Glen consists of a fault running north-east across the Highlands and includes a number of lochs, the most famous being Loch Ness. To complete the crossing, Telford had to build twenty-two miles of canal to join the lochs and twenty-eight locks to carry the canal to the level of the inland lochs, excavating solid rock and carrying the waste away by hand in more than two hundred million wheelbarrow loads. Each lock was designed to be big enough to take a forty-gun frigate. At each end he had to build sea locks, one cut out of solid rock and the other built up above a deep bed of mud. The steepest part of the canal was the eight miles between Loch Eil and Loch Lochy, where the level rises ninety feet (twenty-seven metres) through eight enormous locks in a stretch which Telford christened 'Neptune's Staircase.'

After eighteen years the massive project was completed and on 23 October 1822 the first boat passed through; the North Sea and the Atlantic were now joined and it was no longer necessary to brave the stormy seas to the north of Scotland. It was a fantastic feat of civil engineering but was never in truth widely used. It came too late; the arrival of the railway had put an end to the age of the canal.

## The Road to Holyhead

The road from London to Holyhead on the Isle of Anglesey, from where the ferry crossed to Ireland, was in a terrible state, often no more than a cart track. In 1815 Telford was given the task of rebuilding the whole length of the road.

Telford believed roads should avoid steep climbs in order to allow the horse-drawn traffic to move easily and he made cuttings and built viaducts along the route to achieve his aim, creating gentle gradients even through the mountains of Snowdonia. There he built the graceful 'Waterloo' Bridge at Bettws-y-coed, which he inscribed thus: 'This arch was constructed in the same year as the Battle of Waterloo was fought.' He decorated it with a leek, a thistle, a rose and a shamrock; it was, after all, a bridge built in Wales by a Scot to carry the road from England to Ireland.

His outstanding achievement was the bridge he built across the Menai Straits to avoid the often stormy boat trip between North Wales and Anglesey. He created a giant suspension bridge with wrought-iron chains supporting a span of six hundred feet (one hundred and eighty metres) rising one hundred feet (thirty metres) above the sea, creating another engineering marvel.

The Holyhead road was finished in 1826 when Telford was nearly seventy years old. Telford had worked hard all his life in the new profession of civil engineering and in 1820 he was invited to become the first President of the newly formed Institution of Civil Engineers; it was a fitting mark of his fame and of the respect his fellow engineers felt for him.

He was a life-long bachelor whose only relaxation was dining with his friends. Telford died in 1834 at the age of seventy-seven.

## Telford's Legacy

Telford was perhaps the greatest civil engineer of all time, certainly of his age, and his works remain engineering marvels even today.

His legacy is represented by the canals, the roads, the bridges and the buildings that he constructed, but he should also be admired as one who had risen by hard work and dedicated study from the meanest of beginnings to become the greatest civil engineer in the land, a true and exemplary Enlightenment career.

**Further Reading**
Chris Morris, *On Tour with Thomas Telford*
L.T.C.Rolt, *Thomas Telford*

**Online Resources**
Undiscovered Scotland
http://www.undiscoveredscotland.co.uk/usbiography/t/thomastelford.html

# John Rennie
## 1761–1821

DESIGNER AND BUILDER OF BRITAIN'S CANALS

*'To build! That is the noblest of all the arts.'*

John Rennie became a pre-eminent engineer who blended practical skills with theoretical knowledge to advance the art and profession of civil engineering. He was skilled, as Longfellow wrote in the 'noblest of all the arts,' and was personally responsible for the design and construction of many of the new canals which by the end of the eighteenth century had spread like a spider's web across the country.

Rennie was born in June 1761 on a farm at East Linton about twenty miles from Edinburgh, the youngest of nine children. In a parallel with Telford, his father, James Rennie, died when he was just five years old and the management of the family farm was taken over by his elder brother, George, himself then only sixteen years old. Rennie was already showing where his interests lay, happier building models of boats and simple machinery than playing with other children. In developing these interests, he was lucky that on the family estate lived a miller, Andrew Meikle, who was himself a talented engineer and millwright who designed and built windmills and their machinery, becoming famous as the designer of a new threshing machine which required far fewer people to work it.

Meikle also developed a new design for the sails of the windmills then used to power the milling machinery. At the time, the sails were made of canvas stretched tight over wooden frames and if the wind strength changed, the only way to adjust the trim of the sails was to stop the mill and separately to alter each one. To do this the miller had to stand precariously on a special gallery, and this could be dangerous if a storm suddenly blew up and the miller had to adjust the sails balanced unsteadily on his platform while the wind howled around him. Meikle's solution was to make the sails out of wooden slats connected to a common rod which could be turned to open and close the slats.

Rennie spent much of his spare time at Meikle's workshops and it was perhaps natural that when he reached twelve and it was time to leave the village school, he turned to the workshops of Andrew Meikle for a job, working for two years with the millwright while learning the skills of carpenter, stonemason and bricklayer.

Soon Rennie realised that if he wanted to better himself he needed further education and so after two years of practical instruction, he enrolled as a student at Dunbar High School, a school typical of the excellent education then available in Scotland.

There Rennie flourished, attracting the notice of a visiting dignitary, David Loch the Inspector General of Fisheries, who noted in particular

> *'the singular proficiency [in mathematics] of a young man of the name of Rennie … [who] had then attended [classes] for mathematics for not much more than six months, but [showed] such amazing powers of genius that one could have imagined him a second Newton.'*

Praise indeed...he went on to forecast that this remarkable young man, if spared, 'will do great honour to his country'.

After two years Rennie left school and at the age of eighteen set up his business. His first commission was for his brother George to build a mill on the family estate to house and drive one of the new threshing machines to be supplied by Andrew Meikle. After successfully completing this and a few other commissions, Rennie decided to enrol at Edinburgh University, entering in November 1780. Rennie remained a student for three years, continuing his engineering work in the long vacations. Among his professors he was fortunate to count Joseph Black and John Robison, Professor of Natural Philosophy, who was to become his mentor.

His time at Edinburgh was fundamental to his development as an engineer; it was at university that he learned to solve problems and to design structures using not trial and error but scientific knowledge and methods.


## Boulton and Watt

After university John Rennie spent some time researching engineering structures before eventually approaching the famous and successful engineering firm of Boulton and Watt, where he presented James Watt with a letter of introduction from Professor Robison.

Watt had by then developed the rotating version of his steam engine and was seeking to enter new markets. Boulton planned the construction of a new mill, the Albion Mill near Blackfriar's Bridge in London, to use steam power and act as a show piece for the new Boulton and Watt rotating engines, but there was a snag: the engineers at Boulton and Watt knew a lot about steam engines and their use in powering water pumps, but virtually nothing about milling. Rennie had that knowledge and James Watt offered him the job.

Rennie, then twenty-three, set off for London. The Albion Mill was not only one of the first mills in the country to install a steam engine, but also, one of the largest, with twenty pairs of millstones to grind the corn. Rennie designed all the milling machinery, applying steam power wherever he could and designing a centrifugal governor to control the power output from the steam engine, one of the first times such a device had been installed.

Sir Henry Raeburn, 'John Rennie, Engineer' Scottish National Portrait Gallery

John Rennie
*(detail) see: colour plate 20*

He was so successful that Boulton and Watt commissioned him to design and install new equipment for their Soho works, including a rolling mill and a borer for the cylinders of the steam engines in the factory, a task which had previously been placed out with other companies, resulting in tiresome quality issues.

Rennie had used his experience and his growing reputation from the successful completion of his work at Albion Mill to develop his own business. He was already busy on other projects, designing dyeing machinery for a works in Lambeth and a flour mill in Leith, and receiving a commission to design the Crinan Canal. His reputation had spread widely and he received orders for corn mills in Spain, Portugal and France. He also designed rolling mills for the Royal Mint which rolled the silver or gold into sheets which were then pressed into coins. Matthew Boulton provided the coin presses and Boulton and Watt the steam engines to power the machines.

At that time he wrote rather formally to his brother George to inform him 'that I am about to change my situation in life by marriage.' He had chosen well; the prospective bride came well-endowed with five thousand pounds in investments to be settled as a dowry on the couple by her father, and expectations of a further fifty thousand pounds from an uncle. It all seemed too good to be true, and so it was; the marriage never took place. Instead in 1790 he married the nineteen-year-old Martha Mackintosh; presumably, he had no regrets in the slightest as the couple had nine children.

## Canal Building

Rennie's ambitions soon extended beyond millwork and he developed a business as a civil and structural engineer, surveying a canal from Bishop's Stortford to Lynn; a second linking the Basingstoke Canal to Salisbury and a third linking Bury St Edmunds and Ipswich.

By 1790 Rennie had established a reputation as one of the greatest engineers of his time. He was appointed engineer on the proposed Kennet and Avon Canal.

This waterway, more than fifty-seven miles in length, would require no fewer than twenty-nine locks as it was constructed through hilly countryside. It would be carried on graceful aqueducts across deep and wide rivers, connecting two great rivers, the Thames and the Severn. The completed canal was not just an engineering masterpiece, it was a work of grace and beauty.

Not content with this, Rennie simultaneously served as the engineer for both the Lancaster and the Rochdale Canals, responsible for three major construction projects at one time. To control the work he set up an elaborate chain of command, retaining himself as principal engineer, the overall design responsibility, and with resident engineers working under him, each responsible for a section of the projects and each in turn having his own assistants, some with responsibility for the earthworks and others for the stonemasonry.

The Lancaster Canal was over seventy-five miles long with more than two hundred road bridges, simply and elegantly designed in stone, and twenty-two aqueducts, all different. The Rochdale Canal, shorter at thirty-two miles in length, was structurally more challenging; from Manchester it climbed through Rochdale towards its summit in the Pennines, passing through no fewer than fifty-six locks, on the nineteen-mile climb. The route then descended for thirteen miles through thirty-six locks crossing the River Calder on a graceful four-arched aqueduct until it linked with the Calder and Hebble Navigation Canal.

Civil engineering is sometimes thought of as a rough-and-ready profession, but the maintenance of exact line and level was imperative if the canal was to function. Building a canal required not only precise civil-engineering skills but also hard manual labour. The work comprised the excavation of vast amounts of earth and was largely carried out by hand using the traditional pick and shovel and then running with the heavily laden barrows on plank runways up the sides of deep cuttings to the top, where the earth was tipped into carts or wagons running on light tramways to be carted away. The only aid to manpower was the use of horse-powered ploughs to loosen the earth and scrapers to remove it. A good engineer would balance as far as possible the earth removed to create cuttings with that required for embankments in order to reduce wasted effort.

Rennie was also linked with the redesign and rebuilding of a number of docks and harbours and with the drainage of the Fens in East Anglia where rivers were diverted, new channels were dug, and embankments were built to create farmland from the marshes. Among other projects, in London, Rennie was responsible for the Waterloo, Southwark and London Bridges as well as the Sheerness Docks. In Scotland he designed the Aberdeenshire Canal, Glasgow docks and the harbours at Saltcoats, Montrose and Stranraer.

## Bell Rock Lighthouse

In addition to his work on canals, Rennie worked with Robert Stevenson on the design and construction of the Bell Rock Lighthouse. The Bell Rock, more correctly called the Inch Cape Rock, is situated about eleven miles out to sea in the approach to the Firth of Forth from the north east and is a massive underwater reef with a steep 'cliff' to the north and a sloping sunken reef to the south which is submerged save only for a few hours at low tide. It had long been a danger to shipping and was feared by all who entered the Firth of Forth, particularly when the weather was stormy or the visibility bad, preventing shipping from safely taking refuge in the Forth. It had gained the name 'Bell Rock' because in the Middle Ages, the Abbott of Arbroath had attached a bell to a buoy anchored off the rock which rang out as a warning to shipping. In the fourteenth century the bell was stolen by a Dutch pirate, but in an act of divine justice the vandal responsible was just twelve months later himself wrecked on the Bell Rock and drowned.

After a severe storm in 1799 which lasted more than three days, with some seventy ships wrecked off the coast of Scotland, including several on Bell Rock itself and many more because they feared to run for safety into the Firth of Forth, because of their fear of the Rock, the idea of constructing a lighthouse was proposed. Robert Stevenson, the Engineer to the Northern Light Commissioners, was asked to prepare a report. He created plans for a lighthouse based on Smeaton's design for the Eddystone Lighthouse, but because he was thought inexperienced and his proposal too expensive, John Rennie was called in to advise. Together with Stevenson, Rennie visited the Bell Rock and produced an estimate of cost very close to Stevenson's. His authority and reputation tipped the balance, and in 1806 the Northern Light Commission gave its approval to the construction of a lighthouse built of stone on the Bell Rock with Rennie as chief engineer and Stevenson the assistant engineer.

Together Rennie and Stevenson visited the local quarries and selected Aberdeenshire granite for the project, but the actual work on the rock was supervised by Stevenson. The work was dangerous; the rock was only exposed for a few hours twice a day at low tide and in this time the surface had to be prepared to anchor the stones of the lighthouse. Rennie only visited the rock twice during its construction, both times being seasick, but he kept closely in touch with Stevenson monitoring the progress. The lighthouse was completed in 1810.

## Later Years

John Rennie worked hard, rising at six in the morning and rarely in bed before midnight. He designed and priced everything himself: all the machinery, all the bridges, roads, canals and aqueducts. He produced beautifully drawn designs, coloured as by an artist, and these were then copied to provide working drawings.

He was always honest in his workmanship and priced his work fairly, and he advanced the profession of civil engineering, being a joint founder in 1792 of The Smeatonian Society of Civil Engineers.

As a civil engineer Rennie designed nearly seventy canals and river navigations, and as many bridges and viaducts – indeed many more if all the individual canal bridges are included – and worked on eighty schemes for harbours and docks as well as one lighthouse; on most of these he was also the engineer responsible for the successful completion of the project. He worked on drainage schemes and numerous other engineering projects. It is an amazing portfolio of work.

This all at last took its toll even on his strong frame, and he died, exhausted by a life of labour, in 1821, just sixty years of age.

He was buried in the crypt of St Paul's Cathedral and his grave, fittingly for a man who had used it for his works, was a simple slab of Cornish granite.

## Rennie's Legacy

John Rennie was a man of many parts: he used his training in the application of scientific methods to design mills and their machinery and he became the leading canal engineer of his age, building canals, locks and aqueducts, and designing harbours and ports. His contribution to the construction and equipping of mills and to the development of the transport infrastructure of the country were essential to the development of the Industrial Revolution. His legacy is summed up in the epitaph on his memorial:

> *the many splendid and useful works [built] under his superintending genius are [his] True Monuments.*

**Further Reading**
C.T.G. Boucher, *John Rennie: The Life and Work of a Great Engineer*

**Online Resources**
Undiscovered Scotland
http://www.undiscoveredscotland.co.uk/usbiography/r/johnrennie.html

# Robert Stevenson
## 1772–1850

*Anythin' for a quiet life, as the man said when he took the sitivation at the lighthouse.*

–Sam Weller in Charles Dickens' *Pickwick Papers*

Scotland has nearly four and a half thousand miles of coastline and its coastal waters are scattered with hundreds of islands and submerged rocks. These, coupled with dangerous currents and some of the stormiest seas in the world, made the seas around Scotland perilous for shipping before the development of accurate charts and modern navigational equipment.

Proper charts did not begin to become available until the latter part of the eighteenth century and even as late as the mid-nineteenth century navigation was still largely an art. Sailors relied on the dimly seen outline of the land or a glimpse of a church through the mist or rain as the only guide to where they were. Voyages were dangerous, but Scotland was increasingly reliant on its trade with France and Scandinavia, and later on the import of tobacco and sugar from the New World, and the volume of shipping steadily grew.

Many ships and lives were lost every year. The pressure for improved safety came, however, not from the sailors but from the shipowners, driven not by a Christian concern at the loss of lives but by a more mercenary desire to protect their profits from loss. Better charts and lighthouses were needed to mark the dangerous rocks and reefs so that they could be seen even at night or in the worst of weather.

Eight members of just one family, the Stevensons, over four generations and one hundred fifty years, would design and build more than two hundred lighthouses around the coast of Scotland, working in the wildest conditions, often on uninhabited islets or on rocks only exposed at low tide and lashed by the wildest gales. The first of this famous family of lighthouse builders was Robert Stevenson,

illustration: Matt Collier

Bell Rock Lighthouse off the coast of Angus, Scotland

the father of Alan, David and Thomas, the grandfather of David and Charles and Louis – better known as the writer Robert Louis Stevenson – and the great-grandfather of another Alan, all of whom were involved in the design and construction of Scotland's lighthouses.


## Robert Stevenson

Robert Stevenson was born in June 1772, the only son of Alan and Jean Stevenson, the daughter of a builder. Robert's father was a maltster by trade but already as a young man of twenty had become involved with his brother Hugh in trading with the West Indies. When Robert was two years old, his father and his uncle sailed from Glasgow to the West Indies to advance their business interests. It proved to be a fatal journey as while on the island of St Kitts they were robbed of all their possessions. Hugh set sail in pursuit of the robbers but died at St Christopher in May 1774. Alan had died just one month earlier in Tobago.

Jean Stevenson, not much more than a girl, was left a widow after just three years of marriage, virtually penniless and with a young boy to raise. Determined that despite her disadvantages her son should succeed, Jean moved to Edinburgh to give him the best schooling she could afford. Robert received a godly upbringing and had formal lessons in Latin – and informal lessons on how to survive on very little money.

A keen churchgoer, Jean Stevenson joined a church in the New Town in Edinburgh. Among the congregation was Thomas Smith, a successful middle-aged ironsmith whose first wife Elizabeth, had borne him five children, three of whom had died in infancy, before she herself died of whooping cough. Smith was not much more successful with his second wife, Mary, who bore him only one child before dying of consumption. Undeterred by the high mortality rate among his wives and children, not unusual at the time, and buoyed by the thought of 'third time lucky,' he was looking for another wife. He and Jean were married in 1787.

While Jean Stevenson had hoped her son might become a minister of the church, Robert Stevenson was much more interested in the ironworks of his stepfather, to whom he was formally apprenticed in 1790. The business had by then concentrated on the making of lamps and Smith was largely employed in building street lights for the New Town. Street lights at the time used oil and quickly became covered with dirty grime, giving only poor illumination. Smith experimented with the novel idea of using reflectors to enhance the light, using small slices of mirrors fixed to the inside of a concave sphere to provide more than four times the light of a conventional lamp.

Smith wondered if there could be other uses for his idea – possibly for lighthouses. As he wrote, 'lamp lights with reflectors can be distinguished from every other light in such a manner as to make it impossible to mistake them for a light on shore or on board any other ship.' His ideas were welcomed and in 1787 he had been appointed as the first Engineer to the Northern Lighthouse Trust, the body set up to build and operate lighthouses in Scotland. The Trust, later called the Northern Lighthouse Board, had been established in 1786 under the imposingly titled Act of Erecting Certain Lighthouses in the Northern Part of Great Britain. After many ships from both the naval and merchant fleets had been lost in the wild storms of 1782, it was charged with building four lighthouses, one at Kinneard Head, one on the Mull of Kintyre, one off Harris and one on North Ronaldsay, a small island in the Orkneys. Smith's instructions were simple: he could build them, light them and staff them in any way he chose – provided they didn't cost too much!

The only lighthouse in Scotland had been built in 1636 on the Isle of May, a low-lying islet, just a mile long by one-third of a mile wide at the entrance to the Firth of Forth, and consisted of a coal brazier on a small squat tower. Coal for the light was dropped by boat into the shallows just off the rock and the lighthouse keeper would have to pick the coal out of the sea by hand and winch it in a bucket to the roof of the tower. Not surprisingly, the light often went out, usually when the weather was stormy. It was hardly a blueprint for Smith's assignment. There was even no accepted design for a lighthouse in England where lighthouses had existed for some time.

Smith had to develop his ideas from scratch. He constructed his lighthouses from materials easily available; stone for the thick walls, built to withstand the assaults of wind and sea, and slates and timber. All the materials, even the precious and fragile reflectors mounted in the glass lantern, had to be transported to the site by sea, or in the case of the lighthouse on the Mull of Kintyre, by horseback.

Strict instructions were given to the men who manned these early lights ensuring that the lights were dutifully lit half an hour before sunset and kept burning through the night and that the reflectors were regularly wiped clean, using chalk and a soft rag to polish away the smoky deposits from the oil flame. For this task the reward was typically one shilling per night, free lodging and grazing for one cow! A fine 'sitivation' indeed. During his twenty-one years as Engineer, Smith built a total of eleven lighthouses and updated two more.

The introduction of lighthouses did not secure universal approval. Many people, known as wreckers, looked on a shipwreck as a source of income, some even going so far as to lure ships onto dangerous rocks by providing false lights. Smith was finding his job difficult.

Meanwhile, the business in Edinburgh prospered, providing all types of brassware for the houses being built in the New Town, and Robert Stevenson was proving an able assistant, improving his knowledge by studying civil engineering at Glasgow University. The close relationship between Stevenson and his stepfather was strengthened in 1799 when he married Smith's eldest daughter, Jean.

Robert and Jean had a large family of nine children, but of these only five survived. Three: Alan, David and Thomas, would also become lighthouse builders.

### Stevenson Builds His Career

Stevenson's first assignment was to supervise the building of the lighthouse on Little Cumbrae, in the Firth of Clyde, and he then worked on the construction of two lighthouses on Orkney. In 1797 he took over from Smith the responsibility of making the annual visits to the Board's lighthouses, being formally appointed as Engineer to the Northern Lighthouse Board in 1808, a position he held for a remarkable thirty-four years, during which time he was personally responsible for the design and construction of eighteen major lighthouses around the coast of Scotland, three of them with his father-in-law, and oversaw the construction of many more.

Stevenson was an accomplished leader and organiser who inspired those working for him to great efforts. He actively enjoyed the challenge of building lighthouses in dangerous and inhospitable places, the travel and the harshness of the outdoor life.

He spent a great deal of his time in improving the design of the light, replacing the fragile glass mirrors of the reflectors with silver-coated spheres which gave a stronger and better-focussed beam and using a new form of oil lamp developed by a Swiss scientist to give a brighter and more reliable light.

As the number of lighthouses increased it became necessary for the seafarer to be able to distinguish one light from another. Stevenson developed the idea of rotating the reflectors so that the beam of light appeared as a flash, the timing of which could be varied among all the lighthouses. Rotation was initially manual with the lighthouse keeper given the task of pushing the light around by hand, but by 1806 mechanisation had arrived and a clockwork drive was successfully introduced.

## The Bell Rock

One of Stevenson's first and most challenging tasks was to build a lighthouse on the infamous Bell Rock, a largely submerged reef off the coast of Dundee, which threatens the approach by sea to Dundee, Arbroath and Montrose harbours. He planned to build his lighthouse in the form of a gracefully tapering cycloidal tower to lessen the force of the waves as Smeaton had done on the Eddystone. The tower would be built of granite, each piece dovetailed into the rock to form a solid stone base and each interlocking, so that the first thirty-one feet (ten metres) of the tower would be solid stone, with the apartments and light above. The conditions would not be easy; at the neap tides the highest northern part of the rock is only partially exposed at low tide and only four to six feet above water at low tide during the springs.

Stevenson was still a young man, largely untested, and the commissioners had some doubts. They sought the advice of John Rennie, who agreed that a lighthouse could be built on the Rock and produced a design and cost estimate very similar to Stevenson's. Rennie was appointed chief engineer, with overall responsibility for the project, but it was Robert's design which was eventually approved and it was Robert who actually built the lighthouse. Rennie was generous in recognising the contribution of the young engineer, writing to him in 1807 that the work 'will, if successful, immortalise you in the annals of fame.'

The work started in August 1807. Stevenson had set up a work yard at Arbroath and had commissioned a vessel to take the workers to and from the rock, which he named the *Smeaton*, in honour of the builder of the Eddystone lighthouse. In the first summer, holes were drilled into the rock to build a beacon and a barracks or hut on the rock, in which to house the men and to place the forge and to prepare the foundations of the tower. During this time the workmen were housed on the *Smeaton*, often spending days and nights onboard in mountainous seas while the ship and the rock were lashed by gales, having to row the mile to the rock each day for the few hours' work possible while the rock was above the sea.

The second summer they excavated the rock to make the foundation for the lighthouse, using pick axes to excavate a circle forty-two feet (thirteen metres) in diameter and two feet (just over half a metre) deep in the hard rock into which the first three courses of stone were laid, with the stones carefully cut and dovetailed into each other and into the rock to provide a solid interlocking structure. Each stone, individually shaped and cut and weighing as much as a ton apiece, had to be manhandled from the boat onto the rock and then transported on an elevated cast iron railway to the building site where it was placed in its exact position.

On one occasion the work vessel got loose and drifted away, leaving Stevenson and his men marooned on the rock which was fast disappearing under the rising tide; they were only saved by the lucky visit of a pilot boat which took them off, but Stevenson realised how close they had all been to death.

The third summer, the solid base of the lighthouse was completed comprising twenty-six courses of granite and standing ten metres above the rock. By the summer of 1810 the building of the tower was finished. It stood over one hundred feet (thirty metres) high and just awaited the roof to the lamp room and the lantern for completion. It was time for the sea to make its last protest: a gale lashed the rock for four days, the seas so huge that the waves broke over the top of the tower and cascaded down through the unroofed building, terrifying the men working on the rock, but the tower itself stood firm. The lantern was finally fitted and the lighthouse was complete after four years of hard toil in the most dangerous and arduous of conditions and the Bell Rock lighthouse came into service on the first day of February 1811.

## The Family Firm

Stevenson was now a famous man, hailed as the builder of a modern engineering marvel. Since 1800 he had taken over the management of his stepfather's firm and marine engineering now formed a major part of the business. Stevenson designed a number of harbour improvements, river navigation systems and ferry crossings and also designed and constructed an innovative sea wall using again the profile of a cycloidal curve to more effectively dissipate the energy of the waves. Among all this activity he was appointed Engineer to the Convention of Scottish Burghs and took responsibility for much of the public construction in Scotland, including roads, bridges and canals and work on opening up the New Town in Edinburgh. He became convinced of the superiority of railways over canals as a means of inland transport and advised on a number of railways, including on the line of the Stockton and Darlington Railway, the site in 1825 of the first steam-hauled passenger train, and by 1820 had become the leading authority on horse-drawn railways in Scotland.

## The Stevenson Dynasty

Jane, Robert Stevenson's eldest daughter, worked long hours in the family firm as her father's secretary, transcribing the book he had painstakingly written on his experiences building the lighthouse on the Bell Rock. The book proved a hard task for Stevenson, who was a man of deeds rather than letters, and the *Account of the Bell Rock Lighthouse* was not published until 1824. The gestation may have been long, but Stevenson was pleased with his progeny and wrote to his publisher demanding that each copy should be priced at no less than four guineas, a huge sum in today's money but what he felt it was worth.

To have a daughter in the firm was not enough. Stevenson was determined his sons should become lighthouse engineers and each in turn bore the brunt of his forceful personality. Alan Stevenson, the eldest boy, was a thoughtful, quiet and sometimes sickly lad who liked to disappear on his own with a book of poetry. His father was aghast; what was the point of book learning if you could not construct a lighthouse? At the age of eighteen Alan Stevenson finally bowed to his father's will and entered the firm, becoming a partner in 1832 at the age of twenty-five.

Bob, the second son, resisted more strongly and announced he wanted to be a physician, but David, from the start, entered with enthusiasm into the profession, enjoying the tours round the lighthouses of Scotland which formed a fundamental part of Stevenson's initiation of his sons. They were expected not just to be managers, but to lead by example, joining in the hard physical work. At seventeen David was already working on the Hutcheson Bridge being built over the Clyde, one of his father's most prestigious projects.

Thomas, the youngest, escaped from some of the obsessive parenting suffered by his siblings – perhaps by then Stevenson was at last tiring of his efforts – but although he had ambitions to write fiction producing a 'drawer full' of work, in the end, he too, succumbed to his father's will when told to 'give up such nonsense and mind your business.' Maybe Thomas had realised that he did not have the talent to succeed as a writer as he would have wished - this he would leave to his own son, Louis.

Stevenson's sons began to contribute positively to the business. Continuing to experiment in improving the brightness of the light, Stevenson became aware of the work of the Fresnel brothers in France, who in order to concentrate the beam had placed a lens in front of it in addition to the reflectors behind. Stevenson's recommendation to follow this example was accepted by the Board and the new lights were, cautiously, introduced into the Scottish lighthouses.

He may have discovered the idea, but it was Alan Stevenson who was responsible for the meticulous testing which underlined the technical advance.

## Skerryvore

Skerryvore is a semi-submerged black reef set in the Atlantic twelve miles to the west of the Isle of Tiree. Skerryvore was a fearful threat to sailors; every year ships were wrecked on the rocks and the debris was washed ashore on Tiree, where it was collected by the islanders as their 'harvest' from the sea.

Robert Stevenson had visited the reef twice, once in 1804 and again in 1814 when he had taken Walter Scott with him on a tour around Scotland's lighthouses. Scott wrote a poem to mark his visit to Bell Rock:

> *Far in the bosom of the deep,*
> *O'er these wild shelves my watch I keep:*
> *A ruddy gem of changeful light,*
> *Bound on the dusky brow of night.*
> —Sir Walter Scott, *Untitled*

Scott later described their landing on Skerryvore:

> *There appear a few low broad rocks at one end of a reef, which is about a mile in length. They are never entirely under water though the surf dashes over them … Pull through a very heavy swell with great difficulty, and approach a tremendous surf dashing over black pointed rocks.*

It was to this inauspicious rock that Robert Stevenson returned in 1834 with his sons Thomas and Alan, determined to build a lighthouse.

In many ways Skerryvore was more challenging than even the Bell Rock. Although some part of the reef always appeared above sea level, it was not one land mass but a collection of rocks, of which the largest, Skerryvore itself, had been worn smooth by the pounding of the waves and split and undermined by the action of the sea. The nearest land was Tiree, an island without resources of stone, timber or craftsmen, all of which would have to be shipped in.

Undeterred, Stevenson reported to the Board that building a lighthouse on this desolate spot would be possible. The Board wanted to see for themselves. They visited Skerryvore and soon became convinced of the need for a lighthouse when a fire broke out in the boiler of their steamer and their ship, disabled, drifted helplessly off the wave-lashed rocks!

At sixty-three Stevenson was too old for the hardship of the project so his son Alan was appointed the resident engineer. At twenty-eight, Alan Stevenson had become an experienced lighthouse engineer and had already built seven lighthouses under his father's supervision.

The first task was to build a yard and houses for the workers on Tiree.

Reluctantly, he chose the bay of Hynish as his base, mainly because it provided sight of Skerryvore. In other respects it was far from ideal, exposed as it was to the westerly gales and Atlantic swell. The dock he built has lasted to the present day, but sadly, is of little use because of its exposed position. He opened a quarry on the island, using the hard black granite of Tiree for the lower courses of the lighthouse and building the upper floors of the more easily worked pink granite of Mull.

Exposure to the Atlantic meant that the pressure the seas exerted on the tower could be more than twice that experienced on Bell Rock and, although Skerryvore, at nearly one hundred forty feet (forty-three metres) was forty feet higher than the lighthouse on the Bell Rock. In the severest Atlantic gales giant waves would crash over the top of it, causing the whole structure to shake. He had to make the tower solid while keeping its centre of gravity as low as possible. The tower he eventually built weighed nearly sixty thousand tons, twice the weight of the Bell Rock lighthouse, and the wall at its base was of granite nine-and-a-half feet (three metres) thick. All the stone used in the construction had to be cut exactly to size, transported to the site by ship, offloaded onto the rock in an often hazardous procedure as the boat tossed up and down, and then hoisted into position. The outline of the tower had to be smooth to avoid any resistance to the breaking waves and Alan Stevenson chose to use a hyperbolic curve, not just because it met the engineering requirements but because 'it was pleasing to the eye.'

In the first summer, Alan Stevenson concentrated on preparing the site, providing accommodation for the men by building a barracks — a hut shaped like a rocket with its iron legs set into the rock — erecting a crane to unload the construction materials and stores and setting up a forge on the rock. The work was continually interrupted by storms and the need to wait for supplies to reach them, but in September, after a hard summer, Alan Stevenson sailed for home satisfied with his work. The site had been well prepared for the next season.

His satisfaction would not last long. He had only been back in Edinburgh a few weeks when he received a letter from the storekeeper on Tiree: 'Dear Sir, I am extremely sorry to inform you that the barrack erected on Skerryvore Rock has totally disappeared.' At once Alan Stevenson sailed back to Tiree to see for himself. It was as bad as had been reported. In a wild autumn gale the entire barracks, the forge and the stores had all been washed into the sea and all that remained were the iron legs on which it had stood, twisted and broken beyond repair. What a bitter disappointment; the whole season's work had vanished.

In the second summer, Alan Stevenson constructed an even stronger barracks and anchored it firmly to the rock. He also constructed the foundation for the tower, a pit forty-two feet (thirteen metres) in diameter and fifteen inches deep. The rock in which the pit was set was hard, four times as hard as the Bell Rock, and the only way to excavate the rock was to blast it: drilling holes, filling them with powder and then – after retiring to a safe distance – igniting. The snag with this procedure was that there was nowhere safe to retreat to on the rock! Each time there was an ignition the blasted (in both senses) rock showered upon the men. After more than seven months of hard labour the site was prepared, the base so accurately cut that it was impossible to place a piece of card between the sides of the pit and the stones of the tower. Alan Stevenson was delighted with his work.

The summers of 1841 and 1842 were spent completing the tower. Each piece of stone, which had been individually shaped and cut, slotted exactly into place. By the end of 1843 the glass lantern had been fixed atop the tower and the lighthouse was complete. From February 1844 'and every night thereafter, from sunset to sunrise,' the light on the Skerryvore Rock shined out to protect the ships.

The construction of a lighthouse on Skerryvore had been an exceptional feat of engineering and on Robert Stevenson's retirement in 1842, Alan Stevenson was deservedly appointed Engineer to the Northern Lighthouse Board, a position for which he was well qualified, having already been responsible for the construction of eight lighthouses. In addition to his new responsibilities as Engineer to the Board, which included the annual inspection of the thirty-five lighthouses it now maintained, Alan Stevenson retained responsibility as Resident Engineer for Skerryvore and, in case he had some time to spare, was also charged with writing the history of the project. He had every right to feel just a little tired!

Alan Stevenson worked himself hard, designing and constructing no fewer than ten new lighthouses in the decade after he completed Skerryvore, often working in wild rain and gales on his journeys around the coast of Scotland.

In 1850, at the age of seventy-eight, Robert Stevenson died. He had been a pioneer, inventing almost single-handedly the science of lighthouse construction, a science which his sons would continue and enhance. With the onset of paralysis, Alan Stevenson resigned as Engineer to the Board just three years later. His work had been recognised domestically by his election as a Fellow of the Royal Society of Edinburgh and internationally by the award of a medal by the Emperor of Russia. Despite all the work pressures, he had not totally forsaken his literary tastes, reading works in Italian and Spanish in the original and also being fluent in Ancient Greek. He had given his all and the continuing toil and hardships had taken their toll on his health. He died in 1865. It was time for the next member of the family to pick up the baton.


## Muckle Flugga

Of all Robert Stevenson's sons, David was arguably the one who was the most committed to the business and in 1838 at the age of twenty-three, he had become a partner in the family firm, taking responsibility for the overall management. It was therefore natural that on Alan Stevenson's retirement in 1853, David Stevenson should succeed him as Engineer to the Board.

He was immediately faced with a challenge. Britain in the mid-nineteenth century was challenged by the growing power of Russia and war seemed ever more likely. In its wisdom, or what passed for wisdom, the Admiralty considered sending a fleet to blockade the Russian ports of Archangel and Murmansk and plotted a route for the fleet north of Shetland. A lighthouse would be needed to protect the fleet on this journey and David Stevenson was sent to investigate. His report could be summarised in one word: 'Crazy!' *'It is not practicable,'* he wrote somewhat more politely, *'to erect and maintain a lighthouse upon these rocks'* – and why should you choose to go that far north when there was a perfectly good route between Orkney and Shetland? The Admiralty had, however, made their decision and a lighthouse there must be.

The location they had selected was a rock named Muckle Flugga, a reef rising steeply from the water to the north of North Unst, the most northerly island of the Shetlands. Next stop north is the Arctic Circle.

Mickle Flugga is part of a reef rising from sea level to a maximum height of two hundred feet (sixty metres). The seas in the area are so rough that waves have been known to break over the summit of the rock. On the Admiralty's instructions a temporary light was built upon the rock. They did not realise just how temporary it would be: a winter gale, gusting hurricane force broke the glass panes of the lantern and the seas broke through the living accommodation on the two-hundred foot summit of the rock. A permanent lighthouse was the only possible solution.

David Stevenson decided it would be impracticable to transport blocks of stone to this desolate spot and that, therefore, the tower should be built of brick, three and a half feet thick at the base. No other lighthouse tower built by the Stevensons had used brick. The building was carried out in appalling weather and the workmen often had to crawl about the rock on their hands and knees to avoid being blown away by the fierce winds. Despite these atrocious conditions the lighthouse was completed in 1857. Without doubt it was the worst site ever tackled by the Stevensons.

## Dubh Artach

David Stevenson found the combined pressures of designing and building new lighthouses with the increasing administration of the Northern Lighthouse Board and the work of the private business too great. He proposed firstly that his younger brother Thomas Stevenson should join him in the position of Joint Engineer to the Board and secondly that they should concentrate on engineering, passing the burden of administration and the annual inspection of the lights to a separate administrator. This was agreed and worked well.

In their role as Joint Engineers, Thomas and David Stevenson were responsible over the next twenty-five years for the design and construction of twenty-nine lights around the coast of Scotland. Their fame had spread and they also constructed lighthouses in India, Japan, Canada and Singapore, learning to deal with the new problems these locations raised. Thomas, meanwhile, experimented with the lights, dispensing with the reflectors and instead focusing the light through an immense lens, obtaining great accuracy and a strength of beam far greater than those of the early, primitive systems. Scottish lights were the most accurate and powerful in the world.

Dubh Artach was the main rock of the dangerous ten-mile-long Torran Reef to the south-west of Mull. The semi-submerged reef was a great danger to ships rounding the isle as the currents swept around it like a tide race. Thomas visited in 1854 and found that the rock was only thirty feet (nine metres) above high-water mark and that even in good conditions a landing proved impossible. He supported the project though, as more than thirty ships and fifty lives had been lost on the reef in the previous fifty years. It would prove as great a challenge as Skerryvore.

The first problem Thomas faced was the length of the reef: where should the light be positioned so that it could be most visible? He selected Dubh Artach, a smooth rock about two hundred and forty feet long (just under seventy-five metres), but the problem was that it rose sheer from the water with no landing place or shelter. Thomas chose a design similar to, but smaller than that of Skerryvore, and set up base on Earraid, a tiny isle fifteen miles from the rock and connected to Mull by a spit of sand. Louis, Thomas's son, arrived on the island when the work on the base had been completed, with a pier, sheds and cottages for the workers.

Work on the rock began in April 1867, but little was achieved in the first season because of the appalling weather conditions, with only the barracks completed. So the project continued for four years, with the rock again and again lashed by gales and high seas, until eventually the lamp was lit. Thomas had taken Louis with him to see the progress of the work, but in truth Louis could not wait to return to Edinburgh. He was expected to follow his father into the business of designing and building lighthouses but did not take wholeheartedly to the life, writing of one site, 'I am utterly sick of this grey, grim, sea-beaten hole.' He would later earn great fame as Robert Louis Stevenson. To Thomas's disappointment it was not his own son but David's two boys, Charles and David, who would take over the management of the business; embittered and wearied Thomas died in 1887.

It is perhaps ironic that Thomas Stevenson, who had himself wanted to be a writer but had bowed instead to his father's will, could not accept that his son in turn should choose to renounce lighthouses for the equally uncertain life of an author, and that Thomas is remembered less for his contribution to the design and building of lighthouses than as the father of Robert Louis Stevenson.

The family firm continued to build lighthouses; twenty-three new ones were built in the thirty years after Thomas's death. David Stevenson was the last member of the family to serve as Engineer to the Northern Lighthouse Board, retiring in 1938, the family completing an astonishing one hundred and fifty-one years since Thomas Smith had first been appointed Engineer of the Northern

Lights Board. The last of the lighthouse family, Charles's son Alan, worked as Engineer to The Clyde Lighthouses Trust until his retirement in 1952, but is remembered more as a historian of Scotland's lighthouses than for his engineering achievements.

## The Stevenson Family Legacy

Robert Stevenson's legacy is set in stone, the lighthouses around Scotland's coast which he, his sons and his grandsons built, often in the most remote places and under appalling conditions.

All seafarers who have avoided shipwreck through sighting the light of a Stevenson lighthouse owe their lives to this remarkable family who espoused the virtues of good education, dedication and the power of reason characteristic of the Enlightenment to create the profession and science of lighthouse building.

**Further Reading**
Bella Bathurst, *The Lighthouse Stevensons*
Roland Paxton, *Dynasty of Engineers*

**Online Resources**
Bell Rock Organisation
http://www.bellrock.org.uk/stevensons/stevenson_robert.htm

'PARTHENOPE & EGERIA' (2 pieces)
Eduardo Paolozzi - 1991
King's Buildings, University of Edinburgh
photos: Thomas Haywood

Paolozzi was charged
with creating
sculpture reflective of
the work that would
take place inside the
university medical and
science laboratories.
He produced a critical
observation of the
strange and
sometimes cruel
relationship between
human kind and
medical science.

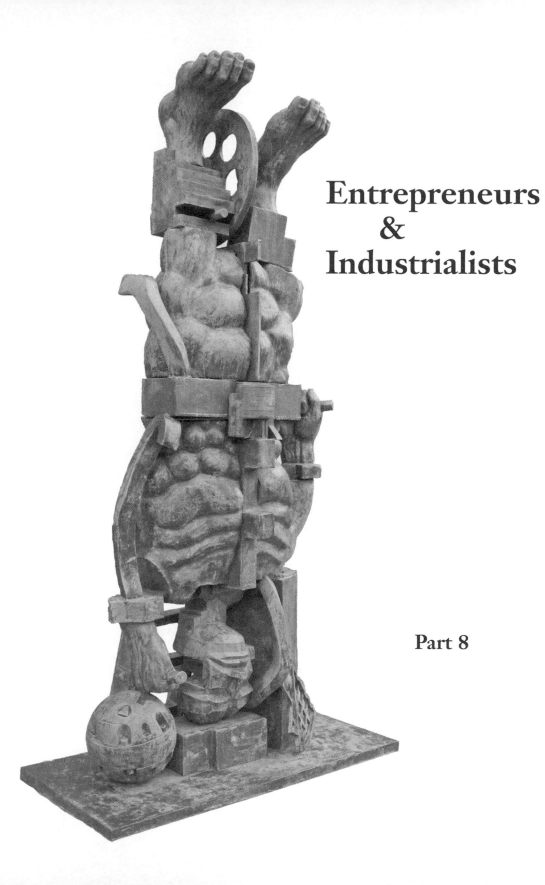

# Entrepreneurs
# &
# Industrialists

Part 8

ENTREPRENEURS
&
INDUSTRIALISTS


**Robert Napier**
*SHIPBUILDER*


**James 'Paraffin' Young**
*THE FIRST OIL MAGNATE*


**Andrew Carnegie**
*INDUSTRIALIST AND PHILANTHROPIST*


**Sir Thomas Lipton**
*GROCER TO THE WORLD*

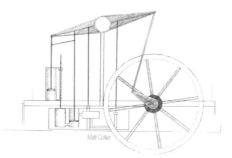

## The Workshop of the Empire

Edinburgh may have built its New Town, inspired by the architecture of Robert Adam, but Glasgow developed its industry.

The Enlightenment is usually thought of in terms of ideas and of the philosophers, the scientists, the artists and the writers who contributed those ideas. It also encompassed major improvements in agriculture, with better understanding of crop rotation, more scientific methods of breeding to improve the quality of livestock and the introduction of mechanisation, albeit primitive, on the farm.

But there was a third strand: a rapid development of industry, which was built on the scientific discoveries of the Enlightenment and on the virtues of good education and hard endeavour embodied within it. Industrialisation would transform the nation, combining the large-scale movement of people away from the land to the growing industrial towns and with increased wealth – at least for the owners and managers. The nineteenth century industrial growth of Scotland was driven in large part by the development of shipbuilding on the Clyde.

Glasgow had taken full advantage of the new freedom to trade with the colonies resulting from the Union to develop extensive trade with the Americas, especially in tobacco where the amount imported more than doubled between 1741 and 1751 to twenty-one million lbs., more than the combined imports of all of the English ports, and requiring a substantial investment in ships.

Before the American War of Independence these ships were built in America using the plentiful supplies of timber available there, but the war brought a sudden end to these supplies. Resourcefully, the Tobacco Lords shifted their orders to the Clyde and a new shipbuilding industry rapidly developed with timber imported from the Baltic. Traditionally, ships had been made of wood and powered by sails, but two changes, the use of iron for building ships and the use of steam engines to power them, in a process which began with the *Charlotte Dundas* of William Symington, revolutionised the shipbuilding industry.

Glasgow was well placed to take advantage of these new methods and grew to become by the middle of the nineteenth century the most important shipbuilding centre in Britain, building half the nation's steamships. Glasgow became the second most important city in Britain and the 'Workshop of the Empire.'

Robert Napier was one of the Clyde shipbuilders who created this industry.

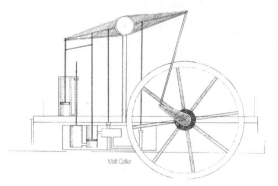

Matt Collier

# Robert Napier
## 1791–1876

SHIPBUILDER

*I have had the pleasure of being carried ... by a pair of your incomparable engines; I trust it will be a satisfaction to hear that they have done their duty well.*

These words were written by a naval captain to Robert Napier as a report on the first Napier engines to have been fitted in Royal Naval ships. It was on such a reputation for quality that Napier built his business.

Robert Napier and his cousin David were just two of a number of shipbuilders to make their fortune on the Clyde, taking advantage of two major developments in the design of ships: the changes from sail to steam and from wooden hulls to iron.

Based on good design and benefiting from a skilled and relatively cheap labour force, many of these Clydeside yards had become major companies by the start of the First World War. The demands of the war brought even more business and by its end, the Clyde was producing more than two and a half million tons of ships, sixty per cent of Britain's entire output. During the inter-war years attention shifted to passenger liners, with both the *Queen Mary* and the *Queen Elizabeth* launched on the Clyde in the 1930s. But after the Second World War a combination of poor management, aggressive unions and new low-cost shipbuilding in countries such as Korea brought the industry to an end.

### Early Days in Dumbarton

Robert Napier was born in Dumbarton in 1791 to James and Jean Napier. Their first-born had died in infancy and Napier was baptised the day after he was born, indicating he may not himself have been a robust baby.

James Napier ran a foundry business with his brother in Dumbarton. Somewhat ahead of their time, they used two steam engines in their factory, one to blow the air into the furnace and the other to power a machine to bore the finished iron castings. Later Robert Napier would say he was 'born with a hammer in his hand.'

Napier was given a good schooling in Dumbarton, learning besides English, Latin and French, the skill of mechanical drawing, and it was this practical skill that really interested him. It had been planned that he should enter the church, but instead at the age of fourteen, he joined his father in the family business.

In those days young men were often seized by press gangs to serve in the ships of the Royal Navy, a rough and ready way of recruiting seamen. Napier himself once narrowly escaped being caught, and since apprentices were free from the threat, he decided in 1809 to become formally apprenticed to his father for five years 'to learn the trade of a blacksmith and an iron founder.' He was given no special favour; for any day he was absent during the five years, he had to make good by working an extra two.

When Napier had finished his apprenticeship he worked for a time for Robert Stevenson, the lighthouse engineer, but in 1815 he decided to set up on his own and bought a small smithy's shop in Glasgow, trading under the title 'Robert Napier, Engineer and Blacksmith.'


## David Napier

In 1815 at the age of twenty-four, Robert Napier married his cousin Isabella, also a Napier, and through her became closer with his cousin David, Isabella's brother. David Napier would also become a famous marine engineer. He was a few months older than Robert and worked in his father's foundry in Glasgow, becoming manager when he was only twenty. One of their customers was Henry Bell and when Bell decided to build his *Comet* paddle steamer, he turned to David to produce the boiler and castings for his new ship.

David realised at once the potential of steam-powered ships and set up a works near Camlachie Burn in the east end of Glasgow. In those early days it was felt that steam engines and iron-built hulls would not withstand the battering of heavy seas and so steamboats did not venture out of the Clyde in stormy weather.

David thought otherwise. He felt the broad blunt bow of existing designs did not give an easy flow through the water and so experimented with hull design in the Camlachie Burn. He made a model of the ship he planned to build and placed on its deck a drum with a cable, to which was attached a weight. He tried shaping the bow of his model ship to move through the water as easily as possible, each time measuring the effect of his design upon the speed through the water by using a constant weight to 'power' the boat. When his experiments were finished, he took his model to a ship designer instructing him to produce a ship to the exact same design. The ship, the *Rob Roy*, amazed everyone by being both speedy and seaworthy. She was set to work on the route to Greenock and David Napier was first to demonstrate that a steamship could safely and securely navigate the open seas.

David made his reputation through this breakthrough in design and began receiving a number of orders for ships, building a new works with a dock and leasing his old foundry, for which he now had no need, to his cousin Robert. In 1826 David reached the peak of his career by designing and building the first 'leviathan' or 'sea monster,' the *United Kingdom*. Huge for the time, she had an overall length of one hundred and sixty feet (fifty metres) and became the wonder of the age. She sailed from the Clyde in July 1826 with one hundred and fifty passengers onboard and made the perilous journey around the north of Scotland to reach Leith sixty-five days later in an impressive demonstration of steam power.

Regrettably, David's workmanship did not always match his dreams and he suffered a number of setbacks, the most disastrous being the 1835 explosion of the boiler on one of his steamships, the *Earl Grey*, as she was building up a head of steam to challenge another steamship in a trial. A number of people were killed or injured by the explosion and David was badly affected by the disaster, both as a businessman and in his health. He moved his ship-building activities down to London, where he died in 1869.

## Becoming a Shipbuilder

Robert Napier had taken over the lease of his cousin's foundry in 1821 and set about building up his business. From David's success, he realised that there was profit in building engines for steamships and in 1823 he got his first order. His first engine was a great success and led rapidly to more. Robert built engines for river boats and larger vessels such as the Belfast steamers. In 1826 he built the *Eclipse*, described as:

*-the most complete vessel of her size ever built on the Clyde; in point of sailing unequalled by any vessel; built of the best British oak, copper-sheathed and fastened, with double side-lever engines warranted equal in construction and workmanship to the best engines made.*

Napier was developing a reputation equal to if not greater than that of his cousin. In 1827 the Northern Yacht Club offered a cup, valued at twenty guineas, to the fastest steamboat over a course from Rothesay Bay around boats moored off the north shore of Great Cumbrae and then back to Rothesay Bay. Napier's entry, the *Clarence*, won the three-hour race and the cup and another of his designs came second. He had become a successful designer, engineer and businessman.

At this time Napier was building paddle steamers, equipped with a full set of sails and wooden hulls. Napier took responsibility for the whole design, but only producing the engines, placing the construction of the wooden hull with another firm, appropriately that of a Mr Wood, who had earned a reputation for constructing wooden ships of great beauty and strength. In this way, he produced a number of vessels for a wealthy private English yachtsman, Mr Assheton Smith, and in 1932 two substantial steamers, the *Dundee* and the *Perth* for the snappily named Dundee, Perth and London Shipping Company. Beating off English competition, he also secured an order to build a steamship for the East India Company.

It is a mark of Napier's growing reputation that in 1838 he was able to secure two orders for engines for the Admiralty, no mean feat as the Admiralty was heavily biased towards its existing English suppliers. Napier engines were installed in HMS *Vesuvius* and HMS *Stromboli*, both of which saw active service. After five years' experience with the engines, the captain of the *Vesuvius* wrote a letter to Robert Napier stating,

> *You will no doubt, and with very good reason, call me a shabby fellow for not writing you since I have had the pleasure of being carried so far by a pair of your incomparable engines; but I trust it will be a satisfaction to hear that they have done their duty well … I am proud to think they have been no expense to Government for repairs since we have been on the station.*

Napier was able to demonstrate to the Admiralty that his engines suffered far lower downtime and cost far less to repair than those of his English competitors and as a result became an approved supplier to the navy. This meant he soon had to expand his business to meet the growing demand, leasing and then buying the Lancefield Works of his cousin David, and bringing in his brother James to manage his commercial affairs.

A talented engineer himself, James had invented the idea of tubular boilers and had with his other brother William started building steamers with iron hulls rather than the traditional wood. James had also taken out a patent for a steam carriage whose influence was seen many years later in the development of the Napier motor car.

### Steamships across the Atlantic

In 1833 Napier was asked for his views on the practicability of using steamships to provide a passenger service to America. In 1819 the *Savannah*, a small sailing ship assisted by paddles, had crossed the Atlantic from the USA, partly under power but mainly under sail. It had not been a great success as she was relatively small and underpowered.

Napier had very different ideas; he visualised a regular service using powered vessels of as much as eight hundred tons to provide a fast and reliable Atlantic crossing. He produced detailed financial estimates for such ships which could carry up to one hundred passengers at a time and make six trips a year from Liverpool to New York and back. He estimated they would cost thirty-four thousand pounds each and earn a profit of ten thousand pounds a year.

A few years later he supplied the engines for just such a ship, the *British Queen*, a magnificent steam vessel whose hull was built by a shipyard on the Thames under direction from Napier. She made her maiden voyage across the Atlantic in July 1839, completing the crossing in a little less than sixteen days.

That year, Napier was approached by Samuel Cunard, a Canadian who wished to start an Atlantic service to carry both passengers and mail. Napier quoted for ships of nine hundred sixty tons with engines of three hundred and seventy-five horsepower and a contract was speedily signed for three such vessels. Napier believed the ships should be even larger but Cunard demurred, saying his funds were limited. This could easily be resolved. Napier and a number of other wealthy Scots subscribed for shares in a company with a name as long as its ambitions and the British & North American Royal Mail Steam-Packet Company came into being with Samuel Cunard as principal shareholder.

Napier initially built four ships for the company, strengthening the hulls with double planking secured by massive iron straps and providing water-tight bulkheads in case they struck an iceberg. The first to be launched, the *Britannia*, made her maiden voyage in July 1840, crossing the Atlantic in fourteen days against strong head winds and returning in a startling ten. Napier had performed a key role in forming what eventually became the famous Cunard Company for whom he would build over forty ships.

### Iron Steamships

Steam engines were becoming so large and powerful it was getting difficult to build wooden hulls strong enough to carry them. Napier realised the answer was to build the hulls of iron and in 1841, he bought some land in Govan to create a works to build iron ships. He recruited William Denny, himself later a famous shipbuilder, to provide the expertise he needed and with his help started to build his first iron vessel, the *Vanguard*, a paddle steamer of seven hundred tons.

The success of the *Vanguard* helped Napier to persuade the British Admiralty, still committed to traditional wooden boats, to purchase three iron-hulled ships, the first iron ships to enter service with the Royal Navy. In 1845 Napier received another order for a propeller-driven iron-hulled frigate, the *Simoom*, which took three years longer to build than planned while the Admiralty argued over design changes for which they then refused to pay. The *Simoom* remained in service as a troop carrier for more than forty years.

### 'Retirement' to West Shandon

By the age of sixty, Robert Napier had built a prosperous and successful ship-building company and he desired partially to retire, leaving the business in the hands of his sons James and John and of his nephew, another James.

Napier had a mansion built for his family, West Shandon, on the Gareloch, and there he entertained generously his family and business friends and the many naval commanders he came to know through his work for the Admiralty. He accumulated a fine collection of paintings, including works by the Italian masters Titian, Veronese and Tintoretto, by Rembrandt and Rubens and by Raeburn and Wilkie. He collected porcelain, including fine specimens of Sevres and Dresden.

Even in retirement Napier remained very much in charge and was deeply involved in the design and building of the *Persia*, the first iron-hulled steamship for the Cunard Company, a ship of over three thousand six hundred tons with an overall length of three hundred and ninety feet (one hundred and twenty metres) and paddle wheels forty feet (twelve metres) in diameter. She was built with an emphasis on strength, which enabled her later to survive a head-on collision with an iceberg, and was sumptuously furnished with accommodation for three hundred passengers. At the time she was considered the largest and finest vessel afloat and was one of the famed 'Atlantic greyhounds,' with a speed of over sixteen knots.

Abroad, Napoleon III had ordered the construction of an ironclad frigate and this move frightened the British Admiralty into action. They asked Napier for a design for a thirty-six gun frigate with a hull encased in armour plating so that it could withstand direct shell fire. The building of this ship was fraught with difficulty as Napier wrestled with the new technology and the *Black Prince*, (a sister ship to the Warrior, now on display in Portsmouth), weighing nine thousand eight hundred tons, was not finished for two years. Napier went on to build ironclad ships for the Danish, Turkish and Dutch navies as well as for the British Admiralty.

Napier built two last paddle steamers for the Cunard Company and two screw (propeller) driven ships for the French, enabling them to wrest the 'blue riband' for the fastest Atlantic crossing from the British.

### Napier's Last Years and Legacy

Robert Napier received many honours in his later life, including some from foreign governments, but surprisingly, despite his services both to shipbuilding and to the Admiralty, he was never knighted. In the autumn of 1875 his wife died, leaving Napier bereft and *'not in a mood to do anything.'* He soon followed her, dying nine months later at the age of eighty-five.

Robert Napier had started as a blacksmith and foundry man, but by the time of his death he had created one of the largest and most successful ship-building companies in the world, overseeing the introduction of steam-powered and in time iron-hulled ships. He completed more than four hundred contracts for engines and ships. Many who worked with him learned their trade through Napier and went on to found their own ship-building companies. Napier was thus largely instrumental in developing the Clyde as a ship-building centre, powering the industrial growth of Scotland.

**Further Reading** - James Napier, *Life of Robert Napier of West Shandon*

**Online Resources** - Glasgow Digital Library
http://gdl.cdlr.strath.ac.uk/mlemen/mlemen069.htm

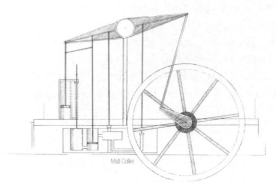

Matt Collier

# James 'Paraffin' Young
## 1811–1883

THE FIRST OIL MAGNATE

A common image of an oil-industry tycoon is a Texan chomping on a fat cigar. While the birth of the oil industry is normally credited to Pennsylvania. One Sunday in 1859, a borehole drilled by the crazy 'Colonel' Drake into the hard Allegheny County rock began to fill, and he had 'struck oil.' The news spread like wildfire through a local church congregation and before the minister could complete his sermon, they had all ridden off to stake their claims. The age of oil had arrived. In its first year the Pennsylvania Railroad shipped just three hundred and twenty-five barrels of the 'liquid gold,' but less than three years later shipments had risen to thirty thousand barrels a month. But the Americans were not the originators of the oil industry. This honour belongs to a Scot, James Young.

## Education

The son of a cabinet maker in Glasgow, Young was soon apprenticed to his father to learn the practical skills of the carpenter and so he might have continued had it not been for Scotland's fine tradition of free education.

Young lived not far from the Andersonian University, now the University of Strathclyde, which had been founded in 1796 by John Anderson with the mission of providing a formal scientific education to those who worked with their hands. John Anderson was the man who had given James Watt his model steam engine to repair, thus bringing about the steam age, and the college he founded was the first of its kind in the world, aimed as it was at educating young artisans in science and technology. Young took full advantage of the opportunity and from the age of nineteen started attending the evening classes of Thomas Graham, Professor of Chemistry. Amongst his fellow classmates were David Livingstone, the missionary and explorer, and Lyon Playfair, who would subsequently give Young his great opportunity. Graham saw the ability of his young student and appointed Young as his assistant. Sometimes Young would take over the lectures, and continued to do so when Graham moved to University College in London.

## The First Oil Well

Young married when he was twenty-seven and decided to leave the academic life in favour of industry, first as a manager in a chemical works near Liverpool and then joining Charles Tennant and Company, a substantial Manchester chemical engineering company.

Then James Young got his big opportunity in the form of a letter from his old classmate Lyon Playfair, who was now a professor of chemistry at the Royal School of Mines. He told Young of an interesting discovery on his brother-in-law's estate at Alfreton in Derbyshire. 'You know,' wrote Playfair,

> *'that mineral naptha [oil] is a rare natural product, no spring of it occurring in this country, all being imported from the Continent or Persia. Lately, a spring of this valuable product has been found on an estate belonging to my brother-in-law near Alfreton, Derbyshire. It yields at present about three hundred gallons daily. The naptha is about the consistency of thin treacle, and with one distillation it gives a clear, colourless liquid of brilliant illuminating power.'*

At once Young realised the opportunity, but first very properly asked his employers if they were interested in developing this find. They declined as they thought the prospect too small, thus missing out on the birth of a new industry. Young decided to develop it himself and set up a partnership with two colleagues – Meldrum, a chemist, and Binney, a lawyer – to exploit the discovery. They proved wise choices, the chemist developing the process and the lawyer defending their patent rights. Together they marketed the oil as a lubricant for the cotton mills of Manchester and as lamp oil for lighting.

Playfair had noticed that when chilled the oil would turn cloudy with a deposit which seemed similar to the solid 'paraffin' that a German chemist had extracted from wood tar. Young extracted the deposit from the naptha in the form of a wax and found it could be made into candles. As the business began to prosper a problem appeared: the oil spring, the source of all their income, was beginning to dry up.

## The First Oil Plant

Young needed another oil source. He thought, wrongly as it turned out, that the oil had been formed as vapour given off when coal had condensed in porous sandstone and so he tried producing oil from the dry distillation of coal, much as William Murdoch had done some years before to produce gas. Oil is in fact formed from the remains of marine plants which have been compressed over millions of years by the pressure from layers of sediment, but nevertheless his idea worked provided the right type of coal was used.

Like Murdoch before him, Young became aware of the 'cannel' coal which was used by the people of West Lothian. They burned coal for heat but also burned a little cannel coal in a brazier beside their fires to provide light. This same coal had been burnt in the brazier in the lighthouse on the Isle of May since 1635. It proved to give the best yield of oil of any coal. Young took out a patent in 1850 to cover his idea of extracting oil from coal.

In his work, he also discovered the principle of catalytic cracking, the process whereby heavy oils can be broken down into lighter oils of lower molecular weight, of which the most common form is petrol. Cracking is still used in oil refineries today.

Young moved back to Scotland to take charge of his new venture and the partnership set up a works at Bathgate for the commercial production of various grades of oil, the first such in the world. The oil was sold for use as a lubricant, as paraffin for lamps – giving him his nickname of 'Paraffin' Young – and in the form of wax to make candles.

Soon business was very profitable and it encouraged a lot of people to copy his ideas and to challenge his patent, arguing that the cannel coal used as raw material for processing was not 'coal' as set out in his patent application. After much scientific evidence from distinguished geologists – and plenty of fees from many expensive lawyers – it was decided that the material Young was using was indeed a form of coal and that the process whereby the coal was gently heated to extract the oil and the subsequent purification of that oil to produce the refined products were indeed the unique inventions of James Young.

## Oil-bearing Shale Deposits

Again Young worried that the supply of raw material, cannel coal, might become exhausted and he began to search for other sources of oil-rich coal. He discovered that shale, effectively compressed sediment in the shape of slates, was also rich in oil. There were large shale deposits around West Calder and Young secretly bought up a number of these sites and in 1865 formed a new company to process the oil shale. He called it Young's Paraffin Light and Mineral Oil Company – a mouthful of a title which set out clear objectives for the business. He asked his old university friend David Livingstone to lay the foundation stone of the new plant.

It proved the formation of an enormous industry. At its peak there were more than thirteen thousand men employed in the mining of oil shale in West Lothian alone, with another thirty thousand employed in the one hundred and twenty manufacturing plants in the area. The total annual output of oil shale reached nearly four million tons.

The uses of the products were manifold: lubricating oils for industry, paraffin oil for lamps and for lighthouses, wax for candles and tapers, naptha for dry-cleaning and the manufacture of rubber, wax for waterproofing coats; the list was almost endless, as it remains today.

In 1870 when he was not yet sixty, James Young retired from the business he had created. He was already an immensely wealthy man and did not need to continue working. Perhaps Young also foresaw the looming threat to his business.

For some time he had believed that oil would be found in reservoirs deep under the earth's surface which could be tapped by drilling. He had even published a paper setting out his theories. Was it the threat from the oil that was beginning to flow from the American oil wells that persuaded him to retire?

The discovery of oil wells, first in America and then in the Middle East, provided a source of oil at a price which could not be matched by the oil-shale process. Inevitably over time, the shale mines closed until by the beginning of the twentieth century there were only thirteen still operating. The last oil-shale mine shut down in 1962.

## Retirement

Young had become an extremely wealthy man with large estates and a number of houses in both Scotland and England. It was time for him to give something back to society. Remembering his own start in life, he funded a number of educational projects, a Chair of Technical Chemistry and a lectureship in Geology at the Andersonian University. Young served as president of the university from 1868 to 1877. He also supported Livingstone, funding his expeditions into the heartlands of Africa. Without Young's support Livingstone would have been unable to make his later journeys.

A modest man who avoided the limelight, Young enjoyed the company of friends, often inviting them on his yacht which, perhaps in tribute to Livingstone, he named the *Nyanza* and on which he cruised the seas around Scotland and as far as St Kilda.

In addition, Young also received a number of honours, becoming a Fellow of the Royal Society in 1873 and an honorary graduate of St Andrew's University in 1879. He died at his house near Wemyss Bay on the Firth of Clyde in 1883.

## Young's Legacy

Naturally occurring pitch or oil had been known for years; Alexander the Great had marvelled at the oil springs he saw on fire at Babylon and pitch had long been used to make wooden ships watertight, but James 'Paraffin' Young was the first oil tycoon, the first man to recognise its potential and to commercialise the production and sale of oil. True to the principles of the Enlightenment, he allied his commercial mind with his scientific skills both to find new sources of oil and to find new uses for its products. The United States Commissioner of Patents in 1864 put it succinctly: 'The manufactures of coal oil in this country had their origin in Dr Young's patents … Previous to Dr Young's discovery petroleum had little or no commercial value.'

Oil remains a fundamental contributor to the modern economy, not just in the form of petrol or diesel in our cars and trucks or as gasoline for jet engines, or even as a form of lubrication, but as a root stock for many other products, from plastics to fertilisers. It is this dependence on oil which poses such a problem for mankind as the finite resources are becoming exhausted.

The production of oil from oil shale, the process discovered and developed by James Young, was driven out of business by the discovery of much cheaper sources from oil wells drilled first in America, then in the Middle East and now all over the world. As the uses of oil have proliferated, so have resources become more scarce and the costs of extraction more expensive. It is ironic that the industry is again looking at the vast worldwide tar sand deposits, particularly in Canada, as a future source for oil. Perhaps James Young was very well a couple of centuries ahead of is time.

**Further Reading**
David Murray, *'Paraffin' Young*

**Online Resources**
Museum of Scottish Shale Oil
http://www.scottishshale.co.uk/HistoryPages/Biographies/JamesYoung.html

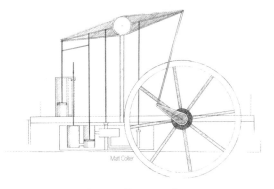

# Andrew Carnegie
## 1835–1919

<small>INDUSTRIALIST AND PHILANTHROPIST</small>

*'Never stop a man making money, but remember that during his lifetime he should always give it back – a man should be ashamed to die rich.' Andrew Carnegie*

Andrew Carnegie lived his life according to his principles. Born into a poor Scots family, he created an industrial empire which made him, in his time, the richest man in the world – and then he gave it all away! Carnegie was born in Dunfermline in November 1835. His father, William, was a weaver of fine cloth and Carnegie would watch fascinated as his father, clad in a white apron, fired the shuttle of the loom to and fro while vigorously pedalling the treadles, often singing traditional Scots ballads. A favourite of Carnegie's was the ballad of Sir Patrick Spens, the sailor who was sent to bring to Scotland the Maid of Norway who when only three years old, had become Queen Margaret of Scotland on the death of Alexander III. The ballad begins:

> *The King sits in Dunfermline towne*
> *Drinking the blude red wine*
> *'Where will I get a steely skipper*
> *To sail this ship o' mine?'*
> Traditional, Sir Patrick Spens

But it was Carnegie's mother, Margaret, who was the dominating influence on his life. She was a very powerful lady and Carnegie remained more than a little afraid of her throughout his life. Unusually, Carnegie did not go to school until eight years old, apparently because he was not 'ready' – which may be a view shared by many children with less forgiving parents – but when he eventually enrolled he found he enjoyed learning. Besides reading and writing, Carnegie also learned about poverty. Life for a hand weaver was getting harder; power looms had been introduced, making hand weaving no longer economic. The Carnegies were struggling to survive and William decided they should make a new start in America. They sold all their possessions, borrowed twenty pounds from Margaret's school friend and booked a trip to New York. They left in May 1848 on the *Wiscasset*, a three-masted sailing vessel, and upon arriving in the USA, journeyed on by river, canal and lake until they reached Pittsburgh.


## Pittsburgh

Pittsburgh was a city whose wealth was based on coal. The city was dirty and grimy and had been devastated by fire just a few years earlier. Smoke from the furnaces got into people's lungs and the soot quickly made newly washed clothes black, but the city had bustle and offered Carnegie a life of opportunity.

Carnegie needed work and found a job as a 'bobbin-boy' at a cotton mill run by a Scotsman, which paid $1.20 a week. He worked hard and the family was soon able to pay back the twenty pounds they had borrowed in Scotland. He also read voraciously from the library of a Colonel Anderson who made his books available free for a week to any poor boy who *'wished to improve himself.'* It was a generous act that Carnegie remembered when he himself became wealthy. Cotton was not an exciting industry. Carnegie realised that the railways, booming with the opening up of America, were the future. When the Philadelphia to Pittsburgh line opened, Carnegie, then sixteen, was asked to join the Pennsylvania Railroad Company as assistant to Thomas Scott, the superintendent.

Scott became a mentor for Carnegie, but surprisingly, when many years later Scott hit financial problems, Carnegie declined to help him as he 'had already too many people dependent on him.' Carnegie said, 'It gave me more pain than all the financial trials to which I had been subjected up to that time.' But many believed he betrayed the man who had given him his chance.

Carnegie was short, only five foot three inches tall (1.6 metres), with a shock of white hair, but like many short men what he lacked in height he more than made up in energy and drive and he was soon doing well. He realised that the way to become wealthy was not to work for a salary, but to invest in companies and projects. He had seen poverty and he wanted to be rich.

In his first investment he backed an entrepreneur who had started a company to make luxury sleeping-car carriages for the railways. Sleeping cars in those days were just wagons kitted with bunks; they were dirty and unsafe and no woman would ever travel in one. The new cars were designed to be carriages by day and cabins by night and would be clean and safe. The investment was a success. The man was George Pullman and his eponymous railway carriages became synonymous with luxury rail travel for more than a century. Within only two years Carnegie's original small investment was bringing an annual income of five thousand dollars, much more than his salary. The Carnegie family began to rise.

## The American Civil War

America was a Union but it was divided. The southern states still practised slavery, using slaves to work the cotton fields, while the North believed slavery was wrong and should be abolished – a view which Carnegie shared. Abraham Lincoln, born a simple farm boy, became President of the United States and vowed to abolish slavery. In response, the states left the Union, forming the Confederate States of America and in 1861 the 'War between the States' began.

Andrew Carnegie at Skibo Castle, 1914

Although he believed war was evil, Carnegie felt that even the horrors of war would be justified if an end was brought to slavery. He realised the railways could provide the key to military success, enabling the generals to move men and equipment rapidly around the country. He was invited by Scott to join the Union war effort and one of his first tasks was to organise the evacuation of the wounded following the defeat of a Union army in Virginia by the southern Confederates; two thousand wounded soldiers were carried by rail back to safety. Then Carnegie became exhausted. He had made a fortune investing in a new oil field and could now afford a holiday. So he went back to Scotland to rest.

Upon his return to America, Carnegie learned with alarm that the war had not gone well from the Union point of view; General Robert E. Lee was poised to capture Pittsburgh from the Union. Carnegie again took control of transport and brought in soldiers and arms by rail. The opposing armies fought at Gettysburg, the battle raging for three days with heavy casualties on both sides, until Lee admitted defeat and the Confederate army withdrew.

This proved a turning point in the war. The Union moved its armies by rail into the Confederate states in the South and, after further defeats, in April 1865 the Confederates surrendered. Peace did not come easily. On 14 April President Lincoln, the one man who might have reconciled the states of the north and the south, was assassinated at the opera in Washington D.C..

## Carnegie's Expanding Business Empire

One result of the war was a shortage of iron. Steam engines had been damaged and bridges destroyed. Carnegie recognised the opportunity and invested heavily in an ironworks, a locomotive company and a company to make iron bridges – he had realised the wooden bridges then in use were not strong enough to bear the weight of the huge new locomotives. One of his first projects was to build a cast-iron bridge over the Ohio River with a three hundred foot span.

No longer needing to work for a salary, Carnegie resigned from the railway; instead he would create his own industrial empire. He and his mother moved away from Pittsburgh to a grand hotel in New York, where Carnegie could think strategically, unbothered by the worries of day-to-day management.

Carnegie realised that the iron rails used throughout America were not up to the harsh weather and heavy traffic. He learned of the new Bessemer process for making steel; whereby air was blown under pressure through molten pig iron to remove the carbon that caused the weakness in iron rails. He invested in a huge new steel works to exploit this new process.

## Marriage and Scotland

Strangely for a man so positive and aggressive, Carnegie's mother had always been a strong dominating influence over him. This perhaps helps explain why he did not form a romantic relationship until he was forty-five, when he met Louise Whitfield, with whom he used to go horse riding in Central Park.

Perhaps in an attempt to get him away from Whitfield, his mother promptly took him back to Scotland. They had a triumphal reception in Dunfermline, where she opened a public library donated by her son, the first of an unbelievable two thousand eight hundred and eleven he would found, principally in America and Britain. Carnegie was at his happiest then, as he said: *'It's a God's mercy I was born a Scotchman, for I do not see how I could ever have been contented to be anything else!'*

But Carnegie was far from romantic. He only wrote once to Whitfield during the seven weeks he was away, but she was patient and their courtship resumed on his return to New York. In 1883 at the age of forty-eight he became secretly engaged, to her, but did not marry until after the death of his mother in 1886; Margaret had remained a dominating figure in his life until the end of hers.

Immediately after their marriage Carnegie and his bride sailed to Scotland. She came to love Scotland, which they would visit for six months every summer, renting a place to stay. After the birth in 1897 of their daughter, predictably named Margaret after Carnegie's mother, they needed a small place they could call their own and so Carnegie bought Skibo Castle and twenty-two thousand acres of land. Carnegie, sixty-two when his daughter was born, was a doting father.

## The Richest Man in the World

In 1892 when a strike at one of Carnegie's plants occured, the Pinkertons were called in to break it. The Pinkertons were a ruthless group of private detectives formed by a Scotsman, Allan Pinkerton. They had a reputation for rough justice and when they arrived at the plant, they were attacked by the angry strikers. In the struggle five strikers and three Pinkertons were killed, and many more were badly injured; the state militia had to be brought in to restore calm. Carnegie tried to distance himself from the event, claiming he was overseas when it all took place, but even while travelling he kept in close touch with business affairs. Deservedly or not the affair stained his reputation.

Things grew worse. He had always declared himself a lover of peace, but when a huge contract to provide armour-plated steel for new battleships for the American Navy was offered, profit triumphed over principle and he accepted. Worse still, the Carnegie Steel Company supplied inferior quality plate and then tried to cover up the faults. Carnegie was fast losing his reputation for ethical business behaviour; perhaps that explains why in 1901 he accepted an offer of four hundred and eighty million dollars from J.P. Morgan for his companies. As Morgan handed over the money he said, 'Mr Carnegie, I want to congratulate you on being the richest man in the world.' And true to his principles, Carnegie then gave it all away.

He spent an amazing three hundred and fifty million dollars endowing libraries, schools, universities and over seven thousand church organs all across the world. He did not believe in giving cash to the poor but preferred to give them access to education and self-improvement in an echo of Enlightenment ideals. It was an extraordinary spate of giving. He also worked hard for peace and was bitterly disappointed when, despite his efforts to persuade the Kaiser, he could not prevent the First World War. He died in the USA in 1919.

## Carnegie's Legacy

While Andrew Carnegie lived long after the Enlightenment, his life embodied its characteristics of reason, application and hard work. He had set out to become wealthy and he had succeeded by ruthlessly building a great industrial empire which he then sold for a huge fortune, which made him the richest man in the world. True to his beliefs, he gave huge sums away, paying back his debt to mankind.

It could be argued, however, that his philanthropy did not extend to his workers, whose efforts he sweated and whose wages he reduced at every opportunity, although in fairness, late in life he did set up a fund for those of his former workers who had fallen on hard times. One former worker wrote, 'Andrew Carnegie sweated the last dollar out of his workers and gave them little in return; his gifts to libraries and other institutions were stolen from the pockets of his labourers.'

Was Carnegie a great philanthropist, ruthless industrialist, or both?

**Further Reading**
Raymond Lamont-Brown, *Carnegie: The Richest Man in the World*

**Online Resources**
http://carnegie.org/about-us/foundation-history/about-andrew-carnegie/

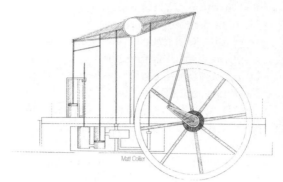

Matt Collier

## Sir Thomas Lipton
### 1850–1931

GROCER TO THE WORLD

Sir Thomas Lipton rose from being the Glasgow-born son of a grocer to found an internationally-famed grocery and tea empire. Lipton's teas are even now sold throughout the world. But perhaps he is best remembered as a challenger for the Auld Mug, the America's Cup.

### The America's Cup

The Royal Yacht Squadron in Cowes, on the Isle of Wight, was formed as the Yacht Club in 1815, receiving its royal status in 1833. By 1851 it had become the home of yacht racing in Britain and by extension the world. It was widely believed – at least in Britain! – that the best racing sail boats were designed in Britain and that they were sailed by the world's best sailors, the British.

This belief received a sharp jolt in 1851 with the arrival at Cowes of the schooner *America*. *America* had been built by John Cox Stevens, an American businessman. His father, Captain John Stevens, had made his money by operating ferry services; he was the first to operate a steam ferry across the Hudson River to New York. John Cox Stevens built sailing yachts to race in New York harbour, later forming the New York Yacht Club of which he was the first commodore. Stevens wanted to challenge the supposedly unbeatable British on their home waters at Cowes.

With friends he sailed the *America* across the Atlantic – in those days racing yachts had to be seaworthy enough to make the perilous ocean crossing – and on arrival in the Solent issued a challenge. He would race any yacht over a course of between twenty and seventy miles with the winner to receive ten thousand pounds, a considerable sum of money in those days. He was greeted by a stunned silence. Who was this upstart American?

Reliance and Shamrock III before the start, Aug. 25, 1903

*U. S. Library of Congress, Prints and Photographs Division, Detroit Publishing Company Collection*

The Royal Yacht Squadron made a suitably gentlemanly counter offer: a race for a challenge cup worth considerably less – just one hundred pounds.

On Friday, 22 August 1851 the race took place and was watched by Queen Victoria. The graceful *America* with her elegant lines and well-cut sails was triumphant, outsailing the best of British design and seamanship.

John Cox Stevens died only six years after his triumph. The cup he had won was donated to the New York Yacht Club and, renamed the America's Cup, was offered for challenge *'for friendly competition between foreign countries.'* It has remained for challenge ever since, although the competition has not always been friendly. How did a grocer's son become a challenger for the America's Cup?

### Lipton's Early Years

Thomas 'Tommy' Lipton was born in 1850 in the Gorbals in Glasgow. His parents had both been born in Ireland, but their families were Scottish. The Liptons, strict Calvinists, had migrated to Ulster in the seventeenth century and his mother's family, the Johnstons, had come from Dumfriesshire. His mother, Frances, and his father, Thomas, were married in their early twenties. Life then in Ireland was exceptionally hard with little work and less food – the potato famine had caused many deaths and many Irish folk had left Ireland.

Despairing of their future in Ireland, his parents had moved in the mid 1840s to Glasgow, then a fast-growing city and the second largest in the British Empire. The Clyde was known as the shipbuilder to the world; over the next twenty-five years two thirds of all ships built in Britain were built on the Clyde.

Life for Frances and Thomas was hard. Of their children only Tommy and his sister Margaret survived to adulthood, with two of their siblings dying in childbirth, a sister in infancy and a brother, John, who was training to become a doctor, at nineteen. Lipton idolised his mother, whom he called 'the best, bravest, the noblest mother God ever sent straight from heaven to be one of his angels on earth.'

When he was not much older than ten, Lipton left school, his parents had just opened a grocer's shop and he would help by sweeping the floor and going down to the quay each Monday evening to collect the supplies for their shop off the boat from Ireland. That is where he got his first taste of the sea. Laden with exotic spices and tobacco, ships would come from all over the world; on the docks he first met Americans, arriving on the passenger ships from the USA, and he found their enthusiasm and vitality infectious.

Inspired by the sea, he built his first boat, carved from the lid of an old wooden chest and fitted with a mast, rigging and sails. He called his boat *Shamrock* in tribute to his Irish roots and he raced her against the model boats of his friends.

He also took a number of jobs working in shops until he followed his love for the sea and became a cabin boy, working on the run from Glasgow to Belfast, for which he was paid eight shillings a week. When he was fifteen he surprised his parents by announcing that he had saved enough money to take a ship to New York and was off there the next day.

Lipton was amazed at the bustle and life of New York but found it difficult to get work. Eventually he went to Virginia where he worked on a tobacco plantation. It was only a few years after the end of the American Civil War and the abolition of slavery. Picking tobacco leaves was hard work and Lipton realised if he were not careful he would be doing it for the rest of his life. He moved around the United States doing a variety of jobs, from working on a rice plantation in South Carolina to driving a tram in New Orleans, until eventually he returned to New York. There he had the experience that would change his life.

He worked in the grocery section of a department store in Manhattan. Although the goods for sale – the hams, eggs and cheeses – were the same as those sold in his parents' shop back in Glasgow, the way they were sold was totally different. The shop was bright and cheerful, the hams and cheeses were piled high, and the friendly sales people would chat to the customers, persuading them to buy. This was what he would do. He would go home and set up a grocery shop.

## Lipton's Market

In May 1871 he opened his first shop in Glasgow. From the start it was a success. The brightly lit windows, the clean, cheerful interior and the friendly staff were far removed from the dark and dingy shops of the time. Lipton himself took a key role. He rose at dawn to meet the boats coming in from Ireland and to fill his cart with fresh cheeses and hams before serving in the shop dressed in an immaculate white apron, always ready for a joke with his customers.

His real flair was for publicity at a time when such a thing hardly existed. He hired an artist to draw cartoons which he would hang in the window of his shop; these would show thin, scrawny people 'before' and the rotund figures of those 'after' the 'Lipton experience.' He hired a swineherd to bring a herd of pigs through the streets of Glasgow to his shop, causing chaos but making everyone aware of Lipton's.

Within four years he opened a second shop and thereafter was no stopping him. He opened shops throughout Scotland, attending each new shop opening in person, serving and chatting with the customers. Under the huge 'Lipton's Market' sign were cartoons of the scrawny 'befores' and the chubby 'afters', and the shop was piled high with hams and cheeses of all kinds.

In 1882 he imported specially made 'jumbo' cheeses from America for Christmas. These were more than sixteen feet (roughly five metres) round and weighed nearly a ton! They were led in procession through the streets to three of his stores, in Glasgow, Edinburgh and the new one in Leeds, the first Lipton's Market in England. He repeated this every year, and in March 1887 offered Queen Victoria a monster cheese weighing five tons, an offer Her Majesty declined. Perhaps she was worried how long it would take for the Royal Family to work their way through it; after all she was the real 'big cheese,' not some upstart grocer.

By the end of the 1880s, there were more than one hundred fifty Lipton's Markets throughout England and Scotland with new stores opening almost weekly. Lipton had already become a very wealthy man, but in 1890 his business took a new turn.

## Lipton's Tea

Tea drinking was popular, particularly in England, but it was a privilege of the better-off as tea was expensive. Lipton started selling tea in his shops, which he bought at auction, thus cutting out the middleman and making it affordable for the masses. But true to character, Lipton did more than just sell tea.

He reasoned that if he could source the tea directly, he could reduce prices even further. In 1890 he sailed to Ceylon (now Sri Lanka), which was not at the time famous for tea. Tea came mainly from China and India but a few years earlier a Scot, James Taylor, had thought the climate and soil of Ceylon would be ideal for

©Corbis Images

Observers of the Shamrock and the Resolute,
during the America's Cup race

tea growing and started the first plantation there. Lipton bought his own plantation and advertised his tea as coming straight from the plantation to the pot; in fact, most of his tea was still bought in India, but why spoil a good story!

Within two years his plantation employed five thousand people, with more employed in Scotland where the tea was blended by Lipton's specialist blenders and attractively packed in cheerful packets, usually with a picture of a smiling Ceylonese girl. His competitors were still selling tea loose, scooped into a paper bag. Lipton's became famous for tea and today the Lipton name, now part of a massive international group, is still found on tea bags throughout the world.

Lipton had made his fortune. In 1898 his company was floated publicly and Lipton received the immense sum of two and a half million pounds, impressive even now but enormous at the time. He did not found libraries or colleges as did Carnegie, although in 1897 he did contribute twenty-five thousand pounds towards an appeal raised by Princess Alexandria to provide a meal for four hundred thousand of London's poor to mark Queen Victoria's jubilee. Each would receive a meat pie, a loaf, some cheese and of course a cup of Lipton's Tea. In 1898 his generosity was recognised; he became Sir Thomas Lipton.

## The Challenge for the America's Cup

Lipton was a great admirer of all things American and had been upset when the Earl of Dunraven, who himself challenged three times for the America's Cup, cried foul after his third challenge was defeated in 1895, causing much ill feeling between the two countries. Lipton wanted to prove that a Briton could play fair and still win the America's Cup.

In 1899 he issued his first challenge through the Royal Ulster Yacht Club. He called his new boat *Shamrock* after his first and chose one Captain Hogarth from the Clyde as his skipper. Specially built for the challenge, *Shamrock* was eighty-nine feet (twenty-seven metres) long at the waterline. There was only time for the briefest of trials before she was strengthened with heavy planks for the sail across the Atlantic.

In those days the challenger had first to be sailed across the Atlantic, a disadvantage as this meant she had to be strong and seaworthy while the defender could be designed as an outright racing boat.

*Shamrock* was a strongly built boat with a greater wetted area than the defender, *Columbia*, and would therefore be better suited to strong winds; *Columbia* was suited to lighter winds and unlike *Shamrock* had been thoroughly tested, giving her skipper Charlie Barr, also a Scot, and her crew plenty of time to learn how best to handle her.

Surrounded by his guests, Lipton watched the races on his motor yacht *Erin*, which he had bought in 1898. She was one of the largest steam yachts of her time, with a highly polished deck, superbly fitted cabins with gilt beds and priceless china ornaments, and a large and elegant state room or dining area.

Unfortunately the winds were fickle, the first five races being abandoned due to lack of wind. In the first real race *Shamrock* took the lead at the start but all too soon, *Columbia* powered ahead, pointing closer to the wind and winning by more than ten minutes. In the next race there was a better wind and *Shamrock* was holding her own until disaster struck – her topmast collapsed, dropping the topsail in the water. Two days' racing and two down! Lipton was staring defeat in the face. *Columbia* easily won the third race, winning the best of five series. Lipton took defeat bravely, issuing another challenge before the final race was even over. *Erin* was eventually commandeered by the Admiralty as a patrol boat in the First World War. She was armed with guns and sank a German submarine before she hit a mine and was herself sunk in 1916.


## The Second Challenge

Lipton's second challenge took place in 1901. *Shamrock II* was launched in April. She had lovely racing lines, suited to skimming the water rather than forcing her way through the waves. Two new defenders were built but in the trials *Columbia*, sailed aggressively by Captain Barr, triumphed. *Shamrock II* was facing a two-year-old design. Surely this time Britain could win.

In the first race Captain Barr seized the lead at the start by aggressive sailing, hounding *Shamrock II* and giving her no room. The race was cancelled as time ran out, but Barr had firmly thrown down the gauntlet. In the next race, the first to count, *Shamrock II* seized the lead and the two yachts raced head to head. *Shamrock II* was in the lead on the final downwind run when the wind died; as *Shamrock II* slowed *Columbia* surged past and held on to win. In the second race *Columbia* stalked *Shamrock II* until the windward leg, when she pointed higher and took the lead. *Columbia* led two to nil. The third race was again close, with both boats taking and losing the lead, but the greater experience and skill of Captain Barr triumphed. The challenger had again failed to win a race.

## The Third, Fourth and Fifth Challenges

In 1903 Lipton challenged again, this time with *Shamrock III*, designed by Wiiliam Fife of Fairlie, the designer of the beaten *Shamrock I*, assisted by George Watson, the designer of the beaten *Shamrock II*. Working together could they design a winning boat?

The design for the new boat was thoroughly tested in a tank of water using a wax model of the hull. She was launched, appropriately enough, on St Patrick's Day. Her lovely hull shape was well suited to the lighter winds found off New York.

While she was being towed across the Atlantic, the American defender, *Reliance*, was being designed and built. *Reliance* was huge, the same waterline length as *Shamrock III* (ninety feet or twenty-seven metres) but with an overall length of one hundred and forty-four feet (forty-four metres). Her mast was one hundred and seventy-five feet (fifty-four metres) high and she had sixteen thousand square feet of sail, five times the area of a modern Admiral's Cup boat. This monstrous boat was captained yet again by the redoubtable Charlie Barr, who won the first three races. Lipton had made three challenges and not won a single race!

*Reliance* was such an extreme design that Lipton realised he could never beat her. He therefore proposed a challenge with a J class yacht, with a maximum waterline length of sixty-eight feet instead of the existing limit of ninety feet, and an overall length of no more than one hundred and ten feet.

*Shamrock IV* was built. She reached New York in 1914, but by then war had broken out.

The challenge took place in 1920. *Shamrock IV*, although an 'old' boat, proved very competitive and won the first two races. Only one more win was needed. The skills of the skipper and crew of the American defender *Resolute* had been well honed in the preliminary races, however, and proved too great for the British, who were outsailed in the final three races.

The fifth challenge took place in 1930. *Shamrock V* was easily defeated in three straight races.

So Lipton had failed in his ambition. He had chosen what he saw as the 'best' team – the best designer, skipper and crew – but perhaps had lost because he was a lone challenger. The defender had been chosen after a tight series of knockout races, the crew was better drilled and the skipper knew his boat in racing conditions. But Lipton had won the hearts of the American people who recognised his sportsmanship. He was presented with a gold cup which on his death he donated to the New York Yacht Club.

## Later Years and Legacy

At the beginning of the twentieth century Lipton had been a very well-known figure heading a vast international business, but after the war, the world had changed and Lipton's did not respond. In 1927 he lost control and the company was sold. Lipton lived another four years, dying in 1931. He had never married; his house was left as a hostel for nurses and his money went to charity.

Through his determination and flair for publicity, Lipton built a vast business empire from his chain of grocery shops and his brand of tea, still recognised throughout the world. He gave generously to charity. But he is best remembered for his America's Cup challenges and for his gracious sportsmanship in defeat.

Sir Thomas Lipton saluting on deck

**Further Reading**
Laurence Brady, *The Man Who Challenged America*

**Online Resources**
Mitchell Library Glasgow
http://www.mitchelllibrary.org/lipton/

photo: Thomas Haywood

Reaching into the future: The Forth Rail Bridge, Scotland (built 1883-1890). This engineering marvel, built during the second half of the Enlightenment period, is still considered a masterpiece as the first major steel structure in Scotland and Britain.

## Scots Who Enlightened the World:
## Their relevance today?

Much has changed since The Scottish Enlightenment. Hutcheson, Kames and Hume were deeply involved in questions of religion. Hutcheson, the son of a Calvinist minister, challenged the harsh certainties of the Calvinist faith, questioning the core belief in a harsh and unrelenting God. He taught instead of an enlightened and caring God, rejecting the concept of predestination and believing instead in a more positive doctrine whereby a man could, by his good deeds, alter his destiny. He taught an early form of humanism in which man strove to do acts which gave happiness and pleasure and 'that action is best which produces the greatest happiness for the greatest number' - a philosophy for life which transcends the idiosyncrasies of individual religions.

Hume analysed religion from a perspective of proof and rationality; he was probably an agnostic rather than an atheist, professing that the existence of God could not be proven by empirical evidence. He thought that the world had not been created by an all-seeing God, but by man acting through knowledge derived from experience, and his rationality led him to question the concept of immortality. This was all very shocking at the time and his views undoubtedly resulted in Hume being overlooked for a number of public posts; they also brought him into conflict with Kames, himself a deeply religious man.

It may be difficult in today's world to realise the depth of feelings aroused by such questioning of the tenets at the very heart of religious faith. We live in a predominately secular world with a far smaller proportion of practising Christians than at the time of the Enlightenment. Even today, the ideas of radical thinkers such as Richard Dawkins, (who question in the same way as Hume had done so many years before belief in a God whose existence cannot be proven), continue to shock and enrage devout believers.

Hutton also cast a considerable spanner in the religious works, demonstrating that the world had not been created around four thousand years before Christ in accordance with a strict interpretation of the Bible, but had evolved over millions of years through geological action. It is disturbing that, despite all the evidence both as to the age of the Earth and of the principle of evolution by natural selection, foreshadowed by Hutton but formalised in Darwin's *The Origin of Species*, there remain a large number of Creationists who believe in a literal interpretation of the Bible in the face of reason and evidence.

Hutton believed that geological and biological processes were interlinked and would have been very comfortable with the Gaia Theory, the hypothesis proposed by James Lovelock that the Earth, incorporating the atmosphere and biosphere, operates as a self-regulating system where living organisms and inorganic matter react to changes in the Earth's environment to return the system to stability, maintaining the equilibrium of the characteristics essential to life. The evidence supporting the Gaia Theory is that over millions of years the surface temperature of Earth has remained within habitable limits despite variations in the energy emitted by the sun; similarly the percentage of oxygen in the atmosphere and the salinity of the sea have through the interaction of living plants and organisms been maintained at levels which permit the continuation of life.

Latterly, the rapidly increasing population and consequent demands upon the Earth's resources, coupled with the effect of the emission of greenhouse gases and global warming, have conspired to destabilize the eco-system. The Gaia Theory proposes that the intrinsic self-stabilizing features of the Gaia system will, over a period of perhaps hundreds of thousands of years, return the environment to long term equilibrium so that the Earth as a living entity will survive. Somewhat less satisfactorily from a human point of view, man's brief footprint upon the Earth might well be obliterated before stability is restored. The ideas of Hume and Hutton still resonate in today's world but perhaps the greatest impact has come from the ideas of Adam Smith which he set out in his masterpiece *The Wealth of Nations*, one of the most influential books of all time.

His beliefs in the virtues of the market, of improved efficiencies derived from the division of labour and of the economic benefits derived from free trade between countries have become the accepted wisdom of economic theory but are nevertheless continually threatened, as Smith had foretold, by interest groups who try to protect their industries through tariffs, by exploiting the possibilities of monopoly power or by profiting through 'meeting together ... in a conspiracy against the public or in some contrivance to raise prices,' thus interfering with the free operation of the market. Smith recognised the danger of leaving markets entirely unregulated, realising that self-interest could threaten the efficient operation of the market; it was exactly this exercise of self-interest and absence of effective regulation that encouraged investment bankers to invent evermore arcane financial instruments, devised, it would appear, principally for the enrichment of the bankers themselves, which led inexorably to the recent banking crash.

Adam Smith would also have recognised that the concept of the Eurozone was inherently flawed, that it would be impossible over time for countries with different fiscal policies and economic circumstances to remain linked within the straitjacket of a fixed currency. Germany has benefited from the euro which has made its exports more competitive than if it had retained the Deutschmark, but the low interest rates appropriate to the German economy fuelled the runaway property booms in countries such as Spain and Ireland, and in these countries it was unbridled private speculation rather than public profligacy which overheated their economies.

It is not just the philosophical ideas of the Enlightenment that changed the world. The discoveries of the scientists, engineers and medics and the works of the authors, artists and builders remain as relevant in the new millennium as when they were first produced. Technology may have progressed so that the inventions of Watt, Murdoch and Symington are now more appropriate to our industrial heritage than to our life today, but who can question the importance of the ubiquitous mackintosh, the telephone or the pneumatic tyre so crucial to our chosen mode of transport, be it the bicycle, the motor car or the aeroplane.

The discoveries of such scientists as Joseph Black, Lord Kelvin and James Clerk Maxwell remain fundamental to our understanding of the world and although in medicine new anaesthetic agents and antibiotics have been developed, the work of James Young Simpson and Alexander Fleming pioneered the way. Anaesthetics are the key to eliminating the trauma of surgery and to easing the pains of childbirth and any patient about to undergo surgery and any mother-to-be owes a real debt to the work of Simpson. Many owe their lives to the use of effective antibiotics, although the development of resistant organisms provides both a threat to the effectiveness of existing antibiotics and an opportunity for a future Fleming to develop the next 'wonder drug.' The work of Joseph Lister remains as relevant today as in the hospitals of his time with the rising prevalence in recent years of 'hospital infections' caused by insufficient attention to antisepsis in the wards of some of our hospitals.

The poems of Robert Burns form the cornerstone of Scottish literature and although the well-crafted but leisurely paced stories of Scott and Buchan have slipped out of fashion in our modern frenetic world, they remain a store of delight while the classic tales of Robert Louis Stevenson still entrance new young readers. The paintings of David Wilkie, Henry Raeburn and Allan Ramsay continue to give pleasure and the creations of Robert Adam, Robert Stevenson and Thomas Telford to impress with their design, their functional beauty and their durability with all these remarkable men and women contributing in their different ways to the world's store of culture.

Such a period of intellectual excitement inevitably came 'off the boil.' The economic and political pull of England meant that many Scots – John Buchan is a good example – sought success outside their homeland. The Empire also provided a fertile opportunity for ambitious and adventurous Scots and there are extensive Scottish populations in the former colonies, especially Canada, the USA, Australia and New Zealand, where Scots have played a significant part in the economic and cultural development of their adopted countries.

I believe this book has shown that the study of the lives of these remarkable men and women of the Enlightenment is indeed relevant to our modern world.

The true legacy of the Enlightenment is not however limited to their ideas and inventions, their writings and their creations. If we can understand the conditions which inspired this flowering of ideas, which encouraged the core belief that anything is achievable given the will and which developed the belief that rational thought is dependent upon reasoned analysis, then perhaps we can create again those conditions which could lead to a Scottish Re-Enlightenment.

## Scots Who Enlightened the World: The Lessons

The men and women whose lives we have examined may be disparate in their achievements but they have many shared characteristics: a good and broad education; a home environment where reading and learning were encouraged; a belief in the power of reason and the acquisition of knowledge derived from observation and experience; a determination to continue a task until it was successfully completed; a burning desire for self-improvement and a conviction that it was their duty to make the very best of the gifts with which they were endowed – as Alexander Graham Bell wrote, 'A man, as a general rule, owes very little to what he is born with – a man is what he makes of himself.'

Is there an over-arching lesson to be learned from their experiences?

The young, often alienated from society, are the keystone for the future. Thomas Aikenhead may have been young and foolhardy when he profaned the name of God, but he was at least following 'an insatiable inclination to truth...' There is a very real danger of an underclass of undereducated and underprivileged youth being created through a cycle of economic and social deprivation who do not accept the values of society; the recent rioting in London showed how thin is the veneer of civilisation. It is fundamental that every effort is made through education and by the encouragement of participation in sport, leisure and community activities to rescue these potential outcasts from society and encourage them to contribute to their own and their country's future.

As I enjoy the late afternoon of my time, I realise all too clearly that one has only one 'shot' at life and that it is therefore the imperative duty of every parent, every teacher; indeed, anybody with authority or influence over the young, to guide them by example and precept to 'make the most of themselves.' This is the greatest challenge to our society.

Education and self-improvement are at the heart of the Enlightenment and every government, whether it be a Scottish parliament with devolved powers or the Scottish parliament of an independent nation, has a fundamental duty to provide its young citizens with the education, the environment and the encouragement to make the very best of their innate abilities.

## The Scottish Referendum — An Enlightened Analysis

*He either fears his fate too much,*
*Or his deserts are small*
*That puts it not unto the touch,*
*To win or lose it all*

— James Graham, Marquis of Montrose

Many millions of years ago as the earth's crust cooled, a part of the North American landmass broke away and collided around four hundred million years ago with a similar landmass which had broken away from Europe. In the violent collision which ensued, the hills of the Borders were created by the force of the impact and England and Scotland became united in one landmass but perhaps in little else.

This 'Rough wooing' was replicated during centuries of bitter conflict when Scotland fought for independence from its powerful southern neighbour until perhaps exhausted by years of battle and worn down by economic pressures, Scotland joined with England in the Act of Union.

Scotland would in time benefit from union, growing in confidence and wealth from the ability to exploit the greater English market, to trade with England's colonies and to participate full heartedly in the expansion of the British Empire. This increase in intellectual self-confidence was one of the defining features of the Scottish Enlightenment.

Three hundred years later Scots, or more correctly those people living in Scotland at the time, will in the autumn of 2014 be given an opportunity to vote in a referendum as to whether Scotland should continue as an integral part of Britain, albeit with its own parliament and devolved powers, or should seek an alternative future as an independent nation.

In these momentous times can the application of the principle of reasoned argument, central to the Enlightenment, assist in assessing the merits of the arguments? I believe it can.

### The Political and Economic Background to the Referendum

The Marquis of Montrose elegantly expressed the choice facing the Scottish people. This book does not attempt to make that choice as it is for those who vote to decide whether they 'dare to put it to the touch,' but the choice should be based upon a realistic examination of the options, based upon facts, not determined by fear of the unknown or dislike of Westminster-centric government. Passion needs to be weighted by reason and reason has to be based on facts. It is facts which are in short supply. A rational assessment of the choices is firmly within the spirit of the Enlightenment and it is in this spirit that a few of the principal issues are examined.

*The International Dimension* — An independent Scotland is often portrayed as small and vulnerable in the modern world, but the converse could be argued as an independent Scotland would not inherit the delusions of a long-lost imperial power. Would an enlightened country have embarked on the military ventures espoused by Britain in recent years?

The study of history should not be just for arcane discussion in the marbled halls of academia, but should be a guide to help us navigate our way through the confusion created by the pressures of events while trapped in the spotlight of twenty-four hour news and comment. A historian such as Hume or Carlyle would have pointed out the dangers in the probably illegal invasion of Iraq and the subsequent invasion of Afghanistan.

The invasion of Iraq took place on the pretext of the supposed existence of weapons of mass destruction and of an unlikely alliance between the intensely secular Ba'ath party and the ultra-religious al-Quaeda. The benefit has been the removal of an oppressive dictator but at the expense of leaving a country racked by ethnic and religious divisions and by continued violence. A historian would have pointed out the artificial nature of a country defined by lines drawn on a map by Gertrude Bell who exhibited an insouciant disregard for the underlying tribal loyalties. This embryo and essentially artificial country had already been under the *de facto* control of Britain in the aftermath of the First World War under a mandate which could only be enforced through bloody repression.

The invasion of Afghanistan has an even more dubious pedigree, redefined as each domino tumbles. First, it was to exact revenge upon al-Quaeda for the World Trade Centre atrocity, then as a mission to defeat the Taliban, then to introduce democracy into an essentially tribal country, then to improve the rights of women and latterly to reduce the supposed 'security threat' to Britain posed by Afghanistan, a threat curiously unspecified. For these 'causes' young British men and women are dying and yet when the troops finally leave they will leave little trace in the sands other than their blood. Do the politicians not remember the two disastrous Anglo-Afghan Wars of the late nineteenth century, after the first of which only one British survivor limped back to the safety of India?

Would an 'enlightened' country have embarked on these ill-starred ventures?

*A Scottish Pound?* — If the Scottish people exercise their opportunity to move to full independence, one fundamental decision will immediately present itself; should Scotland stay with the British pound within the sterling area, join the euro zone or adopt a Scottish pound.

Adam Smith, were he alive today, would point out the dangers of being a part of a currency zone, be it the euro or the pound sterling, with differing fiscal characteristics, so starkly demonstrated by the recent Irish experience where the flames of a runaway property boom were fanned by the low interest rate imposed on the euro zone by the domestic policies of Germany. He would highlight the advantages of a free floating Scottish pound which would give a Scottish government the freedom to adopt the policies best suited for Scotland's own needs, determined solely by the needs of the Scottish economy.

The practical solution he would probably propose would be to link the Scottish pound informally to the British pound so that effectively there would be just one currency operating throughout the British Isles but nevertheless retaining freedom of action should the economic fundamentals diverge.

There is a further issue. If Scots voted for independence, it is by no means certain that Scotland would automatically become a part of the European Union. Which raises the question – should it apply? Membership would give the security of being part of a greater entity with more power in a troubled world but it would also bring with it the burdens of Europe's bureaucracy, the costs of supporting the Common Agricultural Policy and the confusion of European fishing policy. Would an independent Scotland be better advised to take the Scandinavian route and stay discretely outside or to seek a friendly haven in a potentially hostile world by applying to join countries, such as Norway. as a member of the European Eonomic Area, linked to, but not part of the European Union? An informed debate on these issues is surely an essential precursor to a rational vote in the referendum.

***What proportion of the UK National Debt would be apportioned to an independent Scotland?*** — The size of the share of the UK National Debt to be apportioned to Scotland in the event of Scottish independence is also fundamental to rational debate, because an independent Scotland saddled with too great a share of debt would suffer the same currency and economic pressures currently experienced by Spain and Italy in the Eurozone crisis.

The UK National Debt is usually quoted as one trillion pounds, but even this enormous figure considerably understates the UK's true underlying indebtedness, the product of years of spendthrift public spending and loose financial control. Provision for public sector responsibility, for the pension entitlements of the civil service, police, teachers, fire fighters, NHS employees and the like, pension commitments which in the private sector would be required to be fully funded, would more than double the debt to £2.1 trillion. Provisions for unfunded liabilities such as cleaning up the nuclear power stations add a further £100 billion and amounts owing under PFI schemes a further trifling £23 billion, giving a total of over £2.2 trillion. This huge figure still leaves out any outstanding liability for the State Pension which is funded on a pay-as-you go basis.

What would be Scotland's share and would an independent Scotland be able to fund the portion of this Debt graciously 'handed over?' One simple answer would be to allocate a proportion based upon the relative populations. Scotland has 8.4% of the UK population and on this basis would pick up liability for roughly £84 billion of the existing underlying National Debt.

Is this level of debt sustainable? As Lesley Sutton points out in a paper published appropriately by The David Hume Institute, the judgement would depend not on just the absolute size of the Debt but more crucially upon Scotland's perceived ability to fund it, essentially on the ratio of Debt to Scotland's Income. This begs the next question.

***What Would be Scotland's Income?*** — The income of a country, its wealth as defined by Adam Smith, is measured by the total of the goods and services produced by the people and enterprises of that country, essentially its Gross Domestic Product (GDP). Scotland's GDP would crucially depend upon the share of oil revenues appropriated to an independent Scotland. Here the fundamental question is whether an independent Scotland would be credited with a share of UK oil revenues in proportion to population or – arguably more reasonably in an international context – its geographic share?

Although it is often argued, and rightly, that the 'best' years of the oil boom are long gone, the combination of the rising price of oil and the improved technology applied by nimbler operators are extending the life of oil reserves which can be economically recovered. These revenues would give an independent Scotland vital time to develop new sources of income. Oil revenue is crucial to the viability of the Scottish economy and if the benefits of oil were allocated pro rata to population then Scotland could find it difficult to fund its share of the National Debt.

The potential funding problem is not, however, limited to funding the National Debt. The Scottish government has adopted the Scandinavian model of democracy providing a number of 'free' benefits, including free prescriptions, free higher education and free personal care for the elderly, all against the background of an ageing population who will make increasing demands on resources.

In the absence of significant oil revenues, it is questionable whether these benefits could be funded. The apportionment of oil revenues is therefore fundamental to reasoned analysis and a decision should be declared prior to the referendum if there is to be rational debate upon the possible economic future of an independent Scotland.

***Scotland's Financial Sector*** — The question is often asked whether an independent Scotland would have been able to fund the recent rescue of the Royal Bank of Scotland and HBOS. A more pertinent question might be whether an enlightened government would have allowed the toxic brew of investment, sometimes called casino, banking and retail banking to simmer within one entity, but would have reverted to the historic distinction between 'high street' and merchant banks.

Banking has always been given an exaggerated importance and status in England not bestowed upon manufacturing or – dare one say – trade. John Buchan summed the English attitude well in the words of the American Blenkiron, in his novel *Mr. Standfast*: 'You English, have gotten business on the brain, and think a fellow's a dandy at handling your government if he happens to have made a pile by some flat-catching ramp on your Stock Exchange. It makes me tired. You're about the best business nation on earth, but for God's sake don't begin talking about it or you'll lose your power. And don't go confusing real business with the ordinary gift of raking in the dollars.'

In recent years, the health of the country's manufacturing base has been sacrificed on the altar of the City. Short-termism has, in the prescient words of Harold Macmillan, encouraged a 'sale of the family silver' so that the core of British industry, the water companies (but not in Scotland), the power companies, the airports and the burgeoning manufacturing companies, the industrial giants of the future, have been sold to overseas buyers so the City could reap the fees and profits to meet its short term targets and the country could continue to fund a lifestyle beyond its means – 'bought and sold for foreign gold, such a parcel of rogues in a nation' in the words of Burns.

The German emphasis on long term investment in industry and on technological excellence is a model which should be closely studied. Their economy thrives with a large number of small to medium privately-owned companies, providing a sound commercially-based economy with booming exports secured through excellence in design, and competitiveness in manufacture.

***The Education Conundrum*** — One lesson above all that has been learned from studying the lives of the Enlightenment has been the importance of education. Scotland has a fine reputation for education, (not always reflected in current standards), and an emphasis on the quality of education at both school and university level is essential to future prosperity in an increasingly knowledge driven world.

Universities are sometimes parodied for providing elite education with little commercial significance, but in truth, the future of Scotland is dependent upon the talents of its youth. The Scottish Government should therefore be applauded for retaining free higher education, with some caveats.

It is debatable whether a target of fifty per cent of school leavers — going on to university education, is either desirable or attainable, particularly as an unintended consequence of the expansion of universities with declining vocational courses. It is also debatable whether traditional university education meets all the higher education needs of the modern world, or whether students should be encouraged to take degree courses later during their working careers, perhaps building on the model of the Open University to achieve better use of scarce resources using internet technologies.

Free higher education is further complicated by membership of the European Union. While under EU rules it is perfectly proper to differentiate between people within a country, it is not permitted to discriminate between member countries and therefore every European student, other than from England, has the right to obtain free education at Scottish Universities. As a result, roughly eight per cent of places at the fifteen Scottish universities, comprising the 'ancient' universities and the 'new', are now taken by students from the European Union so that effectively, the equivalent of one of Scotland's fifteen universities is dedicated solely to providing free higher education to EU students. It is good that Scotland should be becoming a centre of excellence for education but somewhat less desirable that the education is being provided free. The irony is that were Scotland to become independent but remain within the European Union, English students too would be entitled to free education at Scottish universities while Scottish students who attended English universities would be required to pay.

Whatever the decision in the referendum, this is not sustainable in the long term. Perhaps a solution would be to learn from history – Robert Fergusson was awarded a bursary for the University of St. Andrews where eligibility was limited to those bearing the name Fergusson - and resurrect the concept of bursaries which could be awarded by an 'independent' public body. Charges could then be introduced for university places, but with a little fancy footwork to get around the EU rules, Scottish resident students might still receive free education in true Enlightenment tradition.

## Summary of the Arguments

These thoughts are only intended as a 'taster', in an attempt to challenge some of the accepted 'orthodoxies' and an overview of some of the questions which need to be answered.

One conclusion however is clear. Informed debate can only take place if the facts are known. Without resolution of these issues, any referendum vote must necessarily be based upon emotion rather than rational analysis.

***How Might the Leaders of the Enlightenment Vote?*** — How can one answer that as the burning intellectual questions of the time were very different from those of today? The Act of Union had just been passed, Scotland was entering on a new life as North Britain and Scottish independence was not on the agenda for the great thinkers of the Enlightenment, but nevertheless, it is interesting to speculate as to their views.

Hume was a supporter of the Union, renouncing the Scots' language and even changing the spelling of his name to facilitate its pronunciation by the English. Adam was another who embraced the possibilities of the English market.

Smith, on the other hand, would have probably pointed out the illogicality of a government with spending powers financed by a block grant over which it had no authority and lacking the restraint imposed by the discipline of raising the necessary revenues.

Burns, characteristically, was more caustic, describing those Scots who had signed the Act of Union as 'Such a parcel of rogues in a nation.'

But perhaps the final word should be left to Francis Hutcheson, the 'Father of the Enlightenment.' He wrote in his book, *A System of Moral Philosophy*:

'There is something so unnatural in supposing a large society, sufficient for all the good purposes of an independent political union, remaining subject to the direction and government of a distant body of men who know not sufficiently the circumstances and exigencies of this society; or in supposing this society obliged to be governed solely for the benefit of a distance (sic) country; that it is not easy to imagine that there can be any foundation for it in justice or equity.'

What Hutcheson was in effect saying, is that if a country is big enough to look after itself then it should be self-governing. For Hutcheson the decision would come down to one simple question – is Scotland big enough to look after itself?

## A Scottish Re-Enlightenment –
## The Ideas of the Enlightenment and the World Today

We live in a very threatening world where the pace of change in technological development seems to be ever accelerating with today's product all too quickly becoming tomorrow's obsolescence, and where the 'old order' is rapidly changing. Can the ideas of the Scots Who Enlightened the World provide us with a guide in these uncertain times?

Since the Industrial Revolution, indeed since the Age of Enlightenment, there has been an accepted world order, with the 'white' countries: Europe, America, Australia, New Zealand and the like, having an assured future and a standard of living only dreamt of by others. This is now being challenged by a new economic order and changing much faster than most of us appreciate. The new century could see the emergence of China as the dominant world economy, followed by Brazil and India - if India can unleash its people from a stifling and corrupt bureaucracy. Resources of food, energy and raw materials will become increasingly important as nations compete over dwindling supplies, giving greater power to those countries such as Russia which are rich in energy resources. A world population of seven billion – and rising - will put increasing strains on a planet which can only naturally sustain a much smaller population, placing unparalleled demands upon resources, the environment and human ingenuity, as we endeavour to feed the hungry mouths of a growing world population (already an estimated one billion are living at starvation level). Emerging countries demand the same living standards and goods – the cars and consumer gizmos – as the 'rich' countries enjoy today.

All this implies a very different future for our children. The old economies have no 'God-given right' to be wealthy, but will have to earn their way in an increasingly competitive world in which advantage will have moved to the East. We will have to rethink our objectives as a society; perhaps we will even see the emergence of a fifth form of society, a post-industrialised economy, to add to the four stages identified by Kames.

*The Opportunity for Scotland: A New Form of Society?* — Whatever the outcome of the referendum, for the status quo — with perhaps some enhanced but unspecified powers — or for full independence, the decision should not be based on economic arguments alone. It is not enough for the debate to be dominated by dissatisfaction with the United Kingdom or the perceived oppression of rule by Westminster. The debate should offer a positive and exciting future for Scotland, a future which recognises the challenges and opportunities of a changing world. There can be an opportunity for Scotland, following the lead of Kames, to develop a new form of society.

Such a society should above all be tolerant and equitable and based upon the rule of law, identified all those years ago by Kames as a necessary condition for an advanced society. The objectives of society need to be readdressed – is continued growth the 'be-all and end-all' of society or should we be seeking a self-sustaining economy where economic growth is not the over-arching aim, a mature society where greed is tempered by concern for the general weal and where wealth is shared to support the elderly, the infirm and the poor, a society which is as far as possible self-sustaining, relying on renewable sources of food, energy and materials. Above all, a country which can survive the pressures of the developing new world order?

The balance of power will almost inevitably shift from the 'old' countries, which for centuries have dominated and shared disproportionately in the wealth and resources of our planet, to the new economies. It is a sobering thought that China has twenty-two per cent of the world's population but only seven per cent of its arable land. When Chinese peasants become wealthy enough to demand the improved diet of the Western nations the impact upon the world's supplies of food will be considerable. The emerging countries — China, Brazil, India and others - by flexing their economic muscles could put pressures on world resources which may lead to increasing tension between the new order and the old, exacerbated as burgeoning economic strength is invested in military strength. A frightening corollary to the growing international power of China is its disregard for human rights.

It is ironic that China's economic power has come about as a direct result of the Western economies outsourcing production to China in search of reduced costs, a process driven by capitalism and facilitated by the artificially low exchange rate of the renminbi and the sweatshop working conditions of many Chinese workers who work twelve-hour shifts and a six-day work week for what is in western terms a pittance, importing Chinese products at the expense of local jobs, and of endangering the planet through the consequent pollution. With so much sovereign wealth now in Chinese hands we are indeed hoist by our own petard.

***What Should Scotland Do to Prosper in this New and Potentially Dangerous World?*** — Are there opportunities for Scotland in such a challenging world? Of course, but they need to be identified. This would rely in true Adam Smith spirit upon concentrating on areas where Scotland has a potential competitive advantage rather than trying to compete with low-cost manufacturers based in the Far East.

Scotland has wonderful natural resources: the beauty of her land; the possibility of becoming virtually self-sufficient in food (but perhaps not to the extent of developing a Scottish claret, as not too seriously postulated by Smith); a bountiful (sometimes too bountiful) supply of water; potential self-sufficiency in energy both through green sources such as nuclear power, wind power, tidal and hydroelectric schemes and through resources of fossil fuels, both coal and oil; a strong national identity; and not least, the Scottish intellectual tradition.

The future prosperity of Scotland will depend, as Adam Smith wrote, upon the cumulative efforts and aspirations of all her people driven by the workings of an 'invisible hand,' but the government has a duty to prepare the soil and fertilise the ground in order to let the seeds of new ideas germinate and their flowers flourish.

This first and foremost requires an excellent and widely available education and the creation of a society that embraces the best parts of Calvinism: the desire for self-improvement and a belief that anything can be achieved through hard work. These characteristics are seen again and again in the lives we have studied and underline the vital requirement of a well educated and highly motivated people. It also implies creating an environment of opportunity where the social, economic and fiscal infrastructure encourages the brightest Scots to stay and entices new and exciting overseas talents to settle here.

Whisky should not be Scotland's only world-class industry. One can imagine for example a world in which Scotland could lead in providing education and healthcare of the very best quality, not just for her own people but for people across the world. Scotland also has the potential to develop its tourism industry, and as a country, be recognised as being an attractive place to live. Through positive financial policies, the right environment to create a base for technical expertise could be developed for research teams and the information technologists who will drive industries of the future — as well as provide a cultural home for authors and artists to create the next Harry Potter, Precious Ramotse or DI Rebus.

Scotland also has the potential of competitive advantage in the provision of financial expertise, situated as it is in the time zone between East and West – although we must first wait for the dust to settle on recent banking over-exuberance.

The main lesson is to embrace change. Much as the loss of America from the Empire encouraged the development of shipbuilding on the Clyde, itself in time destroyed by foreign competition, so it must be recognised that the Scotland of the future will be different in very many ways from the Scotland of today. She will have to thrive in new ways and in new industries, some probably not yet even imagined. But whatever these new endeavours may be, they will only succeed through the ambition, energy and intellect of Scots. Those very same attributes ascribed to the giants of the Enlightenment – the benefits of a good and broad education available to all, a belief in one's abilities and the burning desire to make the most of opportunities – will be just as fundamental to the Scotland of the future as they were to the men and women of the Enlightenment.

### A Scottish Re-Enlightenment?

Could all this lead to a Scottish Re-Enlightenment? The essential heart of the Enlightenment was a belief in the power of reason, that the exercise of reason would uncover the Truth. Are we now slaves to fashion in thought or are there still independent minds prepared to ask the questions as yet unasked?

Scotland is recovering its sense of national identity with the start of a new song. A Scottish Parliament is of its essence more receptive to the demands and wishes of the people than a remote parliament based in Westminster, providing a new political environment and therefore an opportunity, much in the way the Act of Union did in the early eighteenth century.

It could also be said, with tongue somewhat in cheek, that Scotland has recently had its 'Darien' moment. The rapid, indeed reckless, expansion of its two premier banks and their subsequent virtual collapse resulted in heavy losses for investors. The reputation of Scots for hard-headed prudence has been severely dented due to the hubris of a few men seduced by power, money and the blandishments of the City.

Even that charming young lady, Prudence herself, was abandoned by her erstwhile admirer, with a period of reckless expansion of public spending uncharacteristic of Scotland's Calvinist roots, causing a burgeoning public-sector deficit in the United Kingdom's accounts well before the 'credit crunch' impacted. Although it could be argued as to whether a financial crisis is a necessary condition for a new Age of Enlightenment, the cuts demanded by the need to return to fiscal rectitude do require a searching reassessment of government objectives and priorities.

Is there the opportunity in today's world for an intellectual explosion of ideas as was seen in the Enlightenment? The main areas for intellectual innovation would undoubtedly be in technology and medicine, as well as in the artistic abilities of Scotland's writers, painters and architects. It was the developments in philosophical thought which provided the initial driving force for the Enlightenment, but there is probably less scope for such intellectual breakthroughs now, although there may be an opportunity for a philosopher to set out the parameters of the fifth state of society, based on a green economy, on self-sustainability in food and energy and on service industries such as health, education, tourism, software design, banking and insurance to provide an expanding outlet for Scottish talents.

A Scotland which through excellence in education inspired its young to achieve could undoubtedly provide the right environment for the emergence of the Re-Enlightenment figures of the future. The essential thing is to realise that the future does not have to mean more of the past.

All this would help, but for a Scottish Re-Enlightenment to take place one further and most important ingredient has to be added to the brew; the appearance of thirty or forty men and women of exceptional talent who can provide its intellectual foundation. Intellectual giants such as Hume, Smith and Black and artistic talents such as Ramsay, Scott and Burns cannot be produced at will.

The Scottish Age of Enlightenment in the last analysis only took place because, like the notorious Number Eleven bus, a number of these remarkable minds came along at the same time.

Andrew Ferguson

# I N D E X

note: Index of names and subjects. Where the subject applies directly to a prominent
biographical figure in the book, that person is identified parenthetically.

# Scots Who Enlightened the World

social media

## Scots Who Enlightened the World
### Facebook fan page

## @ScotsWho
### Twitter

greatscots@scotswho.com

Polwarth Publishing

Inspired by the likes of Scotland's James Young Simpson, Andrew Ferguson is a veteran of the medical manufacturing industry, specialising in anaesthetic surgical equipment – a career highlighted by winning The Queen's Award for Export and Technical Achievement, twice:

"We're an endangered species —
we *made* things."

Andrew studied economics at Cambridge University where he was introduced to the work of Adam Smith. Even earlier, as a young boy taking walks with his father, he was inspirited by the stories of the contributions made to society by the men and women of The Scottish Enlightenment. Now as an author, he shares these passions with you.

Andrew lives and works in the South of England,  and makes regular excursions to Scotland (particularly Murrayfield).

**ANDREW FERGUSON**

contact:
andrewf@scotswho.com